More AMERICAN ROCK'N'ROLL
THE UK TOURS
1973-84

More AMERICAN ROCK'N'ROLL
THE UK TOURS
1973-84

Ian Wallis

MUSIC MENTOR BOOKS
York, England

British Library Cataloguing-in-Publication Data
A catalogue record for this book is available from the British Library.

ISBN-13: 978-0-9562679-3-1

Published worldwide by Music Mentor Books *(Proprietor: G.R. Groom-White)*
69 Station Road, Upper Poppleton, York YO26 6PZ, North Yorkshire, England.
Telephone/Fax: +44 (0)1904 330308   *Email:* music.mentor@lineone.net.

Cover by It's Great To Be Rich, York.

Printed and bound in Great Britain by Bonacia Ltd, Peterborough.

Acknowledgments

A feeling of panic is running through me as I prepare these words of acknowledgement. A great many people have kindly supplied information, encouragement and support during the writing of this book and I just know that I will be unable to bring to mind the names of everyone who is deserving of my thanks. So to all the friends, acquaintances and rock'n'roll nuts who are listed below and those who are not, but who should be, a very big thank you. I hope that you enjoy the finished article as much as I enjoyed writing it.

Anyway here goes. Imagine a trumpet fanfare (or perhaps a Chuck Berry guitar solo) as you read the names of Steve Aynsley, Craig Baguley, Graham Barker, Paul Barrett, Cary Brooks, John Beecher, David Bowell, Rocky Burnette, Trevor Cajiao, Ray Campi, Terry Clemson, Breathless Dan Coffey, Stuart Colman, Barry Dixon, Bob Dunham, Narvel Felts, Rob Finnis, Bob Fish, Laurence Fontaine, Jim Grant, Bill Greensmith, Paul Harris, Martin Hawkins, Ronnie Hawkins, John Howard, Rob Hughes, Tommy Hunt, John Ingman, Willie Jeffery, Geoff Kember, Val Kember, Ken Major, Hugh McCallum, Bill Millar, Arthur Moir, Eleanor Newby, Gary Owens, Colin Phillips, John Poole, Marvin Rainwater, Jean-Pierre Ravelli, Morten Reff, Billy Swan, Ian Tilbury, Keith Tillman, Dave Travis, George White, Lee Wilkinson and Tony Wilkinson.

An encyclopaedia-type book calls for exhaustive research and I ploughed through every page of *New Musical Express* and *Melody Maker* for the full twelve-year period 1973-84. It was not a very inspiring experience because the UK music press had lost interest in rock'n'roll long ago, but necessary, as for much of this period there was no comprehensive rock'n'roll magazine to supply tour information. Periodicals such as *New Kommotion*, *Cat Talk* and *Not Fade Away* tended to appear infrequently and to concentrate on record releases and biographies. Like a dying man seeking water in the desert, I kept looking forward to April 1983 and the emergence of *Now Dig This* (still the greatest rock'n'roll magazine in the world, ever), but even their early issues were far from comprehensive and they missed one Bo Diddley tour altogether, so I have been obliged to gather information from every available source and hope that I have succeeded in keeping errors and omissions to an acceptable level.

Among the magazines, newspapers and fanzines consulted were (in no particular order): *Revival*, *Not Fade Away*, *Sounds*, *Melody Maker*, *Haley News*, *UK Rock*, *Country Music People*, *Now Dig This*, *New Musical Express*, *Radio Times*, *TV Times*, *Cat Talk*, *Blues Unlimited*, *New Kommotion*, *Fireball Mail*, *Lewis Scene*, *Juke Blues*, *Blues & Rhythm*, *Tales From The Woods*, *Crickets File*, *Gene Vincent Fan Club Magazine* and *New Camel Walker*.

Many long hours were spent at both the British Library at Euston and the British Library Newspaper Library in Colindale trawling through dusty back

Acknowledgments

issues of the local papers and in my near-insane fixation for trivia, I spent a whole summer's day at Colindale reading issue after issue of *TV Times* in a desperate attempt to locate some long-forgotten television appearances by Clarence 'Frogman' Henry. At one point, I did reflect that there may be more constructive ways to spend a Saturday and that possibly I may be the only person interested in the outcome of this piece of obscure research, but nevertheless carried on to the bitter end. Perhaps there is a Clarence 'Frogman' Henry fan out there somewhere who will appreciate such attention to detail!

For Joanna

Contents

Introduction

More than half a century ago rock'n'roll arrived unannounced and largely unwanted and the critics gave it no more than six months, after which they predicted that it would be forgotten, a craze as inconsequential as the hoola hoop or the Davy Crockett hat. Today the music survives in a way that nobody could possibly have predicted. There are CD's, DVD's, books and magazines available in abundance and a thriving live music scene throughout Britain.

In 2003, Music Mentor Books published *American Rock'n'Roll – The UK Tours 1956-72*, the first book to ever make a close study of live rock'n'roll music in the UK. It traced the rise of rock'n'roll in Britain and contained details of every UK tour by an American (or Canadian) performer within that period, listing the dates and venues of every known show, the identities of the backing groups, the supporting acts, the names of the promoters and a summary of British TV appearances. There was also a full description of each tour, based on contemporary reports.

As a result of the generous reviews which followed publication, the research has continued and this second volume investigates the changing face of live rock'n'roll music over the twelve year period, 1973-84. It is intended that each book is self-contained. In other words, it is not necessary for you to have read the first volume to enjoy this one, although it is obviously my hope that both will eventually be accepted as an accurate record of live rock'n'roll in Britain.

By the beginning of 1973, rock'n'roll was at a low ebb. Most of the tours around that time were aimed at the cabaret circuit. The primitive excitement and unpredictability of the early years had been ironed out and audiences were wallowing in nostalgia for the hit records of their youth. There was nothing happening to attract younger people to rock'n'roll and the whole scene was becoming stale and undemanding.

Amazingly however, as the Seventies progressed, so the situation changed. Record companies found that there was a market for rock'n'roll and rockabilly and raided their own back catalogues, where they found a host of wonderful recordings, often by artists who were unknown to the general public. Rockabilly made the sounds of the Fifties fashionable again and attracted a new generation of fans to the music of their parents. Suddenly, the scene came alive and much of the action transferred to the clubs, pubs and the holiday camp weekenders which represented the future for live rock'n'roll.

By 1980 there were more and more young musicians performing rock'n'roll again, and during that summer the Stray Cats arrived from New York, a teenage band in the style of Gene Vincent and Eddie Cochran, but with a sound perhaps best described as 'punk rockabilly'. One of the most difficult decisions was whether or not to include them and the other young

American bands in this book. Their music is not strictly Fifties rock'n'roll, but so strong was their influence on this new generation of teenage fans that to exclude them would give a false representation of events. For that reason, the Stray Cats story is contained here alongside the Chuck Berry and Jerry Lee Lewis tours and hopefully this gives a fair perspective, as even their biggest critics must surely concede, the Stray Cats and their contemporaries had a big influence on the live music scene and one which remains very visible more than thirty years later.

It is hoped that this volume will pluck the memory strings and help the reader to relive some great memories of sweaty, boozy nights in a packed crowd listening to pounding pianos, honking saxes and a demented bass player climbing all over his instrument. When the atmosphere is right and the joint is really jumping there is nothing that can beat a live rock'n'roll show. It is, after all, the greatest music in the world.

To close this introduction, here is a small challenge for you. What was the very last song performed on a British stage by the father of rock'n'roll, Bill Haley, before his untimely death in 1981?

The answer is to be found within the pages of this book, but I doubt that many people will guess right!

TECHNICAL NOTE

By the Seventies there were still some promoters such as Henry Sellers and Mervyn Conn setting up rock'n'roll tours, but many of the Americans visiting the UK did so off the back of a single large show like the Caister weekender. Sometimes, small club dates would be added as well, but in many cases there was no one actual promoter bearing the financial risk for the whole tour. For that reason, in this volume, the description 'tour promoter' has been amended to 'tour organiser', which is probably a fairer job description.

CHAPTER ONE

1973

I Want You To Play With My Ding-A-Ling

1973 was very far from being a vintage year for rock'n'roll. The euphoria created by the Wembley rock'n'roll show the previous summer had soon evaporated and the majority of the Americans who toured Britain at this time did so on promoter Henry Sellers' cabaret circuit. The major players like Fats Domino, Chuck Berry – his career unexpectedly boosted by his novelty hit, 'My Ding-A-Ling' – and the Johnny Cash/Carl Perkins show, still retained a foothold for rock'n'roll in the theatres, but otherwise it meant smart clothes (no jeans) and the safe conformity of a visit to see the likes of Del Shannon or the Crickets in some Northern club where everything was becoming just a little too genteel and civilised.

This should not be construed as a criticism of Henry Sellers. After several years of chaos in the mid-Sixties, his arrival on the scene had probably kept rock'n'roll alive through a string of well-organised and professionally publicised tours and there was unquestionably a demand for such shows. The teenagers of the Fifties had grown up and married. Many now liked to dress up for an evening's entertainment where they could sing along to 'Runaway', 'Peggy Sue' and the other songs of their youth while scoffing scampi or chicken in the basket in aesthetically pleasing surroundings.

It was the dangerous side of rock'n'roll which was missing. Sadly, Gene Vincent was no longer alive to ensure a sufficient level of craziness and a few years would elapse before the rockabilly tours came along to provide that much needed energy and excitement again.

In Britain, stalwarts like Screaming Lord Sutch were still out there performing on a regular basis and he opened the Rollin' Rock Club in Harrow to provide regular Thursday nights of rock'n'roll. Newer names like Chuck Fowler, Carl Simmons and Ravin' Rupert were also active on the club circuit while Shane Fenton reinvented himself as Alvin Stardust and somehow managed to gatecrash the glam rock craze with 'My Coo-Ca-Choo' – the first of a series of hit records that were not dissimilar from his earlier work, but which were now aimed squarely at a new generation of teenagers.

Away from rock'n'roll there was plenty of live music. The explosion of interest in country music resulted in tours by several top names including

Don Gibson, Faron Young, Chet Atkins, Jeannie C. Riley and Anne Murray. Bluesmen such as Willie Mabon, Freddie King and Lightnin' Slim were to be found in the clubs, while the cabaret circuit provided an outlet for such diverse talents as Johnny Tillotson, Esther Phillips, the Four Freshmen and Gene Pitney.

BUCK RAM'S PLATTERS

December 1972			15-21	Southend	Talk Of The South
24-30	Sheffield	Fiesta	22-28	Leicester	Cavendish
31	Stockton	Fiesta	30	Stoke	Tiffany's
January 1973			**February 1973**		
1-6	Stockton	Fiesta	1	Birmingham	Barbarella's
7	Spennymoor	Top Hat		Stafford	Top of the World
8-9	Whitley Bay	Sands	2	Birmingham	Barbarella's
10	Chester-le-Street	Garden Farm	3	Birmingham	Barbarella's
11-13	Spennymoor	Top Hat		Stafford	Top of the World
	Peterlee	Senate			
Tour organiser — Danny O'Donovan					

As the year opened, Buck Ram's Platters were part-way through a six-week cabaret tour. Although the line-up did not include even one of the individuals who had been responsible for the success of the Platters in the Fifties, or had participated on any of their hit records, they proved to be a superbly slick and professional outfit. At the Southend show, lead singer Monroe Powell showed perfect pitch and an impressively powerful voice that was ideally suited to their big ballads like 'My Prayer' and 'Smoke Gets In Your Eyes'. Although he sang lead on the majority of the songs, the other group members all contributed as well. Sherman James had a husky voice much better suited to the soul numbers, while it was the deep bass of Gene Williams which brought Paul Robeson's 'Ol' Man River' to life. Hal Howard proved to be the comedian of the group, while Lita Fonza in a tight figure-hugging dress provided a very pleasing physical presence as she danced and shimmied across the stage. 'The Great Pretender', 'Only You', 'With This Ring' and even Mario Lanza's 'Come Prima', were devoured in a well-choreographed set which closed with a frantic 'Land Of A Thousand Dances'.

JERRY LEE LEWIS

The career of Jerry Lee Lewis has flourished through his natural talent, rather than as a result of any well-structured business plan, and on occasion he has suffered badly through lack of attention to such trifling matters as contracts and taxes. For a brief period, he did make a concerted if short-lived attempt at taking care of business with the formation of Jerry Lee Lewis Enterprises Inc, who by the beginning of 1973 were claiming to be a booking agency and talent management firm complete with a publishing arm, production department and expertise in promotion and public relations. They negotiated a new long-term deal for Jerry with Mercury Records, and as a result of this sudden burst of businesslike activity it was announced that he would come to London and record a new rock'n'roll album with a host of British musicians.

Similar projects had been tried successfully by both Chuck Berry and B.B. King, but Jerry Lee's rather more obtuse personality made it less likely that he would be comfortable sharing the limelight with others, so there was considerable apprehension when he arrived at Advision Studios in London on Monday, 8 January to commence work on an album that would become known as *The Session*.

Recording in London.

Producer Steve Rowland's approach was to cram every available musician into the studio and the sessions, which lasted four days and eventually boasted contributions by a staggering array of European musicians including Albert Lee, Chas Hodges, Peter Frampton, Andy Bown, Gary Taylor, Klaus Voormann, Tony Colton, Alvin Lee, Johnny Gustafson, Ray Smith, Pete Gavin, Kenny Jones, Tony Ashton, Matthew Fisher and Rory Gallagher. All these names were further augmented by Americans Kenneth Lovelace, Delaney Bramlett and nineteen-year-old budding drummer Jerry Lee Lewis Jr, while Jud Phillips (representing Jerry Lee Lewis Enterprises Inc) was also on hand to try and make some sense out of the inevitable chaos.

A double album eventually appeared, but the number of musicians jammed onto each track made the exercise more successful in terms of publicity and exposure than actual musical content – though Jerry Lee did his best to tear up the hired Steinway grand piano as they worked through old favourites like 'Sea Cruise', 'Johnny B. Goode' and 'Drinking Wine Spo-Dee-O-Dee' plus new material including 'Jukebox' and 'Music To The Man'. Long-time fans of the Killer were delighted to see him recording rock'n'roll again at a time when he was a major chart act in the field of country music, but would have preferred a less commercial and more traditionally authentic feel to the album.

Tragedy never seems more than an arm's length from Jerry Lee, whose younger son, Steve Allen Lewis drowned in the family swimming pool immediately prior to his comeback tour of Britain in 1962. Only ten months after his participation in the London sessions, Jerry Lee Lewis Jr lost control of his jeep while driving home, hit a bridge support and broke his neck in a fatal accident near Hernando, Mississippi.

CHUCK BERRY

January 1973			February 1973		
15	Glasgow	Green's Playhouse	4	Finsbury Park	Rainbow
16	Bournemouth	Hardrock	6	Manchester	Hardrock
17	Birmingham	Barbarella's	7	Newcastle	City Hall
18	Manchester	Hardrock	8	Doncaster	Top Rank
19	Finsbury Park	Rainbow			
22	Edinburgh	Usher Hall			
29	Kensington	Imperial College			
Tour organisers — Jumpin' Jack & Angelique Enterprises					

'There is an argument for TV producers exercising restraint as to what they put on the family screen at peak viewing time. Otherwise, they will bring down on themselves a censorship that most reasonable people do not want.' The subject of this London *Evening News* editorial was nothing less than Chuck Berry's naughty nursery rhyme, 'My Ding-A-Ling'. The song had been recorded live at the *Lanchester Arts Festival* in February 1972 and by the end of November had finally given Chuck the only No.1 hit single of his long career.

Mary Whitehouse, self-appointed guardian of the nation's morals, was in no doubt at all about the real meaning of the song's innocent lyrics. 'They are intended as deliberate stimulation to self- and mutual masturbation,' she pronounced, firing off a salvo of complaints to the BBC in an attempt to have the record banned. *Top Of The Pops* did drop their film of Berry performing the song and such was the frenzy of righteous indignation that it became front-page news when Jimmy Young, of all people, continued to spin the disc on Radio One.

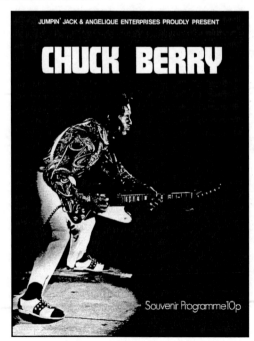

JUMPIN' JACK & ANGELIQUE ENTERPRISES PROUDLY PRESENT

CHUCK BERRY

Souvenir Programme 10p

Chuck himself flew into the UK with his career in a healthy state and 'My Ding-A-Ling' still occupying a spot in the Top 20. The wonderful prospect of Berry and Mrs. Whitehouse appearing together on a TV chat show sadly never materialised, but all the publicity can only have assisted ticket sales.

Support on the tour came mainly from a combination of Baby Whale, Trapeze, the Roy Young Band and Evensong. Chuck's own musicians were lined up to back him, but owing to work permit problems a nucleus of the Roy Young Band – but minus Young himself – deputised on the early shows.

Perhaps not surprisingly there was criticism that the band

seemed ragged and unrehearsed on the opening night at Glasgow. The first house was half-empty and became no more than a warm-up session, but with the late show packed to the rafters, Chuck went to work. From the moment that he hit those familiar opening notes on his brown Gibson, the auditorium came alive and he eased his way through 'Roll Over Beethoven',

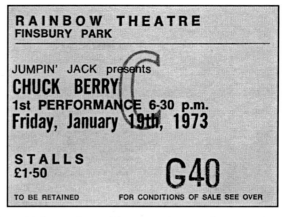

RAINBOW THEATRE
FINSBURY PARK

JUMPIN' JACK presents
CHUCK BERRY
1st PERFORMANCE 6-30 p.m.
Friday, January 19th, 1973

STALLS
£1-50   **G40**

TO BE RETAINED   FOR CONDITIONS OF SALE SEE OVER

'Sweet Little Sixteen' and all the old favourites. Showing plenty of energy, he duckwalked and kangaroo-hopped to the delight of the crowd, who urged him on through 'Carol', 'School Day' and the rest. He briefly dropped the pace for 'That's My Desire' and 'South Of The Border', before accelerating into 'Reelin' And Rockin' ' and finally reached the inevitable 'My Ding-A-Ling'. 'I don't care what Mary thinks,' he pronounced, 'some people just have dirty minds.' His nursery rhyme hit was well received, but it was 'Johnny B. Goode' that had the whole crowd on their feet, clapping and calling in vain for an encore.

The tour was not without its problems though. At Birmingham, Chuck cut his performance to just 20 minutes, claiming that he had been kept waiting by the management before being allowed to go on. He only returned for an encore after the club owner had £200 in cash taken out to him in his car. At Manchester, fog prevented Berry from playing the first house and the second was held up while contract problems were sorted out. The crowd at London's Rainbow Theatre were forced to endure a 45-minute delay after sitting through a tedious set by Baby Whale before Chuck finally appeared, but here again his act ended very abruptly and he failed to reappear for an encore. It was hardly good value for money, and long-time fans were becoming frustrated by his seemingly grasping attitude.

At least the work permit problem was resolved, and for the first time in Britain Chuck Berry was able to work with his own musicians: Billy Peek (guitar), Greg Edick (bass) and Ron Reed (drums). Peek in particular was a real asset, and at the Imperial College in Kensington he traded licks with Berry and contributed enormously to a fine performance.

The original plan was for the British leg of the tour to conclude on 29 January, when Chuck headed off to Europe, but such was the demand for his services that a further four nights were added – including return visits to both Manchester's Hardrock and the Rainbow Theatre in London – ahead of more gigs in Europe. Chuck may have been a controversial figure, but he remained unquestionably the most popular of all the original rock'n'rollers in 1973.

The final word on the 'My Ding-A-Ling' furore was left to a *Record Mirror* reader who observed: *'If Mrs. Whitehouse is correct and it does encourage masturbation, then after selling around eight million copies, there must be an awful lot of wankers around!'*

17

THE COASTERS

January 1973			6	Failsworth	Broadway
21	Bolton	Copperfield's	7-10	Farnworth	Blighty's
	Blackburn	Cavendish		Failsworth	Broadway
22-23	Birmingham	Barbarella's	11-17	Leigh	Garrick
	Birmingham	Rebecca's		Manchester	Fagin's
24-27	Bolton	Copperfield's	18-24	Batley	Variety
28-31	Liverpool	Allinson's	27-28	Birmingham	Barbarella's
	Liverpool	Wooky Hollow		Birmingham	Rebecca's
February 1973			March 1973		
1-3	Liverpool	Allinson's	1-3	Birmingham	Barbarella's
	Liverpool	Wooky Hollow		Birmingham	Rebecca's
4	Failsworth	Broadway	3	Whitchurch	Civic Centre
	Farnworth	Blighty's			
Tour organiser — Henry Sellers					

Twelve months on from their first British tour, the Coasters returned for a second time, but on this occasion confined their appearances to the Northern cabaret circuit, never venturing further south than Birmingham. There was one change to the line-up because founder member Billy Guy had departed to have another stab at a solo career, his place being taken by Jimmy Norman. The 1973 Coasters were therefore Carl Gardner (lead), Earl Carroll (tenor), Ronnie Bright (bass), Jimmy Norman (baritone) and Thomas 'Curley' Palmer (guitar).

The act continued to highlight their classic songs like 'Searchin'', 'Charlie Brown' and 'Poison Ivy', but also included their updated version of the old Clovers hit, 'Love Potion Number 9' and a few newer things like Al Green's 'Let's Stay Together'. Carl Gardner expressed pleasure at their reception when he told *Blues & Soul*, 'We dig playing to British audiences and plan to come over at least once a year.'

Immediately the British dates were concluded, the Coasters flew to Las Vegas, where on 7 March they commenced a season at the International Hotel.

NEIL SEDAKA

January 1973			May 1973		
22-31	London	Talk of The Town	1-5	Southend	Talk of the South
February 1973			6-12	Batley	Variety
1-20	London	Talk of The Town	14-19	Sheffield	Fiesta
March 1973			26	High Wycombe	Caves
25-31	Batley	Variety	June 1973		
April 1973			3-9	Leicester	Bailey's
2-8	Wythenshawe	Golden Garter	July 1973		
15-21	Stockton	Fiesta	4-5	Batley	Variety
29-30	Southend	Talk of the South			
Tour organiser unknown					

Neil Sedaka based himself in Britain for the first half of 1973. His records were back in the UK charts again and his highly acclaimed new album, *Solitaire*, had been recorded in Manchester with members of the

British group 10cc providing the rhythm section. He rented a plush apartment just off London's Park Lane, which provided a home for his wife and two children while he travelled around Britain and Europe for television and cabaret appearances.

On 26 May, he took part in a charity gig for the Samaritans at High Wycombe, appearing alongside Wizzard, the Nashville Teens, Country Fever, the Settlers and Bryan Chalker.

TV Appearances

They Sold A Million (BBC2)	11 February 1973
The Golden Shot (ATV)	15 April 1973
Hey Brian! (Yorkshire)	5 June 1973
Disco Champions '73 (LWT)	15 June 1973
The Rolf Harris Show (LWT)	30 June 1973

CHRIS MONTEZ

February 1973		March 1973	
25-28 Southend	Talk of the South	1-3 Southend	Talk of the South
Tour organiser unknown			

A reissued 45 of 'Let's Dance' had returned Chris Montez to the British charts at the end of 1972 and he made a short trip to Britain as part of an ambitious tour which also took in shows in Germany, Spain, Belgium and Japan. The music press ignored him completely.

TV Appearances

They Sold A Million (BBC2)	8 March 1973

LITTLE RICHARD

It was first announced that Richard would be visiting Britain for two television appearances in March. These were quickly postponed in favour of a more elaborate venture which would involve him in a string of concerts and a major outdoor festival. In the end, it was our friends from the Inland Revenue who intervened, claiming that Richard still owed £4,000 tax in the UK and that a receiving order had been made against him. Inevitably, he declined to come while the threat of bankruptcy was hanging over him.

MARVIN RAINWATER

March 1973	
30 Erdington	Silver Saddle
Tour organiser unknown	

Marvin Rainwater was in Britain to record an album, *Marvin Rainwater Gets Country Fever*, for Philips Records and picked up a solitary live booking for the Silver Saddle Country Music Club in Erdington. They had been seeking a special headliner for their birthday celebrations and it was a considerable coup for them to land Marvin, as few people even knew that he was in the country. Support was provided by Anne & Ray Brett plus the Muskrats.

ROY ORBISON

Roy had an extensive concert and cabaret tour lined up to commence in April 1973. Unfortunately illness prevented him travelling to Britain and the whole project had to be scrapped and then rescheduled later in the year.

FATS DOMINO

April 1973			May 1973		
28	Hammersmith	Odeon	3	Newcastle	City Hall
29	Birmingham	Odeon	4	Preston	Guildhall
			5	Bournemouth	Winter Gardens
			6	Manchester	Hardrock
Tour organiser — Robert Paterson					

Fats Domino's first trip to Britain in March 1967 had been a magnificent occasion during which he had performed for a week at London's Saville Theatre. Six years later, he returned as part of an extensive European tour accompanied by his nine-piece band comprising Walter Kimble (tenor sax), Fred Kemp (tenor sax), Roger Lewis (baritone sax), Maurice Simon (tenor sax), Fred Sheppard (alto sax), Roy Montrell (guitar), David Douglas (bass), Clarence Brown (drums) and Bernard Dunn (drums). Only Kimble, Montrell and Brown survived from the exceptional line-up of 1967, but the new outfit was still a treat for British audiences quite unaccustomed to the sight of a swinging New Orleans band with a battalion of five saxophones.

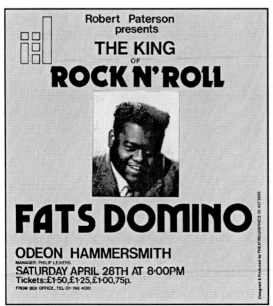

They flew in from Dublin on the morning of 28 April and performed the same evening at the Hammersmith Odeon. The theatre was sold out and Fats made a spectacular entrance wearing a white jacket, white shirt, pink tie and pink trousers. He opened with 'I'm Walkin' ' and proceeded to lead this audience on a journey through the classic songs of New Orleans. 'Blue Monday'

led into 'Stagger Lee', a driving 'Let The Four Winds Blow' and 'I'm In Love Again'. He was not a demonstrative performer, preferring to stay hunched over his piano, building the atmosphere through his music. 'I Want To Walk You Home' was followed by a gutsy 'Shake, Rattle And Roll' and 'My Girl Josephine'. Unfortunately, the enjoyment was to some extent marred by sound problems. At times Domino's vocals were being overpowered by the band. He eventually played for almost an hour, finally closing with 'Ain't That A Shame', 'Jambalaya' and 'So Long'. It was a masterful display and was greeted with an enthusiastic standing ovation.

Immediately following the performance in Manchester, Domino and his entourage flew off for further shows in Germany, Belgium and the Netherlands.

BOB LUMAN

Like several other rock'n'rollers, Bob Luman had reinvented himself as a country singer during the Sixties and by 1973 was a regular in the US country charts with a steady string of hits for Epic Records. He made a brief visit to Britain during May solely to perform at military bases but found time to be interviewed by Bob Powel for *Country Music People*. Luman left no doubts that he was still a rock'n'roller at heart: *'I am still doing the things I have always done. I never could cut with the steels and fiddles – hard-core country – because I have a little rock blood left in me. I guess you could call my material rockabilly.'*

If only his health had held up, Bob Luman would have been a massive draw once the rockabilly craze took off, but sadly this was not to be the case. He never returned to Britain and during 1976 needed surgery for a ruptured blood vessel in the oesophagus. He did continue performing almost to the end, but following a bout of pneumonia passed away on 27 December 1978. Johnny Cash sang at his funeral.

THE CRICKETS

May 1973			June 1973		
19	Margate	Dreamland	1-2	Barnsley	Bailey's
	London	Speakeasy		Sheffield	Bailey's
20-26	Doncaster	Bailey's	3-9	Stockton	Fiesta
	Hull	Bailey's	10-16	Burnley	Rosegrove
27	Sheffield	Bailey's		Eccles	Talk of the North
	Barnsley	Bailey's	17-21	Wakefield	Theatre Club
28-31	Sheffield	Bailey's	22	Boroughbridge	Crown Hotel
				Wakefield	Theatre Club
			23	Goole	Vikings Hotel
				Wakefield	Theatre Club
Tour organiser — Henry Sellers					

The Crickets had spent the early part of January in Britain recording their album, *Bubblegum, Bop, Ballads and Boogies*, which was released on Philips during April. A cabaret tour in the North of England was an ideal opportunity to promote the new record, and the previous line-up of Sonny Curtis, Jerry Allison, Glen D. Hardin and Rick Grech was now augmented by the inclusion of ace guitarist Albert Lee. Steve Krikorian again travelled with them in the role of road manager.

Glen D. Hardin had still to complete a series of shows playing piano for Elvis and arrived after the tour was underway. Perhaps unsurprisingly, the transition from the glamour of Las Vegas to the Northern club scene in Great Britain proved too much of a culture shock. He never really settled back into life as a Cricket and it wasn't long before he packed his bags and returned to the States.

The tour received very little media coverage, but a write-up which appeared in the *Barnsley Chronicle* reported a thoroughly enjoyable night. The Holly classics inevitably made up the bulk of the show, but the introduction of Albert Lee into the band resulted in updated arrangements, a heavier guitar sound and a stronger beat. 'Rockin' Pneumonia And The Boogie Woogie Flu', 'Lovesick Blues' and 'My Rockin' Days' were performed from the new album, and other less obvious Crickets material like 'Stagger Lee' and 'Me And Bobby McGee' included. An hour-long set left the audience on their feet and shouting for more.

Promoter Henry Sellers reported that the tour was a resounding success and revealed plans to bring them back, perhaps in October, to play arenas omitted from the current schedule.

SHA NA NA

May 1973			June 1973		
25-26	Finsbury Park	Rainbow	1	Birmingham	Town Hall
28	Manchester	Free Trade Hall	2	Liverpool	Stadium
			3	Bristol	Hippodrome
			4	Sheffield	City Hall
Tour organiser — Frederick Bannister					

The appeal of Sha Na Na appeared to be wearing a little thin with British audiences by the time of this, their third tour in three years. They were engaged in a lengthy European excursion and flew into London after already playing concerts in Scandinavia, Belgium and France.

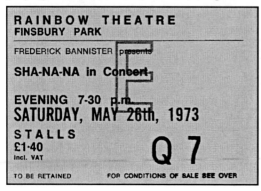

RAINBOW THEATRE
FINSBURY PARK

FREDERICK BANNISTER presents

SHA-NA-NA in Concert

EVENING 7-30 p.m.
SATURDAY, MAY 26th, 1973
STALLS
£1·40
Incl. VAT

Q 7

TO BE RETAINED   FOR CONDITIONS OF SALE SEE OVER

The twelve-man line-up comprised Jocko Marcellino, Bruno Clarke, Lennie Baker, Screamin' Scott Simon, Captain Outrageous (aka Scott Powell), Rich Joffe, Donny York, Elliot 'Gino' Cahn, Jon 'Bowzer' Bauman, Vinnie Taylor, Johnny 'The Kid' Contardo and one other referred to simply as 'Butch'. Originally it was hoped that Commander Cody & His

Lost Planet Airmen would be the support act, but this was never confirmed and instead the pretentious-sounding Esperanto, who described themselves as 'the world's first international rock orchestra', opened each show. Most rock'n'roll fans remained in the bar until after the intermission.

The format of Sha Na Na's act was pretty well unchanged and perhaps the novelty was starting to wear off. They had a new British single, 'Yakety Yak', to promote and the twelve group members worked as hard as ever, dancing, harmonising and powering their way through a set of rock'n'roll classics in an affectionate, if satirical way. The trouble was that, when first seen, the group made a tremendous visual impact, but this effect lessened on each subsequent occasion and it was hard for them to vary the format without losing the whole point of the performance.

There was little interest in Sha Na Na from the media and the tour passed off without much comment. Trouble was also brewing up within the group, and in October 1973 three members – Cahn, Joffe and Clarke – split from the others and commenced legal action in the Supreme Court of the State of New York in an attempt to prevent the remaining members from performing under the name of Sha Na Na without them. It seemed as if the satirists were starting to take themselves a little too seriously.

DEL SHANNON

May 1973				23	Swansea	Townsman
25-26	Stalybridge	Bower		25	Birkenhead	Hamilton
	Hyde	Circles		26-28	Batley	Variety
27-31	Bolton	Copperfield's		29	Bolton	Aquarius
	Failsworth	Broadway		30-31	Purfleet	Circus Tavern .
June 1973				**August 1973**		
1-2	Bolton	Copperfield's		1-4	Purfleet	Circus Tavern
	Failsworth	Broadway		5-11	Stockton	Fiesta
3-9	Burnley	Rosegrove		12-17	Hull	Bailey's
	Eccles	Talk of the North		18	Goole	Vikings Hotel
10	Coventry	Trent Valley			Hull	Bailey's
14-15	Birmingham	Barbarella's		19	Sheffield	Bailey's
16	Bilston	Wolves Supporters			Barnsley	Bailey's
	Birmingham	Barbarella's		20-23	Sheffield	Bailey's
17-23	Liverpool	Allinson's		24-25	Barnsley	Bailey's
	Liverpool	Wooky Hollow			Sheffield	Bailey's
24-30	Manchester	Fagin's		26-28	Oldham	Bailey's
July 1973				29	Salford	Willows
1-7	Birmingham	La Dolce Vita			Oldham	Bailey's
18	Stockport	Warren		30-31	Oldham	Bailey's
19	Warrington	Rugby		**September 1973**		
	Salford	Rugby		1	Oldham	Bailey's
20	Hanley	Heavy Steam Machine		2-8	Leicester	Bailey's
Tour organiser — Henry Sellers						

Promoter Henry Sellers had now added Del Shannon to his roster of rock'n'rollers, and such was the strength of bookings that a tour originally scheduled for ten weeks gradually expanded into three and a half months. Del rented a house in Manchester so that his wife, Shirley Westover, and children, Craig, Jody and Kym, could be with him. Amazingly, almost all of his bookings proved to be inside an hour by train or car from his temporary home. Other than a week's residency at the Circus Tavern at Purfleet, Shannon never ventured into the South of England at all.

Audience reaction was excellent and his performance at the Talk of the North was typical of the whole tour. Backed by Impala, he opened with 'Hats Off To Larry' and 'Handy Man' – both songs designed to highlight his trademark falsetto, which sounded as effective as ever. 'The Swiss Maid' was well received and was followed by 'Hey! Little Girl' and 'Little Town Flirt' before the pace slackened for 'Kelly'. A soulful version of Roy Orbison's 'Crying' led into 'Two Kinds Of Teardrops', 'The Answer To Everything' and 'So Long Baby'. With such quality material at his fingertips, Shannon's success on the cabaret circuit was easily understood. He again slowed the pace for 'Jody' before closing out his act with 'Keep Searchin' ' and 'Runaway'. By now the audience were clambering to their feet and dancing among the tables. As Henry Sellers had clearly observed, there was plenty of mileage left in Del Shannon. Del spent ten days playing in Europe during mid-July, but otherwise it was routine cabaret appearances almost every night.

TV Appearances
The Old Grey Whistle Test (BBC2)   19 June 1973

BO DIDDLEY

Since his first trip to Britain with the Everly Brothers in 1963, poor Bo had not experienced the best of luck. His later tours had been plagued by problems but his many fans were encouraged by the news that he would be returning to the UK for 17 days in June. Unfortunately it was not only Bo's fans who spotted his forthcoming visit, and it was soon reported that a letter from the Inland Revenue was received by him in the States demanding £775 unpaid tax relating to his 1972 Wembley appearance. His manager simply returned the letter to promoter Ray Brown with the words 'Tour cancelled' scribbled across it.

THE DRIFTERS

June 1973			29	Nottingham	Intercon
16	Dunstable	California		Birmingham	Barbarella's
	London	Speakeasy	30	Market Drayton	Swimming Pool
17-19	Batley	Variety		Birmingham	Barbarella's
20	Preston	Top Rank	**July 1973**		
	Batley	Variety	1	Hanley	Top Rank
21	Batley	Variety	6	Leysdown	Island Hotel
22	Doncaster	Top Rank		Margate	Dreamland
	Batley	Variety	7	Dunstable	California
23	Batley	Variety	8-14	Farnworth	Blighty's
24	Jacksdale	Grey Topper		Failsworth	Broadway
25	Reading	Top Rank	15-21	Liverpool	Allinson's
26	Stevenage	Locarno		Liverpool	Wooky Hollow
	London	Gulliver's	22	Eccles	Talk of the North
27	Wolverhampton	Gaumont	23-28	Manchester	Fagin's
	Birmingham	Barbarella's		Eccles	Talk of the North
28	Birmingham	Barbarella's	29	Southend	Talk of the South
Tour organiser — Henry Sellers					

Johnny Moore, Bill Fredericks, Grant Kitchings, Butch Leake and guitarist Butch Mann flew into the UK from Spain on 15 June and tore straight into a long and strenuous programme of club and cabaret work, backed throughout by the John McFlair Band. This was a highly successful period for the Drifters, who notched up capacity crowds almost everywhere they went and during their residency at Batley Variety Club smashed the box office record previously held by Shirley Bassey.

The music press remained uncomfortable with acts who prospered by performing old material and *Melody Maker*, who attended the show at Hanley, criticised the group for playing to the requirements of the crowd, rather than introducing newer songs. The Drifters knew what they were doing though, opening with a sizzling version of Sam Cooke's 'Good News', and mixing their classics like 'Up On The Roof', 'Under The Boardwalk' and 'Come On Over To My Place' with other rock'n'roll standards such as 'My Prayer' and 'Rip It Up'. Kitchings took the lead on an exciting interpretation of 'Dance With Me' and the audience response throughout the night (and indeed the whole tour) left no doubt that the Drifters were just about the most popular act on the cabaret circuit. *Melody Maker* had totally lost the plot yet again.

Left to right: Butch Leake, Grant Kitchings, Bill Fredericks and Johnny Moore.

Some new songs from the group's first album for Bell Records did eventually work their way into the repertoire, including their latest single, 'Like Sister And Brother', while Moore occasionally performed a stylish version of 'I Can See Clearly Now', but unquestionably it was the classic Drifters songs from their days with Atlantic Records which the crowds came to hear.

During their television spot on *The Old Grey Whistle Test*, Kitchings was suffering with a heavy chest cold, but they still gave a good account of themselves performing three of their Atlantic numbers including a highly effective 'Under The Boardwalk'. At Wolverhampton they shared billing with Major Lance.

TV Appearances
The Old Grey Whistle Test (BBC2)   24 July 1973

CHUCK BERRY

July 1973		
21 Buxton	Booth Farm	
Tour organiser — North-West Promotions		

Much to Mary Whitehouse's dismay, the newly recorded X-certificate live version of 'Reelin' And Rockin' ' had been followed by 'My Ding-A-Ling' into the British charts. Chuck, with his name back in the spotlight, was brought in to headline the *Buxton Festival*, earning himself a reported £9,000 for just a single performance – a significant amount of money back in 1973.

The event took place in the open at Booth Farm on a site which was proposed to become Britain's first permanent festival venue. There was a strong support made up of contemporary rock names including Nazareth, Medicine Head, the Groundhogs, the Edgar Broughton Band, Wizzard, Canned Heat and compere John Peel. Berry was backed by Memphis Bend.

An estimated crowd in excess of 16,000 was confronted with bleak conditions and rain so heavy that even the nearby mountain sheep huddled together for shelter. Soon everything had sunk into three inches of mud and to add insult to injury the woefully inadequate PA system kept breaking down. One or two of the less resilient support bands refused to play. Chuck Berry, who knows a thing or two about contracts, arrived, collected his fee in cash and took the stage unrehearsed while the bedraggled audience kept themselves warm by jiving to 'Sweet Little Sixteen', 'Johnny B. Goode' and the rest. Somehow, he managed to rise above the appalling conditions and even the PA seemed to hold up during his set. Not for the first time Berry was the saviour of the show. There was no encore. The rain kept on falling while Chuck climbed straight into a waiting car and was gone.

FREDDY CANNON

August 1973			September 1973		
24	Birmingham	Barbarella's	1	Bolton	Copperfield's
25	Whitchurch	Civic Centre		Failsworth	Broadway
	Birmingham	Barbarella's	2-8	Liverpool	Wooky Hollow
26	Bolton	Copperfield's		Liverpool	Allinson's
	Failsworth	Broadway			
27-28	Failsworth	Broadway			
29-31	Bolton	Copperfield's			
	Failsworth	Broadway			
Tour organiser — Henry Sellers					

This was one of rock'n'roll's forgotten tours. Freddy Cannon had successfully toured Britain in May and June 1960 in the company of Johnny Preston and Conway Twitty, but had last been seen on a British stage in September 1963. His name had dropped right out of sight and was rarely mentioned in the music press until a brief announcement reported that the Clayman Agency were bringing him in for a fortnight of dates commencing 20 July. These never materialised and instead Freddy found himself working Henry Sellers' Northern cabaret circuit a month later.

Cannon did seem a strange choice in some ways. His sledgehammer style of rock'n'roll was far from everybody's taste and frantic versions of 'Buzz Buzz A-Diddle-It' and 'Tallahassee Lassie' were liable to cause the cabaret audiences to choke on their chicken in the basket. The tour went ahead under a complete veil of secrecy and nobody from the media interviewed Freddy, nor reported on his progress. One can only assume that he failed to empathise with the cabaret set, as it would be more than twenty years before his next appearance on a British stage.

JOHNNY CASH
CARL PERKINS

September 1973		
1	Wembley	Stadium
2	Birmingham	Town Hall
3	Manchester	Free Trade Hall
4	Newcastle	City Hall
5	Glasgow	Apollo Centre
Tour organiser unknown		

A crowd in excess of 50,000 gathered at Wembley Stadium on 1 September for the climax of evangelist Billy Graham's ambitious *SPR-E '73*, which stood for *'Spiritual Re-Emphasis'*. A seminar had been held at Earls Court during the preceding week and this culminated with a massive concert headlined by Johnny Cash and Cliff Richard.

Cash's segment was introduced by Cliff and commenced with Carl Perkins singing the Tom T. Hall song, 'Me And Jesus'. Johnny opened with 'Sunday Morning Coming Down', but then surprisingly made the focal point of his act, not a selection of gospel songs, but a medley of rockabilly favourites: 'Hey Porter', 'Folsom Prison Blues', 'Wreck Of The Old 97' and 'Orange Blossom Special'. This did seem an inappropriate choice for a religious gathering, but he ploughed on, duetting with June Carter on 'Jackson', 'Help Me Make It Through The Night' and 'Daddy Sang Bass'. Some of the crowd seemed unsure exactly what to make of Cash, who looked and sounded a little uncomfortable, but there were sufficient of his fans present to ensure he received a warm and hearty response. Backing for Cash and Perkins was provided by the Tennessee Three – Bob Wootton (guitar), Marshall Grant (bass) and W.S. Holland (drums).

CHUCK BERRY

September 1973	
7	Finsbury Park Rainbow
Tour organiser — Peter Bowyer	

Chuck's enduring popularity resulted in a one-off return booking at London's Rainbow Theatre. This was his third UK visit of the year and, judging by the roasting he received in some areas of the music press, it was probably one show more than was needed by all concerned.

New Musical Express savaged Berry unmercifully, describing him as *'an unprofessional, condescending old sham'*. They complained that he took five minutes to get plugged in, that his usually reliable backing group, Memphis Bend, sounded both unrehearsed and out of tune, and that he seemed content to merely slip in and out of songs by means of endless inane, doodling guitar passages. When somebody in the audience called for more rock'n'roll, he retorted, 'I'm playing twenty minutes over time. I've done my forty-five minutes and I can leave any time I want to.' He then took the easy way out and invited the audience onstage to finish the show for him. Chuck's

Chaotic end to a disastrous gig – although Sunglasses Ron seems to have enjoyed himself!

many fans remained frustrated at his attitude. The man appeared to have so much more to offer than was being delivered. The support act at the Rainbow were Fumble.

BOBBY VEE

September 1973						
14	Leigh	Garrick		26	Liverpool	Wooky Hollow
15	Scampton	RAF		27-29	Birkenhead	Hamilton
	Lincoln	Aquarius			Liverpool	Wooky Hollow
16	Eccles	Talk of the North		30	Birmingham	Barbarella's
	Farnworth	Blighty's		**October 1973**		
17-18	Eccles	Talk of the North		1-4	Birmingham	Barbarella's
19-22	Eccles	Talk of the North		5-6	Birmingham	Club Cedar
	Farnworth	Blighty's		7	Failsworth	Broadway
23	Birkenhead	Hamilton			Bolton	Copperfield's
	Liverpool	Wooky Hollow		8	Barrow	99
24	Liverpool	Wooky Hollow		9	Stockport	Warren
25	New Brighton	Tower		10-13	Failsworth	Broadway
	Liverpool	Wooky Hollow			Bolton	Copperfield's
Tour organiser — Henry Sellers						

Bobby Vee remained one of the strongest draws on the Northern cabaret circuit and a regular visitor to the UK. This was his eighth tour since 1962, and even though the chart hits had long since dried up he had retained a solid block of largely female fans who remained loyal and who turned out each time the boy from North Dakota stepped out onto a British stage.

BRENDA LEE

September 1973			October 1973		
16-22	Sheffield	Fiesta	1-6	Stockton	Fiesta
23-29	Southend	Talk of the South	7-13	Glasgow	Rangers FC Social
30	Stockton	Fiesta			
Tour organiser unknown					

Brenda Lee had not toured Britain since 1967. Health complications following the birth of her second child, Jolie, had led to a period of semi-retirement. She flew into Britain on 15 September with her manager, Joe Higgins, to undertake a short cabaret tour and, despite being out of the public eye for so long, still proved to be a box office attraction.

Her act had become a little more sophisticated and the show at Southend could probably be best described as a mixture of schmaltz and nostalgia, with old favourites like 'I'm Sorry', 'All Alone Am I', 'Coming On Strong' and 'Sweet Nothin's' getting the greatest applause.

TV Appearances
Russell Harty Plus (LWT)   23 September 1973

ROY ORBISON

September 1973			October 1973		
16	Stockport	Davenport	1-6	Batley	Variety
17-22	Southend	Talk of the South	7-13	Luton	Caesar's Palace
23-30	Batley	Variety	14-20	St. Agnes	Talk of the West
			21	Derby	Talk of the Midlands
			22-23	Weston-super-Mare	Webbington
			24-27	Derby	Talk of the Midlands
			28	Chatham	Central Hall
Tour organiser unknown					

A bout of illness had caused the cancellation of Roy's tour, which had originally been scheduled for April and May. Now fully recovered, he underlined his long-term commitment to his British fans with six weeks on the cabaret circuit. His long run of hit records had dried up four years earlier, but the strength and enduring popularity of numbers like 'Blue Bayou' and 'Oh, Pretty Woman' ensured a welcome for Orbison wherever he appeared in the UK. The only disappointment was the late cancellation of his show at London's Rainbow Theatre, where he had been scheduled to appear with the Majestics on 29 October.

At the end of his stay, Roy flew home to Nashville for a few days' rest before embarking upon a lengthy US tour for promoter Richard Nader.

BEN E. KING

September 1973			November 1973		
28	Leysdown	Island Hotel	1-3	Liverpool	Wooky Hollow
	London	Ronnie Scott's		Liverpool	Allinson's
29	Margate	Dreamland	4	Manchester	Placemate
30	Sheffield	Fiesta	5	Hanley	Heavy Steam Machine
October 1973					
1-6	Sheffield	Fiesta			
7	Leigh	Garrick			
8-13	Manchester	Fagin's			
	Leigh	Garrick			
14-20	Eccles	Talk of the North			
21	Jacksdale	Grey Topper			
23	Redcar	Top Deck			
24	Doncaster	Outlook			
25	London	Pheasantry			
26	Torquay	Paradise Hotel			
27	Dunstable	California			
	Peckham	Mr. Bee's			
28-31	Liverpool	Wooky Hollow			
	Liverpool	Allinson's			
Tour organiser unknown					

Ben E. King, formerly lead vocalist with the Drifters, had been a top attraction on the UK club and ballroom circuit during the Sixties and had toured Britain at least once every year since 1964 with an act that comprised a mixture of soul music and those vocal group classics which made the Drifters perennial favourites with UK audiences. In truth, however, his period of dominance on the club scene had passed by the time he returned in September 1973. There was still plenty of work for him though, and very little time off during his five-week stay.

TONY ORLANDO

Dawn were still proving a popular act with British record buyers, and Tony Orlando, Telma Hopkins and Joyce Vincent flew into Britain on 1 October for a week of promotion including three BBC-TV appearances. Their fifth British hit, 'Say, Has Anybody Seen My Sweet Gypsy Rose', was still in the charts and Orlando promised to return early in the new year for a series of live dates. What he really needed was to find himself another song of the calibre of 'Halfway To Paradise' if he was going to reawaken the interest of the rock'n'roll fans.

TV Appearances

It's Lulu (BBC1)	13 October 1973
The Two Ronnies (BBC2)	? October 1973 (screened 20 December 1973)
Top Of The Pops (BBC1)	? October 1973 (screened 25 December 1973)

THE DRIFTERS

November 1973			December 1973		
9	Shrewsbury	Music Hall	1-2	Wythenshawe	Golden Garter
	Birmingham	Barbarella's	3	Liverpool	Wispa
10	Whitchurch	Civic Centre		Liverpool	Allinson's
	Birmingham	Barbarella's	5	Birmingham	Barbarella's
11-13	Leicester	Bailey's		Birmingham	Club Cedar
14	Northampton	Salon	6	Enfield	Picketts Lock
	Leicester	Bailey's		London	La Valbonne
15-16	Leicester	Bailey's			
17	Jacksdale	Grey Topper			
	Leicester	Bailey's			
18-21	Batley	Variety			
22	Rotherham	Tiffany's			
	Batley	Variety			
23	Batley	Variety			
24	Goole	Vikings Hotel			
	Batley	Variety			
26-30	Wythenshawe	Golden Garter			
Tour organiser — Henry Sellers					

Things were really buzzing for the Drifters. Their new Bell recording, 'Like Sister And Brother', had reached the UK Top 10 during August and this ensured another full datebook when they returned for their second British tour of 1973. Johnny Moore, Bill Fredericks, Grant Kitchings and Butch Leake again worked with the John McFlair Band and sold out time and again on a mixture of club and cabaret dates. The support act at Barbarella's on 5 December were Jimmy James & The Vagabonds.

CHAPTER TWO

1974

Don't Knock The Rock

Cabaret rock'n'roll was at its peak in 1974. A constant flow of American artists toured the UK, the likes of Del Shannon, Bobby Vee, Neil Sedaka and the Drifters each making more than one visit. Away from the cabaret circuit, however, things were less rosy. Not for the first time it needed Bill Haley & His Comets to stir up the excitement and general mayhem that inevitably accompanied their British appearances, so the Haley tour was a welcome contrast to the rather sterile scene elsewhere.

If live rock'n'roll was not especially exciting, there were at least signs for renewed optimism. The record companies were dusting down and reissuing old hits, and all manner of vintage material was becoming available, some for the very first time. Both Haley and the Crystals reappeared on the British charts as their old recordings found a new lease of life. Specialist records shops like Rock On, Vintage Record Centre and Moondog's were springing up to cater for the rock'n'roll fans' insatiable demand for product. Even *New Musical Express* carried a lengthy article about rockabilly music in their issue on 4 May.

There were some who felt strongly about the need for live rock'n'roll. A gentleman named Ronald Elvis Presley was arrested after running naked through a housing estate in Winsford, Cheshire in protest about his namesake's continuing failure to visit the UK.

A big package show headlined by Billy Fury and Marty Wilde, and also featuring Tommy Bruce, Heinz, Carl Simmons and the New Tornadoes, set out around the theatres in February and did such good business that it was relaunched for a second stint in May. Alvin Stardust – the former Shane Fenton – enjoyed a highly successful year with four big hit records. His live shows were pandemonium, with screaming girls, some fainting and others throwing their underwear onto the stage and a set list that included rock'n'roll standards like 'Rip It Up' and 'Johnny B. Goode'.

Some of the more interesting country acts to tour Britain included Doug Kershaw, John D. Loudermilk, Glen Campbell and Jimmy Payne, while black music was represented by Sonny Terry & Brownie McGhee, Eddie Holman, Ike & Tina Turner and, on a memorable evening at London's 100 Club, a virtuoso appearance by guitarist Mickey Baker.

THE COASTERS

January 1974			8	Doncaster	Top Rank
26	Dunstable	California		Sheffield	Bailey's
29-31	Oldham	Bailey's	9	Goole	Vikings Hotel
February 1974				Sheffield	Bailey's
1-2	Oldham	Bailey's	10-16	Cardiff	Tito's
3-7	Sheffield	Bailey's			
Tour organiser — Henry Sellers					

Carl Gardner, Earl Carroll, Jimmy Norman and Ron Bright spent nearly a month performing for the cabaret set and had a new British album released to coincide with the tour. *On Broadway* was a recently recorded collection of rock'n'roll, R&B and soul material, but inevitably it was their old hits which were the backbone of the act. There was no media interest in their visit, which once again was concentrated away from London and the South of England.

DOCTOR ROSS

January 1974			10	Glasgow	Apollo Centre
27	Nottingham	Imperial College	11	Manchester	Free Trade Hall
28	London	City of London Poly	12	Liverpool	University
31	Bangor	University	13	Sheffield	Polytechnic
February 1974			15	Lancaster	University
1	Coventry	Technical College	16	Durham	University
2	Bristol	University	17	Birmingham	Repertory
3	Euston	Shaw Theatre	19	London	100 Club
4	Keele	University	20	Bangor	University
5	York	University	21	Portsmouth	Polytechnic
6	Aberystwyth	University	**March 1974**		
8	Brighton	Polytechnic	7	Birmingham	University
9	Loughborough	University	10	Newcastle	Guildhall
Tour organiser — Big Bear Promotions					

Bluesman Isiah 'Doctor' Ross became a cult hero to rockabilly fans during the Eighties when several of his primitive-sounding recordings such as 'The Boogie Disease' and 'Cat Squirrel' were elevated to hit status in the clubs and ballrooms. In 1974 however, he was still working blues clubs and colleges, and for the majority of this lengthy tour appeared as part of a package titled *American Blues Legends '74*, on which he was joined by Big John Wrencher, Chicago guitarist Eddie 'Playboy' Taylor, George 'G.P.' Jackson (also known as 'Kansas City Bo Diddley') and New Orleans pianist Cousin Joe Pleasant.

The capacity crowd of mainly students who packed into Coventry's Lanchester Technical College particularly enjoyed a powerhouse version of 'Doctor Ross Boogie' and fine interpretations of 'Good Morning Little Schoolgirl' and Sonny Boy Williamson's 'Sugar Mama', each performed in the Doctor's highly unusual style, his guitar played both left-handed and upside down.

NEIL SEDAKA

February 1974			March 1974		
2	London	Royal Festival Hall	10-16	Usk	Helmaen Int'l.
9	Chatham	Central Hall	17-23	Batley	Variety
10	Manchester	Opera House	24	Farnworth	Blighty's
11	Stoke	Jollee's	26-30	Farnworth	Blighty's
13	Glasgow	Apollo Centre	**April 1974**		
14	Southport	Theatre	14-20	Charnock Richard	Park Hall Hotel
15	Croydon	Fairfield Halls	22	Farnworth	Blighty's
16	Bournemouth	Winter Gardens	24-27	Farnworth	Blighty's
17	Oxford	New	**May 1974**		
19	Birmingham	Town Hall	5-11	Batley	Variety
21	Bristol	Colston Hall			
22	Brighton	Dome			
23	St. Albans	City Hall			
Tour organiser — Henry Sellers					

Polydor Records released 'A Little Lovin' ' to coincide with Neil's lengthy stay in the UK, and his renewed popularity helped the record into the British charts during February. Perhaps surprisingly, this was the first time that he had played a substantial series of one-nighters in Britain, and many venues sold out very quickly.

At the Royal Festival Hall, he was dressed in a smart white suit and gave an immaculate performance mainly comprising his newer material. Opening with 'Standing On The Inside' and 'Love Will Keep Us Together', he worked through 'Solitaire', 'Sad Eyes' and 'Ease My Suspicion'. After the interval, Neil was joined by the full Royal Philharmonic Orchestra for songs like 'Superbird', 'I'm A Mean Old Man', 'This Will Be Our Last Song Together' and 'Laughter In The Rain'. There were even a few screams when he turned the clock back and eased his way into 'Oh! Carol', 'Stairway To Heaven' and 'Little Devil', during which he had to fight hard against some rhythmless clapping from the enthusiastic audience. An album, *Live At The Royal Festival Hall*, was released by Polydor in November.

TV Appearances

The Old Grey Whistle Test (BBC2)	3 February 1974
Saturday Request (BBC2)	16 February 1974
Look – Mike Yarwood (BBC1)	15 May 1974 (screened 1 June 1974)

TONY ORLANDO

Tony Orlando and Dawn were lined up for a fortnight of shows in the UK during February, although Oxford was the only venue which had been revealed to the public before the whole project became a victim of the energy crisis. The revised plan saw Orlando and Dawn limit their stay to a couple of days and telerecord a special from the Talk of the Town for later transmission by the BBC.

TV appearances
Top American Stars (BBC2) 16 February 1974 (screened 24 February 1974)

BILL HALEY & HIS COMETS

February 1974			April 1974		
28	Islington	City University	1	Ilford	King's
March 1974				Ilford	Green Gate
1	Margate	Dreamland	2-3	Jersey, CI	Behan's (West
	Leysdown	Island Hotel			Park Pavilion)
2	Leeds	University	4	Cleethorpes	Pier Pavilion
3-9	Liverpool	Allinson's		Immingham	Mayflower
	Liverpool	Wooky Hollow	5	Nottingham	Lucky 7
10	Glasgow	Apollo Centre		Jacksdale	Grey Topper
11	Stafford	Top of the World	6	Little Paxton	Samuel Jones
	Wolverhampton	Lafayette	7	Southend	Talk of the South
13	Morecambe	Bowl	8	Southend	Talk of the South
14	Stevenage	Locarno		Ilford	Palais
15	Lanchester	Polytechnic	9-13	Southend	Talk of the South
16	Loughborough	University	14	Lowestoft	South Pier Pavilion
	Twycross	Country	17-18	Derby	Talk of the Midlands
17	Brighouse	Stardust	19	Doncaster	Top Rank
	Farnworth	Blighty's	20	Whitchurch	Civic Centre
18	Brighouse	Stardust		Birmingham	Barbarella's
	Oldham	Candlewick	21	Sheffield	Fiesta
19-23	Brighouse	Stardust	22-27	Stockton	Fiesta
	Farnworth	Blighty's	28-30	Leicester	Bailey's
25	Hammersmith	Palais	**May 1974**		
	Kensington	Biba's	1	Hucknall	WMC
27	Nelson	Imperial		Leicester	Bailey's
	Bury	Basement	2	Leamington	Royal Spa Centre
28	Bedworth	Civic Hall		Leicester	Bailey's
	Birmingham	Barbarella's	3-4	Leicester	Bailey's
29-30	Coventry	Chrysler UK	5	Failsworth	Broadway
	Birmingham	Barbarella's	6	Birmingham	Barbarella's
31	Leicester	Palais	7	Blackpool	Locarno
			12	Purfleet	Circus Tavern
Tour organisers — Patrick Malynn and Henry Sellers					

Twenty years after 'Rock Around The Clock' was recorded, Bill Haley returned to Britain for a highly successful tour on which an estimated 95% of the dates sold out. He was accompanied by his wife Martha and long-time Comets Rudy Pompilli (saxophone), Nick Nastos (lead guitar) and Ray Cawley (double bass) plus newcomers Ray Parsons (rhythm guitar) and Freddy Moore (drums). They made such an impact as they travelled the country, that a reissued 'Rock Around The Clock' swept back into the British charts again midway through the tour, peaking at a highly respectable No.12 on 20 April.

Haley arrived in the UK on 25 February and embarked upon a rapid round of radio and television promotions which included *The Old Grey Whistle Test*, *Top Of The Pops* and Radio Two's *My Top Twelve* and *Open House*. The first show at London's City University set the pattern for the whole tour with a packed house, including many students who would have hardly been born when Bill and his Comets first came to Britain in 1957.

In fact, the University had tried to restrict the sale of tickets to students only by initially not advertising the gig, but inevitably there were several Teddy boys mingling with the students when Bill ran on stage smartly attired in a sparkly jacket, dress shirt and tie, and carrying his trusty Gibson horizontally under his arm. As soon as the Comets broke into 'Shake, Rattle And Roll', the whole place erupted with a feverish display of jiving, jitterbugging, handclapping and foot-stomping. Haley has always been easy to ridicule – his unhip appearance and never-changing stage act, along with an image which could not have been further from the contemporary world of rock music in 1974 – but yet again the sheer excitement of the music reached out to a new generation of youngsters and the tour was off to a rip-roaring start.

Each night was like a throwback to 1957 as the Comets travelled back and forth across the country. In Brighouse, the compere was showered with coins and beer mats when he brought one show to an abrupt close, while at Doncaster the Comets went on so late that some irate fans had to leave before the show got underway. The tour itself was open-ended and bookings came flooding in, eventually extending the itinerary well into May. Shakin' Stevens & The Sunsets provided the support at Glasgow and at several other venues, while the Kinks opened for Haley at Leeds, and Flying Saucers at Stevenage.

One of the more unlikely dates took place on 6 April at the tiny village of Little Paxton, near to St. Neots. Bill and the Comets were booked by the works social committee of Samuel Jones Ltd, who twice sold out their 300-capacity hall for shows at 7.00 pm and 1.00 am. The *St. Neots Advertiser* was on hand to witness a perspiring Haley and an excited bunch of revellers dancing the night away. No comment was made as to the level of absenteeism from work the following morning, however.

Olivia Newton-John met up with Bill in London and presented him with an award commemorating the sixth entry into the UK charts of 'Rock Around The Clock'. While in Leeds, Haley visited Elland Road and sat in the front of the directors' box for the Football League match against Burnley. Leeds manager Don Revie returned the compliment by attending one of the shows at Brighouse. Eye-Line Films were at one stage poised to make a 90-minute movie of the tour, but sadly in the end this project failed to materialise.

In the same way that the Royal Albert Hall had been the focal point of Haley's 1968 tour, so the gig at the Hammersmith Palais on 25 March proved to be the occasion which grabbed the lion's share of the publicity six years later. Queues had started forming some hours before showtime and eventually stretched for several hundred yards as considerably more people than the legal limit struggled to gain admittance. By the time Bill and the Comets followed the Wild Angels and Rock Island Line onto the stage, there were an estimated 4,000 fans in the Palais, packed in like

GREAT WESTERN FESTIVALS & HENRY SELLERS
IN ASSOCIATION WITH PATRICK MALYN PRESENT

BILL HALEY & THE COMETS
HAMMERSMITH PALAIS
MONDAY 25TH MARCH AT 7.30 p.m.
£1.25 IN ADVANCE
£1.50 ON DOOR **N⁰** **0101**

sardines and sweating profusely in the oppressive heat.

The Hammersmith gig was recorded for an album that was later released by Antic as *Live In London*. For this reason, Haley extended his usual show to include 'Rock-A-Beatin' Boogie', 'The Saints Rock'n'Roll', 'Rock The Joint' and 'Rip It Up'. As usual, the Comets were each featured in turn, Nick Nastos's flying fingers demonstrating 'Guitar Boogie Shuffle', while drummer Freddy Moore took the spotlight for 'Caravan'. Ray Cawley sang 'Hey Mama'. Ray Parsons scored with 'Rockin' Robin' and 'Memphis, Tennessee', and Rudy contributed 'Kansas City' as well as blowing up a storm with 'Rudy's Rock'. The atmosphere throughout was electric, and as Bill closed out the show with 'Rock Around The Clock' the audience went wild. His long-time fans knew that Haley rarely performed encores, but after the Comets had triumphantly climbed the backstage stairs to the safety of their dressing room, the chant of 'We want Bill!' echoed around the packed hall.

Eventually glasses, bottles and even chairs were hurled at the stage when a young policeman made a futile attempt to disperse the crowd, only to be pelted with missiles for his trouble. *The Sun* reported the proceedings under the banner headline, 'Haley Fans Rip It Up Again'.

All in all, the tour was an extraordinary success. If nothing else it demonstrated yet again that the rock'n'roll monster was very much alive and there were still plenty of great days yet to come.

Sadly, however, this was the last occasion that British audiences would enjoy the fine saxophone playing of Rudy Pompilli. Rudy had accompanied Bill on every one of his British tours stretching right back to 1957 and he had proved a loyal friend to Haley during the many lean times that had followed his enormous success all those years ago. Rudy became ill the following year and finally succumbed to lung cancer on 31 January 1976. Bill Haley & His Comets would never be quite the same again.

TV Appearances

Today (Thames)	26 February 1974
The Old Grey Whistle Test (BBC2)	26 February 1974
Nationwide (BBC1)	27 February 1974
Top Of The Pops (BBC1)	27 February 1974
Wheeltappers and Shunters Social Club (Granada)	20 April 1974

THE DRIFTERS

March 1974			May 1974		
15	Wolverhampton	Lafayette	1-4	Liverpool	Wooky Hollow
	Hanley	Heavy Steam Machine		Liverpool	Allinson's
16	Dunstable	California	6	Caerphilly	Double Diamond
17-23	Leicester	Bailey's	7	Jersey, CI	Behan's (West
24-30	Nottingham	Heart of the Midlands			Park Pavilion)
April 1974			9	Torquay	Paradise Hotel
?	Kensington	Biba's	11	Dunstable	California
3	Sheffield	Fiesta	12	Leigh	Garrick
4	Stevenage	Locarno		Farnworth	Blighty's
5	Birmingham	Rebecca's	13-18	Manchester	Fagin's
	Birmingham	Barbarella's	19	Bolton	Copperfield's
6	Bedworth	Civic Hall	20	Derby	Talk of the Midlands
	Birmingham	Barbarella's	22	Spennymoor	Variety
7	Dudley	Caesar's Palace	23	Birmingham	Barbarella's
8	Hinckley	Tiffany's	24	Birmingham	Rebecca's
9	Purley	Tiffany's		Birmingham	Barbarella's
	Birmingham	Barbarella's	25	Whitchurch	Civic Centre
10	Morecambe	Bowl		Dudley	Caesar's Palace
11	Stafford	Top of the World	26	Batley	Variety
13	Margate	Dreamland	27	Barnsley	Civic Hall
	Leysdown	Island Hotel		Batley	Variety
?	Ilford	Tiffany's	28-29	Batley	Variety
19	Peterborough	Wirrina Stadium	30	Rotherham	Tiffany's
20	Eastbourne	King's		Batley	Variety
21-27	Southend	Talk of the South	31	Doncaster	Top Rank
28-30	Liverpool	Wooky Hollow		Batley	Variety
	Liverpool	Allinson's	**June 1974**		
			1	Batley	Variety
Tour organiser — Henry Sellers					

The massive display of support for the Drifters continued throughout this long and arduous tour. Their latest single, 'Kissin' In The Back Row Of The Movies', was promoted every night and duly charted in Britain during June, eventually reaching No.2, only failing to dislodge 'She' by Charles Aznavour from the top spot.

Most of the gigs were played to capacity audiences and the show at Biba's was probably typical of the whole tour. Fans had to be bodily restrained from swamping the stage, while at one point Bill Fredericks had to stop the proceedings and appeal for the audience to return to their seats. They opened the act with 'Come On Over To My Place', following which Fredericks and Johnny Moore divided up the lead vocals as they moved through the likes of 'Under The Boardwalk', 'At the Club', 'Saturday Night At The Movies' and 'On Broadway'. The whole set was superbly slick and brilliantly choreographed. Butch Leake drew screams of encouragement as he embarked on a crazy, rubberlegged dance. However, the highlight of a memorable evening was Grant Kitchings' remarkable and moving interpretation of 'My Prayer'.

Rock'n'roll may have been struggling for survival during the spring of 1974, but the Drifters seemed more popular than ever and were now totally committed to their British audiences.

TV Appearances

Sunday Night at the London Palladium (ATV)	14 April 1974
They Sold A Million (BBC2)	7 July 1974

Del performing at unknown UK venue, 1974.

DEL SHANNON

March 1974			7	Glasgow	St. Roch
29-30 Driffield	Rex		8-11	Coatbridge	Casanova
April 1974			14-20	Leicester	Bailey's
1-5 Derby	Bailey's		22-27	Swansea	Townsman
6 Jacksdale	Grey Topper				
Derby	Bailey's				
Tour organiser — Henry Sellers					

Musical fashions have a nasty habit of dictating the fortunes of entertainers. Audiences can be notoriously fickle and at a whim can discard a former favourite for no good reason other than a collective desire to embrace something new or different. Del Shannon was always a quality performer and as a creative artist tried throughout his life to develop his career with new recordings in a variety of different styles. The hit records of the early Sixties became like a millstone around his neck, stifling any chance of being allowed to progress, yet at the same time providing a safe haven which allowed him to feed his family and remain in the music business. He was not alone in struggling to find work in the States, where old rock'n'rollers were still a long way short of being fashionable again. The loyal British fans may have frustrated him by constantly calling for the old hits, but Del, like all singers, gained strength from the roar of the crowd and the UK would be his second home for several years to come. Times would change and things would open up for him again in the future, but the British cabaret scene was there when he needed it.

WANDA JACKSON

April 1974		
13 Wembley	Empire Pool	
	Tour organiser — Mervyn Conn	

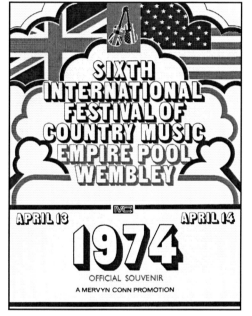

The *6th International Festival of Country Music* was a two-day event held over the Easter weekend and Wanda was one of the stars on the opening night. The other acts comprised Kitty Wells, Bill Anderson, Bill Monroe, Tompall Glaser, Jeanne Pruett, Terry Stafford, Johnny Wright, Ray Lynam, Philomena Begley, the Jonny Young 4, Rankarna & Mats Rådberg (from Sweden), the Hillsiders, Kathie Kay and compere Murray Kash. The festival had now become an established part of the music calendar and, although far from full, there was a sizeable crowd, many of whom had travelled considerable distances to attend.

This was not Wanda Jackson's first visit to Britain, as she had participated on the Capitol Records showcase, *Country Music Caravan*, in April 1970 along with Tex Ritter and Buck Owens. Both occasions proved enjoyable, if frustrating experiences for the rock'n'rollers among the audience: Wanda's distinctive voice was as strong and powerful as ever, but rock'n'roll only comprised a small portion of her act.

Backed by the Jonny Young 4, it was her 1961 country hit, 'Right Or Wrong', which drew the greatest applause, although the rock'n'rollers unquestionably preferred her gutsy 'Let's Have A Party'. Wanda even delivered a brief sermon (which received a round of applause), before breaking into 'I Saw The Light'. She closed her short spot with a burst of yodelling on 'I Betcha My Heart I Love You'.

TV Appearances
Up Country Festival (BBC2)   13 April 1974 (screened 24 April 1974)

NARVEL FELTS

April 1974		
14 Wembley	Empire Pool	
	Tour organiser — Mervyn Conn	

Narvel Felts has an impressive rock'n'roll pedigree. He had been performing the music since 1956, but apart from one minor chart entry with 'Honey Love' in 1957 had failed to find the elusive hit record that would elevate his career out of the clubs and bars and into the big time. Finally, by the Seventies, he had switched to recording country and had been rewarded with three successive hits in the US charts and a first trip to England to appear on Day Two of the *6th International Festival of Country Music* at Wembley.

He was still coming to terms with his new-found success and was somewhat in awe of the array of country stars with whom he travelled from the States. A limousine journey through London to the hotel in the company of Jeanne Pruett and Bill Monroe was a memorable experience for him, and more than thirty years later he still vividly remembered being scared almost to death as disc jockey Bob Powel drove him at speed through the London traffic on the way to an interview at the studio of BBC Radio London. At Mervyn Conn's pre-festival banquet, Felts was seated next to Wanda Jackson and her husband, Wendell Goodman, and this was the first occasion that the two former rock'n'rollers had met. At that stage, neither Wanda nor Narvel could have imagined that in future they would both return to Britain many times to perform for specialist rock'n'roll audiences.

Wembley in 1974 was a whole different scene, however, and Felts was only one name among a sizeable list of performers. George Jones and Tammy Wynette were scheduled to headline Sunday evening, but in the early hours of the morning George received a phone call from his daughter with the tragic news that his mother had died. He and Tammy chartered a plane and flew home immediately. Bill Anderson, who had already performed the night before, took his place.

In addition to Narvel, the show comprised Johnny Rodriguez, the Oak Ridge Boys, Mac Wiseman, David Rogers, Pasty Sledd & The Jones Boys, Jimmy Payne & The Kelvin Henderson Country Band, Larry Cunningham, Caroline Hall, Czech Country Beat, Miki & Griff and Frisco.

Narvel only had a fifteen-minute spot to impress an audience who were largely unfamiliar with his music. Efficiently backed by the Jonny Young 4, he naturally included his three recent country hits, 'Drift Away', 'All In The Name Of Love' and 'When Your Good Love Was Mine', plus 'Look Homeward Angel', a track from his latest album, and, as a tribute to his rock'n'roll roots, a rockin' 'Blue Suede Shoes'.

Back in 1964, Felts had met up with Carl Perkins at a club in Poplar Bluff, Missouri shortly after the latter returned from his first UK tour and reported how overwhelmed he had been by the magnificent reception he received from his British fans. This undoubtedly inspired him to include the Perkins song in his set. Audience response had been good until he switched to rock'n'roll, whereupon a vociferous minority hollered out for him to 'Keep it country'. There were many rockers among the Wembley audience, but it would be another decade before they got the opportunity to hear a full-blooded rock'n'roll show from Narvel the Marvel.

TV Appearances
Up Country Festival (BBC2)   13 April 1974 (screened 1 May1974)

WAYLON JENNINGS

Waylon had been advertised to appear at the *6th International Festival of Country Music* but dropped out with the promise of a concert tour in May as compensation. Country music journalist-turned-promoter Larry Adams announced dates in Manchester, Oxford, Liverpool, Norwich and Belfast, with more still to be confirmed, but by the end of April the whole venture had collapsed. Jennings was reported to be suffering with an infected ear and vague plans for a rescheduled tour in September came to nothing.

THE CRYSTALS

April 1974			May 1974		
19	Birmingham	Club Cedar	4	Lincoln	Aquarius
	Birmingham	Rebecca's		Goole	Vikings Hotel
20	Peckham	Mr. Bee's	5	Spennymoor	Top Hat
21	Stoke	Tiffany's	6	Whitley Bay	Sands
23	Kenilworth	Blaise's	7	Chester-le-Street	Garden Farm Hotel
24	Camden Town	Dingwalls		Whitley Bay	Sands
	London	Gulliver's	8	Stanley	Huntingdon
26	Doncaster	Bailey's		Whitley Bay	Sands
27	Lakenheath	USAF	9-10	Spennymoor	Top Hat
28	Jacksdale	Grey Topper	11	Hebburn	Trade & Labour
29	Kingswinford	Summerhill House Hotel		Spennymoor	Top Hat
	Wolverhampton	Lafayette	12	Manchester	Mr. Smith's
30	Porthcawl	Stoneleigh			
Tour organiser — Paul Dainty					

The Phil Spector Sound, which had been so popular a decade earlier was again attracting interest in 1974. Reissued 45s had introduced both the Ronettes and the Crystals to a new generation of record buyers and the Crystals flew into the UK for almost a month of one-nighters. Only Dee Dee Kennibrew survived from the original group and was joined by Louise Bethune and Peggi Blu. The two new girls had recently joined from the Sandpebbles and had never even met Spector. Backed throughout the tour by State Express, they gave a good account of themselves wherever they played.

At Doncaster they participated in a sizeable promotion, appearing alongside the Detroit Emeralds, Mac & Katie Kissoon and J.J. Barnes.

PHIL EVERLY

The Everly Brothers had ceased working together in July 1973 and Phil made a short promotional visit to the UK during May in the company of his wife, Patricia. He was now going out as a solo act and interviews appeared in both *The Sun* and the *Daily Express*. He stayed near Haslemere in Surrey and, with Patricia expecting a baby in September, was even considering buying a house there.

Phil did not appear on television, but surprised his loyal fans by joining international fast bowler John Snow in a charity cricket match at Hove.

BOBBY VEE

May 1974			June 1974		
10	Leysdown	Island Hotel	1	Derby	Bailey's
11	Birmingham	Barbarella's	2-8	St. Agnes	Talk of the West
12	Jacksdale	Grey Topper	9-12	Farnworth	Blighty's
13-18	Southend	Talk of the South		Oldham	Bailey's
19-25	Charnock Richard	Park Hall Hotel	13-15	Bolton	Copperfield's
27-31	Derby	Bailey's		Oldham	Bailey's
Tour organiser — Henry Sellers					

Bobby Vee spent five weeks performing in cabaret and gave a good account of himself, as usual. Like Del Shannon and Roy Orbison, Vee had settled comfortably into a touring routine which enabled him to earn a worthwhile living off his old hits. One or two British tours each year were now a regular part of his schedule.

THE CRICKETS

May 1974					
31	Leysdown	Island Hotel	13	Glasgow	St. Roch
	London	Speakeasy	14-15	Edinburgh	Baron Suite
June 1974			16-22	Charnock Richard	Park Hall Hotel
1	Birmingham	Barbarella's	25	Guildford	*unknown venue*
2-8	Wakefield	Theatre Club	26	Stanmore	Queen of Hearts
9	Helensburgh	Drumfork		London	Speakeasy
10	Coatbridge	Casanova	27	Kensington	Biba's
11	Edinburgh	Swinging Goblet	28	Coventry	Chrysler UK
12	Kirkaldy	Glenrothes Forum	30	Jacksdale	Grey Topper
Tour organiser — Henry Sellers					

The Crickets, who for so long had seemed to lack musical direction, had made a move into the world of country rock via an album which they cut in Nashville for Bob Montgomery titled *Remnants*. For some time, both Jerry Allison and Sonny Curtis had worn beards and long hair, and one sensed that they wanted to break free from the umbilical cord which since the birth of the group had permanently joined them to their late leader and inspiration, Buddy Holly.

Nevertheless, Henry Sellers' cabaret circuit allowed little room for such innovations. The 'scampi in a basket' brigade wanted to hear the hit records, not modern songs or even modern interpretations of the old ones.

The 1974 Crickets comprised Sonny Curtis, Jerry Allison, Rick Grech and Albert Lee, plus Californian Steve Krikorian, who had travelled with the group previously as roadie, but who now joined his colleagues onstage, contributing both guitar and harmonica,

The show at Stanmore was typical of the whole tour and the five-man Crickets seemed to be operating on cruise control. It wasn't that they were failing to put in the effort, rather that it was all too easy for them. Sonny was incredibly laid-back but sang well enough, while Albert filled in with all the familiar solos and Grech and Allison made a very strong rhythm section. They worked through all the familiar numbers, closing strongly with a pumping 'Rave On'.

At Birmingham they co-starred with Del Shannon. A second show at the same venue was pencilled in for 28 June but did not go ahead, soul singer Doris Troy replacing them. Mike Berry was in the audience for the two gigs on 26 June.

TV Appearances
Wheeltappers and Shunters Social Club (Granada)   17 August 1974

DEL SHANNON

May 1974			July 1974		
31	Birmingham	Barbarella's	5	Edinburgh	Swinging Goblet
June 1974			7-13	Liverpool	Bailey's
1	Bedworth	Civic Hall	14-20	Hanley	Bailey's
	Birmingham	Barbarella's	21	Manchester	Maine Road Social
2-8	Sheffield	Fiesta		Bolton	Copperfield's
9-14	Batley	Variety	24	Manchester	Radcliffe
15	Goole	Vikings Hotel		Salford	Willows
	Batley	Variety	25	Stockport	Warren
16-17	Stockton	Fiesta	26	Hull	Willows
18	Stockport	Warren		Filey	Blue Dolphin
	Stockton	Fiesta	27	Hull	Phoenix
19-22	Stockton	Fiesta		Filey	Blue Dolphin
23	Leigh	Garrick	28-31	Blackburn	Cavendish
24-29	Manchester	Fagin's	**August 1974**		
	Leigh	Garrick	1-3	Blackburn	Cavendish
Tour organiser — Henry Sellers					

This was the second of three British tours by Del Shannon during 1974. His audiences were as enthusiastic as ever and many of the venues were full to capacity. On 1 June he shared billing with the Crickets at Birmingham, while at Stockton he appeared with comedian Les Dennis, and at Stockport with the Fantastics, an American soul group with an interesting pedigree. They had started life in the Fifties singing doo-wop as the Velours, charting in 1957 and 1958 with 'Can I Come Over Tonight' and 'Remember' respectively. Now based in the UK, they were a popular soul act on the ballroom circuit, but in years to come would revert to their original name and perform for the rock'n'roll set again.

BO DIDDLEY

Yet another attempt was made to bring the elusive Mr. Diddley back to Britain, and Biba's issued a press release stating that he would be appearing at their London club on 17 June. Long-term fans had no sooner made the appropriate entry in their diaries when a statement from Phonogram, Bo's UK record company, scotched the plan. They made it clear that no contract was in place for UK dates during June, although something might be forthcoming later in the year.

DUANE EDDY

July 1974			August 1974		
11	Leysdown	Island Hotel	4	Salford	Cumberland
13	Gristhorpe	Caesar's Palace	7	Stockport	Warren
	Hull	Phoenix	8	Bedworth	Civic Hall
14	Leicester	Bailey's		Birmingham	Barbarella's
21-28	Manchester	Fagin's	9	Coventry	Chrysler UK
29	Kensington	Biba's		Birmingham	Barbarella's
31	London	Lyceum	10	Birmingham	Barbarella's
			11	Jacksdale	Grey Topper
				Blackpool	Tiffany's
Tour organiser — Henry Sellers					

The latest participant on Henry Sellers' cabaret circuit was guitar man Duane Eddy. Accompanied on this trip by saxophone player Brad Bauder and a young Californian lady, Deed Abbate, who both sang and played rhythm guitar, he otherwise worked with British musicians. At least two different bands were used, namely the Second Showband at Leicester and Trash at London's Lyceum. Eddy himself was looking fit and well and sporting a full beard.

The show at the fashionable Biba store in London's Kensington was staged upstairs in the Rainbow Rooms – a rather grand ballroom-cum-restaurant. Duane stuck to a playlist that featured many of his biggest hits and really scored with a vibrant 'Peter Gunn'. Brad Bauder's excellent sax playing was featured on 'Yakety Sax' and added considerably to hard-hitting

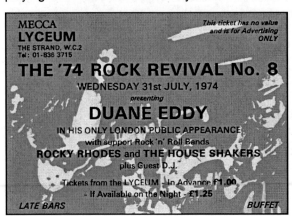

versions of 'Ramrod', 'Forty Miles Of Bad Road' and 'Pepe', while Deed contributed vocally to '(Dance With The) Guitar Man' and her solo rendition of 'Will You Love Me Tomorrow', although earlier in the tour a throat infection had prevented her from singing. Audience reaction was very good, and by the close of proceedings some of the more adventurous were dancing frantically on top of the highly polished tables, much to the dismay of the management. Support at Biba's was provided by Kilburn & The High Roads, featuring Ian Dury, and at the Lyceum by the Houseshakers.

When the British dates had all been completed, Duane flew off for further shows in New Zealand and Australia.

THE RONETTES

July 1974			2	Birmingham	Barbarella's
27	Taunton	Camelot		Birmingham	Rebecca's
	Bristol	Yate Centre	3	Dunstable	California
29	Kingswinford	Summerhill House		Birmingham	Barbarella's
		Hotel	4	Blackpool	Tiffany's
	Wolverhampton	Lafayette	5	Kensington	Biba's
30	Colwyn Bay	Dixie Showbar	6	Portsmouth	HMS Collinwood
31	Croydon	Scamps	10	Wigan	Casino
August 1974			12	Liverpool	Timepiece
1	Widnes	Bumble's	16-17	Spennymoor	Top Hat
	New Brighton	Bumble's			
Tour organiser — Barry Collins					

The Ronettes had toured Britain twice in 1964, when they were a current chart act enjoying hits like 'Baby I Love You' and '(The Best Part Of) Breaking Up'. Subsequently, their reputation had taken something of a battering after several fake groups performed under their name around the Northern clubs, and many people assumed that the 1974 line-up was yet another trio of impostors. It would have been helpful if the music press had clarified the position in advance of the tour, as this version of the Ronettes contained original lead singer Ronnie Spector (née Bennett), along with two new members, Denise Edwards and another girl merely identified as Marilyn, plus their drummer and musical arranger, Michael Cook.

Ronnie was newly separated and soon to be divorced from the eccentric record producer Phil Spector, and appeared anxious to re-establish her reputation with British audiences. The tour did not start very well however. At least one of the opening gigs drew a paltry crowd of around fifty people and the *New Musical Express* dismissed Ronnie's efforts as being awkward and graceless, even though she remained as beautiful as ever and described her as *'a poor, East Side cabaret version of Tina Turner'*. Tiny though the audience was, their reaction to the Ronettes was ecstatic.

Things did improve, and at Croydon a very sexy version of 'The Loco-motion' noticeably aroused the crowd. It was hard to interpret the Spector sound with only the three girls plus a trio of guitar, bass and drums, but Ronnie's unique voice and stage presence helped to overcome such inherent difficulties. The guitarist got lost during 'You Came, You Saw, You Conquered', but overall the audience went away happy.

Ronnie became ill during the show at Portsmouth and scheduled performances at Cambridge, Basildon and at London's Playboy and La Valbonne clubs had to be axed, but happily she recovered sufficiently to finish the remainder of the tour.

ROY ORBISON

July 1974			11-17	Solihull	New Cresta
28-31	Batley	Variety		Dudley	Caesar's Palace
August 1974			18-24	Frimley Green	Lakeside
1-10	Batley	Variety			
Tour organiser — Henry Sellers					

Roy flew in on 27 July for a short cabaret tour and a TV appearance to promote his new 45, 'Sweet Mama Blue'. Proposed gigs at Southport and Stoke did not materialise.

TV Appearances
Wheeltappers and Shunters Social Club (Granada)   10 August 1974

BEN E. KING

August 1974			7	Taunton	County
6	Cambridge	Corn Exchange		Yate	Sterling Suite
16	Nantwich	Civic	9	Liverpool	Timepiece
	Shrewsbury	Music Hall	10	Conway	Palace
17	Dunstable	California		Asaph	Stables
18-24	Liverpool	Wooky Hollow	12	Buckley	Tivoli
	Liverpool	Allinson's	13	Wrexham	Fagin's
26	Goole	Vikings Hotel		Widnes	Bumble's
28	Strood	Amega	14	Bolton	Nevada
29	Stockton	Inn Cognito		Manchester	Carib
30-31	Spennymoor	Top Hat	15	Willesden	Apollo
September 1974			16	Shrewsbury	Tiffany's
1	Sutton in Ashfield	Golden Diamond	17	Gloucester	Tracy's
	Peckham	Mr. Bee's	18	Basildon	Sweeney's
2	Coventry	Mr. George		London	La Valbonne
3	Camden Town	Dingwalls	19	Mablethorpe	Gables Cricket Club
4	Stanmore	Queen of Hearts		Skegness	Variety Bar
	London	Playboy	20	Birmingham	Barbarella's
5	Hanley	Heavy Steam		Birmingham	Rebecca's
		Machine	21	Whitchurch	Civic Centre
6	Cambridge	Corn Exchange		Birmingham	Barbarella's
	Watford	Spider's Web	22	Leeds	International
Tour organiser unknown					

Ben E. King's stamina was tested to the limit on this marathon tour of one-nighters, backed as usual by the John McFlair Band. The show at Goole on 26 August was a soul all-dayer on which he co-starred with the Exciters.

MARVIN RAINWATER

August 1974			September 1974		
16-17	Birkenhead	Kingsland	?	Palmers Green	Intimate Theatre
		Restaurant	11	New Brighton	Old Tavern
			15	Wimbledon	Tennessee CMC
Tour organiser — Lou Rodgers					

Marvin's six-week UK tour mainly consisted of appearances at US military bases, though he did manage five public shows at country music venues. However, without the benefit of any advance publicity whatsoever, his rock'n'roll fans never even knew that he was in Britain.

At London's Intimate Theatre he was backed by Jellystone Park and gave an enjoyable 50-minute show which included such solid country material as 'Truck Driving Man', 'Okie From Muskogee' and 'Is Anybody Goin' to San Antone'. His rich, nasal voice had changed little over the years and he seemed totally relaxed and unflustered even when a microphone malfunctioned. 'Running Bear', 'Wabash Cannonball' and 'Whole Lotta Woman' were all well received by the attentive audience of about 200 country enthusiasts, but the high point of the evening was the fine version of his 1957 US hit, 'Gonna Find Me A Bluebird'. Sounds Country opened the show.

PHIL EVERLY

Phil made his second UK visit of 1974 during August. Now signed as a solo artist by Pye Records, he was hard at work on his forthcoming album, *Invisible Man*, but still found time for several interviews, and sizeable articles appeared in both the London *Evening News* and the music press. His strained relationship with brother Don was still the main topic of interest, but Phil's future recording plans also attracted some coverage, especially as the Hollies had only just scored a major UK hit with the song, 'The Air That I Breathe', which had been lifted from his first solo album, *Star Spangled Springer*. While in the UK, Phil rented a flat in Cadogan Place, Knightsbridge.

TV Appearances
Cilla (BBC1)   26 August 1974

JOHNNY & THE HURRICANES

Johnny & The Hurricanes were lined up for an extensive British tour during September 1974, but at a fairly early stage several of the European dates, including a two-week engagement in Germany, fell through and the whole project was aborted.

TONY WILLIAMS' PLATTERS

September 1974			October 1974		
8-14	Birmingham	La Dolce Vita	1-5	Liverpool	Bailey's
	Leicester	Bailey's	6-12	Oldham	Bailey's
15-21	Derby	Bailey's		Blackburn	Cavendish
	Stoke	Bailey's	13-19	Watford	Bailey's
22-28	Bristol	Bailey's			
29-30	Liverpool	Bailey's			
Tour organiser unknown					

A most unexpected but welcome visitor to the UK during September 1974 was Tony Williams, fronting his own version of the Platters. This may not have been the official group, as the name was owned by their long-time manager Buck Ram, but Williams, who had left for a solo career in 1960, had been the lead singer on all their great hits of the Fifties and his was the authentic sound of the Platters.

Tony Williams' Platters comprised Tony on lead vocals, his wife Helen Williams, Ricky Williams (their son?), Ricky Black and the bass voice of Bobby Rivers. Those who studied carefully the comings and goings of the US vocal groups would have spotted that Rivers was also a member of the Invitations soul group and had toured the UK during 1967 as part of a totally bogus set of Drifters.

At Birmingham, the audience quickly learnt that Williams had lost none of his magnificent phrasing, nor his unique and wonderful voice. Working closely with Black and Rivers, he moved effortlessly through a classy doo-wop set featuring 'The Great Pretender', 'Harbour Lights', 'The Magic Touch' and 'Heaven On Earth'. His versions of 'Only You' and 'Twilight Time' were just breathtaking, and for six weeks cabaret audiences were privileged to enjoy the enormous talent of one of doo-wop's greatest vocalists.

Regrettably, Tony Williams never again recaptured anything even approaching the success he had enjoyed with the original Platters line-up. He died in New York on 14 August 1992.

JOHNNY RIVERS

September 1974			9	Manchester	University
9	Kensington	Biba's	10	Sheffield	University
October 1974			11	Uxbridge	Brunel University
4	Hanley	Heavy Steam Machine	12	Bristol	University
5	London	School of Economics	14	Canterbury	University of Kent
Tour organiser unknown					

The Johnny Rivers Boogie Band comprising Rivers (vocals), Ned Doherty (guitar), part-time Cricket Rick Grech (bass), Zoot Money (keyboards) and Jim Keltner (drums) kicked off their European tour at Biba's in Kensington, where the appalling acoustics partially disguised their attempts at 'Tracks Of My Tears', 'Maybelline' and 'Memphis'. Rivers varied the pace and sang 'Geronimo's Cadillac' accompanied by just his own guitar, but it was the climax of the act featuring both 'Sea Cruise' and 'Rockin' Pneumonia And The Boogie Woogie Flu' which had the audience clapping along and stomping their feet.

Rivers never made much impact in Britain – certainly nothing approaching the success he enjoyed back in the States – and by the time he returned on 3 October after a series of shows in Europe, his Boogie Band was assuming a somewhat fluid appearance with continual personnel changes and upheavals. Gigs at Hanley and at Leeds University were scrapped and by 18 October Johnny had returned to the USA, the whole venture having fallen apart. Support on most of the shows was provided by the Mike Storey Band.

TV Appearances
The Old Grey Whistle Test (BBC2)   8 October 1974

TOMMY ROE

September 1974			October 1974		
20-21	Spennymoor	Top Hat	1	Swansea	Townsman
22-28	Liverpool	Allinson's	3	Birmingham	Barbarella's
	Liverpool	Wooky Hollow			
Tour organiser — Henry Sellers					

A short cabaret visit by Tommy Roe was the latest addition to Henry Sellers' ever-expanding programme. Tommy had acquired a lot of British fans during his extensive tours in the Sixties, many of whom returned to hear him perform 'Sheila', 'Dizzy' and his other hits. Comedian Les Dennis provided the support at Liverpool's Wooky Hollow club.

THE CRICKETS

September 1974			October 1974		
22	Sunderland	Empire	2	Purley	Tiffany's
23	Hull	Tiffany's	3	Borehamwood	Civic Hall
25	Hemel Hempstead	Pavilion	4	Aldershot	Prince's Hall
26	Great Yarmouth	Tiffany's	5	Halifax	Civic Hall
28	Chatham	Central Hall			
29	Southport	Floral Hall			
Tour organiser — Henry Sellers					

This was another of rock'n'roll's lost tours. Barely publicised at all, it was overlooked even by many of the Crickets' most ardent fans and was probably scheduled too soon after their previous visit only three months earlier.

At the opening gig in Sunderland, there were four Crickets on stage, namely Sonny Curtis, Jerry Allison, Rick Grech and Albert Lee, but Rick was in such poor shape as a result of alcohol and drugs misuse that he was no longer able to perform to the required standard. By the time they reached Hemel Hempstead only three nights later, both Grech and Lee were gone and road manager Steve Krikorian was again filling in, this time on bass guitar.

The show was opened by Ronnie Storm & The Typhoons, who featured throughout the tour, plus the Earthquakes. The three Crickets made an immediate visual impression as they were smartly dressed in matching white suits. Curtis introduced each song in his deep Texan drawl and led the audience through memorable versions of 'Oh Boy!', 'It's So Easy' and 'It Doesn't Matter Anymore'. The set was entertaining, if totally predictable, but it was precisely what the audience wanted and the show finished strongly with 'Peggy Sue', 'That'll Be The Day' and, as an encore, 'Keep A-Knockin' '.

THE DRIFTERS

September 1974			16	Stockton	Globe
27	Telford	John Hunt School	17	Birmingham	Barbarella's
	Birmingham	Barbarella's		Derby	Bailey's
28	Dunstable	California	18	Wolverhampton	Lafayette
29-30	Caerphilly	Double Diamond	19	Eastbourne	King's
October 1974			20	Hanley	Victoria Hall
1-5	Caerphilly	Double Diamond	21-26	London	Talk of the Town
6	Blackpool	Tiffany's	28-31	London	Talk of the Town
7-12	Wythenshawe	Golden Garter	**November 1974**		
13	Batley	Variety	1-2	London	Talk of the Town
14-15	Liverpool	Allinson's			
Tour organiser — Henry Sellers					

Another new Drifters single, 'Down On The Beach Tonight', roared into the British charts during October while the group were engaged upon their latest, highly successful visit. This was the seventh time that the line-up of Johnny Moore, Bill Fredericks, Butch Leake and Grant Kitchings had toured the UK since 1971 and their slick, well-choreographed act remained as popular as ever. Backing was provided once again by the John McFlair Band.

At Dunstable, on a hot, sticky night, they opened with an energetic version of Sam Cooke's 'Good News'. The bulk of the set inevitably comprised a run-down of the group's greatest hits, and the five-man backing band, complete with twin saxes, ably assisted as they worked through 'Come On Over To My Place', 'Under The Boardwalk' and 'Saturday Night At The Movies'. Interestingly, there was no attempt to embrace soul music within the act, and when they did move away from their own material it was rock'n'roll classics 'Charlie Brown', 'Blue Moon' and even a brief 'Let's Twist Again' which were featured. The whole performance was superbly crafted and highly professional. Baritone singer Fredericks injected just the right level of humour between songs when he told the audience, 'We spent the summer in Monte Carlo, but all the time we were saying "Man, I wish we were in Dunstable!".'

The tour was frighteningly successful, selling out at several venues. At Birmingham they appeared alongside the Fortunes and comedian Jimmy Jones, while at Wolverhampton they were supported by British rock'n'rollers Yakety Yak. Sadly, Bill Fredericks left the group after their season at London's Talk of the Town. The Drifters flew off to the Bahamas, but he remained in Britain to pursue a solo career as a cabaret performer.

DOCTOR ROSS

October 1974			5	Redcar	Top Deck
8	London	100 Club	6	Doncaster	Outlook
November 1974			7	Cheltenham	Pavilion
4	London	100 Club	9	Portsmouth	Polytechnic
Tour organiser unknown					

Doctor Ross reappeared for his second UK visit of 1974, lining up alongside Ann Peebles at the 100 Club on a show labelled *30 Years of Memphis Soul – A Tribute to Memphis Music from Sun to Hi*. Gradually, more people were discovering the great unknowns and soon the less prominent names of Memphis rockabilly would be given the opportunity to play to UK audiences – still a seemingly impossible dream in 1974.

The Doctor spent the remainder of October gigging around Europe before returning for a further handful of British dates, on at least some of which he shared billing with New Orleans pianist Cousin Joe Pleasant.

DEL SHANNON

October 1974			18	Manchester	Valentines
11	Margate	Dreamland		Wythenshawe	Yew Tree
	Leysdown	Island Hotel	19	Manchester	Valentines
12	Dewsbury	Pickwick	22	Kensington	Biba's
17	London	Speakeasy	24	Birmingham	Barbarella's
			25-26	Spennymoor	Top Hat
Tour organiser — Henry Sellers					

Backed on this trip by the Birmingham band Impala, Del was in fine form at the prestigious Central London gig at the Speakeasy. Opening with 'Hats Off To Larry', he churned out near-perfect renditions of his hits including standout versions of 'Hey Little Girl', 'Swiss Maid' and 'Little Town Flirt'. Between numbers, he was clearly visible taking a few slugs from a bottle of Jack Daniels, but this in no way hindered a fine performance. He introduced his latest single, 'I'm The Music', and included an excellent 'Runaround Sue', eventually closing with 'Keep Searchin' (We'll Follow The Sun)' and 'Runaway'.

At Kensington's Biba's, Del shared billing with Dr. Feelgood.

Unknown UK venue, 1974.

BOBBY VEE

November 1974		
1	Birmingham	Barbarella's
	Hanley	Heavy Steam Machine
2	Hatfield, Yorks	Cromwell's
	Dewsbury	Pickwick
10-16	Liverpool	Bailey's
18	London	Speakeasy
19	Swansea	Townsman
Tour organiser — Henry Sellers		

This, the second Bobby Vee tour of 1974, ran into organisational difficulties when there was a delay in granting his work permit. An appearance had been scheduled for 11 October at the Vikings Hotel, Goole, and presumably other dates were also in the course of being finalised, but without the necessary paperwork in place the whole project had to be moved back to November and the good people of Goole had to be content with Jess Conrad as a late substitute.

When the tour finally got underway in Birmingham, Vee was his usual chirpy self. His audience wanted to hear the hits and he duly obliged, with 'Sharing You', 'Take Good Care Of My Baby' and 'Rubber Ball' gaining more than their share of the applause.

LINK WRAY

It was announced that guitar hero Link Wray would make his British debut at London's 100 Club on 12 November – news that was received with some excitement by instrumental fans who had been disappointed in the past when an earlier visit failed to materialise. Link had recorded a new album in San Francisco during February, featuring Boz Scaggs and the Tower of Power horn section, which included a remake of his classic, 'Rumble'. The chance to hear it performed live was a mouth-watering prospect, but annoyingly the booking fizzled out with no real explanation for the frustrated fans who were left high and dry once again.

THE CRYSTALS

November 1974			December 1974		
15	Worksop	Variety	1-7	Oldham	Bailey's
16	Leysdown	Island Hotel		Blackburn	Cavendish
17-23	Liverpool	Bailey's	8-14	Derby	Bailey's
24	Leicester	Bailey's		Stoke	Bailey's
	Birmingham	Bloomers			
25-30	Leicester	Bailey's			
	Birmingham	La Dolce Vita			
Tour organiser — Paul Dainty					

This was a second 1974 visit from Dee Dee Kennibrew, Louise Bethune and Peggi Blu, and the reason for the increased activity was the surprise reappearance of 'Da Doo Ron Ron' in the British Top 20 during October and November. So rapidly was this tour thrown together that the girls had only one day to pack and prepare for their flight, but their renewed chart status ensured them an enthusiastic welcome. Founder member Dee Dee even confessed that, if all went well, they would be getting together again with producer Phil Spector in Los Angeles during February to start work on some new recordings.

CHARLIE RICH

For years the music of Charlie Rich had remained a closely guarded secret known only to a small number of rock'n'roll fans who coveted his US recordings like 'Lonely Weekends', 'Whirlwind', 'Mohair Sam' and 'I Washed My Hands In Muddy Water'. Some of his work had been released in the UK, but it was not until 'The Most Beautiful Girl' gave him his first British hit in February 1974 that he became accepted by the public at large. A tour was announced for November, including shows in London, Liverpool, Southport and Glasgow, but was soon cancelled again owing to Rich's heavy recording commitments in the States.

JOHNNIE ALLAN

South Louisiana rock'n'roll, often referred to as swamp pop, had received very little exposure in the UK up to this time. It can best be described as a potent mixture of New Orleans rhythm & blues with hillbilly melodies, added to both traditional Cajun and creole music. Johnnie Allan was a leading exponent of swamp pop and had been performing in that style since the Fifties, although rarely straying far from Lafayette, Louisiana, where he also held down a day job as Assistant Principal at the Acadian Elementary School.

Writer and broadcaster Charlie Gillett issued an album of swamp pop and Cajun music in the UK on his Oval Records, titled *Another Saturday Night* and curiously it was future pop mogul Pete Waterman who picked out the Johnnie Allan track 'Promised Land' and started playing it at the Soul Hole record shop in Coventry. This unique arrangement of the Chuck Berry rocker, complete with a frenzied accordion solo, was soon issued as a single and sold in sufficient quantities that a major British hit looked a distinct possibility.

Contact was made with Allan in Louisiana and an offer made for him to visit the UK for a promotional tour. He was all set to travel, but unfortunately the Lafayette Parish Board refused him leave of absence. His disappointment must have been further compounded when only six weeks later Elvis Presley's version of the same song was released and swept into the Top 10, killing his potential hit stone dead. He did at least still have his teaching job, even if that trip to Britain had to wait for quite a while longer.

ROY ORBISON

December 1974		
1-2	Sheffield	Fiesta
3	Stockton	Globe
4-5	Sheffield	Fiesta
Tour organiser — Henry Sellers		

The principal reason for Roy's return to the UK at this time was to tape a BBC television show in Manchester on 12 December titled *Roy Sings Orbison*. He performed eleven songs which included his biggest hits plus 'Penny Arcade', 'Mean Woman Blues', 'Candy Man' and a new song, 'Hung Up On You'. When the show was finally aired several months later, 'Hung Up On You' was edited out, even though it was Roy's latest release at the time.

Six nights in cabaret in Sheffield and Stockton preceded the television work. His audiences knew precisely what to expect from the Big O, and as always he delivered a quality act, albeit with few surprises. On at least one occasion at Sheffield, Roy performed 'Pretty Paper' – a hit for him in 1964, but a song he rarely sang live.

TV appearances
Roy Sings Orbison (BBC1)   12 December 1974 (screened 11 July 1975)

NEIL SEDAKA

December 1974		
8-21	Batley	Variety
Tour organiser — Henry Sellers		

This was a much shorter trip for Neil Sedaka, and his third visit of the year to the prestigious Batley Variety club. His second wave of hit records was coming to an end, but he remained one of the premier names on the cabaret circuit.

TV Appearances
45 (Granada)   25 December 1974

BUCK RAM'S PLATTERS

December 1974			January 1975		
16-24	Southend	Talk of the South	1-4	Usk	Helmaen Int'l.
26-28	Southend	Talk of the South	5-11	Farnworth	Blighty's
29-31	Usk	Helmaen Int'l.		Failsworth	Broadway
			12-18	Liverpool	Shakespeare
Tour organiser unknown					

Legal ownership of the Platters name was held by their veteran manager, Buck Ram, via his company 'Five Platters, Inc.'. Such legal manoeuvring was vital, owing to the large number of bogus acts cashing in on the group's reputation and illegally performing as the Platters. As recently as 24 May 1974, Ram had won a restraining order in a Colorado court preventing Zola Taylor from using the group's name. Zola had left in 1964, selling out her interest in Five Platters, Inc. at that time. Unfortunately, none of the original line-up remained in Buck Ram's group and their British tour came only three months after Tony Williams' Platters had been seen around the cabaret circuit. Ram may have owned the name of the Platters, but Williams would always be the voice of the Platters – which did make life difficult for Buck and his ever-changing line-up.

The 1974 Platters who toured the UK were built around lead singer Monroe Powell. The rest of the group were Willie Lewis (tenor), Quibar Shurat (bass), Hal Howard (baritone) and the glamorous Lita Fonza. Henry Lee Parilla doubled up as both guitarist and musical director.

Possibly it was the recent chart revival of 'Only You' by Ringo Starr which had reminded listeners of the vastly superior original, but this tour did extremely good business, Buck Ram claiming that their album, *The Platters In Person*, was selling around 150 copies a night. Great songs like 'Harbour Lights', 'My Prayer' and 'Smoke Gets In Your Eyes' continued to weave their special magic with audiences.

THE COASTERS

December 1974		
24	Leysdown	Island Hotel
	Margate	Dreamland
26	Scunthorpe	Baths
31	Dunstable	California
	London	Speakeasy
Tour organiser — Henry Sellers		

The year finished as it began with a short visit from the Coasters. Carl Gardner, Earl Carroll, Jimmy Norman and Ron Bright were nearing the end of a long and tiring European tour. A little advance publicity would have not gone amiss, but nevertheless the four stalwarts rocked their way through their usual repertoire and the less-than-capacity audiences always received their money's worth. Jimmy Powell & The New Dimensions were the support act at Scunthorpe.

CHAPTER THREE

1975

Let's Rumble

Rock'n'roll was not very visible to the general public during 1975, although below the surface there was a great deal of often frenzied activity. The wholesale reissue of vintage material continued and resulted in renewed chart appearances by such unlikely candidates as Brian Hyland and Chubby Checker.

More significantly, increasing amounts of rock'n'roll – and particularly rockabilly – that had never previously been available in the UK, invariably by obscure artists who were completely unknown except to the privileged minority, were finding their way into the marketplace. Sales were insufficient to make hit records a realistic possibility, although even that would change in the near future, but enough copies were being sold to encourage even the most obdurate of the major labels to allow access to their back catalogues. For the British rock'n'roll fans it was an exciting time. Material that had previously only been accessible through rare and high-priced US 45s could now be obtained on compilation albums or as repro singles (although admittedly in many cases, of dubious legality).

During January, Texan rockabilly singer Johnny Carroll gained a UK release for his 'Black Leather Rebel', an exciting tribute to Gene Vincent, while Charly Records, soon to become the UK's top rock'n'roll reissue label, was launched in August. The *New Musical Express* seemed more than a little bemused when, in their edition for 13 September, they quoted Ted Carroll of the specialist record shop, Rock On, as listing Dion's 'The Wanderer', Jerry Byrne's 'Lights Out' and Hank Mizell's 'Jungle Rock' as their most sought-after oldies. Dion, they could understand: 'The Wanderer' was a fine record and had been a big seller in the UK during 1962 – but Jerry Byrne and Hank Mizell. What was that all about? They had never had records released in Britain at all. Something was happening below the surface all right, and before long the floodgates would open.

Among the rock'n'roll tours in 1975 came the British stage debuts of Link Wray and Charlie Rich – very different talents, but each eagerly anticipated by fans who had followed their careers since the Fifties. The incredible popularity of the Drifters continued unchecked and they played to capacity crowds almost everywhere they went. In contrast, both Chuck Berry and Little Richard lost sight of what their audiences wanted and seriously harmed their reputations with some truly dreadful performances.

One man who slipped quietly into Britain without any fuss or publicity was Arthur 'Guitar Boogie' Smith, who spent Easter in Britain with his wife, travelling from their home in Charlotte, North Carolina to celebrate their wedding anniversary. Smith had written the influential 'Guitar Boogie', on which so many rock'n'roll instrumentals were based, as well as composing the more recent hit, 'Duelling Banjos', featured in the 1972 movie, *Deliverance*. He and Mrs. Smith were in the audience to enjoy both Marvin Rainwater and Wanda Jackson at Wembley.

Country music fans were again rewarded with tours involving leading acts such as Charley Pride, Glen Campbell and George Jones, although Willie Nelson cancelled his May tour after a change of management. Less prominent names like Patsy Montana, Hank Locklin and the 'King of Bluegrass', Bill Monroe could be found on the club circuit. Black music was well represented by acts as diverse as Barry White, Major Lance, the Tymes and the Stylistics. Even the old crooner Perry Como played a string of British concerts. To many people it seemed as if bad old rock'n'roll had finally disappeared, but like a painful boil it remained just below the skin, throbbing away in time to that infectious beat.

SHA NA NA

January 1975		
26	Hammersmith	Odeon
27	Birmingham	Odeon
Tour organiser — Harvey Goldsmith		

A British tour had been set up for Sha Na Na in December. Dates were announced for shows in Birmingham, Manchester, Liverpool and Newcastle, but the whole project was aborted after the group split from their management company. They finally arrived a month later, but had only two dates on the revised agenda and were no longer considered very newsworthy.

The ensemble had shrunk to a ten-man line-up comprising Screamin' Scott Simon, Jon 'Bowzer' Bauman, Lennie Baker, Jocko Marcellino, Donny York, Elliot Randall (alias Enrico Ronzoni), Captain Outrageous, Johnny Contardo, Denny Greene and Chico Ryan. Their original guitarist, Elliot 'Gino' Cahn, was now working as a writer for *New Musical Express*, having previously sued the group, while another ex-member, Vinnie Taylor, had died of a heroin overdose not long before.

Nevertheless, the sign outside the Hammersmith Odeon confirmed that the theatre had sold out and the act opened as always with a whirl of frenzied activity as the group covered every inch of the large stage for 'Rock Around The Clock' and 'Yakety Yak', before pausing for breath and cruising into 'Silhouettes'. A deadpan 'Tell Laura I Love Her' preceded 'Splish Splash', complete with a blitz of soap bubbles, and then a dramatic and quivering, 'All Shook Up'.

The trouble was that the audience had seen it all before. Sha Na Na provided an affectionate satire of Fifties rock'n'roll and they did it to perfection, but every introduction, every joke and even the sight of Bowzer flicking the grease off his comb and into the audience, had been in the act previously. The magic had escaped, and in the absence of anything new they were definitely flagging. The audience enjoyed the show, which also featured impressive versions of 'La Bamba', 'Runaway' and 'At The Hop', but it was clear that Sha Na Na were nearing the end of the road.

NEIL SEDAKA

February 1975			March 1975		
12	Brighton	Dome	1	Manchester	Free Trade Hall
14	Bristol	Colston Hall	2	Leicester	De Montfort Hall
15	Cardiff	Capitol	5	Eastbourne	Congress
16	Oxford	New	8	Southport	New
17	Southport	New	9	Hull	City Hall
18	Stoke	Jollee's	10	Sheffield	City Hall
20	Portsmouth	Guildhall	15	London	Royal Festival Hall
21	Croydon	Fairfield Halls	16	Stockport	Davenport
22	Bournemouth	Winter Gardens	21	Hammersmith	Odeon
23	Birmingham	Hippodrome	23-29	Usk	Halmaen Int'l.
25	Newcastle	City Hall	30-31	Farnworth	Blighty's
26	Edinburgh	Usher Hall	**April 1975**		
27	Aberdeen	Capitol	1	Failsworth	Broadway
28	Glasgow	Apollo Centre	2-6	Farnworth	Blighty's
			7-12	Batley	Variety
Tour organiser — Barry Dickins					

For the last few years Neil Sedaka had been focusing a lot of his energy on success in Britain and had been rewarded with seven hit singles and some healthy album sales during the period 1972-74. Just prior to this tour, his recording of 'Laughter In The Rain' topped the *Billboard* listings, giving him his first US hit since 1966. From now on, he would spend more time concentrating on the home market.

Although distinctly unhip as far as teenagers were concerned, Neil was immensely popular with the older set, who appreciated his well-crafted songs and easy-going personality. This extensive tour sold out rapidly at nearly every venue. At Southport, tickets were at such a premium that a second night was added in to the itinerary.

The prestigious booking at London's Royal Festival Hall even attracted Elton John, who was spotted among the packed audience thoroughly enjoying a classy act in which Sedaka interspersed contemporary material like 'Our Last Song Together' and 'Laughter In The Rain' with several of his early rock'n'roll hits. Other highlights were a moving rendition of 'The Other Side Of Me' and his latest (and, as it would turn out, last) British hit, 'The Queen Of 1964'.

TV Appearances
Lulu (BBC1)   8 February 1975
In Concert (BBC2)   26 April 1975

DUANE EDDY

A two-week promotional visit to Britain commencing in mid-February proved to be time well spent for Duane. His new single, 'Play Me Like You Play Your Guitar', was already starting to make some noise and another hit record was looking like a distinct possibility. As well as radio and television appearances, he also found time to complete the work on his new album with producer, Tony Macaulay.

TV Appearances

Top Of The Pops (BBC1)	27 February and 13 March 1975
The Old Grey Whistle Test (BBC2)	28 February 1975

Opening night of the tour at Lewisham Odeon.

CHUCK BERRY

February 1975			27	Southampton	Gaumont
19	Lewisham	Odeon	28	Cardiff	Capitol
20	Southport	New	**March 1975**		
21	Glasgow	Apollo Centre	1	Gloucester	Odeon
22	Manchester	Free Trade Hall	2	Birmingham	Odeon
23	Coventry	Theatre	6	Hammersmith	Odeon
26	Finsbury Park	Rainbow			
Tour organiser — Mervyn Conn					

After a break of seventeen months, Chuck returned to Britain for a series of concert dates which succeeded in further tarnishing his reputation. Backed throughout by Gilson Lavis (drums), John Spurling (bass) and Lance Dixon (keyboards), he seemed unwilling to do more than go through the motions and was slaughtered by the music press and fans alike. Instead of enjoying the spectacle of one of the great rock'n'rollers in full flow, audiences and critics were in many cases left angry by his apparent lack of effort and the resultant debate centred more on the questionable length and dubious content of his shows, rather than a celebration of his great songs. The support act were Maxim, while the compere throughout the tour was Bob Stewart.

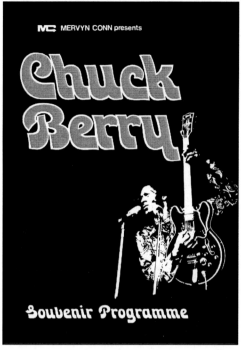

Reporting on the opening night at Lewisham, *New Musical Express* described the efforts of Maxim as being both embarrassing and tediously incompetent, so the show did not get off to a good start. Chuck's contribution was equally unsatisfactory. His voice and guitar drowned out the rest of the band, and although every so often he produced a few bars of the guitar playing which had been so inspirational in the past, for most of the time he was content to just clown about. A dire version of 'My Ding-A-Ling' was padded out for almost 20 minutes, and although things did eventually improve when he opened the throttle for a powerful 'Back In The USA', he was soon back wasting his enormous talent by instructing the audience to sing 'School Day' for him. It was very sad and completely avoidable. At the end of his allotted time, he departed abruptly with no bow and no encores.

Even the national press got in on the act after the Manchester show. On this occasion, Berry spent the best part of five minutes tuning his guitar, allowed his daughter Ingrid to perform two or three songs and then brought some thirty dancers up on stage from the audience. One of them apparently swore at him, so he unplugged his guitar and walked off leaving the majority of the audience howling for more. They eventually held a 'sit in' and the police had to be summoned to clear the theatre. At the subsequent inquest, Chuck's publicist claimed that he had already exceeded his 45-minute time slot, while others claimed that his whole act had lasted less than half an hour.

On the final night at Hammersmith, there was more controversy. It was not the exciting versions of 'Sweet Little Sixteen' and 'You Never Can Tell' which were the abiding memories, but Chuck's mid-song departure when the theatre manager refused to turn on the house lights. Once again, the argument raged. Had he sung for 58 minutes as he claimed, or were the audience being short-changed? Whatever the truth of the matter, Chuck Berry was alienating many of his long-time fans and doing his reputation no good at all.

THE DRIFTERS

March 1975					
14	Birmingham	Barbarella's	24	Birmingham	Barbarella's
15	Eastbourne	King's		Hanley	Heavy Steam Machine
16-22	Luton	Caesar's Palace	25	Barrow	Maxim's
23	Hammersmith	Palais		Morecambe	Bowl
24	Stoke	Jollee's	26	Birmingham	Barbarella's
25	Caerphilly	Double Diamond	28	Wolverhampton	Lafayette
27	Nottingham	Palais		Stafford	Top of the World
29	Hull	City Hall	29	Southend	Talk of the South
30-31	Batley	Variety	30	Southampton	Top Rank
April 1975			**May 1975**		
1-5	Batley	Variety	1	Jersey, CI	Behan's (West Park Pavilion)
6	Liverpool	Allinson's	2	Bedworth	Civic Hall
7-9	Liverpool	Wooky Hollow	3	Chester	Celebrity
	Liverpool	Allinson's	4	Farnworth	Blighty's
10-11	Liverpool	Allinson's	6	Farnworth	Blighty's
12	Liverpool	Wispa	7-8	Manchester	Fagin's
	Liverpool	Allinson's		Farnworth	Blighty's
19	Dunstable	California	9-10	Farnworth	Blighty's
20	London	Palladium	11	Leicester	Tiffany's
21	Shrewsbury	Tiffany's	18-24	Wakefield	Theatre
22	Derby	Bailey's	26-31	Wythenshawe	Golden Garter
23	Stockton	Fiesta	**June 1975**		
			1	Wythenshawe	Golden Garter
Tour organiser — Henry Sellers					

Throughout their long and glorious existence, the personnel of the Drifters has rarely stayed constant for very long. Indeed, the period from the summer of 1971 until late 1974, during which Johnny Moore, Bill Fredericks, Butch Leake and Grant Kitchings entertained British audiences on seven lengthy tours, saw about as much stability as the Drifters ever managed.

However, Bill Fredericks was now pursuing a solo career, so this was the first opportunity for UK fans to see his replacement, Clyde Brown, a baritone from Cincinnati, Ohio, in action. Brown had a background in gospel music, but had most recently been signed to Atlantic Records as a solo performer. His four singles for the label had failed to make the grade, so he had travelled to Freeport in the Bahamas and successfully auditioned for the vacancy in the Drifters on the recommendation of Atlantic's Barbara Harris. Johnny Moore was quick to express his delight at acquiring such a talented colleague. 'We've always been pacesetters and that is how we can be again, now that Clyde is in the group,' he explained.

The London Palladium was the high spot of the tour and few of the capacity audience would even have noticed a different face on stage as the four men sang and danced their way through a superb selection of Drifters favourites including their latest British hit, 'Love Games'. Batley Variety Club, where they shared the billing with comedians Cannon & Ball, was yet another of the venues where the 'House Full' notices were posted, while tickets for the three nights at Liverpool's Wooky Hollow club were all snapped up within days of going on sale. Clyde Brown could hardly have believed his change of luck as they packed their bags at the beginning of June in preparation for an extensive tour of the Far East and Australasia.

MARVIN RAINWATER

March 1975			April 1975		
27	New Brighton	Old Tavern	17	New Brighton	Old Tavern
30	Wembley	Empire Pool	18	Liverpool	Frontier Bar
Tour organiser — Mervyn Conn					

Mervyn Conn's *7th International Festival of Country Music* was held at Wembley over the Easter weekend and initially the bill held no great interest for rock'n'roll fans. However, late changes to the Sunday evening line-up brought about the inclusion of erstwhile rockers Marvin Rainwater and Wanda Jackson – news which ensured a last-minute scuffle for tickets. Rainwater was already in Britain playing military bases, plus a few country clubs in the Liverpool area and was brought in to replace the legendary Lefty Frizzell, who was seriously ill. Frizzell never recovered and passed away in comparative obscurity during July.

Backed at Wembley by Country Fever, which included Albert Lee on piano, Marvin was given a lengthy spot which was generally well received. *New Musical Express* described his style as being 'heavy metal rockabilly', a reflection of the fact that his own guitarwork was a good deal more gutsy than the rest of the show. He opened strongly with 'Running Bear' and a punchy 'Whole Lotta Woman', and made an immediate impact with the audience. He tore through 'It's Good To Be Back Home Again' and 'Oklahoma Hills' before closing his set with a controversial pro-Vietnam war song, 'The Troubles My Little Boy Had', which he prefaced with a few sneering remarks about hippies. He encored with a rocking take of Merle Haggard's 'Mama Tried'.

WANDA JACKSON

March 1975	
30 Wembley	Empire Pool
Tour organiser — Mervyn Conn	

Wanda was a late addition to the Wembley bill and her booking was a direct result of the marriage break-up of George Jones and Tammy Wynette. With divorce proceedings getting underway, Tammy chose not to accompany her husband to Britain, giving Mervyn Conn another headache as he struggled to finalise the acts for his festival. When the dust had settled, in addition to Wanda the Sunday evening line-up comprised George Jones, Melba Montgomery, Marvin Rainwater, Barbara Mandrell, Red Sovine, Jimmy Payne, Larry Cunningham and Frisco, plus George Hamilton IV as compere.

Wanda followed Marvin Rainwater on stage and was probably backed by Country Fever. She delivered a quality performance ranging from a bouncy 'Silver Threads And Golden Needles', through powerful versions of 'Let's Have A Party' and 'Turn Your Radio On' and her gospel numbers, 'He Is My Everything' and 'Jesus Put A Yodel In My Soul'. She closed strongly with 'I Betcha My Heart I Love You'.

BEN E. KING

April 1975	
5 Liverpool	Empire
6 Manchester	Opera House
9 Bristol	Colston Hall
10 Southampton	Gaumont
11 Birmingham	Hippodrome
12 Ipswich	Gaumont
13 Croydon	Fairfield Halls
16 Oxford	New
17 Hammersmith	Odeon
Tour organiser — Arthur Howes	

The record 'Supernatural Thing' had restored Ben E. King to the US charts and given his career a welcome boost. He had recently re-signed with Atlantic Records and this tour, which also featured the Detroit Spinners, Sister Sledge and the Jimmy Castor Bunch, was titled *Soul Explosion*. It was very much a showcase for Atlantic acts and had also promised participation from Margie Joseph and Arthur Conley, both of whom dropped out before the first curtain. Emperor Rosko was engaged as compere.

At Liverpool, Ben opened with a smooth rendition of Rufus's 'Once You Get Started', while the classy backing from the Jimmy Castor Bunch provided a Latin feel. Even on a soul show, the main body of his act was made up of 'Don't Play That Song', 'Stand By Me' and 'Spanish Harlem'. Audience response was excellent and his all-too-brief spot ended with a hypnotic version of 'Supernatural Thing'.

King was happy to be in the charts and restored to the Atlantic stable.

He also went to great lengths to stress that this brief excursion around the theatre circuit did not mean he was deserting his club audiences. 'They stuck with me down through the years when my name stopped meaning a thing on record. I'll never forget them,' he insisted. 'I'm not gonna desert those people now, even if it means turning down a few highly paid concert gigs, because they'll still be there to support me when all the fuss has died down.'

Jimmy Castor is worthy of a passing mention. In 1975, his act was strictly soul and of no interest whatsoever to the rock'n'roll fraternity. However, he had started out performing doo-wop, and back in 1958 had recorded with Lewis Lymon (younger brother of Frankie) as second tenor in his group, the Teenchords, while four years later he had supplied the saxophone to Dave 'Baby' Cortez's US instrumental hit, 'Rinky Dink'.

TV Appearances
The Old Grey Whistle Test (BBC2) ? April 1975 (screened 5 July 1975)

JACKIE WILSON

June 1975					
4	London	La Valbonne	10	London	100 Club
5	Halesowen	Tiffany's	11	Batley	Variety
	Birmingham	Barbarella's	12	Colwyn Bay	Dixie Showbar
6	Birmingham	Rebecca's		Rhyl	Stables
	Birmingham	Barbarella's	13	Stockton	Inn Cognito
7	Hanley	Heavy Steam Machine	14	Wigan	Casino
	Birmingham	Barbarella's		Marchamley	Hawkstone Hall
9	Wolverhampton	Lafayette	15	Salford	Willows
			?	Wallasey	*unknown venue*
Tour organiser — Henry Sellers					

Looking back on Jackie Wilson's second UK tour is a melancholy experience. Unquestionably, he was one of the greatest stage performers of all time, yet British audiences never had the opportunity to see him in his prime. Hit songs like 'Lonely Teardrops', 'Reet Petite' and 'To Be Loved' are rock'n'roll classics and would have been guaranteed show-stoppers if Jackie had appeared on any of the package tours in the early Sixties. Instead, his only exposure to British audiences had been via a poorly publicised and chaotic tour of nightclubs and ballrooms in 1972.

Rumours of a second British tour started early in the year with promoter Danny O'Donovan at the helm. Indeed, a date at Wigan Casino in May was even advertised, but not for the first time it was Henry Sellers who finally pulled it all together.

Wilson arrived in the UK following a week of playing US military bases in Germany and was accompanied by his heavily pregnant girlfriend, Lynn Crochet. Their daughter Li-Nie would be born in August. He brought his own band, namely Larry Blassingame (guitar), George Farrimond (bass), John 'Peanut' Glenfox (drums) and Vince Willis (keyboards/ trumpet).

At Birmingham's Barbarella's his dynamic act was restricted by a carpeted stage, but he still squeezed every drop of emotion out of 'To Be Loved', falling to one knee, and later in the set performed some precision pirouettes. At the 100 Club in London he played for a full hour, mixing soul and rock'n'roll, blues and ballads, but inexplicably failed to attract anything close to a capacity crowd.

The mid-Seventies were a difficult time for rock'n'roll. The early years were now a distant memory and even a spectacular performer like Jackie Wilson, with the added bonus of soul music credibility, was forced to endure almost unbelievable humiliation for his craft. Things would soon improve again, but if any one date need be selected as rock'n'roll's saddest moment, then try 11 June 1975. That was the night when the great Jackie Wilson played at Batley Variety Club – but as support for those plastic Teddy boys, Showaddywaddy.

His performance at Batley was quite magnificent. He was dressed in a neat tan leather outfit, looking lean and fit, tight curly hair replacing the greasy style in the older photos. His vast vocal range and assured stage presence were immediately apparent and he effortlessly moved between the easy-paced 'Lonely Teardrops', the soulful 'I Get The Sweetest Feeling' and the more raucous 'I'll Be Satisfied'. His dance routines were an integral part of the act and he seemed to glide effortlessly around the stage, ending with a 360-degree spin during the instrumental break on 'That's Why (I Love You So)'. Guitarist Larry Blassingame excelled himself during a slow 'Stormy Monday Blues' and Jackie mesmerised his audience with everything from 'Danny Boy' to 'Talk That Talk' and never let up for a moment, dancing, strutting, spinning and sliding back and forth, using every inch of the stage. Goodness knows what the Showaddywaddy fans made of it all. He closed with an emotional '(Your Love Keeps Lifting Me) Higher And Higher', complete with splits and twirls, dancing on one foot, down on his knees, up and into a back flip until finally he was gone.

Unlike the 1972 tour, Henry Sellers had done well enough this time that another Jackie Wilson tour was lined up for November, with week-long engagements scheduled on the Bailey's cabaret circuit. He even re-entered the British charts in July with 'I Get The Sweetest Feeling', but in the end the rather bizarre double booking which paired a barbecue at Hawkstone Hall Monastery in Marchamley, Shropshire with an all-night rave for the Northern soul fans at Wigan Casino, followed by a low-key appearance in a Salford nightclub, proved to be his swansong for British audiences.

On 29 September he was on stage at the Latin Casino in New Jersey, and was reportedly halfway through 'Lonely Teardrops'. As he sang the words *'My heart is crying, crying....'*, he suffered a massive heart attack. Jackie Wilson, the man they dubbed 'Mr. Excitement', lapsed into a coma from which he never awoke. For eight and a half years he remained in a semi-comatose condition at the Cherry Hill Medical Centre in New Jersey before finally passing away on 22 January 1984.

TV Appearances
Top Of The Pops (BBC1)   ? June 1975

LINK WRAY

June 1975		
5	London	Lyceum
Tour organisers — Virgin Concerts and Alick Lesley		

Several failed attempts had already been made to lure North Carolina's guitar hero on to a British stage, but when it finally happened it was almost by accident. Reportedly, Link had already visited the UK for business talks during which he made the acquaintance of singer Kevin Coyne, which directly led him to a guest spot at the Lyceum in London along with the Kevin Coyne Band and Unicorn.

A large proportion of the audience had assembled specifically to see Link's UK debut, but sadly the whole event was marred by a truly atrocious sound system which was totally unable to cope with the requirements of a man who started every show by spinning the volume controls completely off the dial. Link opened with the infamous 'Rumble', and that slow, repetitive and vaguely threatening sound of his 1958 US hit reverberated around the auditorium. The heavy bass lines were provided by John Greaves of the band Henry Cow, who stood silently alongside the menacing figure of Wray, surely one of the darker characters in rock'n'roll.

The sound problems got worse and worse. On 'Backwoods Preacher Man' his vocals were so slurred as to be incomprehensible, while Ray Charles's 'Unchain My Heart' was taken too fast for comfort. A steamy version of 'Mystery Train' was performed without too many subtleties, although the closing number, 'Jack The Ripper', overcame the sound difficulties and showed just what a superb guitar player he was.

The wider public had a first opportunity to see the Linkster in action when he made a guest appearance on *The Old Grey Whistle Test*.

TV Appearances
The Old Grey Whistle Test (BBC2)   14 June 1975

DEL SHANNON

June 1975			July 1975		
8	Douglas, IoM	Palace Lido	1-5	Wakefield	Theatre Club
12	Stockport	Warren	6-8	Cleethorpes	Bunny's Place
13	Coventry	Chrysler UK	10-12	Cleethorpes	Bunny's Place
24	Leigh	Garrick	13	Salford	Willows
25	Birmingham	Barbarella's			
26	Morecambe	Bowl			
27	Taunton	Camelot			
28	St. Neots	*unknown venue*			
	St. Ives	*unknown venue*			
29	Canvey Island	King's			
30	Wakefield	Theatre Club			
Tour organiser — Henry Sellers					

Del Shannon's popularity on the ballroom and cabaret circuit remained as strong as ever and most of the dates sold out on this his first UK tour of 1975. At Coventry, he shared billing with the soul group Limmie & The Family Cookin', but usually it was just the enduring nature of his reputation plus nostalgia for those vintage hit records that kept a smile on the face of promoter, Henry Sellers.

DUANE EDDY

June 1975			11	Newcastle	City Hall
12	Chelmsford	Chancellor Hall	12	Spennymoor	Top Hat
13	Wolverhampton	Lafayette	14	London	Cambridge
14	Chester	Celebrity	15	Aldershot	Prince's Hall
15	Douglas, IoM	Palace Lido	16	Greenham Common	USAF
17	London	100 Club	17	Croughton	USAF
18	Birmingham	Barbarella's		Heyford	USAF
20	Newport, Salop	Village Disco	18	Alconbury	USAF
21	Winsford	Civic Centre		Chicksands	USAF
27	Nottingham	Playhouse	19	Lakenheath	USAF
July 1975			24	Leicester	De Montfort Hall
4	West Runton	Pavilion	27	London	New Victoria
6	Cardiff	Top Rank	30	Manchester	Palace
8	Bristol	Colston Hall	August 1975		
9	Stockport	Warren	1	Glasgow	Apollo Centre
Tour organiser — Danny O'Donovan					

One of the surprise hits of 1975 was 'Play Me Like You Play Your Guitar', which brought Duane Eddy back to the UK Top 10 at the end of March. A tour was hastily put together, although a little too hastily as it turned out, because work permit difficulties resulted in the cancellation of the first batch of dates – an eerie reminder of similar problems which had prevented Duane's group, the Rebels, from playing for much of his 1963 tour with Little Richard.

On this occasion however, he was backed by British musicians, namely Rob Townsend (drums) and Charlie McCracken (bass) from Medicine Head, Roger Saunders (guitar), Dave Rose (piano) and Rex Morris (sax). Interestingly, Morris, a onetime member of Lord Rockingham's XI, had participated as one of the Rebels on the 1963 tour as well. Accompanying Duane from America were his vocalists, the Rebelettes, in the shapely form of Deed Abbate and Kin Vassy. All the ingredients were in place for a quality act.

Unfortunately, publicity for the tour was decidedly patchy and consequently attendances were often disappointing. Duane worked extremely hard and could not be faulted in any way. The show at Bristol was probably typical. It was arranged at short notice and tickets were only on sale for three days before the event, so the sparse turnout could hardly have been a surprise.

The early part of the act was a celebration of Duane Eddy's classic hits. Opening with a raucous 'Moovin' n' Groovin' ', he steamed through 'Detour' before slowing the pace for 'The Lonely One'. After rocking through 'Forty Miles Of Bad Road' and 'Shazam!', he introduced his new record, 'Man With The Golden Guitar', and adjusted the tempo again for '3.30 Blues'.

After that, the show moved into a fascinating history lesson as Duane explained the origins of rock'n'roll music via blues, country and gospel. He played banjo for 'Will The Circle Be Unbroken', switched to steel guitar as Deed and Kin sang 'Beer Drinkin' Music' and a couple of Hank Williams songs. He even duetted with Kin on 'Hey Good Lookin' '. Kin then moved on to a hip-wiggling 'Heartbreak Hotel' and this sequence concluded with the two girls singing Roy Orbison's 'Crying'.

An excellent evening's entertainment then built to a climax with another feast of twang. 'Because They're Young' was followed by '(Dance With The) Guitar Man' and an amazing 'Peter Gunn' on which Rex Morris played quite brilliantly. The 75-minute show concluded with 'Play Me Like You Play Your Guitar' and a storming 'Rebel Rouser'. Encores were demanded and Duane obliged with 'Cannonball', Chet Atkins' 'Trombone' and an explosive 'Some Kinda Earthquake'.

Better organisation would surely have helped enormously. The gig at Barbarella's in Birmingham had been scheduled three times before it finally took place, and the sound system was appalling. Duane did play a charity gig at the Cambridge Theatre in London for Save The Children, sharing the bill with Lulu, Alvin Stardust, Billy Fury, Helen Shapiro and Osibisa. But overall his efforts deserved a greater level of success. However, one clue hints that this may have been a happy period of Duane's life: he had remarried during 1973 and Rebelette Deed Abbate had become the new Mrs. Eddy.

LITTLE RICHARD

June 1975		
20	Lewisham	Odeon
21	Newcastle	City Hall
22	Hammersmith	Palais
24	Dunstable	Queensway Hall
	London	La Valbonne
Tour organisers — John Martin and Patrick Malynn		

Most rock'n'roll fans remember the 1972 Wembley spectacular and the fiasco which surrounded Little Richard's portion of the show, as a result of which he was booed by a section of the crowd. Few, however, can now recall his even more ignominious return to the UK three years later – which is probably just as well, as his reception was unbelievably hostile, and if ever a performer would prefer a tour to be airbrushed from his curriculum vitae, this would be the one.

Richard arrived in London on 20 June after shows in Belgium, France, Germany and Scandinavia. He was accompanied by his own American seven-piece band and two back-up singers. He was already in a confrontational mood and refused to accept his hotel accommodation, demanding he was moved to the Hilton. He also declined the offer of a sound check and insisted on going for a meal, thereby delaying his journey through South London for the first show at Lewisham until the height of the evening rush hour. Needless to say, he arrived late.

What followed was an evening of what the *Melody Maker* described as *'mounting chaos and absurdity'*. The Wild Angels, who provided the support on all but the Newcastle show, were severely restricted by a painfully inadequate PA system, but battled their way through a set consisting mainly of rock'n'roll standards. After an uncomfortably long interval, the Little Richard Band walked on stage and were immediately greeted with a chorus of boos. There was a large proportion of Teddy boys among the audience and they were not impressed by a procession of afro hair styles and slashed-to-the-navel jumpsuits.

Perhaps more than at any other time, style and appearance were of fundamental importance to rock'n'roll fans during the mid-Seventies. You not only had to sound right, but look right as well.

Unfortunately, the Little Richard Band did not sound right either. Instead of a saxophone-based sound, they played in a contemporary rock style with an organ very much to the fore, and as they worked their way through a couple of unidentified and unappreciated instrumentals, an atmosphere of doom and despondency descended over the proceedings.

Richard finally made his grand entrance, his hair piled high on his head, dressed in a skin-tight scarlet catsuit and teetering on white platform shoes. He climbed on top of the grand piano and blew kisses and waved peace signs to the stunned audience. When he finally launched into a breakneck 'Lucille' it was so overladen with throbbing guitars, screeching organ chords and insanely frantic drums that the overall effect was similar to the engine room of an ocean liner. He was actually in good voice, still easily hitting those whooping top-notes that have always been his trademark, but the absence of a sound check was proving disastrous. At one point, he stopped playing and pleaded for the sound man to do something about the echo which was bouncing back at him, and to rectify the complete lack of balance and clarity.

The Teds were far from sympathetic, and as he struggled through 'Tutti Frutti' and 'Rip It Up' there were shouts of 'The band's too loud' and 'Get rid of the bloody drummer'. 'Blueberry Hill' was ruined by the muzziness of the speakers and during a chaotic 'Be-Bop-A-Lula' a bottle flew past Richard's head and smashed against the back of the stage. This seemed to galvanise him into increased activity and he tore through 'Jenny Jenny' as if his life depended on it. 'Long Tall Sally' started like an attempt on the land speed record and got faster, until halfway through he leapt up from his piano stool, waved to the audience and departed to a chorus of 'Rubbish, you're finished' and 'Bring back Jerry Lee'. It was totally depressing to witness one of rock'n'roll's greatest stars endure such a humiliating experience.

Things did not improve much either. Richard refused to travel by train to Newcastle and hired himself a limousine at the promoters' expense. At La Valbonne in London he claimed that he had been underpaid for the tour until Paddy Malynn proved that he had not, although squabbles over money persisted. On 24 June he also had a date with a Registrar in Chambers on a bankruptcy petition arising from unpaid tax left over from the 1972 Wembley show. By the time Richard left for home he was an undischarged UK bankrupt. Malynn had cancelled his air ticket against uncontracted expenses incurred by Richard and his party and TWA refused to accept his cheque. He had to pay them £2,000 cash before his entourage could fly home to Los Angeles.

It would be ten years before Little Richard returned to Britain. How could a man with so much talent make such a mess of things?

BRIAN HYLAND

Against the odds, 'Sealed With A Kiss' returned to the British charts on 28 June and Brian Hyland stepped back into the limelight. He arrived in the UK on 24 July in time for an appearance on *Top Of The Pops*, along with the usual round of interviews and promotion. Talks took place with promoter Henry Sellers with a view to a tour of personal appearances later in the year.

TV Appearances
Top Of The Pops (BBC1)   24 July 1975

THE DRIFTERS

July 1975			August 1975		
18	Stanton Wolverhampton	Hines Heath Farm Wheel	3-9	Sheffield	Fiesta
19	Farnworth Bolton	Blighty's Copperfield's	10-16	Purfleet	Circus Tavern
20	Leigh Blackpool	Garrick Football Club			
21	Hanley	Bailey's			
22	Derby Nottingham	Bailey's Commodore			
23-24	Stockport	Poco			
25	Bridlington	Royal Hall			
26	Inverness	Aviemore Centre			
29	Batley	Variety			
30	Charnock Richard	Park Hall Hotel			
31	Leigh Chester	Garrick Celebrity			
Tour organiser — Henry Sellers					

Nobody could criticise the Drifters when it came to work rate. Seemingly they never stopped touring. With an exhausting visit to the Far East and Australasia behind them, Johnny Moore, Butch Leake, Clyde Brown and Grant Kitchings soon slotted back into their usual routine, and as the UK's most popular ballroom act of the period there were always more offers of work than could be accommodated. Their latest single, 'There Goes My First Love', entered the British charts in September.

TV Appearances
Pop Proms (Granada)   6 August 1975

ROY ORBISON

August 1975			October 1975		
10-16	Weston-super-Mare	Webbington	1	Southend	Cliffs Pavilion
17-30	Batley	Variety	2	Taunton	Odeon
31	Derby	Talk of The Midlands	3	Paignton	Festival
September 1975			4	Bristol	Hippodrome
1-7	Birmingham	Night Out	5-17	Luton	Caesar's Palace
8-13	Stoke	Jollee's	18	Hornchurch	Queen's
14	Southport	New		Luton	Caesar's Palace
15	Chester	ABC			
16	Hull	ABC			
17	Peterborough	ABC			
18	Stockport	Davenport			
19	Croydon	Fairfield Halls			
20	Nottingham	Theatre Royal			
21-27	Caerphilly	Double Diamond			
28	London	Palladium			
29	Brighton	Dome			
30	Chatham	Central Hall			
Tour organiser — Billy Marsh					

This was one of Roy's longest UK tours, lasting an exhausting 70 nights without a single break, and he remained as popular as ever. He arrived a week early, accompanied by his wife, Barbara, and young son, Roy Orbison Jr, and travelled to Manchester, where he reportedly recorded six songs for an as yet unidentified TV special which also featured Duane Eddy, Phil Everly and Alvin Stardust.

Like several other American rockers, Roy enjoyed the benefit of an active British fan club who provided much-needed support for his career, especially now that his days as a regular chart act were over. As the grand finale of this highly successful tour, a special matinee show was held for fan club members only at the Queen's Theatre in Hornchurch. Over 300 people attended, some travelling from as far afield as Belgium and Holland. Roy arrived nearly forty minutes late, but after a brief press interview opened this special show with 'Only The Lonely', 'Crying' and 'Dream Baby'.

The atmosphere and mood throughout his near-two hour set was quite different from usual. He clearly felt that he was among friends and talked a lot between songs, even offering to sing requests. Mixed in among the expected 'Ooby Dooby', 'In Dreams', 'Mean Woman Blues' and 'Running Scared' came less obvious material such as 'Leah', 'Drift Away', 'Lana' and 'Evergreen'. At one point, he even invited the audience to join him in a rousing 'Happy Birthday' for Roy Jr on the occasion of his fifth birthday. Earlier in the week, a gold disc had been presented to Orbison onstage at Caesar's Palace in Luton to commemorate sales of his *All-Time Greatest Hits* album, and this was proudly displayed for his fan club members. A very relaxed and highly enjoyable afternoon concluded with an instrumental of 'Ooby Dooby' and the inevitable 'Oh, Pretty Woman'.

Roy's enduring popularity in Britain was further underlined when a TV-advertised album, *The Best of Roy Orbison*, was released by Arcade and went to No.1 on the British charts at the end of 1975.

BRIAN HYLAND

September 1975		
7-13	Leicester	Bailey's
15-20	Birmingham	Abigail's
Tour organiser — Henry Sellers		

Brian had been playing a gig on an Indian reservation when the news reached him during July that 'Sealed With A Kiss', his 1961 hit record, was enjoying a new lease of life and climbing the British charts again. Life for a teenage idol can become difficult when the spotlight moves elsewhere, but Hyland seemed philosophical about his fluctuating fortunes. 'I still get $2,000 cheques occasionally from 'Sealed With A Kiss' because it is on several compilation albums, but I don't spend much money. I live in a cabin by the sea in Oregon which is very peaceful,' he explained.

In the end, not much of a tour materialised. His record may have picked up fresh sales, but the image of Brian Hyland was not right for a prolonged comeback in 1975. He was soon back home again, free to enjoy that Oregon sunshine.

DOCTOR ROSS

September 1975			29	London	100 Club
7	Birmingham	Repertory	30	Bracknell	Arts Centre
24	Durham	University	**October 1975**		
25	Sunderland	Roker Park	1	Bridgwater	Arts Centre
26	Darlington	College of Art	3	Bingley	College of Education
27	Camden Town	Dingwalls	7	Birmingham	Barbarella's
28	Basildon	Arts Centre			
Tour organiser unknown					

Doctor Ross arrived in the UK to participate in the *Brum Folk '75* festival in Birmingham, after which he continued a lengthy European tour, reappearing later in the month for a fortnight of mainly college gigs. There were a few rock'n'rollers mingling with the blues fans, as the Doctor's one time connection with Sun records of Memphis was attracting the curious, but it would still be a few more years before he became a favourite of the rockabilly crowd.

WANDA JACKSON

September 1975					
8	Belfast	ABC	19	Hammersmith	Odeon
12	Peterborough	ABC	20	Southampton	Gaumont
13	Ipswich	Gaumont	21	Norwich	Theatre Royal
14	Coventry	Theatre	24	Aberdeen	Music Hall
18	Liverpool	Empire	25	Glasgow	Apollo
			26	Hull	ABC
Tour organiser — Mervyn Conn					

Two successful appearances for Mervyn Conn at his 1974 and 1975 country festivals in Wembley led to a spin-off theatre tour for Wanda, headlined by George Jones and with additional support from Vernon Oxford and compere Murray Kash. All did not proceed smoothly, however. Oxford dropped out completely and Jones lived up to his 'No Show Jones' reputation by failing to make it for the Irish leg of the tour, claiming that his daughter was undergoing surgery and his presence was therefore required at home. Wanda fulfilled the dates in Belfast and Dublin, but the show scheduled for 11 September in Gloucester was scrapped.

Happily, George finally arrived along with a new line-up of his band, the Jones Boys, who also backed Wanda, after which the remainder of the tour proceeded on schedule. Despite this, attendances at some venues were disappointing.

At the Hammersmith show, Wanda nearly brought the house down with her vocal gymnastics on 'Yodelling Cowboy', but complained about a head cold picked up in Liverpool the previous night. Her powerful and distinctive voice, so well suited to country music, excelled with 'In The Middle Of A Heartache' and 'Right Or Wrong', but even though she had time for a longer act than at Wembley, she still kept to a strictly country format, with only the inclusion of 'Let's Have A Party' reminding the audience of her rockabilly past. The Jones Boys were not the most sympathetic of backing groups for Wanda and their shortcomings did take some of the edge off her performance.

JOHNNY CASH

September 1975		
17	Edinburgh	Usher Hall
18	Glasgow	Apollo
20	London	Royal Festival Hall
21	London	Palladium
22	London	Royal Albert Hall
Tour organisers — Adrian Hopkins and Artists Consultants		

Johnny Cash flew into Britain as part of a short European tour which had already included shows in Austria, Switzerland and Germany. He was accompanied by the Tennessee Three – Marshall Grant, Bob Wootton and W.S. Holland – who were augmented by pianist Larry McCoy and fiddle player Gordon Terry. Support came from Johnny's wife, June Carter, sisters-

in-law Anita and Helen Carter, and daughter Rosanne Cash. The whole operation was very much a family affair, although a very noticeable absentee was Carl Perkins, who had been a fixture of every previous Cash tour since 1968 but had now ventured out on his own again.

Three London dates underlined the level of Cash's popularity and both houses at the Palladium were recorded for an album eventually released under the title *Strawberry Cake*. There was a bomb scare during one performance, which meant that the venue had to be cleared, and the bomb announcement can even be heard on the album. Lonnie Donegan was in the audience, which is perhaps what inspired Johnny to include his version of 'Rock Island Line'.

At the Royal Albert Hall, the cosy family atmosphere prevailed when first the Tennessee Three performed a couple of songs, before being joined by the sweet and gentle Rosanne Cash. She in turn gave way to her Aunt Anita, undoubtedly the Carter sister blessed with the most beautiful voice. A duet with her husband, Bob Wootton, was followed by a short spot by Anita, June and Helen before finally the familiar words 'Hello, I'm Johnny Cash' heralded the arrival of the star turn.

For more than an hour, the audience were taken on a rollercoaster ride through a seemingly endless series of great songs. 'Ring Of Fire' and 'Man In Black' contrasted with the more intricate 'Lady From Baltimore'. Cash's deep baritone voice roused the rockers in the audience with flawless renditions of 'Big River' and 'Folsom Prison Blues', until the pace of the show changed yet again when June Carter returned to the stage for duets on 'Jackson' and 'If I Were A Carpenter'. He carried on through 'San Quentin' and 'I Got Stripes', eventually reassembling all the cast for a rousing, 'Were You There When They Crucified My Lord'. He had held back 'I Walk The Line' for the encore and left the

GREATER LONDON COUNCIL
ROYAL FESTIVAL HALL
DIRECTOR: JOHN DENISON, C.B.E.

JOHNNY CASH WITH
SUPPORTING ARTISTS

SAT., 20 SEPTEMBER, 1975
9 p.m.
Management: Chrysalis Promotions Ltd.

TERRACE
£3.00

GANGWAY 9
ROW   SEAT
N   27

RED
SIDE

Please enter the auditorium by
DOOR
5
LEVEL
5

stage to tumultuous applause which was richly deserved.

The following day, the Johnny Cash show moved on to Dublin. The rock'n'roll crowd had cheered as hard as the country fans, but there was no escaping the fact that Carl Perkins had been sorely missed.

CHARLIE RICH

September 1975		
20	Ipswich	Gaumont
21	Stockport	Davenport
24	Newcastle	City Hall
25	Southport	New
27	Hammersmith	Odeon
28	London	Royal, Drury Lane
Tour organiser — Jeffrey Kruger		

The massively talented Charlie Rich had been a closely-guarded secret for years. His first hit in the States, 'Lonely Weekends', had been released as long ago as 1959 on Sun's sister label, Phillips International, while plenty of excellent material including 'Rebound', 'Whirlwind', 'I Washed My Hands In Muddy Water' and the rock'n'roll novelty, 'Mohair Sam', had seeped across the Atlantic in later years without ever making any serious impact on the British charts. Rich finally established himself in the big league with 'Behind Closed Doors' and 'The Most Beautiful Girl', firmly aimed at the middle-of-the-road country market. He was now deservedly a big star and had even broken into the Top 10 in Britain during early 1974.

It was no surprise when, at the second attempt, a short British tour eventually brought the Silver Fox to the UK, and many rock'n'roll enthusiasts were in the front of the line when tickets became available. Support came from Sarah Johns, but the rockers in the audience were dismayed to see that Rich was to be backed by a 29-piece orchestra, which even included a lady harp player in a long evening dress. Nobody expected a rockabilly combo – but it had been hoped that at least a portion of the act would

The
CHARLIE RICH
SOUVENIR PROGRAMME
September 1975

feature his rock'n'roll material.

Charlie did bring his own orchestra conductor, Lenny Stack, and guitarist David Mayfield, but perhaps not surprisingly the show was heavily slanted towards his new 'countrypolitan' style.

At Ipswich, he opened with 'The Most Beautiful Girl' and 'I Take It On Home', and then performed 'Lonely Weekends' newly adapted for an orchestral arrangement. His distinctive and mellow voice was superb and he effortlessly moved through 'Nice 'N' Easy', 'My Elusive Dreams' and 'Midnite Blues'. After a short contribution from the Little Foxes vocal backing group, Charlie returned to the stage with 'River Stay 'Way From My Door' and, in medley form, 'A Very Special Love Song', 'There Won't Be Anymore', 'I Love My Friend' and Harlan Howard's 'She Called Me Baby'. Even his son, Allan Rich, was brought on for one song. Charlie did rock things up a little with a solid 'Memphis And Arkansas Bridge' and Jimmy Reed's 'Big Boss Man', which was quite wild, showcasing his piano and David Mayfield's guitar. The set closed with 'Mohair Sam' and a faithfully re-created 'Behind Closed Doors'. For an encore, Rich left the audience with the haunting 'I Feel Like Going Home', a stunning end to a classy show.

On the final night at London's Drury Lane Theatre, Charlie met with some resentment from the rockers in the audience, who tried to express their views on the inclusion of the lady harpist. He also seemed unexpectedly nervous and came across as rather awkward when he attempted his patter between songs. The opinion of many was expressed loudly by one anonymous voice from the stalls, who called long and hard for 'Whirlwind' during a particularly tender orchestral break. It was never going to happen though. Charlie Rich had starved for too many years playing rock'n'roll. This was payback time and a highly polished show designed for the Las Vegas crowd.

TV Appearances
In Concert (BBC2)   22 September 1975

BUCK RAM'S PLATTERS

September 1975			17 Croydon	Fairfield Halls
22-30 London	Talk of the Town		20-25 Birmingham	Night Out
October 1975			26-31 Frimley Green	Lakeside
1-4 London	Talk of the Town		**November 1975**	
5-11 Batley	Variety		1 Frimley Green	Lakeside
Tour organiser unknown				

Buck Ram's Platters returned to the UK with just one change to the group who toured at the end of 1974: Monroe Powell, Hal Howard, Chili Lewis and Lita Fonza were joined by Tommy Ellison from Las Vegas, and once again their slick and well-rehearsed act was perfect for cabaret venues such as London's Talk of the Town, a favourite spot for tourists and businessmen alike.

They opened with a rousing 'Put Your Hands Together' before sliding effortlessly through their own hits like 'Twilight Time', 'Harbour Lights' and 'Smoke Gets In Your Eyes', interspersed with other Fifties' classics including 'Sixteen Tons', 'Personality' and 'Who's Sorry Now'. A few new songs were featured, such as 'My Ship Is Coming In' and 'Love Train', but the audience really responded only when the three biggies, 'Only You', 'The Great Pretender' and finally 'My Prayer' were reached at the climax of the act. They deserved greater appreciation for a superbly crafted slab of pure nostalgia.

THE DRIFTERS

September 1975			October 1975		
26	Birmingham	Barbarella's	1	Hull	Bailey's
27	Dunstable	California	3-4	Frimley Green	Lakeside
29	Bristol	Bailey's	5-11	Liverpool	Allinson's
30	Leicester	Bailey's		Liverpool	Wooky Hollow
			12	Hammersmith	Odeon
			13	Blackburn	Bailey's
			16	Morecambe	Bowl
			17-18	Chesterfield	Aquarius
			19	Southend	Talk of the South
Tour organiser — Henry Sellers					

The schedule of almost non-stop touring undertaken by the Drifters inevitably wore down many of the participants, as there are few who can sustain life on the road for an indefinite period. Grant Kitchings, formerly of the Ravens and the Ink Spots, had reached the end of his days as a Drifter and was replaced by a felsty New Yorker, Billy Lewis, who had worked in the States during the mid-Sixties in one of the many versions of the Drifters, only leaving after he was conscripted into the United States army.

In the future, Lewis would lock horns with their manager, Faye Treadwell, after the formation of his own group of Drifters and their dispute would eventually occupy time within the British courts, but in the late summer of 1975 he lined up alongside Johnny Moore, Butch Leake and Clyde Brown for a series of high-energy shows in Britain. The opening night at Birmingham was his debut with the group.

TV Appearances
Top Of The Pops (BBC1)   25 September 1975

BEN E. KING

There was brief mention in *New Musical Express* of a tour by Ben E. King scheduled to commence on 24 October in Birmingham. Although eight gigs were listed, including venues in Ilford, Chester, Barrow, Southampton and Birkenhead, most if not all were cancelled and, as no references appeared elsewhere, it seems probable that the whole operation was aborted.

DEL SHANNON

October 1975			16-19	Cardiff	Spotlight
31	Leigh	Garrick	20-22	Cardiff	New Tito's
	Bolton	Copperfield's		Cardiff	Spotlight
November 1975			27	Stockport	Warren
1	Leigh	Garrick	29	Whitley Bay	Sands
	Bolton	Copperfield's		Spennymoor	Top Hat
2	Coventry	Chrysler UK	30	Liverpool	Allinson's
5	St. Helens, Lancs	Plaza	**December 1975**		
6-8	Batley	Variety	1-6	Liverpool	Allinson's
12-15	Stoke	Jollee's			
Tour organiser — Henry Sellers					

Del's second UK tour of 1975 took him back to many familiar cabaret venues that he had played on previous trips. The audiences kept coming back, but he was increasingly frustrated at the lack of interest in his new material from both fans and record companies alike. The nostalgia for those old hits was very much a double-edged sword.

BILLY SWAN

Born in Cape Girardeau, Missouri, Billy Swan was still at school when he wrote the Clyde McPhatter hit, 'Lover Please'. He later produced 'Polk Salad Annie' for Tony Joe White and was an original member of Kris Kristofferson's band. His own success came with 'I Can Help', an international hit which figured in the UK Top 10 during January 1975.

With a new album, *Rock'n'Roll Moon*, to promote, Swan was lined up for a short European tour which included a solitary UK date at London's Royal Festival Hall on Monday, 3 November. Advance publicity was somewhat half-hearted and the project was allowed to quietly fizzle out with no explanation offered for the cancellation.

HANK BALLARD

During the mid-Fifties, Detroit-born Hank Ballard and his group, the Midnighters, enjoyed a run of hits in the USA with rockin' R&B like 'Work With Me Annie' and 'Sexy Ways'. Then, after a lean spell, he reached out to an even wider audience with a series of dance records including 'Let's Go, Let's Go, Let's Go', 'Finger Poppin' Time' and the original, pre-Chubby Checker version of 'The Twist'. None of this made much impact with the majority of record buyers in Britain, where despite the undoubted quality of his work, his tally of hits in the UK remained at precisely zilch.

Nevertheless, by 1975 there was a sizeable minority in Britain who were familiar with Ballard's work and this included the rock'n'roll fraternity, so news of ten proposed UK dates commencing at the Liverpool Empire on 9 November was greeted with considerable interest. Hank would obviously perform his old hits, but otherwise the touring package, titled *The All Platinum Roadshow*, contained a selection of contemporary soul acts including Shirley & Company (in the Fifties, Shirley Goodman had been one half of the

R&B duo, Shirley & Lee), Chuck Jackson (a former member of the Del Vikings doo-wop group) and the Moments.

Disappointingly though, the tour was scrapped during October with no real explanation. The All Platinum label had just acquired the Chess/Checker catalogue in the States, so possibly this had an effect. Interviewed by *Blues & Soul*, Chuck Jackson implied that the old problem of work permits had arisen yet again. There was some vague talk about rescheduling dates early in 1976, but sadly the project was never mentioned again.

THE DRIFTERS

November 1975			December 1975		
13	Blackburn	Bailey's	1	Halesowen	Tiffany's
	Oldham	Bailey's	2	Bristol	Bailey's
14	Newcastle	Mayfair	3-4	Watford	Bailey's
15	Carlisle	Cosmo	5	Wolverhampton	Lafayette
16-22	Batley	Variety	6	Ashford, Kent	Stour Centre
24	Stafford	Top of the World	8-10	Derby	Bailey's
	Birmingham	Abigail's	11	Hanley	Bailey's
26	Camden Town	Nero's Palace	12-13	Derby	Bailey's
27	Hanley	Bailey's			
28	Liverpool	New Grafton Rooms			
30	Chester	ABC			
Tour organiser — Henry Sellers					

Four British tours in 1975 told everything about the popularity of the Drifters. Johnny Moore, Clyde Brown, Butch Leake and Billy Lewis had a new 45 to promote and 'Can I Take You Home Little Girl' entered the charts in November, eventually reaching the Top 10 in January 1976. Additionally, both *24 Original Hits*, a collection of their Atlantic classics, and the newly recorded *Love Games*, featured in the album charts. These were indeed exciting times for the group, who always delivered a slick, well-choreographed performance wherever they played.

They were the opening attraction at Nero's Palace, a new theatre-restaurant in North London, the site of which was formerly a BBC studio, while support at the two Hanley gigs came from first Linda Carr and the Love Squad and on their second visit, from Georgie Fame. At Chester they shared billing with the Exciters.

MARVIN RAINWATER

November 1975			29	Welford	USAF
14	Grays	Queen's Hotel	30	Keynsham	Fry's
15	Mildenhall	USAF	**December 1975**		
16	Bury St. Edmunds	Theatre Royal	1	Tetbury	Town Hall
21	Hemel Hempstead	Adeyfield	2	Scunthorpe	Tiffany's
22	Alconbury	USAF	3	Liverpool	British Legion
23	Matlock	Town Hall	4	Colchester	Woods Leisure Centre
24	Kerry	Anchor Inn	5	Chicksands	USAF
27	Torrington	Globe?	6	Chichester	Lavant Hill
28	Greenham Common	USAF	7	Southwick	Ponderosa

December 1975 (continued)			15	Cleethorpes	Bunny's Place
8	Stoke	Keep It Country	16	Wellington	Cleve Hotel
9-10	Amesbury	High Post Hotel	18	Croft	Country
12	Holsworthy	Memorial Hall	19	Horsham	Capitol
13	Bentwaters	USAF	20	Redcar	Coatham Bowl
14	Haywards Heath	Clair Hall			
Tour organiser — Lou Rodgers					

Country music promoter Lou Rodgers was able to cash in on Marvin's highly acclaimed appearance at the *7th International Festival of Country Music* at Easter by putting together a lengthy tour of clubs, pubs, assembly halls and military bases on which he worked with Jon Derek, plus Jeannie Denver and her J.D. Band. The range of venues was quite extraordinary. Rodgers seemed to find bookings in the most unlikely places and Marvin travelled to small towns like Kerry (Powys), Holsworthy (Devon) and Croft (Leicestershire) where American performers – indeed foreigners of any description – were a decided novelty.

This was strictly a country music tour, although every night Marvin would crank up the volume for a rocking 'Whole Lotta Woman', which probably caused a few frowns at hard-core country venues such as Stoke's Keep It Country club. He may have been playing in the rock'n'roll wilderness, but the rockers had not forgotten him. The tide was turning, and more and more people of all ages were discovering rockabilly music for the first time in Britain.

On 2 and 3 December Marvin and Country Fever recorded the album *Especially For You* at September Sound Studios in Huddersfield, which included re-recordings of both 'Whole Lotta Woman' and 'I Dig You Baby'. It was released in April 1976 by Westwood Records.

TV Appearances
Unknown (Southern)   19 November 1975

DEE CLARK

Arkansas-born Delecta Clark had enjoyed consistent chart action in the States between 1958 and 1963, with his biggest hit, 'Raindrops', on Vee-Jay only narrowly missing the No.1 spot. In Britain however, his only success had been in 1959, when 'Just Keep It Up (And See What Happens)', had briefly charted, so it was a complete surprise to everyone – including Clark himself – when his 1975 soul recording, 'Ride A Wild Horse', became a big favourite in the UK discos and sold consistently enough to register in the Top 20 during October.

A tour was hurriedly thrown together and a string of dates announced for December, commencing at Rascals in Chester, but Clark failed to materialise and the whole project disintegrated amidst allegations that he had been sent the funds for his air ticket to England but had run off with the money. He denied this slur on his character, but what is not in dispute is that the incident put paid to any chance for UK fans to see him perform live. He soon dropped out of the limelight and eventually succumbed to a heart attack in Atlanta, Georgia on 7 December 1990.

CHAPTER FOUR

1976

Jungle Rock

1976 was the year when rock'n'roll started to come back after several years in the doldrums. Invaluable research by music historians like Bill Millar, Colin Escott and Martin Hawkins had resulted in large quantities of Fifties' rock'n'roll and rockabilly becoming available in the UK, often for the first time, as more and more record companies were cajoled into re-examining their back catalogues. Names such as Charlie Feathers, Ray Campi and Billy Lee Riley were unknown in the UK until years after they made their classic recordings, but now they were starting to emerge as heroes to a new generation of rock'n'roll enthusiasts.

The American rock'n'rollers would soon be dragged away from the cabaret circuit and into the holiday camps, bars and ballrooms. The new breed of teenagers wanted the rough edges to return, and it was the ready availability of all this great music that made it possible. Amazingly, by 1976 there were more rock'n'roll records on sale than at any time in the past. Rock'n'roll was not about to change the world as it had done twenty years earlier, but did gather sufficient momentum to dent the British charts again. Even more importantly, enough of this new generation of teenagers who discovered rock'n'roll during the Seventies would stay with the music to ensure an audience for live rock'n'roll for many years to come. Suddenly everything looked exciting and dangerous again. If only Gene Vincent could have survived long enough to reclaim his throne.

The Wild Wax Show was a three-man rock'n'roll disco featuring Roy Williams, Runaround Stu Wester and Jailhouse John. They held down a residency at the Lyceum Ballroom in Central London which strove to keep the dancers on the floor between the live acts and they were always on the lookout for new sounds. Wester located 'Jungle Rock' by Hank Mizell on an obscure Dutch album and it was soon being played up to five times a night as the dancers voted with their feet. Williams met with Charly Records and talked them into releasing the record on a 45. Largely through his persistence, plus support from Roger Scott at Capital Radio, it entered the charts, peaking at No.3 on 24 April. A hastily released cover version by Shakin' Stevens grabbed some of the sales and probably prevented Mizell from reaching the very top. Rockabilly music had now finally arrived in Britain.

On 15 May rock'n'roll fans stormed the BBC. Some 5,000 people led by organisers Stuart Colman, Geoff Barker and Teddy boy Sunglasses Ron

Staples, marched through Central London with an enormous petition demanding a regular show on national radio. Both Duane Eddy and Carl Perkins had signed the petition, which was estimated to contain more than 50,000 names, and stalwarts Flying Saucers performed live from the back of a truck as the invasion successfully terrorised the weekend shoppers along the whole length of Oxford Street. It was no surprise to see Screaming Lord Sutch and a scantily clad female companion at the front of the procession. A somewhat stunned Teddy Warwick, then assistant head of Radio One, accepted the petition, following which more than 3,000 people squeezed into Picketts Lock Centre at Edmonton for a concert by Crazy Cavan & The Rhythm Rockers, the Hellraisers and Flying Saucers. The resultant BBC radio show, *It's Rock'n'Roll*, hit the airwaves on 25 September.

More and more clubs and pubs around Britain were opening their doors to live rock'n'roll again and the leading UK bands, which included the Riot Rockers, Matchbox and the Wild Angels, were becoming increasingly in demand. A Johnny Kidd memorial concert to mark the tenth anniversary of his death was held at the Loughborough Hotel in Brixton and was headlined by the irrepressible Lord Sutch.

Away from rock'n'roll, country music visitors included Buck Owens, Marty Robbins, Don Williams and Johnny Bond, plus more contemporary acts like the Ozark Mountain Daredevils and the Flying Burrito Brothers. Soul and blues tours during 1976 featured Memphis Slim, Freddie King, Marvin Gaye and Natalie Cole. Johnny 'Guitar' Watson returned for the first time since his 1965 tour with Larry Williams, but sadly he was now peddling disco soul and of no interest to the rock'n'rollers.

One of the most interesting tours of the year took place in February and featured new country star Emmylou Harris. She made her UK debut before sell-out audiences, a large proportion of whom were there to see her musicians, the Hot Band, who included not only ex-Cricket Glen D. Hardin, but also rock'n'roll guitarist James Burton, who had played on classic records for Ricky Nelson, Dale Hawkins, Bob Luman and more recently, Elvis Presley.

BRENDA LEE

Attempts were made to set up a tour for Brenda Lee during January. She had not appeared in Britain since 1973, and with so many hit records to her name would always have been welcome around the Northern clubs. Two nights were advertised at the Spotlight in Cardiff, but were soon cancelled again. Brenda had a young family growing up back in Tennessee and that was now her top priority.

LINK WRAY

Link had finally made his British stage debut in June 1975 and returned to the UK at the beginning of February to work on an album for Virgin Records. Recording took place in the East End of London and the finished article, *Stuck In Gear*, was released in April. It included a live cut of 'Jack The Ripper' which emanated from that first UK appearance at the Lyceum.

TONY WILLIAMS' PLATTERS

Blues & Soul made brief mention of a proposed second tour by Tony Williams' Platters scheduled to take place in March 1976. Quite why the project was dropped is unknown, but as Williams' first tour in September 1974 had been well received, there would certainly have been mileage in a return booking. Perhaps the ongoing battle for the right to use the Platters name caused promoters to back off. Long-time manager Buck Ram was actively pursuing bogus Platters groups through the US courts and in October 1976 won a further round in this long-running saga when acts described as 'Platters '76' and 'Tommy Cook & The Platters' were barred from using the name in the States.

THE DRIFTERS

March 1976			May 1976		
12	Newcastle	Mayfair	1	Batley	Variety
13	Manchester	Free Trade Hall	3	Stafford	Top of the World
14	Wolverhampton	Civic Hall	4	Mexborough	Jesters
15	Eastbourne	King's		Chesterfield	Aquarius
17	Southport	New	5	Chesterfield	Aquarius
18	Glasgow	Apollo	6	Burslem	Queen's Hall
19	Spennymoor	Top Hat	7	Blackpool	Locarno
20	Hull	City Hall	8-9	Ayr	Darlington Hall
21-27	Batley	Variety	10	Wakefield	Theatre Club
28-31	Sheffield	Fiesta	11	Middlesbrough	Madison
April 1976			12	Wakefield	Theatre Club
1-3	Sheffield	Fiesta	13	Portsmouth	Locarno
6	Purley	Tiffany's	15	Bournemouth	Village
8	Coventry	Tiffany's	16	Reading	Top Rank
9	Birmingham	Barbarella's	17-19	Watford	Bailey's
10	Ipswich	Gaumont	20-22	Derby	Bailey's
11-12	Caerphilly	Double Diamond		Leicester	Bailey's
13	Jersey, CI	Behan's (West Park Pavilion)			
15	Nottingham	Palais			
17	Dunstable	California			
18	London	Palladium			
20	Charnock Richard	Park Hall			
21-22	Farnworth	Blighty's			
23-24	Failsworth	Broadway			
	Farnworth	Blighty's			
25-30	Batley	Variety			
Tour organiser — Henry Sellers					

Surprisingly, this tour by the Drifters included the first occasions when they performed in Scotland. The show at Glasgow's Apollo Theatre proved such an attraction that queues for the box office stretched round the block and the demand for tickets eventually forced promoter Henry Sellers to sanction a second performance on the same night. The audience were not disappointed and, along with their classic recordings, the group included their new British hit, 'Hello Happiness', and even sang 'Please Stay', a 1960-vintage Drifters number which rarely featured on their set list.

Left to right: Johnny Moore, Joe Blunt, Clyde Brown and Billy Lewis.

The 1976 Drifters included new member Joe Blunt, a rhythm & blues stalwart who had been a member of the Chancellors during the Sixties. He replaced Butch Leake, who stepped down after more than four years, resulting in a line-up of Johnny Moore, Clyde Brown, Billy Lewis and Joe Blunt. Support on the concert dates came from the Dooley Family.

TV Appearances
Top Of The Pops (BBC1)   1 April 1976

FATS DOMINO

March 1976		
24 London	New Victoria	
Tour organiser — Patrick Malynn		

Fats and his nine-piece New Orleans band included just one date in the UK as part of their hectic European tour, but what a great occasion it proved to be.

The band comprised Lee Allen and Walter Kimble (tenor saxes), Herb Hardesty (tenor sax and trumpet), Curtis Wright (baritone sax), Dave Bartholomew (trumpet), Roy Montrell and David Douglas (guitars), Nat Williams (bass) and Joe 'Smokey' Johnson (drums). The Mal Gray Band (Mal was formerly vocalist with the Wild Angels) provided the support, while disc jockey Tommy Vance acted as compere.

After an overlong intermission, the second half of the show

DUDLEY RUSSELL, by arrangement with PATRICK MALYNN presents

DOLPHIN
Concert Productions Limited

FATS

DOMINO

with guest
MAL GRAY and his BAND

New Victoria Theatre
WILTON ROAD, LONDON, SW1

Wednesday 24th March at 6.45 & 9.00 p.m.

Tickets £3.00 £2.50 £1.75 & £1.25

From Box Office, Tel. 01-834 0671
AND USUAL AGENTS

commenced with the Domino band playing two instrumentals and a swinging version of 'Way Down Yonder In New Orleans' on which Dave Bartholomew provided the vocals. Then Fats himself was introduced as the 'King of Rock'n'Roll'. He walked over to his piano, smartly attired in a bright-blue suit with coloured braid edging and went straight into 'I'm Walkin' '. The audience responded with a roar of enthusiasm which was maintained through 'Blue Monday', 'Let The Four Winds Blow', the slower-paced 'Walking To New Orleans' and 'I'm Gonna Be A Wheel Someday'. During 'Shu Rah', which evolved into 'Lil' Liza Jane', the band walked down into the audience, still playing at a furious pace, and by the end of this number the antics of Allen and Kimble were injecting a touch of comedy into the proceedings.

A superb rendition of 'I'm In Love Again' was followed by 'I'm Ready', and 'Ain't That A Shame'. 'My Girl Josephine' really had the theatre jumping before the familiar introduction to 'Blueberry Hill' slowed the pace again. As this excellent show drew to a close, the whole band marched offstage to the strains of 'When The Saints Go Marching In'. Fats himself heaved the piano several feet and then proceeded to sing a bluesy 'Sentimental Journey' before walking off to thunderous applause. He encored with 'The Fat Man' and an untitled boogie woogie which included snatches of 'Ain't That Just Like A Woman', then insisted upon a round of applause for promoter Paddy Malynn, the man who had brought him to London. Domino was on excellent form and, as expected, his fine band – especially soloists Kimble, Hardesty and Allen – supported him magnificently.

A reissued 45 of his 1956 hit, 'Blueberry Hill', briefly re-entered the UK charts during April and May.

WANDA JACKSON

April 1976		
17 Wembley	Empire Pool	
Tour organiser — Mervyn Conn		

This was the third consecutive year that Wanda had been featured on Mervyn Conn's Easter country festival. Clearly she was popular, but nevertheless her inclusion did raise a few eyebrows, as she was not one of the biggest ticket-sellers with the country audience. In reality, Conn was experiencing enormous problems trying to land his first-choice acts and, as more and more of his intended line-up were sidelined, so Wanda became viewed as a safe pair of hands who would not let him down, and from whom he was guaranteed a quality performance.

So, it turned out that the Saturday bill for the *8th International Festival of Country Music*, finished up with Tammy Wynette, Don Williams, Connie Smith, Jeannie Seely, Vernon Oxford, Jim & Jesse, Jack Greene, Ray Lynam, Philomena Begley, Tex Withers, Leapy Lee and Jeannie Denver. Wanda was slotted in shortly after the intermission, when the audience were still buzzing from a show-stopping performance by Don Williams. Dressed in a bright orange outfit, she tore through a shortened version of 'Let's Have A Party', as if she wanted it out of the way as quickly as possible. The remainder of her act was politely received, but was far from being one of the highlights of the evening. 'Jesus Put A Yodel In My Soul' was still on the set list and sadly there remained no place for 'Fujiyama Mama' or 'Honey Bop'.

TV Appearances
Sing Country (BBC2)   17 April 1976 (screened 26 May 1976)

CARL PERKINS

April 1976		
19 Wembley	Empire Pool	
Tour organiser — Mervyn Conn		

Wembley 1976 was the first occasion post-Cash that Carl Perkins appeared in the UK. In an attempt to widen the scope of the *8th International Festival of Country Music*, Mervyn Conn was experimenting with an evening of contemporary country on Easter Monday and Carl was placed on a bill which included such diverse talent as Buffy Sainte-Marie, the Ozark Mountain Daredevils, the Dillards, John Hartford, Dick Damron, Andy Fairweather-Low, Kenny Johnson & North Wind, Country Gazette, plus comperes Roger Scott and Dave Cash. As the content of Carl's act was some twenty years short of being contemporary, the thinking was probably that he would appeal more to the younger country rock or folk-country fans, than to the mainstream 'Keep it country' brigade, who favoured the likes of George and Tammy, and who would become visibly stressed if any performer varied one iota from their rather narrow perception of country music.

Introduced by Capital Radio's Roger Scott, Carl was backed by Jeannie Denver's group – the J.D. Band – and he was given a very warm reception as he kicked off his short set with a gutsy 'Matchbox'. From there, he moved quickly into 'Boppin' The Blues' and a restrained and thoughtful 'Turn Around'. Between songs, he talked briefly about Sun Records and rockabilly music, all of which brought great cheers from the audience. 'Honey Don't' preceded a tribute to Hank Williams in the form of 'Kaw-Liga'. He then rocked his way through 'That's All Right' and closed with an energetic and much appreciated 'Blue Suede Shoes'.

The J.D. Band did an excellent job backing Carl and it was reported that he was so pleased with their efforts that he presented his Fender guitar to their leader, Stuart Barnes. 'Never in my life have I worked with such a professional outfit,' he commented. 'We met only twice, yet the sound they managed was just great.'

TV Appearances
Sing Country (BBC2)   19 April 1976 (screened 9 June 1976)

WAYLON JENNINGS
RICK NELSON

Mervyn Conn's problems in finalising the acts for his *8th International Festival of Country Music* can best be understood by looking at the names who dropped out. Billed at various times to appear were Hoyt Axton, Willie Nelson, Fairport Convention, Gene Pitney, Jessi Colter and, of greater interest to rock'n'roll enthusiasts, both Waylon Jennings and Rick Nelson. Nelson in particular would have been a strong ticket-seller, as he had only once appeared in Britain, back in February 1972. Sadly, his many British fans were disappointed yet again.

NEIL SEDAKA

April 1976			May 1976		
18-24	Batley	Variety	1	London	Royal Festival Hall
27	Glasgow	Apollo	2	Hammersmith	Odeon
28	Southport	New	4	Bristol	Colston Hall
30	Bournemouth	Winter Gardens	5	Manchester	Palace
Tour organiser — Barry Dickins					

This was almost a rerun of Sedaka's 1975 tour, as he played many of the same venues as a year earlier. The re-recording of his 1962 hit, 'Breaking Up Is Hard To Do', had given him another big chart success in the States, so his career remained in good shape.

The British dates followed on from concerts in France, Germany and the Netherlands, and reports from the Hammersmith Odeon indicated that

Neil was in fine form during the second house, opening with just his own piano accompaniment on 'The Other Side Of Me', before bringing in the band for a selection of his hits old and new, including pleasing renditions of 'Oh! Carol', 'Little Devil', 'Bad Blood' and 'The Hungry Years'. Dressed rather bizarrely in what looked like an orange romper suit, he nevertheless retained the ability to excite his loyal female fans and his podgy wiggling induced near-hysteria in the stalls. He encored with an extended version of 'Love Will Keep Us Together'.

Even an amiable character like Neil Sedaka cannot keep everyone happy though. *Sounds* printed a letter from an irate fan in Gravesend, Kent, who had attended the first house at Hammersmith. He accused Sedaka of dashing off his hits in medley form to preserve his energy for the second show, and further berated him for spending the majority of his act doing embarrassing little dances around the stage and posing for photographs. He claimed to be disgusted by the whole affair.

BILLY SWAN

April 1976		
23 London	New Victoria	
Tour organiser — Asgard		

Billy Swan and his American band, which comprised David Kielhofner (tenor sax), Tim Krekel (guitar), Bill Donohue (piano), Rick Boyer (bass) and Jimmy Bower (drums), were announced as the supporting act for a series of six shows in the UK, opening in Birmingham on 20 April and starring Willie Nelson. For unexplained reasons, the tour shrank to a single gig, which was a shame because both Swan and Nelson were on fine form.

Billy's stage attire was a white Elvis Presley T-shirt and black slacks, plus a pair of green socks which were allegedly once owned by the King himself. He does not have the strongest of voices and his set started unspectacularly, really only coming alive when he moved into his slowed-down, dragged-out version of 'Don't Be Cruel'. This finally got the audience going and he finished strongly with his hits, 'Everything's The Same (Ain't Nothing Changed)' and 'I Can Help'. Other high points of an enjoyable act were a raucous 'Blue Suede Shoes' and a swinging 'Lover Please' (written by Swan, and a 1962 hit for Clyde McPhatter), complete with a rasping saxophone break.

At the conclusion of Willie Nelson's long set, Billy was recalled to the stage to join in a rousing finale with 'Will The Circle Be Unbroken'.

BOBBY VEE

April 1976			May 1976		
30	Jersey, CI	Behan's (West Park Pavilion)	1	Jersey, CI	Behan's (West Park Pavilion)
			5-8	Farnworth	Blighty's
			9	Whitehaven	Haven
			18-22	Bedford	Nite Spot
			?	London	Speakeasy
			25	Whitley Bay	Sands
			26	Chesterfield	Aquarius
			28-29	Caerphilly	Double Diamond
Tour organiser — Henry Sellers					

An energetic and cheery Bobby Vee bounced his way around the UK during May sporting a full beard and an act that was a mixture of his own pop-rock hits and some classic Buddy Holly songs.

Audiences at trendy London clubs like the Speakeasy were often cynical and unkind to acts they did not consider suitably 'cool', but the enormous enthusiasm and good humour with which Vee approached his task rapidly won over his detractors. He was backed by Smackee, who were not only competent musicians, but also able to deliver the vocal harmonies and chants of 'bouncy, bouncy' when required. Bobby scored strongly with a slow version of 'Take Good Care Of My Baby', a lively 'Peggy Sue' and a fast-moving 'The Night Has A Thousand Eyes'. A new song, 'That's The Way It Is, That's The Way It Goes', was also well received.

ROSE MADDOX

A month-long tour of Britain and Ireland was announced by country music promoter Lou Rodgers. Commencing 4 May, with backing provided by Ray Dexter & The Raylettes, this would have been the first real opportunity for UK audiences to enjoy a live appearance by Rose Maddox, truly a country music legend and a lady of increasing interest to rock'n'roll fans as a result of her rockabilly recordings for Capitol during the Fifties. Rose had made a cameo appearance at London's Nashville Room during 1969, in the midst of a tour of US military bases, but had yet to present her full act to British fans. The 1976 itinerary even included the fascinating prospect of a show in Wakefield, where she was scheduled to share billing with US country veteran Eddie Noack.

Sadly, the tour was cancelled, with Rodgers blaming the untimely closure of the West Country booking agency, R.W. Promotions. A good portion of the tour had been scheduled through their intermediary and insufficient time remained to book replacement dates.

CHUCK BERRY

May 1976			June 1976		
13	Sheffield	Fiesta	1	Stoke	Jollee's
15	Bournemouth	Winter Gardens	2	Newcastle	City Hall
21	London	New Victoria	3	Leicester	Bailey's
30	Batley	Variety	4	Stoke	Bailey's
31	Paignton	Festival	5	Liverpool	Empire
			6	Douglas, IoM	Palace Lido
Tour organiser — Derek Block					

News of another Chuck Berry tour first surfaced at the end of January. Promoter Mervyn Conn announced a series of dates for the second half of May to fit around Chuck's European commitments. Mr. Berry is never the easiest of people to conduct business with, and before long the Conn tour sank without trace, only to be resurrected by rival promoter Derek Block. Conn was not amused and *Sounds* reported threats of legal action against his rival, alleging that Block had induced a breach of contract.

After some chopping and changing of the itinerary, Chuck eventually opened in Sheffield on 13 May, though he spent much of the next fortnight in Europe. He was backed on all the UK shows by a four-piece band called Sunweel.

It had been proposed to include a concert at Croydon's Fairfield Halls on 16 May, but the theatre's General Manager, David Shimell, refused to accept the booking, stating, 'We don't really think Chuck Berry is suitable for this type of hall.' He did, however, add that he was not against rock concerts as such, and that Elton John was still scheduled to appear there. Promoter Derek Block commented, 'I am sure the Croydon ratepayers will be interested to hear that the concert is being turned down because they don't like Chuck Berry as a person.'

Happily, the controversy which plagued Chuck's last UK tour was avoided and generally everyone seemed satisfied. At Paignton's Festival Theatre he performed a good cross-section of his classic songs and even slipped in an exciting version of his rarely-performed 'Don't Lie To Me', as well as less obvious material like 'Ramblin' Rose' and 'South Of The Border'. His daughter, Ingrid, joined her father on stage and he accompanied her as she sang the blues standards 'Key To The Highway' and 'Got My Mojo Working'. They then closed the show by duetting on a raunchy version of 'Reelin' And Rockin' '. Chuck had played for the best part of 90 minutes. For once, nobody had been short-changed and his audience went home happy.

Jackie Lynton was the support act for the main London gig at the New Victoria, while Chuck's appearance at Douglas, Isle of Man coincided with the TT motor cycling *Race Week*, where he headlined on a sizeable bill which also featured Crazy Cavan & The Rhythm Rockers, the Hellraisers and Remember This.

DEL SHANNON

May 1976			June 1976		
14-15	Leigh	Garrick	6-12	Cleethorpes	Bunny's Place
	Chorlton	Valentines	13	Leicester	Beaumont
16	Eastbourne	King's		Nuneaton	Co-op
19	Ilford	King's	15-19	Bedford	Nite Spot
21	Spennymoor	Top Hat	20	Bournemouth	Maison Royale
	Whitley Bay	Sands	21	Chesterfield	Aquarius
22	Retford	Aquarius	22	Bentwaters	USAF
	Lincoln	Aquarius	23-26	Batley	Variety
23	Whitehaven	Haven	27	Rugeley	Lea Hall
24	Manchester	*unknown venue*			
25	Melton Mowbray	WMC			
26-29	Farnworth	Blighty's			
Tour organiser — Henry Sellers					

Del Shannon flew back to England on 13 May for six weeks of club and cabaret work. By this stage in his career he was becoming very disillusioned with the music business, and perhaps more than most of the big names of the Fifties and early Sixties was unhappy with his failure to add further hit records to his quite impressive tally of chart entries on both sides of the Atlantic. Island Records had signed him some months earlier, but even though he had worked hard writing new material – some in collaboration with ELO's Jeff Lynne – the company seemed only half-hearted in their efforts to promote him. So, it was back on the cabaret trail again. Support at Whitehaven was provided by Sixties chart act, the Casuals.

HANK MIZELL

On 20 March 1976, 'Jungle Rock' entered the British charts and launched the rockabilly craze that would revitalise the whole rock'n'roll scene in Europe.

William 'Hank' Mizell was born in Daytona Beach, Florida in 1923 (not 1924 or 1928, as has been variously claimed). He dabbled on the fringes of country music and by 1954 had his own radio show in Montgomery, Alabama. Two years later, and after moving to Chicago, he began performing rock'n'roll. 'Jungle Rock' was written by Mizell and cut in 1958 for the tiny Eko label, before being picked up and re-released by King Records of Cincinnati.

Neither sold at all well and Hank's chance of fame seemed to have passed for ever. He carried on playing the Chicago clubs until the early Sixties, when he left show business and worked variously in a paint shop, as a preacher, a truck driver and in a furniture store. His rock'n'roll days were a long way behind him when he got a call from record company executive Shelby Singleton, during April, summoning him to his office in Nashville.

Not surprisingly, Mizell was completely astounded to learn that his 18-year-old flop was moving rapidly towards the British Top 10 and that, in the wake of its UK success, it was now being issued right across Europe (it went to No.1 in the Netherlands) and reissued in the USA. Within days, Singleton had Hank in the studio recording an album and plans were soon afoot for him to undertake a British tour.

The original idea was for Mizell to fly to London for a series of shows in May, but everything was far too rushed and the first set of dates had to be scrapped when a US booking agency erroneously reported that he was not available. A revised itinerary was worked out whereby he would spend a few days doing promotion before setting out on a series of one-nighters commencing at the beginning of June.

He flew into London around 22 May and mimed to 'Jungle Rock' on *Top Of The Pops*. His album was already mixed and ready for release by Charly Records, who were eager to push the new single, 'Kangaroo Rock', even before its predecessor had fallen from the charts. Everything was moving at an alarming rate and poor Hank was struggling to keep up. Adam Komorowski from *New Kommotion* met up with him at the Holiday Inn in Swiss Cottage, North London and found him eager to please, if more than a little dazed by his newly acquired stardom.

With his promotional duties completed and a few free days stretching ahead of him before the first of his live shows, Hank took advantage of the return ticket that had been provided for him and flew home for a short break to recharge his batteries.

Carousel Promotions, who were setting up the tour in conjunction with Charly Records, were less than amused by Mizell's unscheduled departure. One set of dates had already been cancelled and venues were already reluctant to rebook in case of another false alarm. They had gigs lined up at Chelmsford, Derby, Huddersfield, Sunderland, Margate and Bedford, plus a London appearance at Alexandra Palace on the same bill as Crazy Cavan & The Rhythm Rockers and Shakin' Stevens & The Sunsets. Not all the dates were confirmed, however, and with 'Jungle Rock' finally sliding down the charts, neither they nor anybody else were prepared to pay to bring their absentee star back to Britain. A spokesman for Charly Records said, 'If he comes back, it won't be for us. We're just not interested in setting up another tour. The whole affair has been very embarrassing and if it happened again, we'd look plain stupid.'

So, the Hank Mizell tour became a cautionary tale on how not to proceed. 'Kangaroo Rock', the follow-up single, bombed and the world moved on. Hank was left sitting at home to contemplate the vagaries of fame.

TV Appearances
Top Of The Pops (BBC1)   27 May 1976

FREDDY FENDER

June 1976		
13 London	New Victoria	
Tour organiser — Harvey Goldsmith		

Baldemar Huerta was born in the Rio Grande Valley town of San Benito. After three years in the Marines, he started playing the Texan honky tonks and dance halls, and in 1957 scored a hit record in Mexico and South America with a Spanish-language version of Presley's 'Don't Be Cruel'. After a change of name to Freddy Fender, his 1960 recording of the rock'n'roll ballad, 'Wasted Days And Wasted Nights', was just breaking out nationally in the States when he and his bass player were arrested in Baton Rouge and busted for possession of marijuana. He spent the next three years in Angola State Prison, Louisiana.

It was many years before Fender's career recovered, but in April 1975 his recording, 'Before The Next Teardrop Falls', went to No.1 on the US country charts and by the time of his British debut at London's New Victoria Theatre he was at the peak of his popularity.

He was nearing the end of a world tour which included Australia (but not New Zealand, where his drug bust prohibited his entry) and arrived tired and late from Berlin. The theatre was no more than half-full and the opening act, Roy St. John, made no impact whatsoever. Backed by his 'Friends' including Dave Wendells on guitar and B.J. Cole on pedal steel, Fender delivered a varied and fascinating show. On the one hand, he included his recent recordings for ABC/Dot, 'My Rancho Grande', 'Lovin' Cajun Style' and 'Before The Next Teardrop Falls', but interspersed them with the songs which had served him so well during nearly twenty years in the bars and roadhouses. 'Big Boss Man' and 'Get Out Of My Life, Woman' were almost unbearably funky, while others including 'Mathilda', 'Since I Met You Baby' and 'Wasted Days And Wasted Nights' reeked of steamy Bayou nights and tiny stages protected by chicken wire.

He gazed out at the English audience and tried to explain, 'This is not a floor show where some kid does a bunch of songs from the Fifties. These are songs I used to sing so that I could eat back in the Fifties.' Then it was on through 'Donna', 'A Thousand Miles Away', 'Earth Angel', 'Cherry Pie', 'We Belong Together' and his own 'Holy One'. The scattered fans made their appreciation known and Freddy retired with applause ringing in his ears.

Interviewed by David Redshaw for *New Musical Express*, he was asked to confirm if his music should be defined as 'Tex-Mex rockabilly'. 'I don't know what "rockabilly" means,' he replied. 'I've always done rhythm & blues. 'Wasted Days And Wasted Nights' to me was always rhythm & blues. I'm not an Anglo. I'm a Mexican American, and I sing without a Southern accent.'

CHUBBY CHECKER

'Let's Twist Again' had returned to the British Top 10 at the end of 1975, and this may have had a bearing on the announcement from promoter Danny O'Donovan that a five-week tour of one-nighters was being arranged for the Twist King, Chubby Checker, commencing 27 June. His enthusiasm for the project was apparently not shared by others, as nothing further was ever heard on the subject.

MARVIN RAINWATER

Marvin returned to the UK during July 1976 and recorded eleven songs for Westwood Records. They remained unissued until 2001, when they were included on a Bear Family CD release, *Rock Me – The Westwood Recordings.*

JOHNNY CASH

It was rumoured that Johnny Cash and Emmylou Harris would jointly top the bill at a major open-air concert to be held during July or August at Wembley Stadium. The story got as far as a mention in *New Musical Express*, but no further.

THE CRYSTALS

August 1976					
5	Lyneham	RAF	17	Dentwaters	USAF
6	Middleton	Civic Hall	18	Clacton	101 Disco
7	Bristol	Yate Centre	20	Upper Heyford	USAF
	Gloucester	Roundabout	21	Mildenhall	USAF
8	Dalston	Four Aces	22	Greenham Common	USAF
9	Salford	Willows		Bournemouth	Maison Royale
	Birkenhead	Hamilton	24	Charnock Richard	Park Hall
10	Southend	Talk of the South	25	Hucknall	Miners' Welfare
11	Ilford	King's	26	Wood Green	King's Arms
	Tottenham	White Hart		London	Playboy
12	Middlesbrough	Inn Cognito	27	Retford	Porterhouse
13	Sunderland	Annabelle's	28	Alconbury	USAF
14	Manchester	Russell's		Chicksands	USAF
	Widnes	Bumble's	29	Wigan	Rugby
16	Colchester	Copford Windmill		Manchester	Palace
Tour organiser — Barry Collings					

Dee Dee Kennibrew had kept the name of the Crystals alive during the Seventies and had visited Britain on two occasions during 1974 in the company of new recruits Louise Bethune and Peggi Blu. It is probable that the same three girls returned for this lengthy tour, although the total lack of detailed press coverage makes it difficult to be completely certain.

The Spector hits 'Da Doo Ron Ron', 'He's A Rebel' and 'Then He Kissed Me' formed the cornerstone of an act which also featured more contemporary soul material from the likes of Ike & Tina Turner, the O'Jays and Gladys Knight. The audience reaction around the country was generally good, as the girls cleverly adapted their act to the different requirements of discos, pubs and cabaret lounges.

At Bournemouth they co-starred with Mike Berry & The Outlaws and the Nashville Teens.

BEN E. KING

September 1976			October 1976		
17	Middleton	Civic Hall	1	Stockton	Inn Cognito
18	Manchester	Russell's	2	Mildenhall	USAF
	Widnes	Bumble's		Ipswich	Tracy's
19	London	Q	3	Bentwaters	USAF
20	Colchester	Copford Windmill			
21	Runcorn	Cherry Tree Hotel			
	Birkenhead	Hamilton			
22	Tottenham	White Hart			
	Ilford	King's			
23	Wood Green	King's Arms			
	Camden Town	Dingwalls			
24	Alconbury	USAF			
	Chicksands	USAF			
28	Southend	Talk of the South			
29	Norwich	Cromwell's			
30	Bedlington	Lucifer's			
	Sunderland	Gasthoffen			
Tour organiser — Stuart Dingley					

Ben E. King was no longer the Number One draw on the ballroom and nightclub circuit as he had been a few years earlier, but still retained a loyal body of fans who greatly appreciated his warm personality and his seemingly effortless act – a mixture of rock'n'roll ballads and soul music – always delivered with great charm and professionalism.

At Dingwalls in London he bounced on stage, smartly dressed in a white double-breasted suit and black shirt, opening with Lou Rawls' 'You'll Never Find Another Love Like Mine' and a sparkling rendition of Tavares' 'Heaven Must Be Missing An Angel'. Backing was supplied by an anonymous six-piece band from Scotland, augmented by Ben's own pianist, Al MacGruder, while the main body of the act consisted of two lengthy medleys. The first comprised 'The Way We Were', 'Stand By Me', 'There Goes My Baby', 'Cupid' and 'Wonderful World', after which he talked about Sam Cooke and what a great influence he had been on his music, before continuing with 'Save The Last Dance For Me', 'Don't Play That Song' and 'Spanish Harlem'. An enjoyable and well-crafted set closed with 'Supernatural Thing', and as an encore, a faithful recreation of the Sam Cooke hit, 'Bring It On Home To Me'.

THE DRIFTERS

September 1976			November 1976		
24	Newcastle	Mayfair	2	Burnley	Cat's Whiskers
25	Ayr	Darlington Hall	3-4	Chesterfield	Aquarius
27	Aberdeen	Ruffles	5	Glasgow	Apollo
29-30	Watford	Bailey's	6	Cleethorpes	Bunny's Place
October 1976			7-13	Wakefield	Theatre Club
1	Sheffield	City Hall	16	Middlesbrough	Madison
2	Southport	New	17	Farnworth	Blighty's
3-9	Batley	Variety	20	Farnworth	Blighty's
10	Charnock Richard	Park Hall	21-27	Luton	Caesar's Palace
12	Middlesbrough	Madison	28	London	Palladium
14	Stoke	Bailey's	29	Charnock Richard	Park Hall
15	Birmingham	Barbarella's	30	Liverpool	Grafton Rooms
	Birmingham	Abigail's	December 1976		
16	Frimley Green	Lakeside	1	Eastbourne	King's
17	Nottingham	Commodore	2	Coventry	Tiffany's
19	Portsmouth	Locarno		Birmingham	Barbarella's
21	Blackpool	Tiffany's	3	St. Ives	Recreation Centre
22	Morecambe	Winter Gardens	4	West Runton	Pavilion
23	Leigh	Garrick	5	Reading	Top Rank
24	Southend	Talk of the South	6	Charnock Richard	Park Hall
25-30	Leicester	Bailey's	7	Bradford	Locarno
31	Wolverhampton	Civic Hall	9	Edinburgh	Playhouse
			10	Spennymoor	Top Hat
Tour organiser — Henry Sellers					

This long, arduous tour saw the Drifters further cement their reputation as the biggest draw on the club and ballroom circuit. Full houses were the order of the day and the high level of repeat bookings spoke volumes for the popularity of the group. Johnny Moore, Clyde Brown, Joe Blunt and Billy Lewis delivered a quality show night after night, and a letter from a Julie Newton of Gateshead printed in the magazine *Blues & Soul* adequately conveyed the atmosphere of a Drifters' live show:

'I'd like to thank the Drifters for their fantastic performance at Newcastle's Mayfair recently. The very overcrowded club, where there was no seating at all, didn't allow them to see their audience through the smoke and some sections of the crowd behaved very badly as they fought their way to the front, crushing and pushing those who had been waiting from 7.30 until midnight. After singing all their hits for nearly two hours in these appalling conditions, the Drifters deserved twice as much money as they received.'

The latest Drifters record, 'You're More Than A Number In My Little Red Book', a duet between Clyde Brown and Johnny Moore, entered the British charts during this tour, eventually peaking at No.5 on 18 December. It was the last major hit single for the group in the UK.

TV Appearances
Top Of The Pops (BBC1)   23 September 1976

The Drifters go through their paces at Batley Variety Club.

THE SHANGRI-LAS

September 1976			11-16	Leicester	Bailey's
30	Middlesbrough	Inn Cognito	18-24	Birmingham	La Dolce Vita
October 1976			29	Retford	Porterhouse
1	Middleton	Civic Hall	November 1976		
	Widnes	Bumble's	1	Runcorn	Cherry Tree Hotel
4	Colchester	Copford Windmill			
Tour organiser unknown					

New York girl group the Shangri-Las had been all set to tour the UK with Del Shannon in March 1965, but pulled out at the last minute owing to the sudden illness of Mary Weiss. The fact that they finally made it to Britain more than a decade later was entirely due to the unexpected chart reappearance of their most famous song, 'Leader Of The Pack', which found its way back to the UK Top 10 during July 1976.

Sadly, only three of the original Shangri-Las remained, because Mary Ann Ganser had died of an epileptic seizure in 1970, leaving her twin sister Margie Ganser and sisters Mary and Betty Weiss to perform as a trio. Had they toured in 1965 as originally planned, the girls might have made some impact with British audiences, but by 1976 there was only a lukewarm reception, despite the fact that their act included such group favourites as

'Remember (Walking In The Sand)', 'Give Him A Great Big Kiss', 'I Can Never Go Home Anymore' and, of course, 'Leader Of The Pack'. On 12 October at Leicester, they co-starred with Tavares.

The Shangri-Las ceased to function as a group shortly after returning home, the three girls making no more than spasmodic appearances together, preferring to concentrate on family life.

DOCTOR ROSS

October 1976		
1	Middlesbrough	Town Hall
7	Oldham	Birch Hall
11	Camden Town	Dingwalls
Tour organiser unknown		

The Doctor spent a short time in the UK as part of a lengthy European tour and at Dingwalls shared billing with the Tequila Brown Blues Band. He opened the proceedings himself with 'Good Morning Little Schoolgirl' and a rather spiritless version of 'That's Alright' before giving way to the band. At the conclusion of their set he returned and got the whole club boogieing along to 'Baby Please Don't Go' and 'The Harmonica Boogie'. His harmonica stand collapsed in a heap during 'Baby Stop Crying', but he recovered and the audience, which contained many Sun Records enthusiasts, were delighted to hear him perform 'The Boogie Disease' at the climax of the show.

MARVIN RAINWATER

October 1976					
1	Adeyfield	Country	22	Greenham Common	USAF
2	Alconbury	USAF	23	Welford	USAF
3	Southwick	Ponderosa	25	Whitcombe	Whitcombe House Hotel
7	South Ockendon	Hospital	26	Birkenhead	Hamilton
8	Peterborough	Esterlaid	28	West Ham	Upton Park
9	Bentwaters	USAF	29	Upper Heyford	USAF
10	Bury St. Edmunds	Theatre Royal	30	Lakenheath	USAF
15	Chicksands	USAF	31	Palmers Green	Intimate
16	Mildenhall	USAF	**November 1976**		
17	Maidstone	Hazlette	1	Tetbury	Ormond Hotel
19	Aberdeen	Double Two	3	Bracknell	Hale School
21	Gorleston	Ocean Rooms	5	Cadwell	New Village Hall
			6	Woodbridge	Cinema
Tour organiser — Lou Rodgers					

Marvin topped his 1975 tour by visiting some even more obscure venues than last time, along with his British backing group, Tennessee Stud, and Jon Derek. Do many American entertainers play South Ockendon Hospital, the New Village Hall at Cadwell near Grays in Essex, or Hale School in Bracknell, Berkshire? Promoter Lou Rodgers scored full marks for his ingenuity and lateral thinking, but the trip that really must have made this a tour to remember for Marvin was the show at Maidstone in Kent, followed by the drive to Aberdeen, and then straight back down to entertain the good folk at the Ocean Rooms in Gorleston, near Great Yarmouth.

Rainwater had, of course, topped the bill at the London Palladium during his first visit to Britain in 1958, so the contrast with this ragbag of a tour must have been only too apparent, but, always the true professional, he sent his audiences home happy on a diet of traditional country music and just a sprinkling of rockabilly. He was, however, a little bemused when on more than one occasion he got requests for such obscurities as 'Hot And Cold' and 'Boo Hoo'. Hell, he hadn't sung those old songs for years. Surely nobody really wanted to hear that old rockabilly stuff again after all this time?

WANDA JACKSON

October 1976			19	Chatham	Central Hall
13	Wolverhampton	Civic Hall	20	Ipswich	Gaumont
14	Southport	New	21	Croydon	Fairfield Halls
15	Barrow	Civic Hall	22	Oxford	New
16	Hull	City Hall	23	Portsmouth	Guildhall
17	Corby	Festival Hall	24	Folkestone	Leas Cliff Hall
Tour organiser — Mervyn Conn					

Perhaps as a reward for her continuing support of his Wembley festivals, Mervyn Conn sent Wanda Jackson out on a short UK theatre tour, as well as gigs in both Sweden and Norway. Support was provided by Vernon Oxford and Culpepper County.

This was strictly a country tour and the rock'n'roll enthusiasts who had initially flocked to see Wanda now largely stayed away. She seemed disinclined to sing more than throwaway versions of her great 'Let's Have A Party' and would not perform any of her other rockabilly material. Like Marvin Rainwater, Wanda had yet to realise that there was a very real audience for those old rock'n'roll songs.

DEL SHANNON

October 1976			November 1976		
15-16	Leigh	Garrick	3	Ilford	King's
18	Colchester	Copford Windmill	4	Birkenhead	Deerstalker
21	Hull	Bailey's	5-6	Farnworth	Blighty's
22	Burton	Allied		Manchester	Valentines
23	Whitley Bay	Sands	7-13	Watford	Bailey's
Tour organiser — Henry Sellers					

This was Del's second UK tour of 1976. He was now such a regular attraction on the club and cabaret circuit that his arrival provoked no reaction from the music press and media. His fourteen British hits may have all been in the charts more than a decade earlier, but he still had the ability to entertain his many fans who happily came out to see him over and over again.

103

BILL HALEY & HIS COMETS

December 1976		
3 London	New Victoria	
5 Southport	New	
Tour organiser — Patrick Malynn		

Bill Haley had seemingly lost the will to carry on after the death in February of his friend and long-time saxophone player, Rudy Pompilli. They had travelled the world together for almost twenty years with a succession of different musicians. The personnel of the Comets had evolved, but Rudy had been the one constant factor and his loss was almost unbearable. The two men had jokingly made a pact that, when one of them was gone, the other would lay down his instrument for ever, and for a while Haley behaved as if this would become reality, hiding away at his home in Veracruz in the Gulf of Mexico, where he could not even be contacted by telephone.

Eventually, a European tour was put together at short notice, culminating in two appearances in the UK. Bill seemed less than enthusiastic but accepted the bookings, despite the fact that the Comets had been inactive for so long that he was obliged to recruit a completely new band to accompany him. Bill Turner (lead guitar), Jim Lebak (double bass), Wayne Stephens (drums), Herb Hutchinson (rhythm guitar) and George Baker (saxophone) were the least-prepared Comets to leave the United States, and when compared to their illustrious predecessors were a long way short of perfection.

If Haley and his Comets were below their usual exacting standard, there was no lack of enthusiasm from the British fans, and the Teddy boys

turned out in force. There were two shows scheduled for the New Victoria, and early in the second house it became clear that the theatre security team would have their work cut out. The Teds were leaving their seats and dancing in the aisles almost as soon as Haley commenced his set, but before long some started climbing down into the orchestra pit in readiness for a full-scale assault on the stage. The resultant riot was reminiscent of Bill's infamous appearance at the Royal Albert Hall in 1968, but this time the safety curtain was lowered only eight songs into the act and the show abandoned as fighting between the Teds and the bouncers got out of hand. An array of missiles came hurtling down from the circle causing those seated in the front stalls to dive for cover, and several people made appearances at Horseferry Road Magistrates' Court the following morning facing charges that ranged from threatening behaviour to obstructing the police.

London's *Evening News* gave the debacle prominent coverage under the banner headline 'Battle of the Teds' and 23-year-old Dave Jones described the proceedings from his perspective. *'It was a rotten end to the show. There were quite a few broken noses and geezers were coming out of the orchestra pit with blood pouring from their faces. It made that punk rock lark look like a kid's nursery.'*

Happily, the Southport gig passed off without incident and Bill flew home on 6 December. He

---

New Victoria Theatre
WILTON ROAD, S.W.1
Telephone No. 834 0671/2

John Martin for Classic Concerts by arrangement with Patrick Malynn presents

Bill Haley & The Comets

Evening 9.00
FRIDAY
DECEMBER **3**

STALLS £3

N⁰ C 29

No ticket exchanged nor money refunded
This portion to be retained
NO RE-ADMISSION

---

may have been a reluctant visitor, and his Comets the least accomplished ever, but his music still had the effect of stirring up his audiences. Rock'n'roll could still provoke trouble, even in the punk era.

As an interesting footnote to this tour it should be mentioned that the support act on the UK gigs was Flying Saucers, one of the top British rock'n'roll bands. Among their ranks was saxophone player Jacko Buddin, who was ideally placed to observe the Comets in action. In the future, after Haley's death, he would front a re-formed 1955 Comets revealing a singing voice uncannily close to that of the father of rock'n'roll.

CHAPTER FIVE

1977

Rockin' At The Ritz

In the period since 'Jungle Rock' had brought Fifties' rockabilly into the British charts, interest in the more obscure names from rock'n'roll's past had accelerated at an amazing pace and long-time fans were being joined by a new generation, attracted by the barrage of vintage recordings which had previously only been available on rare and highly priced 45s. It was now clear that for every rock'n'roll king like Elvis, Carl or Jerry Lee, there had been literally hundreds of foot soldiers. These were the local heroes who had sprung up in every town across the United States, performed at high school dances, recorded for record labels with often very limited distribution and achieved little or no real success, until in many cases they had left music for more rewarding ways to earn a living.

It was also apparent that it wasn't always the best records or the most deserving artists who hit the big time. Fate is a lottery in every aspect of life, but in popular music even more so. Many talented performers failed to get that lucky break and wonderful records passed by unheard and unappreciated. In 1977, European rock'n'roll fans started to redress the balance. Those rock'n'rollers who had been overlooked or forgotten would henceforth be enthusiastically resurrected and their work reassessed. One by one they would be invited to Europe to perform live and, as a result, many of the greatest rock'n'roll shows of all time had still to take place.

The *Sun Sound Show*, held over two nights at London's Rainbow Theatre at the end of April 1977, was by far the most significant event for live rock'n'roll music since the big Wembley spectacular nearly five years earlier and was important in two ways. This was an ambitious project involving four American singers and it carried a considerable financial risk, yet it was promoted by a rock'n'roll fan, Graham Wood. Rock'n'roll was finally becoming self-sufficient. In addition, two of the artists, Warren Smith and Charlie Feathers, were unknown in the UK outside the specialist rock'n'roll world. Neither man had any records released in Britain during the Fifties and interest had built as a direct result of bootlegs, and eventually legal releases of their classic recordings, which most fans had only heard for the first time during the Seventies.

In mainstream popular music, 1977 was the year that punk invaded the charts and ruffled the feathers of the Establishment by cursing, gobbing and snarling at everyone and everything. Rock'n'roll had overcome the mods and the hippies, so cheerfully rose to the challenge of this new phenomenon, with fighting regularly reported between punks and young Teddy boys especially around the Kings Road area of Chelsea. In reality, these two factions had much in common and in the future the punk influence on rockabilly would become apparent in some of the next generation of British rock'n'roll bands.

There was one ill-advised attempt to put together a 'punk-ted' gig at the Global Village in London's Charing Cross during September. The show was to be jointly headlined by Shakin' Stevens & The Sunsets and the American punk band, Johnny Thunders & The Heartbreakers. No promoter would take it on, so Track Records announced that they would organise the show themselves. This was about as sensible as the disastrous Chuck Berry gig with the Who in 1969, but happily no blood was shed on this occasion because Track pulled the plug on the whole exercise after receiving reports of a proposed punch-up of mega proportions.

British rock'n'roll gigs were increasing in number. Marty Wilde and Bert Weedon toured the theatres in February, while the likes of Joe Brown, Jet Harris and Mike Berry were working regularly throughout the year. Johnny Spence, Mick Green and Frank Farley re-formed Johnny Kidd's Pirates and adapted his original sound to a more contemporary Seventies style, while names like Yakety Yak, Vernon & The G.I.s and the Hellraisers were amongst the newer faces on the steadily widening rock'n'roll circuit. Britain's first authentic doo-wop group, Darts, had evolved out of Rocky Sharpe & The Razors and charted in November with 'Daddy Cool'.

Elsewhere, country music was represented by live shows from Kenny Rogers, Don Williams and Faron Young, plus contemporary acts like the Dillards, Dr Hook & The Medicine Show and the country rock band, the Eagles. The Western swing group Asleep At The Wheel made their British debut at the Hammersmith Odeon during April.

Blues and soul fans enjoyed gigs by Barry White, Smokey Robinson, Muddy Waters and George Benson, and perhaps less predictably Etta James, Louisiana Red, James Booker and Dr. Feelgood (alias Piano Red) – all acts with more than a flavour of rock'n'roll. Variety and choice were very much the name of the game in 1977, and for rock'n'roll followers things were getting better all the time.

HERB REED'S PLATTERS

January 1977		
9-16 Luton	Caesar's Palace	
Tour organiser — Henry Sellers		

Herb Reed, the bass voice on the Platters' hits, had not visited Britain since May 1962, but was in the UK to record a new album for PVK Records, with his own version of the group, comprising Nate Nelson (an ex-member of the Flamingos), Ron Austin, Duke Daniels and Regina Coco.

A week at Luton's Caesar's Palace gave British fans the chance to enjoy their classy, cabaret-styled act, which opened with Daniels singing lead on 'Don't Take Away The Music'. Regina took over for a spirited 'Heatwave' and duetted with Duke on 'That's Where The Music Takes Me'. With the audience now warmed up, the lead vocal passed to Nate Nelson for a trio of Platters' hits – 'Twilight Time', 'Harbour Lights' and 'The Great Pretender' – before Ms. Coco smouldered her way through 'Enjoy Yourself'. All five Platters took it in turns to sing lead on 'Heaven Must Be Missing An Angel' before leaving the stage to quite an ovation. They encored with 'The Way We Were', sung by Regina, and killer versions of 'Only You' and 'My Prayer', performed by Nate. Herb Reed's Platters were the perfect nightclub act, cleverly blending both old and new material in a highly entertaining fashion.

BOBBY VEE

Arrangements were being made to bring Bobby Vee back to Britain and a gig was advertised for Ragamuffins in Camberley on 12 February by promoter Terry King. The project was aborted around the end of January however, and patrons at Ragamuffins were instead entertained by Marty Wilde, who could at least perform his cover version of 'Rubber Ball', in the absence of Mr. Velline to provide the original.

THE FLAMINGOS

February 1977		
14-17	Leicester	Bailey's
	Derby	Bailey's
18-19	Leicester	Bailey's
24-26	Oldham	Bailey's
	Blackburn	Cavendish
Tour organiser unknown		

The Flamingos were formed in Chicago as long ago as 1952 and had been among the leading rock'n'roll vocal groups in the USA during the Fifties and early Sixties, with a string of hits including the popular stroller 'I Only Have Eyes For You'. However, their chart success had never been replicated in Britain, where only 'The Boogaloo Party' had been a modest hit in 1969.

This same record was the reason for the group's short UK tour of 1977, as 'The Boogaloo Party' had become a dance-floor hit in the Northern soul clubs. Ex-member Tommy Hunt, by then a UK resident and a popular performer on the cabaret circuit, found out that his erstwhile colleagues were visiting Britain and caught up with them in Leicester.

Original members Jake and Zeke Carey, Jake's son, J.C. Carey, and latter-day Flamingo Frank Ayers had made the trip to the UK, where they were performing all their old hits. For British fans this was a rare opportunity to enjoy classy renditions of 'A Kiss From Your Lips', 'Lovers Never Say Goodbye' and 'Golden Teardrops', plus the wonderfully evocative 'I Only Have Eyes For You'.

Doo-wop has never approached the same level of popularity in Britain as in the USA, and with the exception of the various line-ups of Drifters, Coasters and Platters, few black vocal groups had visited the UK up to this time. This short tour by the Flamingos was a notable exception to the rule.

JERRY LEE LEWIS
LINDA GAIL LEWIS

February 1977		
25	Manchester	Belle Vue
26	Birmingham	Odeon
27	Finsbury Park	Rainbow
Tour organiser — Bob England		

Jerry Lee's return to Britain after an absence of nearly five years was an eagerly awaited event in the rock'n'roll calendar. However, at one stage it looked as if his many fans were going to be disappointed. He was suffering from a stomach disorder, but happily this cleared up sufficiently for him to make the trip. His younger sister, Linda Gail Lewis, opened each show as well as contributing back up vocals and tambourine, while Jerry's group, the Memphis Beats comprised Kenneth Lovelace (guitar and fiddle), Joel Shumaker (electric bass) and Bobby Brown (drums). Nobody in the media picked up on the fact that Brown was the brother of Jerry Lee's ex-wife, Myra, thereby missing an ideal opportunity to re-spin the story of the 1958 'child bride' scandal yet again.

The Manchester gig was a great success despite a less-than-capacity crowd. Linda opened the proceedings with 'Rollin' In My Sweet Baby's Arms' and was halfway through a spirited version of Presley's 'Teddy Bear' when her brother strolled out on to the stage, sat down at the piano and rocked straight into 'Down The Line' and an energetic 'What'd I Say'. He was on great form vocally and his piano playing as exciting as ever. His long show lasted nearly 90 minutes, during which he sang old rockers like 'Great Balls Of Fire' and 'High School Confidential' with genuine enthusiasm, threw in some gospel with 'I'll Fly Away', a bluesy 'Trouble In Mind', and a selection of his country hits including 'She Even Woke Me Up To Say Goodbye' and 'Another Place, Another Time'. Other highlights included a torrid 'Chantilly Lace' and a fine interpretation of Jimmie Rodgers' 'Waiting

RAINBOW THEATRE
FINSBURY PARK **33**

Goodearth presents
JERRY LEE LEWIS
at 7.30 p.m.

Sunday **FEB. 27**

CIRCLE

Including VAT **£4.00**

B 27

TO BE RETAINED   For conditions of sale see over

For A Train'. He closed an outstanding show with a medley of 'Whole Lotta Shakin' Goin' On' and 'Boogie Woogie Country Man'.

At Birmingham, Jerry opened with 'Roll Over Beethoven' and included an inspired version of Bobby Helms' 'Fraulein', a slow and hypnotic 'Me And Bobby McGee', and a thundering 'Ubangi Stomp' which sent the audience wild. He switched back and forth between rock'n'roll and country. In 'What'd I Say' he snarled the classic lines *'Tell your mama, tell your paw – gonna shake your ass back to Arkansas'* before decelerating into a sentimental 'Country Church'. Then it was 'I'll Fly Away', during which Linda shook both her tambourine and her shapely butt for the audience, before a storming 'Drinking Wine Spo-Dee-O-Dee'. He even worked in snatches of 'Don't Be Cruel' and 'Mean Woman Blues' into his closing 'Whole Lotta Shakin' Goin' On'. There was perhaps a little less rock'n'roll in this show than at Manchester, but enough to keep everyone happy.

The more obstinate side of Lewis's nature came to the fore at London's Rainbow Theatre, where an excitable crowd quickly tired of his slower country songs. It was another lengthy performance and still contained a measure of rock'n'roll, but there was just too much country for many in the audience, who started to barrack him and shout for rock'n'roll tunes as he worked through 'Green Green Grass Of Home', 'Who's Gonna Play This Old Piano' and a somewhat mediocre 'You Belong To Me'. Jerry Lee was unimpressed and at one stage addressed the barrackers: 'Here's a lovely Gene Autry tune, which I hope you'll enjoy. And if you don't like it, you can learn to love it.' He then broke into 'Mexicali Rose' and pointedly ignored the boos and catcalls. Jerry Lee has never been one to compromise, and by the time he closed his act with a superb version of 'The Old Rugged Cross' most of the audience were with him, but there was a degree of disappointment that the show had not contained a greater proportion of rock'n'roll.

Support on this short tour was provided by the new British doo-wop group, Darts. They worked hard to overcome the natural opposition of Jerry Lee's fans, who are famously intolerant of inadequate opening bands, and gained genuine applause for their efforts.

DEL SHANNON

February 1977			14-19	Portrush	Arcadia Leisure Centre
25	Eastbourne	King's	23	Leicester	Eyres Monsell
	Kenilworth	Chesford Grange			Community Centre
26	Frimley Green	Lakeside	27	Whitehaven	Haven
28	Charnock Richard	Park Hall Hotel	**April 1977**		
March 1977			1	Manchester	Valentines
1	Charnock Richard	Park Hall Hotel	2	Salford	Willows
2-3	Nottingham	Commodore		Manchester	Valentines
9-12	Farnworth	Blighty's	10-16	Glasgow	Rangers FC Social
			23	Leicester	Beaumont

Tour organiser — Henry Sellers

1977 was not a good year for Del Shannon. He had long been frustrated by his inability to move his career forward. Some artists were content to make an acceptable living performing their past hits, but he was bursting with new ideas and could not understand why successive record companies viewed him solely as an oldies act and would not entertain any radical change of direction.

This frustration was the probable cause of tensions in his private life. His wife, Shirley, accompanied him on this, his latest British tour, but their relationship was strained and he was drinking heavily. Every night his audience would clap and cheer for 'Runaway'. He did his show as best he could, but his heart was not in it. Smackee provided the backing throughout the tour.

THE DRIFTERS

February 1977			May 1977		
26	London	Talk of the Town	1-3	Charnock Richard	Park Hall Hotel
March 1977			4-7	Farnworth	Blighty's
1-13	London	Talk of the Town	9	Stoke	Jollee's
20-26	Batley	Variety	12	Gloucester	Leisure Centre
28	Watford	Bailey's	14	West Runton	Pavilion
April 1977			15	Southend	Talk of the South
1-2	Watford	Bailey's	16	Derby	Bailey's
3	Maesteg	Four Seasons	17-18	Cleethorpes	Bunny's Place
4-7	Wythenshawe	Golden Garter	19-21	Leicester	Bailey's
9	Wythenshawe	Golden Garter	22	Nottingham	Commodore
10	Nottingham	Commodore	23-28	Birmingham	Night Out
11	Morecambe	Bowl	29-31	Luton	Caesar's Palace
12	Nottingham	Commodore	**June 1977**		
13	Birkenhead	Deerstalker	1-4	Luton	Caesar's Palace
14	Nottingham	Commodore	5	London	Palladium
15-16	Frimley Green	Lakeside	6	Skegness	Sands Showbar
17	London	Royal, Drury Lane	8	Chesterfield	Aquarius
20	Plymouth	Castaways	9	Birkenhead	Hamilton
22	Brighton	Top Rank Suite	10	Blackburn	Bailey's
23	Saltburn	Philmore Disco	11	Douglas, IoM	Villa Marina
24-30	Wakefield	Theatre Club			

Tour organiser — Henry Sellers

The hit records may have dried up for the Drifters, but demand for their live shows remained exceptional. This long tour included bookings at most of the top cabaret venues in the country, commencing in London at the prestigious Talk of the Town before moving to the North of England's premier nightspot at Batley Variety Club. Johnny Moore, Clyde Brown, Joe Blunt and Billy Lewis worked hard to please their audiences, while promoter Henry Sellers had no difficulty in setting up just as many shows as they could handle.

Photo by Paul Harris

The Big O at the Brighton Dome.

ROY ORBISON

February 1977					
27	Bristol	Hippodrome	17	Aberdeen	Capitol
28	Croydon	Fairfield Halls	18	Glasgow	Apollo
March 1977			19	Birmingham	Odeon
1	Brighton	Dome	20	Manchester	Opera House
2	Liverpool	Empire	21-26	Watford	Bailey's
3-4	Cleethorpes	Bunny's Place	27	London	Royal, Drury Lane
5	Oxford	New	28	Chatham	Central Hall
6	Nottingham	Commodore	29	Blackburn	King George's Hall
7-12	Stoke	Jollee's	30	Bournemouth	Winter Gardens
13	Bridlington	Royal Hall	**April 1977**		
14	Newcastle	City Hall	1	Belfast	ABC
15	Sheffield	City Hall	3-9	Batley	Variety
			10	Sunderland	Empire
Tour organiser — Derek Block					

Roy returned to Britain on 23 February for a lengthy theatre tour after an absence of nearly two years. Support on all the shows except those at Bristol, Aberdeen and Glasgow was by Sydney Devine.

He spent the first three days undergoing the usual round of interviews and radio sessions to promote the tour, including a television spot in Birmingham on *Saturday Night At The Mill* in which he performed 'Running Scared' and 'Oh, Pretty Woman'. The tour itself involved a gruelling schedule and very little free time, but his voice was in excellent shape and he remained as popular as ever. There were reports that his face appeared an unreal, death-mask white and, with his jet-black hair, white suit and familiar dark glasses, he did present a somewhat strange image, but as always with Orbison, it was the songs and his unemotional and haunting interpretations that counted most.

Each night of the tour Roy opened with 'Only The Lonely' and closed with 'Oh, Pretty Woman'. The rest of the hour-long set varied a little, but centred around his Sixties' hits. At Chatham there were outstanding versions of 'Candy Man' and 'Lana', while at Newcastle he rocked hard through 'Mean Woman Blues' and 'Ooby Dooby'. The London show at the Theatre Royal in Drury Lane included an amazing 'Penny Arcade' and memorable versions of both 'Running Scared' and 'Blue Bayou'. Orbison never disappointed his fans and always gave excellent value for money. As soon as the UK tour came to an end, Roy flew home and went straight back on the road for a string of dates across American and Canada.

TV Appearances
Saturday Night At The Mill (BBC1)   26 February 1977

THE DIAMONDS

March 1977		
7-12 Sheffield	Fiesta	
14-16 Leicester	Bailey's	
17-19 Derby	Bailey's	
Leicester	Bailey's	
Tour organiser unknown		

The Diamonds had enjoyed no fewer than sixteen hit records in the USA during the period 1956-61, which made them arguably the most successful white doo-wop group ever, although only 'Little Darlin' ', a Top 10 record in 1957, had caught the attention of British record buyers. The original group had all been Canadian, but by the time of their British tour they were led by long-time member John Felton, a Californian. He was joined by Gary Owens, Jim Blaine, Jerry Honeycutt, Paul Callaghan (drums) and Mike Dorsey (piano), for a brief taste of the Northern night club circuit and a short residency in Dublin.

The act was polished and well choreographed, and featured a selection of their hits such as 'The Stroll', 'Walking Along' and Little Darlin' ' interspersed with rock'n'roll classics like 'At The Hop', 'Blue Moon' and 'Only You'. Sadly, there was no publicity for the tour whatsoever and few rock'n'roll enthusiasts even knew that the Diamonds were in the country at all.

The group continued to work regularly in the States, but were badly hit in May 1982 when John Felton, who had been with the Diamonds since 1959, tragically perished in an air crash in Nevada.

FATS DOMINO

March 1977		
27	London	New Victoria
Tour organiser — Patrick Malynn		

Fats Domino
European Tour March 1977
SOUVENIR
PROGRAMME

Fats and his band arrived from France towards the end of a month-long tour of Europe, having already played shows in six different countries. His ten-piece line-up included Dave Bartholomew (trumpet), Lee Allen (saxophone), Smokey Johnson (drums) and Roy Montrell (guitar), while support was supplied by the Mal Gray Band, for whom Sha Na Na's Chico Ryan guested on a couple of songs.

Domino opened his show with 'My Girl Josephine'. He was fetchingly attired in a yellow jacket and olive-green trousers, while his musicians were clad in orange-pink suits, so visually the effect was quite stunning. Unfortunately, the sound system let them down during the early stages, but happily this was largely sorted out by the time they reached 'I Want To Walk You Home', which gave the rhythm section the opportunity to demonstrate their skills. The set stretched to 21 songs, including memorable renditions of 'Let The Four Winds Blow', 'I'm Ready', 'Blueberry Hill' and 'Red Sails In The Sunset'. In addition to his own material, Fats even worked 'Stagger Lee' and 'Shake, Rattle And Roll' into the programme. It was a quality performance by a great rock'n'roller, only marred by the erratic sound system and some rather boorish behaviour from a section of young Teddy boys in the audience.

RONNIE SPECTOR

April 1977		
6	Finsbury Park	Rainbow
Tour organiser unknown		

Ronnie had been lead singer of hit girl group the Ronettes, who twice toured the UK in 1964, with a dazzling and sexy stage act that thrilled audiences the length and breadth of the country. By 1977 she was three years on from a painful divorce from the group's Svengali-like producer, Phil Spector, and was still trying to repair and rebuild her life. She had visited

Britain as recently as summer 1974 with a new line-up of Ronettes, but had failed to re-establish the group as a credible force in contemporary rock music.

Ronnie was attempting to make it as a solo singer when she made a guest appearance at a gig at the Rainbow Theatre by Southside Johnny & The Asbury Jukes, with whom she had already played shows back in the States. She had a new single, 'Say Goodbye To Hollywood', to perform, but her act had moved away from that early Ronettes sound and was of no more than passing interest to the rock'n'rollers.

CONWAY TWITTY

Audiences had become used to last-minute additions to, and cancellations from, Mervyn Conn's annual Wembley country festival, but when Conway Twitty dropped out at the eleventh hour after having been billed as the headliner on Saturday, 9 April, it left his many British fans bitterly disappointed.

What was not known at the time was the reason for his absence. Two days before he was due to fly to London, Conway was at his second floor office in Hendersonville, Tennessee when a man burst into the building shouting, 'I want to kill Conway Twitty! I have put a bomb in the building.' He then ran out and vanished. However, the threat was taken very seriously. Conway ordered the building to be evacuated and the FBI were notified. Bomb experts searched, but found nothing. A very shaken Twitty still refused to fly to London, as he was afraid to abandon his family to a potential terrorist.

CARL PERKINS

April 1977			27	Croydon	Fairfield Halls
9	Wembley	Empire Pool	28	Brighton	Dome
16	Peterborough	ABC	29	Bournemouth	Winter Gardens
17	Oxford	New	30	Ipswich	Gaumont
21	Aberdeen	Music Hall	**May 1977**		
22	Liverpool	Empire	1	Norwich	Theatre Royal
24	Coventry	Theatre			
Tour organiser — Mervyn Conn					

Although sneering criticism of country music was a regular occurrence in the rock press, it was unusual to see the specialist country publications joining in. It was therefore a fair indication that all was not well on the Saturday night of Mervyn Conn's *9th International Festival of Country Music*, when respected journalist Alan Cackett described the proceedings in *Country Music People* as being the worst of all the Wembley concerts that he had seen. A line-up that included Loretta Lynn, the Oak Ridge Boys, Jody Miller, Tommy Overstreet, Carroll Baker, Don Gibson, Dennis Weaver, the Cotton Mill Boys, the Frank Jennings Syndicate, Tex Withers and rock'n'roller Carl Perkins looked strong enough on paper, but according to Cackett it took Perkins to bring any life to the proceedings.

Photo by Paul Harris

Carl at the Brighton Dome.

Interestingly, this was the first occasion that Carl appeared in the UK with his own band, and it included his sons, Greg (bass) and Stan (drums). The line-up was completed by pianist Lee McAlpin and the versatile David

Sea, who switched between guitar, saxophone and harmonica as required.

After Wembley, Carl and his band remained in the UK for a theatre tour along with the funky, electrified bluegrass of the Dillards, plus country diva Billie Jo Spears, who was at that time still coasting off the back of her 1975 smash, 'Blanket On The Ground'.

At Croydon, he opened with 'Matchbox', unusually containing a harmonica break, but showed off his innovative guitar playing on 'Boppin' The Blues', 'Turn Around' and a torrid 'Honey Don't'. The audience were enthralled and listened intently as he talked about the influence of Hank Williams on his music, leading into a spirited 'Kaw-Liga'. Up to this point Carl had duplicated his 1976 Wembley show, but now served up a mouth-watering rendition of 'Blue Moon Of Kentucky' complete with a fiery guitar solo that for many was the high point of the evening. 'Blue Suede Shoes' signalled the climax of his act, but the capacity crowd demanded an encore and Perkins obliged with a gospel medley after making reference to the recent passing of his father. He sang with great emotion through shortened versions of 'Amazing Grace', 'Will The Circle Be Unbroken', 'I'll Fly Away' and 'Old Time Religion'. By the end, he had achieved the difficult task of satisfying both the rock'n'roll and country enthusiasts.

Carl's show stayed fairly constant throughout the tour, although 'Daddy Sang Bass', 'I'm So Lonesome I Could Cry' and even 'Down By The Riverside' were performed on one or more occasion. On 19 April he played in Kilburn without the rest of the package, while seven days later Dave Travis visited him at his hotel to discuss publishing business and spent an enjoyable three hours listening as Carl played and sang to him. It had long been rumoured that Perkins cut the song 'Rattlesnakin' Daddy' on Sun – a fact which he happily confirmed, even performing an impromptu version at the hotel for a startled Travis.

TV Appearances
Sing Country (BBC2)   9 April 1977 (screened 19 May 1977)

DON EVERLY

April 1977		
11 Wembley	Empire Pool	
Tour organiser — Mervyn Oonn		

The Everly Brothers had not performed together since July 1973 and this was the first occasion Don went out as a solo act in the UK, on a bill which included Emmylou Harris, Mickey Newbury, Crystal Gayle, the Dillards and Larry Gatlin as part of the Easter Monday segment of the *9th International Festival of Country Music*. His backing was supplied by the Frank Jennings Syndicate, augmented by guitarist Albert Lee.

Perhaps inevitably, it was the old Everly Brothers hits which the audience craved, rather than Don's newer solo recordings. He dressed in denims with a prominent confederate scarf and opened with 'T For Texas' and, from his album of the same name, 'Brother Juke-Box'. However, it was the third song, 'So Sad', which brought the crowd alive and from then on he had them in the palm of his hand as he moved through 'Bye Bye Love', 'Walk Right Back', '('Til) I Kissed You' and 'Cathy's Clown', Albert Lee filling in on the harmonies in the absence of brother Phil. The press called it a *'triumphant return'*.

TV Appearances
Sing Country (BBC2)   11 April 1977 (screened 12 May 1977)

CHUCK BERRY

April 1977		
29	London	New Victoria
May 1977		
1	Batley	Variety
3	Belfast	ABC
5	Birmingham	Odeon
6	Manchester	Apollo
7	Sunderland	Empire
8	Liverpool	Empire
Tour organiser — Derek Block		

If there had ever been a better weekend for live rock'n'roll in London, few could remember when. With two nights of the eagerly awaited *Sun Sound Show* to come, old Crazy Legs himself was in town to kick off on the Friday evening at the New Victoria, backed by Flying Saucers and with strong support from the Pirates.

Chuck opened as usual with 'Roll Over Beethoven'. He looked terrific, his hair cut short and resplendent in a yellow shirt, string tie and black slacks and toting his cherry-red Gibson guitar. During the early part of the set he seemed to be sizing up his audience and doing no more than going through the motions. There was a lot of tension in the theatre and some were fearful that trouble was brewing, but happily the crowd, which included a considerable number of young Teddy boys, did not let things get completely out of hand. For once, the theatre security did not get too heavy-handed with those dancers who were incapable of remaining in their seats. Chuck worked through his hits including 'Memphis, Tennessee', 'Rock And Roll Music' and 'Brown Eyed Handsome Man', before losing the plot completely during 'Carol'. He returned to the mike after his guitar solo, obviously forgot which song he was doing and started singing the middle section of 'Little Queenie'. Flying Saucers coped well with this and every other minor emergency as the elusive Mr. Berry improvised at will, leaving them to keep up as best they could.

The audience were calling out for requests and Chuck surprised everyone by announcing that he was going to do a number that went at 78 rpm and then steamed through his rarely performed 'Too Much Monkey Business' without once fluffing the words – no mean feat. The show was briefly halted as a young lady from Phonogram Records presented him with a silver disc to commemorate 250,000 sales in the UK of his 'greatest hits' album, *Motorvatin'*. Chuck looked suitably pleased, but later admitted that he did not know which record it was for.

The ceremony seemed to spur him on and he threw everything into 'Nadine' and then 'Sweet Little Sixteen', duckwalking and kangaroo-hopping across the stage as the audience went wild. The inevitable 'My Ding-A-Ling' spoilt the mood, but a memorable night was completed by a long version of 'Johnny B. Goode', which ended with the crowd on their feet and Chuck duckwalking off the side of the stage to an unbelievable roar of applause.

WARREN SMITH

April 1977			May 1977		
30	Finsbury Park	Rainbow	1	Finsbury Park	Rainbow
Tour organiser — Graham Wood					

The *Sun Sound Show* was one of the most important rock'n'roll events ever to be staged in the UK. It was arranged for the fans by a fan and vividly illustrated that there was a real demand to see original American performers such as Warren Smith and Charlie Feathers, who at that point were totally unknown to the general public. It was time for the rock'n'roll family to grow up and stand on its own feet. Big-time agents and promoters would still be needed for tours by the heavyweight acts like Jerry Lee or Chuck Berry, or to service the Northern cabaret circuit, but eventually it would

be the drive and determination of rock'n'roll enthusiasts that would bring to Britain so many incredible performers over the years to come.

Graham Wood, a writer, folk music promoter and small-time impresario, was the man behind the *Sun Sound Show*. He had dabbled on the fringes since 1970, when he promoted a short UK tour by Buddy Knox, and was also author of the book, *An A to Z of Rock'n'Roll*, published the following year. Wood had set up a company called Rock Exhibitions along with his partners Mike Harrison and Dave Cox, with the somewhat ambitious intention of staging a rock'n'roll display at the Exhibition Hall in London's Olympia. When this scheme proved a non-starter, he turned his attention to staging a

Photo by Paul Harris

BBC Radio London, April 1977.

live show that would honour Sun Records, the greatest rock'n'roll label of them all.

The plan was to secure Carl Perkins as headline act, and for a time it seemed as if Wood had pulled it off, until rival promoter Mervyn Conn announced that Carl was already contracted to him for a three-week tour with Billie Jo Spears. After much speculation, the bill was finalised with four North American acts – Jack Scott, Buddy Knox, Warren Smith and Charlie Feathers – plus the Welsh band Crazy Cavan & The Rhythm Rockers.

Of the headliners only Knox had visited the UK previously, while neither Knox nor Scott had any connection with Sun Records. Nobody was complaining though, and it is fair to say that many long-time rock'n'roll enthusiasts were viewing what Graham Wood advertised as 'The Greatest Rockabilly Show' with excited disbelief.

Smith, Feathers and Scott flew into London on Thursday, 28 April, but Knox missed his flight and arrived the following day. British performer and music publisher Dave Travis had put together a band to back the main acts consisting of Roger James (lead guitar), Doug Perry (bass), Howard Tibble (drums) and Travis himself (rhythm guitar). For all four men, the Friday before the show was a real slog, first accompanying Warren Smith as he recorded a session for *It's Rock'n'Roll* at the BBC's Maida Vale studios and then a solid four hours of rehearsals at the Regent Park studio. The whole troupe dined that evening at an Italian restaurant in Piccadilly.

When the Saturday night show finally got underway before a near-capacity crowd, it was Crazy Cavan & The Rhythm Rockers who opened the proceedings with a frantic display which included 'Teddy Boy Boogie', 'Old Black Joe' and their latest release on Charly Records, 'My Little Sister's Got A Motorbike'. They went down a storm and really fired-up the already excited crowd, who were having great difficulty in containing their enthusiasm.

The first American act to appear was Mississippi-born Warren Smith, who had been one of the stalwarts of Sun Records, cutting his first record, 'Rock'n'Roll Ruby' at the famous studio at 706 Union Avenue, Memphis as early as February 1956. He had briefly charted in the USA with 'So Long, I'm Gone' the following year, and also enjoyed some success in the country charts after switching to Liberty in 1959, but by the time of his first trip to England was completely out of music and was working as a personnel officer in Longview, Texas.

From the body of the auditorium the sight of Warren Smith walking out on stage was a truly magic moment. Rock'n'roll had been put down by so many for so long, that for the minority who had stayed loyal for more than twenty years, this seemed like a dream come true. It was as if the audience sensed that this was a seminal occasion and somehow Warren's presence brought everybody to their feet. He stood before them, a tall, thick-set man in a dark suit, his hair greased back with a quiff and sideburns and clutching an acoustic guitar. Before he had opened his mouth, the applause rang out and went on and on for several minutes during which he stood silently and visibly stunned. He remarked later that he had never enjoyed such a standing ovation throughout his whole career, yet here in England it had occurred before he had even sung a single note!

When the level of noise finally subsided, Warren rocked straight into 'Ubangi Stomp' and a highly charged 'Rock'n'Roll Ruby'. He spoke a few words between songs, but the noise from the audience made them largely unintelligible. After working through 'Blue Suede Shoes' and 'That's All Right', he threw in a few impressions of country stars like Johnny Cash, Hank Snow and even Kitty Wells before closing his very short set with a burst of 'Baby Let's Play House'. After encoring with a second 'Ubangi Stomp', he left the stage, still looking totally bemused by the whole experience and with applause still ringing in his ears. Without a doubt Warren Smith's British debut at the Rainbow Theatre was one of rock'n'roll's most extraordinary moments.

With work commitments in Texas, Warren's stay in the UK was a brief one. He flew home on 2 May and one can only wonder at the thoughts that must have filled his head on the long journey back to reality

BUDDY KNOX

April 1977			May 1977		
30	Finsbury Park	Rainbow	1	Finsbury Park	Rainbow
			3	London	100 Club
Tour organiser — Graham Wood					

As Texan Buddy Knox was the only one of the headline acts on the *Sun Sound Show* to have visited Britain before, he at least should have been able to anticipate the requirements of the audience. Back in Canada where he was domiciled, such fervent support for authentic Fifties' rock'n'roll did not exist, and in any case he had previously suffered a dose of audience hostility when he had included too many country numbers on the opening gig of his 1970 tour. His first show at the Rainbow Theatre did not go much better.

Image and appearance were so important and Warren Smith, with his cool Fifties' persona, had received such an incredible response that probably nobody could have followed him anyway. Knox was bearded and sported a semi-Afro hairstyle, so the image police were on to him right from the start. His set commenced with his biggest song, 'Party Doll', but there were

Photo by Paul Harris

Buddy *(right)* with broadcaster Charlie Gillett at BBC Radio London.

significant sound and balance problems which persisted throughout, his guitar almost drowning the vocals on occasions.

Buddy ran through 'Rock Your Little Baby To Sleep', 'Lovey Dovey' and 'I Think I'm Gonna Kill Myself' before switching into a medley of 'Maybelline', 'Peggy Sue' and 'That'll Be The Day'. British audiences are rarely fond of medleys and this one sank like a lead balloon, his cause not being aided by the persistent feedback problems. Buddy, ever the professional, gave it his best shot, but knew that it was not his day. 'It's not my audience tonight,' he was heard to comment as he left the stage.

On the second night at the Rainbow, Knox fared much better. He reorganised his set and did not experience the same sound difficulties, but unfortunately the attendance on the Sunday evening was considerably less. It seems that not everyone was supporting Graham Wood's vision of rockabilly paradise and a mystery figure had gone around London slapping 'Sold Out' notices on all the billboards advertising the show. Why, or who was involved, has never been discovered.

For Knox's fans, it was his appearance at the 100 Club in London's Oxford Street that was the high point of his visit. In the more intimate club setting, he delivered a first-rate set to an enthusiastic crowd including standout versions of 'Hula Love' and 'Somebody Touched Me'. He flew back to Vancouver on 6 May.

CHARLIE FEATHERS

April 1977				6	Tottenham	Crepes and Drapes
30	Finsbury Park	Rainbow		7	Southend	Queen's Hotel
May 1977				8	Yate	Stars and Stripes
1	Finsbury Park	Rainbow		9	Birmingham	Barbarella's
3	London	100 Club		10	Camden Town	Dingwalls
5	Fulham	Greyhound				
Tour organiser — Graham Wood						

The appearance of Charlie Feathers on a British stage in April 1977 seemed totally surreal at the time to everybody, including Charlie himself.

Born in Holly Springs, Mississippi, Feathers first recorded for Sun in 1954, but cut his finest rockabilly for King and Meteor. His unusual vocal technique, complete with hiccups and stutters, was instantly recognisable and he was much loved by the purists, especially as he never recorded anything that was even remotely commercial. There was never any danger of Charlie Feathers 'selling out'. He was the real deal and is still a name only properly known and appreciated by the most committed fans.

Photo by Paul Harris

Outside the Rainbow Theatre.

Charlie's whole career had been played out in a series of drop-down-and-drag-out clubs and bars, so had probably never performed in an auditorium like the Rainbow before, let alone thousands of miles from home. An unsophisticated and poorly educated man, this was an ordeal of frightening proportions and as it came closer to the time for him to make his appearance on the *Sun Sound Show*, he seemed to freeze. Eventually Jack Scott had to literally propel him out onto the stage as the audience waited in anticipation for a first sight of the great man.

Smartly dressed in a white suit which matched his prematurely grey hair, Feathers was accompanied on guitar by his son, Bubba. With the audience cheering wildly, he strummed the opening bars of 'Bottle To The Baby' on his acoustic guitar, but halfway through the song stopped and spoke to the audience. His words were hard to pick out through all the surrounding noise, but his nerves seemed to be getting the better of him. The band found it increasingly difficult to follow him as he kept stopping and starting and dodging from one number to another. Classic rockabilly gems like 'Get With It', 'Good Rockin' Tonight' and 'When You Decide' were consequently disjointed and unsatisfactory. What should have been Feathers' finest moment sadly fell a long way short. The audience were kind to him, but it has to be said that he failed to live up to the not-inconsiderable hype which had preceded his act.

FIRST BRITISH
CLUB GIG - SUN STAR ▬
CHARLIE
FEATHERS
AT THE 100 CLUB
100 OXFORD ST. LONDON W.I.
TUESDAY 3ʳᵈ MAY
SUPPORTED BY BUDDY
ALL TICKETS AT DOOR
(£3·00 OPEN 7·30) KNOX
TUESDAY 17ᵗʰ — JACK SCOTT
TUESDAY 31ˢᵗ MAY — THE DARTS

By the Sunday show, Charlie appeared to have tamed his demons. He seemed more confident and relaxed and cut down the spurious chatter. Concentrating on the music, he delivered fine versions of 'I've Been Deceived', 'I Forgot To Remember To Forget' and 'One Hand Loose'. He closed with a furious 'Tongue-Tied Jill' and went a long way to repairing the damage caused to his reputation the night before.

A bunch of one-nighters to follow the Rainbow gigs had been thrown together at short notice and with inadequate publicity. This was much more familiar territory for Feathers, who clearly felt most at home in an intimate club atmosphere. He was sensational at the 100 Club, showing just why he was held in such high regard by rockabilly enthusiasts. 'Stutterin' Cindy', 'Peepin' Eyes', 'Flip, Flop And Fly' and 'I've Been Deceived' were just some of the high points of a most memorable show. Charlie's lack of sophistication did surface for a moment as he recounted a story between songs in which he uttered the N-word while referring to black people. A startled Dave Travis quickly hauled him away from the microphone to the amusement of the audience. The world of Charlie Feathers in rural Mississippi was a wholly different place from London, England in 1977.

During his time in the UK, Charlie recorded radio sessions at the BBC for John Peel, Charlie Gillett, and for *It's Rock'n'Roll*. He was highly suspicious of the whole process and needed much persuasion that he would receive his money and that he was not about to be bootlegged. On 10 May he cut five songs, including 'Blue Moon Of Kentucky', 'Knoxville Girl' and 'Milk Cow Blues' at TPS Studio in London's Denmark Street, insisting that Graham Wood pay him in cash upfront. This session would eventually be included on the Rockstar album *Wild Wild Party* in 1987.

At the gig in Birmingham, the small audience included Led Zeppelin's Jimmy Page and Robert Plant, both huge rockabilly fans who were eager to see Charlie Feathers on stage. However Feathers reserved his best performance for the final night at Dingwalls, where he gave a splendid display to close his first British tour. Unfortunately, the wrangles over money persisted and were only resolved when members of the band backed Graham Wood up against a wall and forcefully insisted upon payment of the outstanding fees. This merely highlighted the somewhat unprofessional nature of the tour organisation. If rock'n'roll was to become self-sufficient, there needed to be a greater level of planning and expertise in future events.

JACK SCOTT

April 1977			May 1977		
30	Finsbury Park	Rainbow	1	Finsbury Park	Rainbow
			7	Southend	Queen's Hotel
			8	Yate	Stars and Stripes
			9	Birmingham	Barbarella's
			12	Fulham	Greyhound
Tour organiser — Graham Wood					

Photo by Paul Harris

BBC Radio London, April 1977.

The best-known of the participants on the *Sun Sound Show* was Jack Scott, who in the period 1958-61 had scored an impressive 19 hit records in the USA, four of which also charted in Britain. There had been a half-hearted attempt to bring him to the UK in April 1960, but in fact this was his first appearance in Europe, a strange omission for such a massively talented performer.

Jack was rightly perceived as the true headliner and had been allocated the final time slot of the evening. However, before he commenced his show, the house band were required to perform a fifteen-minute spot on their own. This was really a pointless exercise, as the audience were now so fired-up that they were not prepared to listen, and as guitarist Roger James, a conspicuous figure in dark glasses and fashionably modern hairstyle, sang what appeared to be a rock'n'roll parody, a succession of young Teds threw beer over him. Bizarrely, the luckless James just stood there soaking wet and carried on singing while the rest of the band fled the stage. Eventually, the curtains were briefly closed in an attempt to restore some semblance of order.

It was against this background of mayhem that Jack Scott, from Windsor, Ontario, made his British stage debut. A solid, tough-looking man with dark hair and a shaggy beard dressed all in black, he exuded charisma and instantly silenced the audience with the opening bars of 'Baby She's Gone'. More than anybody else on the *Sun Sound Show*, Scott just oozed star quality. He performed his hits including 'Leroy', 'Midgie', 'My True Love' and the hypnotic 'Geraldine'. The band were augmented by Jack's own guitarist, Vernon, and an English sax player, Derek Whitehall.

ROCK EXHIBITIONS

PRESENTS

THE SUN SOUND SHOW

FROM THE U.S.A.
TOGETHER FOR THE FIRST TIME
IN EUROPE!

JACK SCOTT - CHARLIE FEATHERS

WARREN SMITH - BUDDY KNOX

PLUS

CRAZY CAVAN & THE RHYTHM ROCKERS

AT THE RAINBOW THEATRE
ON SATURDAY APRIL 30 + SUNDAY MAY 1, 1977

DOORS OPEN 6.30 p.m. — 7.45 p.m. – 10.45 p.m.
LICENSED BAR   SNACKS   RECORD STALL

TICKETS £3.50 UNRESERVED – Mail or Callers only

ADVANCE TICKETS BY POSTAL APPLICATION OR CALLERS TO:

ROCK EXHIBITIONS   ROCKABILITY MANAGEMENT
11/17 LUDGATE HILL   OR   278 SEVEN SISTERS ROAD
LONDON, E.C.4.   LONDON, N.4.
Telephone: 01-236 6781   Telephone: 01-272 9122

Postal Order or Money Order with stamped addressed envelope (essential)

He rolled off the familiar songs one after another. 'Two Timin' Woman', 'The Way I Walk', 'What In The World's Come Over You' and a torrid 'Go Wild Little Sadie' were each greeted with sustained applause which continued through to the conclusion of his final encore, 'Burning Bridges'. Jack Scott was the star of the *Sun Sound Show* and he proved it with a simply electrifying performance.

Scott remained in Britain for some further dates and even turned up in the audience at London's 100 Club to watch Charlie Feathers and Buddy Knox in action on 3 May. His next stage appearance was at Southend, where all did not go so well. The guitarist got drunk and Jack was less than happy with the proceedings, at one stage refusing to go on at all. The stage monitors were not working properly and he restricted his act to a mere twenty minutes before walking out of the club and leaving behind an understandably agitated audience.

This was the only low point of the tour, however. At Yate, near Bristol, a small crowd were rewarded with a wonderful show and at Fulham he really had the fans rocking, including excellent versions of 'Geraldine', 'Leroy' and 'Goodbye Baby' in an outstanding act.

An album, *Four Rock'n'Roll Legends*, featuring Jack Scott, Warren Smith, Charlie Feathers and Buddy Knox live at the *Sun Sound Show*, was released by Harvest Records in 1978.

NEIL SEDAKA

May 1977		
16-22	London	Palladium
23	Glasgow	Apollo
Tour organiser — Barry Dickins		

This was billed as *Neil Sedaka and Songs – A Solo Concert* and promised a two-hour show in which Neil would perform solo and unaccompanied except for his piano. It would trace his 25-year career in show business and eventually was preserved for posterity via a double live album of the same name on Polydor.

In the end, Sedaka's performance spanned an unbelievable 2½ hours, during which he sat smiling at the piano in a crumpled suit, as always the most unlikely looking rock'n'roll star imaginable. That he was able to maintain the attention span of his audience for such a long period was simply down to the strength of his songs, plus his genial and easy-going personality.

Not surprisingly, he performed just about all of his best-known material from 'I Go Ape', 'Oh! Carol' and 'Calendar Girl', through 'Stupid Cupid', 'Happy Birthday, Sweet Sixteen' and 'Breaking Up Is Hard To Do', even including a rare outing for 'Gone With The Morning'. Later favourites included 'Solitaire', 'The Queen Of 1964', 'Our Last Song Together' and '(Is This The Way To) Amarillo'. There are few performers in any sphere of music able to sustain a show of this length and have the quality of material to do so. Neil Sedaka kept his audience entranced and entertained right to the end of a memorable act.

HERB REED'S PLATTERS

May 1977			June 1977		
28-29	London	Sound Circus	2	Weston-super-Mare	Webbington
			3	Bournemouth	The Village
			4	Burnley	Martholme Grange
			5-7	Rhyl	Tito's
			8	Cleethorpes	Bunny's Place
			9-10	Luton	Caesar's Palace
			11	Cleethorpes	Bunny's Place
Tour organiser unknown					

Herb Reed's Platters returned to Britain on 19 May and spent the first week of the tour concluding work on their new album which had commenced in January. Their opening gig was a special Royal Charity Gala event in aid of St. John's Ambulance, then the following night they played an orthodox concert at the same venue. PVK released a 45, 'Can't Help Falling In Love', to tie in with their visit.

BEN E. KING

June 1977			25	Alconbury	USAF
9	Stockton	Inn Cognito		London	Clouds
21	Greenham Common	USAF	**July 1977**		
22	Upper Heyford	USAF	22-23	Hammersmith	Odeon
24	Mildenhall	USAF	30	Edinburgh	Usher Hall
	Bentwaters	USAF			
Tour organiser — Harvey Goldsmith					

After several warm-up gigs, Ben E. King travelled out to Switzerland at the beginning of July and appeared at the prestigious *Montreux Jazz Festival* on a bill which also featured the likes of the Average White Band, Jess Roden, Linda Lewis and John McLaughlin. This led straight into a series of European dates with the Average White Band to promote their joint new Atlantic album, *Benny and Us*.

At Hammersmith, it was King who opened the show, mixing his old favourites like 'Spanish Harlem' and 'Don't Play That Song' with more contemporary numbers such as 'Everything Must Change' and 'Show Me The Way To Go'. Although his vocals were as exciting as ever, he did suffer through a rather disjointed backing group. The Average White Band followed him with a long set lasting well over an hour and brought King back in the middle for a duet on 'Get It Up For Love'. So great was the applause for this interlude that he reappeared again at the end of the show and sang the closing number, 'TLC', finally leaving the stage to rapturous applause.

JANIS MARTIN

Promoter Graham Wood had planned to follow up the *Sun Sound Show* with a first-ever British tour for Janis Martin in September 1977. Janis had recorded for RCA during the Fifties and had been labelled 'The Female Elvis'. After several years away from the music business, she was reported to be ready to rock'n'roll again and would have made an intriguing visitor.

Unfortunately, the somewhat amateurish and haphazard organisation of the two concerts at the Rainbow Theatre and the spin-off club dates which followed had left a rather sour taste. The inexperience of the promoter, plus disputes over money, effectively put an end to Graham Wood's entrepreneurial ambitions and he emigrated to Canada shortly after. British fans had to wait a further five years to see Janis.

RONNIE SPECTOR

September 1977		
10	Crystal Palace	Bowl
Tour organisers — Harvey Goldsmith and Michael Alfandary		

Ronnie Spector was still hanging out with Southside Johnny & The Asbury Jukes and made a brief guest appearance at their gig in South London on the afternoon of 10 September. Billed as *The Garden Party*, the show was headed by Santana and also featured Elvis Costello & The Attractions, Brand X and Crawler.

HERB REED'S PLATTERS

September 1977			22-24	Usk	Helmaen Int'l.
10	Frimley Green	Lakeside	26	Stoke	Jollee's
11	Margate	Winter Gardens	**October 1977**		
14	Ilford	King's	2	Purfleet	Circus Tavern
16-17	Heathrow	Airport Hotel	5	Cleethorpes	Bunny's Place
18	Margate	Winter Gardens			
Tour organiser unknown					

This was the third UK visit of 1977 by Herb Reed's Platters. Herb had remained with Buck Ram's group longer than the other original members, only leaving in 1969 along with ex-Flamingo Nate Nelson, both men having participated on the Platters' final round of US hits, 'With This Ring' and 'Washed Ashore (On A Lonely Island In The Sea)' in 1967. The continuing battle by the Platters' manager, Buck Ram, to keep control of the group's name became especially confusing when applied to Herb, who had been with the group from its inception in 1953 and who claimed to have dreamed up the 'Platters' name himself.

Furthermore, when leaving the group, Reed did not cash in his stock in Ram's corporation, Five Platters, Inc, preferring to scrap for use of the name that he had invented. The lawyers had been kept busy, securing a temporary injunction against him in 1969 which was finally dissolved in 1976, on the understanding that Herb would bill himself as either 'Herb Reed of the Original Platters' or 'Herb Reed, formerly of the Platters'. Needless to say, many of the adverts that appeared for the 1977 UK tours referred solely to 'The Platters'.

THE CRICKETS

September 1977	
14 Kilburn	Gaumont State
Tour organiser — Paul McCartney	

The publishing rights to the Buddy Holly songbook were the reason for this highly enjoyable evening in North London, set up ostensibly to commemorate what would have been Holly's 41st birthday. Ex-Beatle Paul McCartney now owned the Holly songs and had created *Buddy Holly Week* the previous year to raise awareness and presumably increase sales. MCA even joined in the fun by reissuing 'Maybe Baby' on a 45 to tie in with the celebrations.

In fact, Buddy's birthday would have been on 7 September, and it was on this day that the Crickets, comprising Jerry Allison, Sonny Curtis and Joe B. Mauldin, flew into the UK. Interestingly, this was Joe's first time back in Britain since touring with Holly in March 1958, and the venue for the

★ BUDDY HOLLY NEWS ★

Vol 1 No 2   September 7th-14th 1977.

Buddy Holly Week is here again

For the second year running, thousands of fans and members of the rock music industry will have the opportunity to pay tribute to one of rock 'n' roll's legends, Buddy Holly.

The decision to make Buddy Holly Week an annual event follows the phenomenal success of the first 'week' in 1976. Last year's event was originally designed to celebrate what would have been Buddy Holly's fortieth birthday. The commemorative week featured many memorable events, notably a lunch whose guests included leading music and show business personalities. The Guest of Honour at the lunch and during the week was Norman Petty,

Holly's manager, co-writer and record producer. He and his wife Vi won many friends during their visit and everyone looks forward to their return in the future. London's Lyceum was the host to 3,000 rock 'n' roll fans who listened and danced into the early hours of the morning to Buddy Holly music.

This year we are delighted to be able to welcome Buddy Holly's original group The Crickets featuring Jerry Allison, Joe Mauldin and Sonny Curtis. They will be doing a very special concert at the Kilburn State during their stay – further details will be announced later.

concert, the Gaumont State cinema in Kilburn, had been the scene for Holly and the Crickets' second show on that never-to-be-forgotten tour.

On Sunday, 11 September, Radio London's *Honky Tonk* show was broadcast live from Clapham Common and presenter Charlie Gillett introduced several guests, including Ray Sawyer and Dennis Locorriere from Dr. Hook, plus the three Crickets, who were interviewed on stage, much to the delight of a sizeable crowd.

The concert itself was free. Applicants had only to present themselves at the box office to secure up to four tickets each, so not surprisingly the auditorium was filled to capacity. As well as Paul McCartney, the audience included such rock music names as Eric Clapton, Denny Laine, Mick Jagger, Ronnie Wood and Lol Creme, but it was the Teddy boys and girls who created much of the atmosphere.

The support act was Mike Berry & The Outlaws, featuring Billy Kye (guitar), Chas Hodges (piano), Dave Peacock (bass) and Mick Burt (drums), and they got the show off to a fine start with a selection of the lesser-known Holly songs. Within a couple of years Hodges and Peacock would be regulars in the charts under their new name of Chas & Dave.

The Crickets could not fail. An incredibly supportive audience cheered everything they did, and at times they seemed visibly stunned by the reception. Sonny Curtis, who had the onerous task of substituting for Holly, looked more like a bank manager than a rock'n'roll star. Plump, balding and conservatively dressed in a dark suit, he made no attempt to copy Buddy, but merely let the hit songs speak for themselves. A bearded Jerry Allison, his face half-hidden under a cowboy hat, showed once again what a fine drummer he is, while Joe B. Mauldin stood quietly to the side playing his electric bass with his usual puzzled expression. For the last five songs, he switched to a stand-up bass – a move that drew a loud cheer from the audience.

Chas Hodges had played piano for much of the Crickets' set, and eventually Mike Berry and the remaining Outlaws came back on stage and joined the Crickets for a rousing finale which threatened to tear the house down. Berry led the entire cast through 'Rave On' before Sonny Curtis returned to centre stage for the inevitable 'That'll Be The Day', which finally brought the proceedings to a very satisfactory close.

JERRY NAYLOR

September 1977			October 1977		
28	Greenham Common	USAF	1	Bentwaters	USAF
	Welford	USAF	2	Kenton	7-11
30	Mildenhall	USAF			
Tour organiser — Dee Barnes					

A fortnight after the high-profile Crickets gig in London, one of their former members was undertaking a somewhat less-visible tour of the US military bases, plus one public show at Kenton, near Harrow. Jerry Naylor had fronted the Crickets when they visited Britain in 1962 and was now working as a country singer. He had enjoyed small hits in the States with 'Is This All There Is To A Honky Tonk?' and 'The Last Time You Love Me', but was featuring mainly Crickets material in his act in Europe. However, there was little hard edge to his voice and his performances were closer to Bobby Vee than Buddy Holly. Backing was supplied for most of the tour by Muskrat, although Virginia substituted at Welford.

THE DRIFTERS

October 1977			10	Bristol	Webbington
1	Wolverhampton	Civic Hall	11	Liverpool	Empire
2	Chester	Deeside Leisure Centre	12	Blackburn	Cavendish
3-8	Wythenshawe	Golden Garter	13-19	Caerphilly	Double Diamond
9-15	Wakefield	Theatre	20-26	Batley	Variety
17-22	Birmingham	Night Out	27	Farnworth	Blighty's
26-29	Nottingham	Heart of the Midlands		Stockport	Quaffers
30	Chester	Deeside Leisure Centre	28	Farnworth	Blighty's
31	Stockton	Fiesta		Failsworth	Bee's Knees
November 1977			29	Farnworth	Blighty's
1	Stockton	Fiesta		Stockport	Quaffers
2	Nottingham	Commodore	30	Farnworth	Blighty's
3	Aberystwyth	University	December 1977		
4-5	Eastbourne	King's	1-3	Farnworth	Blighty's
7	Stoke	Jollee's	4	Glasgow	Apollo
8	Stafford	Trentham Gardens	5-10	Watford	Bailey's
9	Chesterfield	Aquarius			
Tour organiser — Henry Sellers					

Two or three UK tours per year was now the regular pattern for the Drifters. Recording success was deemed less important than the steady income from cabaret bookings. Johnny Moore, Clyde Brown, Billy Lewis and Joe Blunt were a class act and the audiences just kept on coming back for more.

DEL SHANNON

October 1977			November 1977	
23	Liverpool	Wooky Hollow	3-5 Oldham	Bailey's
30	London	Palladium		
31	Bristol	Snuffy's		
Tour organiser unknown				

Del Shannon returned to the UK in October, but instead of his usual itinerary of cabaret dates, only played a handful of live shows on this occasion. Publicity was non-existent and, indeed, the music press were advertising Ray Stevens for the Palladium on 30 October. Dave Travis noted in his diary that he attended Del's Palladium show, but years later had no specific memories of the occasion. This was Shannon's problem. He had visited Britain so many times that public and media alike were taking him very much for granted and his profile was becoming invisible.

RAY CAMPI
MAC CURTIS

December 1977			24	Southend	Minerva
15	Southgate	Royalty	27	Aylesbury	Civic Centre
16	Rotherham	Clifton Hall	28	South Shields	Tavern
17	Yate	Stars and Stripes	29	Southgate	Royalty
19	Dunstable	Queensway Hall	31	Tottenham	White Hart
22	Wolverhampton	Civic Hall			
Tour organiser — David Harris (Rollin' Rock UK)					

Ray Campi

Rollin' Rock Roadshow 77

Rollin' Rock Records was the brainchild of an eccentric Italian American named Ronny Weiser. Based in Los Angeles, California, he had commenced operations in 1972, initially licensing obscure rockabilly recordings by the likes of Jimmy Patton, Alvis Wayne, Ray Campi and Groovey Joe Poovey – names that were known in Europe only to dedicated record collectors. Weiser's reissue programme made available all manner of primitive rockabilly that was unknown in Europe outside auction listings. He later set up a recording studio in his living room and cajoled former rockabilly artists like Campi, Jackie Lee Cochran and Mac Curtis to record again in the old style. Most of his sales were in Europe, where

Photo by Paul Harris

Ray works up a sweat at the Southgate Royalty.

interest in rockabilly was greatest and in December, hot on the heels of the *Sun Sound Show*, came the *Rollin' Rock Roadshow '77*, organised by David Harris, the label's UK representative.

Ray Campi is the artist most synonymous with Rollin' Rock. He was born in New York, but grew up in Austin, Texas and cut wonderfully obscure rockabilly in the Fifties for labels such as TNT, Dot and Domino. He continued recording unsuccessfully over the next decade, by which time he was living in Los Angeles. After meeting Ronny Weiser, he became the backbone of Rollin' Rock, cutting fine records himself with songs like 'Eager Boy' and 'Pan American Boogie' in Ronny's living room studio, as well as providing instrumental backing for many of his other rockabilly projects.

The other Rollin' Rock artist to visit Britain for the first time was Texan Mac Curtis. His initial career as a rock'n'roller had been more commercially successful than Campi, his King recording of 'You Ain't Treatin' Me Right' having been deemed worthy of a UK release on Parlophone (at a cost of five shillings and seven pence a copy!), but had been so poorly received and is consequently so rare, that it now ranks as one of the highest-priced UK releases and is much sought after by collectors.

Neither Curtis nor Campi had ever enjoyed the luxury of an appearance on the *Billboard* 'Hot 100' chart, although Curtis did see some action in the country listings, recording extensively in that style for Epic, GRT and Ranwood during the period 1967-76. Running parallel to his career as a recording artist, Curtis also worked in radio and it was while he was a deejay

Photo by Paul Harris

Mac at the Royalty.

on KLAC, a country station in Los Angeles, that he had run into Weiser and reactivated his role as a rock'n'roll artist. For both men this first UK tour was an enormous mental leapfrog.

The advance billing promised Ray Campi & His Rockabilly Rebels, plus Mac Curtis and his band, but in reality the Rockabilly Rebels worked with both acts and comprised Americans Colin Winski (guitar and vocals), Kevin Fennell (guitar) and Jerry Sikorski (guitar), augmented by local musicians Stuart Colman (electric bass) and Tom Riley (drums). The US contingent flew into Gatwick on the morning of 14 December and within a few hours were rehearsing in Putney, the first show being scheduled for the following evening.

15 December proved to be a busy day, as the morning was spent at the BBC's Maida Vale studios recording a session for Radio One's *It's Rock'n'Roll*, following which the whole contingent moved on to Southgate in readiness for the opening gig. There was a momentary panic when it was discovered that Campi's double bass was broken, but a replacement was located and the show proceeded on schedule.

Nobody had any idea what to expect, but Ray and the Rockabilly Rebels were both energetic and entertaining. Kevin Fennell turned out to be a competent lead guitarist, while Sikorski and especially Winski were animated and visually exciting. Campi and his double bass were the focal point of the proceedings, however, and he incorporated all the antics that British audiences had first enjoyed back in 1957 when watching Al Rex, bass player for Bill Haley's Comets: he rode the bass, climbed on it, swung it around and used every trick in the book while tearing through his Rollin' Rock repertoire, highlights of which included 'Rockin' At The Ritz', 'Tore Up', 'Eager Boy' and 'Pan American Boogie'.

Mac Curtis was more controlled, delivering powerful versions of

'Grandaddy's Rockin' ', 'You Ain't Treatin' Me Right', 'Amarillo Killer', a storming 'If I Had Me A Woman' and a moving rendition of 'Only You'. He probably grabbed the honours on the first Royalty gig, as Campi was feeling a little below par because of a throat infection. Overall though, both men proved equally popular with the enthusiastic audiences up and down the country.

In Rotherham, on a very wet and cold night, the size of the crowd was disappointing, but the reception outstanding. Yate, near Bristol, was a sell-out, as was South Shields, probably the best gig of the tour. Curtis was on top form at Dunstable on a very foggy night which ended with a big punch-up in the audience. At Southend, on Christmas Eve, the management provided a generous turkey supper, while the second show at the Royalty attracted another big crowd and on this occasion Campi was superb.

Ray, Mac and Kevin Fennell spent Christmas Day with Stuart Colman and his family at their Surrey home, while Winski and Sikorski chose to sleep late at their hotel. Not everything ran smoothly, however. There were squabbles over money, and at one point Colin Winski got drunk and hit David Harris, the promoter. On the penultimate night of the tour, they spent a free evening at London's Astoria Theatre watching Shakin' Stevens in Jack Good's production of the *Elvis* musical, before a final blast at Tottenham in front of another packed house and the unlikely scenario of Ray Campi performing a rockabilly 'Auld Lang Syne' as the clock reached midnight.

The *Rollin' Rock Roadshow '77* had been a great success. There was clearly a demand for more of the same and many people were now openly speculating about which other Americans could be persuaded to return to their rock'n'roll roots. The floodgates were opening.

CHAPTER SIX

1978

Gonna Rock'n'Roll Tonight

In January 1978, *New Musical Express* published their predictions for the coming year. They bemoaned the fact that punk had gone commercial and announced that rockabilly would be 'next year's thing', along with video discs, new wave psychedelia and pavement pizzas. They were way off-line of course, and happily we were at least spared the new wave psychedelia, but rockabilly music did continue to attract a new, younger audience without ever really threatening to become more than a cult interest.

British rock'n'roll groups were becoming increasingly image-conscious. Whirlwind were careful to describe themselves as 'greaser cool' and not a 'ted band', while the rockabilly outfit Levi Dexter & The Rockats toured the UK in April playing to both punk and rockabilly audiences. There were more mainstream rock'n'roll bands on the circuit than ever before, as the likes of Shades, Gina & The Rockin' Rebels and Matchbox joined established names like Flying Saucers and Shakin' Stevens at the forefront of the live scene. 1978 was the big year for Darts, who occupied the British charts almost continuously with a string of doo-wop hits and turned up regularly on television with a well-choreographed and zany stage act.

Several American rock'n'roll greats toured the UK during the year including Carl Perkins, Fats Domino, Jerry Lee Lewis and Bo Diddley, while both Warren Smith and Mac Curtis returned after impressive debuts in 1977. British audiences got their first chance to enjoy the dynamic Carl Mann when he made his first UK stage appearance in March, although another Sun artist, Ray Smith, made a somewhat less auspicious impression when he headlined the *Rock'n'Roll Festival '78* in November.

Some interesting country acts came to Britain, including Emmylou Harris, Merle Haggard and the controversial Joe Ely, who defied description with a repertoire that owed more than a little to rock'n'roll, but as always it was the annual *International Festival of Country Music* at Wembley over the Easter weekend that registered the greatest interest for country fans.

The great Roy Brown appeared at London's Drury Lane Theatre in February and included both 'Let The Four Winds Blow' and 'Good Rockin' Tonight' in an act which was otherwise strictly blues, while Professor Longhair demonstrated the intricacies of New Orleans piano but seemed to lack any discernible stage personality. Other blues and soul acts who appeared in Britain during the year included Martha Reeves, Tina Turner, Gladys Knight and the exciting George Thorogood & The Destroyers.

Link Wray *(left)* with Robert Gordon.

ROBERT GORDON
LINK WRAY

January 1978			February 1978		
28	Glasgow	Strathclyde University	1	Plymouth	Woods Centre
29	Liverpool	Eric's	2	Swansea	Nutz
			3	Birmingham	Barbarella's
			4	Sheffield	Polytechnic
			5	London	Astoria
Tour organiser unknown					

Robert Gordon had been lead singer with the Tuff Darts, a New York punk group, until he cut an album for Private Stock Records in April 1977 with Link Wray on guitar. It comprised a collection of classic rockabilly songs first associated with the likes of Gene Vincent, Sanford Clark and Billy Lee Riley. Robert's powerful vocals and Link's sizzling guitar-work made a lot of people sit up and take notice.

Nobody who attended the concert held at London's Astoria Theatre on 5 February 1978 is ever likely to forget the experience. It was simply the loudest rock'n'roll show ever staged in the UK and probably responsible for collective deafness on a mass scale.

British rockabilly combo Whirlwind opened the proceedings and they played uncomfortably loud, but it was after an intermission when Gordon and Wray, plus bassist Jon Paris and drummer Anton Fig, came on stage that the volume was cranked up to lunatic proportions. *New Kommotion* magazine later speculated that Battersea power station had probably struggled to sustain the voltage for the duration of the show.

Gordon was dressed in a black vest and slacks, his hair greased back and piled high on his head and looking every bit the New York street punk. He opened with 'The Way I Walk' and his big, strong voice filled every corner of the theatre. Behind him, the brooding figure of Link Wray, long, lank hair brushed back under a heavy leather motorcycle jacket, stood menacingly, his back to the audience, only turning round to deliver a stinging solo that seemed to rattle the foundations of the building.

The set included 'Twenty Flight Rock', 'I Wanna Be Free' and 'My Baby Left Me' before Robert let Link take centre stage for a blood-curdling 'Rumble'. Writing in *New Musical Express*, Cliff White accurately described it as *'a skin-stripping, distorted wall of sound, like jagged lumps of scrap metal being raked back and forth across a pit of empty oil drums'*, but most of all it was just so very loud. Wray continued through an uninspired 'Baby What You Want Me To Do', a demonic figure, expressionless behind his dark shades.

Gordon returned with 'Sea Cruise' and 'Summertime Blues'. His powerful voice was most impressive, but he did seem to lack any real stage presence. The set continued with 'Fire', his latest release, and a punchy 'Baby Let's Play House'. The show was wrapped up with 'Red Hot' and a superb 'Endless Sleep', plus encores of 'Blue Suede Shoes' and 'Flyin' Saucers Rock & Roll', after which the audience staggered out into the cold night clutching their ears and trying to unscramble their brains. Robert Gordon's UK debut had certainly been a memorable one.

CARL PERKINS

February 1978			March 1978	
19	London	Nashville Room	26 Wembley	Empire Pool
28	Gateshead	Progressive		
Tour organiser — Mervyn Conn				

With a new record deal and an album, *Ol' Blue Suede's Back*, to promote, Carl made a promotional trip to the UK in February.

Jet Records hosted a reception for him at London's favourite honky tonk, the Nashville, where around 250 fans turned out in force to pay tribute to one of rock'n'roll's most likeable characters and a star-studded line-up of musicians was assembled to play with him, including Dave Edmunds (guitar), Stuart Colman (bass), Carlo Little (drums), B.J. Cole (steel guitar) and both Alan Price and Geraint Watkins (piano). Carl performed two sets and, as well as his usual repertoire, rocked his way through 'Mean Woman Blues', 'C.C. Rider' and a pulsating 'Kaw-Liga'.

Later in the month, while on a promotional trip to Newcastle upon Tyne, Carl was persuaded to leave his hotel press conference and make an unscheduled visit to the North-East Rock'n'Roll Society, who were holding their regular Tuesday evening session at the Progressive Club in Gateshead. Much to the delight of the disbelieving audience, he joined the local band, the Revelation Five, on stage for a brief workout featuring 'Matchbox', 'Blue Suede Shoes' and 'That's Right'.

On 23 March, his own band, now known as C.P. Express and featuring Stan Perkins (drums), Greg Perkins (bass), Lee McAlpin (piano) and David Sea (saxophone, harmonica and guitar) flew into London. Carl had been rebooked after his fine performance in 1977 at Wembley, and again scored well despite a very limited time slot on the Saturday bill for the *10th International Festival of Country Music*. Also appearing that evening were Marty Robbins, Ronnie Milsap, Donna Fargo, Skeeter Davis, Lloyd Green, Charlie McCoy, Hargus 'Pig' Robbins, Lynch & Lawson and Dave & Sugar.

TV Appearances

Sing Country (BBC2)	26 March 1978 (screened 27 June 1978)
Carl Perkins Sings Country (BBC2)	? March 1978 (screened 12 September 1978)

Photo by Paul Harris

FATS DOMINO

March 1978
19   Hammersmith   Odeon
Tour organiser — John Martin

For the third year running, Fats Domino's spring itinerary included an extensive European tour, although the schedule only allowed room for one UK date. The usual star-studded band accompanied him, on this occasion featuring Dave Bartholomew (trumpet), Roy Montrell (guitar), David Douglas (guitar), Lee Allen (sax), Walter Kimble (sax), Fred Kemp (sax), Roger Lewis (sax), Thomas Johnson (trumpet), Carlton McWilliams (bass) and Smokey Johnson (drums). The supporting act at Hammersmith was the Mal Gray Band.

Photo by Paul Harris

Fats's band opened with a typical New Orleans instrumental and a rousing rendition of 'Kansas City' on which Dave Bartholomew handled the vocals. Then Fats walked on stage and after settling himself at the piano rocked straight into 'I'm Walkin'', followed by an energetic 'Blue Monday'. With the exception of his 1950 R&B hit, 'The Fat Man', the set favoured his rock'n'roll classics from the 1955-59 period and he effortlessly worked his way through them one by one, including standout versions of 'I'm Ready', 'Blueberry Hill' and 'Shu Rah', the latter featuring some tremendous sax playing. He also treated the audience to a couple of songs not normally associated with him, 'Shake, Rattle and Roll' and a feisty 'Stagger Lee'.

The whole performance was highly professional and ran for close to 90 minutes. Domino was on top form and seemed in excellent spirits. After encoring with 'It Keeps Rainin'', he left the stage for what was scheduled to be his final departure, but the audience would not let him leave. The sustained applause eventually forced him to return, wearing his overcoat, which he removed for a final burst of 'Whole Lotta Loving'.

JOHNNIE ALLAN

Louisiana rocker Johnnie Allan narrowly missed out on a British tour in 1974, when his recording of Chuck Berry's 'Promised Land' just fell short of the British charts. Four years later, the same record had been reissued by Oval/Stiff and was again getting plenty of airplay, so he made a week-long promotional trip to London over Easter.

Johnnie got to meet Paul McCartney at a Capital Radio awards programme and turned up at Dingwalls on 21 March along with Dave Edmunds, Nick Lowe and Dr. Feelgood frontman Lee Brilleaux to watch Carl Mann's British stage debut. He even put in an appearance at Ronnie Scott's on the occasion of Professor Longhair's press reception the following evening.

CARL MANN

March 1978
21   Camden Town   Dingwalls
Tour organiser — Dave Travis

Carl Mann from Huntingdon, Tennessee was the last rock'n'roller to find fame at Sun Records, when his revival of 'Mona Lisa' on Sun's subsidiary label, Phillips International, broke into the US Top 30 during the summer of 1959. By the time Carl made his UK debut nearly twenty years later, he was semi-retired from music and spending much of his time working in the family logging business.

He had been brought to Europe by Bert and Frances Rockhuizen to record an album in Amsterdam and to headline their *10th Rockhouse International Rock'n'Roll Meeting* in Tilburg. In all, he played four shows in Holland, Belgium and Germany before arriving in Britain on 20 March along with the Rockhuizens, his manager Bob Robinson and Dave Travis's Bad River Band, who provided backing for the whole tour.

The Dingwalls show created considerable interest and the star-studded audience included not only Johnnie Allan and Dave Edmunds, but also Carl Perkins, who called in to wish his namesake the best of luck, but could not take up the offer to do a song with him owing to a dinner engagement elsewhere.

The set opened with Mann playing rhythm guitar on an explosive 'Ubangi Stomp', and it was immediately apparent that the backing was spot-on – in particular the guitar playing of Eddie Jones, who was perfectly replicating the solos in the distinctive style of Carl's original guitarist, Eddie Bush. They worked through 'South Of The Border', 'Look At That Moon' and a lively 'I'm Coming Home', after which Carl switched to play some nifty lead guitar on 'Matchbox' and 'Blue Suede Shoes'. It was a most dynamic performance and a real treat to hear songs like 'Pretend' and 'Rockin' Love' so close to the original recordings.

With the club really heaving, Carl further demonstrated his versatility by moving to the piano for 'You Win Again', 'Red Sails In The Sunset' and 'Mean Woman Blues', before laying down a torrid 'Whole Lotta Shakin' Goin' On', which was one of the high points of the night. An excellent show closed with 'Mona Lisa' and 'Gonna Rock'n'Roll Tonight'.

Carl flew back to the States the day after the Dingwalls show, having made a most favourable impression and leaving a memento of his short trip in the shape of the album which he had recorded in Holland and which Rockhouse released as *Gonna Rock'n'Roll Tonight!* Interestingly, this was the first studio pairing of a UK band with an American rockabilly singer to appear on record, though this combination would be attempted many times in the future.

THE DRIFTERS

March 1978			7-8	Eastbourne	King's
22	Northampton	Salon	10-15	Sheffield	Fiesta
25	Birmingham	Night Out	17-22	Manchester	Fagin's
30	Nottingham	Commodore	23-29	Batley	Variety
April 1978			30	Purfleet	Circus Tavern
1	Manchester	Fagin's	May 1978		
3-4	Stockton	Fiesta	1-6	Purfleet	Circus Tavern
5	Nottingham	Commodore	15-20	Birmingham	Night Out
6	Norwich	Cromwell's			
Tour organiser — Henry Sellers					

By 1978 the number of 'Drifters' groups performing around the world had expanded to epidemic proportions. Charlie Thomas, Dock Green and Bill Pinkney were only a few of the ex-members who continued to trade on the group's reputation and earn a healthy living from live performances. The disputes and squabbles over use of the name kept the lawyers well fed, with Thomas taking legal action against Green in the States to prevent him from working as 'The Drifters'. As a result, he moved his base of operations north into Canada where Dock Green's Drifters continued to thrive. Clearly, there was enough work for all the many 'Drifters' and the public had long since given up identifying with individual group members.

The Drifters who regularly performed in Britain had a strong claim to authenticity: Johnny Moore was the common thread that linked them back to the glory days of the Fifties and Sixties at Atlantic Records. The present line-up of Moore, Clyde Brown, Joe Blunt and Billy Lewis did not even have a record deal, having finished with Arista some months previously, but were as popular as ever on the nightclub circuit

DON EVERLY

March 1978			April 1978		
25	Wembley	Empire Pool	1	Peterborough	ABC
29	Gloucester	Leisure Centre	2	Norwich	Theatre Royal
30	Oxford	New	4	Inverness	Eden Court
31	Middlesbrough	Town Hall	6	Hammersmith	Odeon
			7	Bournemouth	Winter Gardens
Tour organiser — Mervyn Conn					

For the second year running, Don Everly appeared at Wembley over the Easter weekend, having been granted a return booking for the *10th International Festival of Country Music*. He shared the billing with Don Williams, Vernon Oxford, Barbara Fairchild, Jody Miller, George Hamilton IV,

Freddie Hart, the Wilburn Brothers, Carl Smith and Carroll Baker. Backing for this and the subsequent dates was provided by Barbary Coast and guitarist Albert Lee.

After the Wembley show, at which he virtually repeated his 1977 set, Don went out on a short tour as support for Marty Robbins. Also on the package were the Duffy Brothers and West Virginia – the latter appearing as a reward for winning the *Marlboro Talent Contest*.

The audience at Hammersmith had mainly turned out to see Robbins, who entertained them with a virtuoso performance lasting some 80 minutes. He even gave a nod to his brief time as a rock'n'roller with a solid 'Big Boss Man' and completely overshadowed all the rest of the show.

Don did not really seem in the mood at all. His set was distinctly lacklustre and his chat between numbers failed to project his personality. The old Everly hits, 'Walk Right Back', 'So Sad' and 'All I Have To Do Is Dream' were interspersed with his solo offerings 'Brother Juke-Box' and 'Yesterday Just Passed My Way Again', and, although he was politely received, the act never really took off.

TV Appearances
Sing Country (BBC2)   25 March 1978 (screened 1 August 1978)

HERB REED'S PLATTERS

April 1978			May 1978		
9-15	Purfleet	Circus Tavern	2	Cleethorpes	Bunny's Place
16-22	Frimley Green	Lakeside	7-13	Batley	Variety
23	Bedford	Nite Spot			
24	Maesteg	White Wheat			
25	Oakengates	Jubilee 77			
26	Ilford	King's			
29	Harlesden	New Roxy			
Tour organiser — Henry Sellers					

The enduring popularity of the Platters' classic hits, 'Only You', 'My Prayer' and the rest, ensured that they were always a welcome name on the cabaret circuit. This was original member Herb Reed's fourth time in the UK in a little over a year, and although there was not a flicker of recognition or interest from the music press, attendances and audience response remained positive for their slick and well-choreographed act.

Half-hearted attempts were being made to rebrand the act as Herb Reed & Sweet River, but it was the Platters name which sold the tickets, so Herb just kept his head down and churned out the old hits for the umpteenth time. PVK Records issued a new 45, 'The Next Best Thing', to coincide with the tour.

Ironically, the Platters' album, *20 Classic Hits*, entered the British charts on 8 April and eventually made the Top 10. Nobody bothered to interview Herb Reed though, and it is doubtful if the music journalists even knew he was in the country.

BO DIDDLEY
CARL PERKINS

April 1978			19	Chatham	Central Hall
12	Inverness	Eden Court	20	Southgate	Royalty
13	Newcastle	City Hall	21	Lewisham	Odeon
14	Glasgow	Apollo	22	Weymouth	Pavilion
15	Liverpool	Empire	23	Bournemouth	Winter Gardens
16	Birmingham	Odeon			

Tour organiser — Mervyn Conn

Photo by Paul Harris

Bo gets a hero's welcome at the Southgate Royalty.

Carl had performed at the *10th International Festival of Country Music* over the Easter weekend and was now joined by Bo Diddley and Matchbox on a package that was aimed directly at the rock'n'roll fans, rather than the country audience.

Matchbox were a very strong opening act. They were emerging as one of the UK's top groups and the exposure they received on this tour further increased their reputation. They were, however, an odd choice to back Bo Diddley on his first UK tour for nearly six years, and they never seemed truly comfortable together. Initially, they were alarmed to find that Diddley was proposing a funky, cabaret-styled act that was quite inappropriate for the fanatical Teddy boy audiences, but fortunately his manager, Marty Otelsberg, intervened and steered him back to his old style.

Bo was a really down-to-earth guy and good company on the road. At one stage, the tour bus broke down, and in no time he had his sleeves rolled up and was busily occupied with his head inside the engine, trying to locate the fault.

At Lewisham, his short set included a slow version of 'I'm A Man', lots of his distinctive guitar on 'Bo Diddley', and a rather lifeless 'Mona'. He recounted a story about his Cadillac and how the girls wouldn't ride with him because he was always running out of gas, but really only hit the spot with a blistering 'Road Runner'.

Carl in action at the Royalty.

Carl and C.P. Express were on top form. His guitar playing was better than ever and he scored with a delicious rendition of his rarely performed 'Movie Magg', rocking takes of 'Boppin' The Blues', 'Gone, Gone, Gone' and an exciting 'Put Your Cat Clothes On'. The pace only dropped for 'Turn Around' and his rather sickly Elvis tribute, 'The Whole World Misses You'.

Bo Diddley did not play the penultimate night of the tour at the Weymouth Pavilion, where the support act were Danny Wild & The Wildcats.

BILLY SWAN

April 1978		
13	Glasgow	Apollo
15	Birmingham	Hippodrome
16	Manchester	Apollo
18-19	London	Royal Albert Hall
Tour organiser unknown		

Billy returned to the UK along with Kris Kristofferson and Rita Coolidge and performed three songs including his 1975 hit, 'I Can Help', at the start of each show. His main function was to play rhythm guitar in Kristofferson's band, which did at least keep him visible at centre stage for the majority of the proceedings.

JERRY NAYLOR

Ex-Cricket Jerry Naylor made a fleeting visit to the UK during May, playing a number of US military bases as well as guesting on Bob Powel's Radio London show, *London Country*. He even had a UK release of the old Buddy Holly favourite 'Rave On', but seems not to have performed at any public shows on this occasion, though there are some rather confused reports about a gig on board a ship somewhere in the Southampton area. Details are extremely sketchy and memories alcohol-affected, but such a show does appear to have taken place at some stage, though this may have been on his earlier visit in September 1977.

DEL SHANNON

May 1978			June 1978		
16	Telford	77	1	Colchester	Copford Windmill
18	Grimsby	New WMC	3	Whitchurch	Leisure Centre
19-20	Manchester	Valentines	4	Birmingham	Allens Cross Social
22	Hereford	Crystal Room	5	Rugby	Railway
29	Harrogate	USAF	6	Birmingham	Macadown
31	Stoke	Olympic Variety	7	Wolverhampton	University
			8	Northampton	Sunnyside Hotel
			9	Bedworth	Labour
			10	Willenhall	Social
Tour organiser unknown					

This ragbag of dates at social clubs and the like was a real comedown for Del, who had worked so successfully on the UK cabaret circuit throughout the Seventies. His drink problem had intensified as demand for his services reduced, and he was now scratching around for work to keep himself afloat.

ROBERT GORDON
LINK WRAY

June 1978		
14	Camden Town	Music Machine
Tour organiser unknown		

Only five months after their first UK tour, Gordon and Wray were back in Europe promoting their second album together, *Fresh Fish Special*, culminating with a single UK gig in Camden Town.

The show was opened by the Bishops, who had recently changed their name from the Count Bishops, following which the audience were treated to the intimidating sight of Wray and Gordon walking on stage clad in long, black leather coats. An ear-splitting feedback whine heralded the start of the act as Robert launched himself into 'The Way I Walk'. He seemed less self-conscious than on the first tour and his powerful voice filled the whole auditorium.

Shortly into the act, an announcement was made that this was to be their last gig together and that Link Wray and Robert Gordon would go their separate ways when they returned to the States. Inevitably, this raised the temperature, and when Robert briefly left the stage, Link performed 'Rumble', during which he broke and repaired a guitar string while still playing. The applause was such that he played it again at a faster tempo, following which bass player Rob Stoner sang a decent version of 'That's All Right'.

Robert returned and continued to impress with his more confident approach, scoring strongly with 'Fire', 'Sea Cruise' and 'Red Hot'. For the encore he was joined by American punk singer Johnny Thunders, who mutilated 'Blue Suede Shoes' and 'Summertime Blues'. Link then sang 'It's All Over Now, Baby Blue' and Robert brought the show to a close with an exhilarating 'Endless Sleep'.

TV Appearances
The Old Grey Whistle Test (BBC2)   13 June 1978

EDDY CLEARWATER

July 1978
21   Hammersmith   Odeon
Tour organiser — Straight Music

London's Hammersmith Odeon was the venue for *Blues Festival '78*, a package which was originally scheduled to feature Buddy Guy & Junior Wells, Clifton Chenier & His Red Hot Louisiana Band and the Chicago Blues All Stars. Three weeks before the show, however, Chenier dropped out suffering with respiratory problems and was replaced by the delectable Koko Taylor.

For rock'n'roll fans the interest was in the Chicago Blues All Stars, who comprised guitarists Hubert Sumlin and Jimmy Johnson, vocalist Andrew 'Big Voice' Odom, bass player Dave Myers and drummer Odie Payne, plus, for the first time in the UK, blues rocker Eddy Clearwater. They were not to be disappointed, as he proved to be one of the hits of the evening.

The show started slowly. Sumlin, renowned for his work as Howlin' Wolf's guitarist, seemed unable to get himself together and left the stage midway through his second number. After a brief period of confusion, he was replaced by the tall, imposing figure of Clearwater, smartly attired in a white suit and suddenly the whole proceedings came alive. He was only featured on three numbers, but played them Chuck Berry-style, including an animated 'Johnny B. Goode', during which he performed a backwards head-over-heels, as well as playing the guitar on his head. The audience were ecstatic.

He returned later in the show to back blues singer Koko Taylor, who turned in a wild version of 'Wang Dang Doodle', and reappeared again for a jam session at the end of the evening during which he and Taylor ground their way through an animated jitterbug dance.

Eddie Clearwater rocks Hammersmith.

ROY ORBISON

August 1978		
21-26	London	Palladium
28	Liverpool	Aintree Race Course
Tour organiser unknown		

On 18 January 1978 Roy Orbison had a triple bypass heart operation carried out at St. Thomas Hospital, Nashville, Tennessee. His condition had been very serious and his family tried to keep private all news of his illness from fans and media alike. In May it was reported that he had sold his Nashville-based recording studio to country singer Ronnie Milsap, and those with knowledge of his health problems were wondering if this was a prelude to retirement.

Happily this turned out not to be the case, and Roy returned to the UK for a week of live shows and appeared to be fully recovered. His loyal fans flocked to the London Palladium to enjoy his cabaret act, which was little changed from previous visits. At one stage Emmylou Harris was in the frame to be support act for the Palladium shows, but contractual difficulties eventually prevented her involvement. Roy also participated on the third day of the *Aintree Festival*, held on Bank Holiday Monday, in which he co-starred with Suzi Quatro and Gladys Knight & The Pips.

Orbison's name was back in the news during February 1979, when it was reported that he had been attacked by a jealous husband after a concert in Las Vegas and that the man had to be overpowered by two doormen. Apparently his assailant's wife had stated during a marital spat, that Roy was just the type of man she would like to have married, which sent him into an uncontrollable rage.

MAC CURTIS

August 1978			September 1978		
24	Bristol	Tiffany's Music Hall	1	West Runton	Pavilion
25	Southend	Minerva	4	Sunderland	Boilermakers
26	Hull	City Hall	6	Southall	White Hart
28	Southgate	Royalty	8	Carshalton	Chick-a-Boom
29	Leicester	TUL			
31	Southgate	Royalty			
Tour organiser — David Harris (Rollin' Rock UK)					

Mac Curtis was probably at the peak of his popularity with British audiences at the time of this, his second tour. He was also fortunate to have been paired with Matchbox, who were fast becoming one of the UK's leading rock'n'roll bands. By the end of 1979 they would be a chart name and no longer available as a support or backing group to visiting Americans, but for the duration of this tour they contributed significantly to Mac's success with some top-quality rockabilly performances.

Rehearsals took place at the Bisons Club in Feltham on 23 August, following which the tour moved rapidly around the country. Curtis repeated the same act which had served him well on his first visit, and again scored best with his King material such as 'If I Had Me A Woman' and 'You Ain't Treatin' Me Right'. On 28 August he headlined an all-dayer at the Royalty which also featured Crazy Cavan & The Rhythm Rockers, Flying Saucers and Shades.

THE DRIFTERS

September 1978			October 1978		
15	Weston-super-Mare	Webbington	2-7	Wythenshawe	Golden Garter
16	Eastbourne	King's	9-10	Stockton	Fiesta
17-23	Wakefield	Theatre Club	11-14	Luton	Caesar's Palace
25	Stoke	Jollee's	16-21	Birmingham	Night Out
27	Cleethorpes	Bunny's Place	25-28	Caerphilly	Double Diamond
28	Southampton	Salon	**November 1978**		
29-30	Frimley Green	Lakeside	12-18	Wakefield	Theatre Club
			December 1978		
			10-12	Stockport	Quaffers
Tour organiser — Henry Sellers					

On the face of it, this was another routine Drifters cabaret tour, revisiting many of the scenes of earlier triumphs. The impetus from their numerous sell-out tours again ensured both quality bookings and sizeable audiences, but if everything appeared tranquil on the surface, in reality the group were in crisis and the reason was the sudden decision by Johnny Moore to leave for another shot at a solo career.

The Drifters had been formed in May 1953 as a vehicle for the wonderful voice of Clyde McPhatter, but the personnel of the group never stayed constant for very long and Moore had signed up for his first stint as a Drifter late in 1954. He came and went several times over the next decade, but since April 1963 had been the cornerstone of the group, and in later years had been the only link with their glorious era at Atlantic Records. With Moore gone, the Drifters lacked a great deal of credibility.

Johnny Moore's departure was studiously ignored by the music press but was readily apparent to long-time fans. Clyde Brown, Billy Lewis and Joe Blunt were joined by Ray Lewis, a Californian solo singer (no relation to Billy). The act continued to be as professional and entertaining as ever, but the absence of Moore's distinctive lead vocals left a void that was impossible to fill.

RAY CAMPI

Ray's successful British debut in December 1977 and the increasing popularity of his Rollin' Rock records made him an obvious candidate for a return tour. An itinerary was put together for a series of shows in September 1978, opening in Plymouth, which would feature Ray and the Rockabilly Rebels, plus the British R&B band Dr. Feelgood. Ray fell sick with hepatitis and so the project had to be cancelled.

MAC CURTIS

October 1978		
23 Rayleigh	Croc's	
26 Southgate	Royalty	
Tour organiser — David Harris (Rollin' Rock UK)		

Mac Curtis played a gig at Hilvarenbeek in the Netherlands on 21 October, following which he returned to the UK only six weeks after the conclusion of his previous tour. His third appearance at the Royalty in as many months was a sure indication that he was a hot act with the rockabilly crowd. Backing and support was again provided by Matchbox. At one stage there had also been vague talk of recording the Southgate show for a live album to be released on Rollin' Rock, but this never materialised.

BUCK RAM'S PLATTERS

November 1978			December 1978		
1	Birmingham	Barbarella's	2	Ipswich	Gaumont
13-18	Wythenshawe	Golden Garter	3	Slough	Fulcrum Centre
19-25	Caerphilly	Double Diamond	4	London	Quaglino's
29	Wrexham	Leisure Centre	5	Birmingham	Odeon
30	Southampton	Gaumont	6	Taunton	Odeon
			7	Corby	Festival Hall
			8	Dundee	Town Hall
			9	Aberdeen	Capitol
			10	Edinburgh	*unknown venue*
Tour organiser — Henry Sellers					

Monroe Powell again fronted the Buck Ram version of the Platters who returned to Britain after a three-year absence. Powell had succeeded Sonny Turner as lead vocalist in 1970, but had of course arrived on the scene long after their classic hits were recorded in the Fifties. The identity of the 1978 group was never made public, but most likely comprised Powell, Hal Howard, Edwin Cook, Gene Williams and Geri Holiday. They appeared at some quality venues and, as with each generation of Buck Ram's Platters, served up a slick, professional cabaret act.

Ram's continual struggle to keep exclusive use of the Platters name would take a bizarre twist in October 1979 when a banner headline in the *News of the World* proclaimed: 'Sex King's ex-wife is facing a £1m battle'. Instead of his usual litigation against former group members masquerading as Platters, Ram was now claiming a cool million in compensation for breach of contract and punitive damages from his own Platters.

Apparently, lead singer Monroe Powell had married Jean Raymond, ex-wife of Soho strip club owner Paul Raymond, and then left the group. The other four members soon followed and started working together under the name Luxury, leaving the embattled Ram to threaten court proceedings – a course of action which did not wash with Jean Raymond. 'Mr. Ram is saying that I used my feminine sexual charms to entice my husband away from the group. Well, it won't work. I shall be fighting for the rights of wives,' she threatened.

DUANE EDDY
JERRY LEE LEWIS

November 1978		
9	Margate	Winter Gardens
19	Finsbury Park	Rainbow
20	Birmingham	Odeon
Tour organiser — Jeffrey Kruger		

Jerry Lee Lewis returned to the UK with the Memphis Beats, comprising Ken Lovelace (guitar and fiddle), David Mayfield (guitar), Joel Shumaker (bass) and Ron Norwood (drums). This was part of a wider European tour, and between the shows in Margate and Finsbury Park he

Photo by Paul Harris

Jerry Lee at the Rainbow.

appeared in Amsterdam, Oslo, Lyon, Stockholm, Copenhagen and Gothenburg. There had been an attempt to book Jerry into the London Palladium, but the owners, Moss Empires, were having none of it. Twenty years on from the infamous 'child bride' scandal, he was still considered too great a moral risk, even in the midst of the punk era.

At Margate, the Memphis Beats opened, with guitarist David Mayfield immediately catching the eye. He had toured the UK with Charlie Rich in 1975 and laid down a sizzling 'Dixie Pie' before Lewis strolled out to a roar of applause from the audience. He opened strongly with 'Mean Woman Blues', included an exciting 'C.C. Rider' and surprised everyone with a raving 'Just Because'. The show was the usual mixture of rock'n'roll and country, and the range of material quite incredible. Nobody, least of all the band, knew what was coming next and Jerry performed like a human jukebox. Other highlights included 'Me And Bobby McGee', which started slowly before speeding up into a wild rocker, 'Boogie Woogie Country Man', and a belter of 'I'll Find It Where I Can'. Around this period, Jerry performed possibly the most varied material of his long career and every show was totally different.

Jerry appeared to be drunk during the early show at the Rainbow and gave a mediocre performance, but for the second house got it together, launching himself into 'Put No Headstone On My Grave', a wild version of 'Tennessee Saturday Night' and even 'Blue Christmas' (a little early in mid-November). He quietened the mood with 'Touching Home' and 'Who's Gonna Play This Old Piano', but overall it was one of his best rock'n'roll sets in the UK for several years, the act climaxing with 'Meat Man', 'Great Balls Of Fire' and an uptempo 'Hey Good Lookin' '.

Photo by Paul Harris

A beaming Duane Eddy plays the Rainbow.

The Birmingham shows were also drink-affected. Jerry performed an extraordinary ragtime version of 'Great Balls Of Fire' and talked rather incoherently to the audience between songs, at one point inviting somebody – possibly an ex-wife – to 'Kiss my ass, darlin' '. He sang a superb gospel version of 'Life's Railway To Heaven' and a rousing 'Folsom Prison Blues'. As the evening progressed he seemed a little hoarse, but his voice held up enough for quality takes of 'You Win Again', 'Think About It Darling' and a superb 'Walk A Mile In My Shoes'.

There was some comment in the press about ticket prices. £10 to see Jerry at the Rainbow was a great deal of money in 1978, but at least fans had the opportunity to enjoy a quality support act. Duane Eddy did not have the luxury of utilising his own musicians and seemed a trifle under-rehearsed at times, but still excelled with a short set which, in contrast to Jerry, did not vary much from show to show. It was based around his hits and included 'Moovin' 'n' Groovin' ', 'The Lonely One', 'Peter Gunn', 'Shazam!' and 'Rebel Rouser'. His three Rebelettes supplied the vocals for '(Dance With The) Guitar Man' and 'Play Me Like You Play Your Guitar' and he also found room for his classy interpretation of '3.30 Blues'. It made a pleasant change for Jerry Lee's loyal fans to sit and enjoy the support act, rather than crowding into the bar so as to avoid some unspeakable irrelevance, as had happened so many times in the past.

TV Appearances (Duane Eddy)
Top Of The Pops (BBC1)   ? November 1978

RONNIE HAWKINS

GMC Promotions of Basingstoke, Hampshire announced an ambitious project titled *Rock'n'Roll Festival '78*, an all-day event of non-stop rock'n'roll to be held at the New Roxy Theatre in Harlesden, North London on

11 November. Headliners were to be Ronnie Hawkins & The Hawks, featuring Jack DeKeyser (guitar), Stan Szelest (piano), Bob Johnston (bass) and Gary Oatridge (drums). Although Hawkins had visited the UK previously, this was scheduled to be his long-awaited stage debut, so there were a lot of long faces when it was reported only days before the show that he had been rushed to hospital in Toronto suffering with a recurrence of his heart problems.

The festival went ahead with Sun rockers Warren Smith and Ray Smith replacing Ronnie, so his loyal fans were left to wait even longer for the Hawk's first show in Europe.

WARREN SMITH

November 1978		
11 Harlesden	New Roxy	
Tour organiser — GMC Promotions		

The extraordinary welcome afforded to Warren Smith on the occasion of his UK stage debut in April 1977 made it inevitable that he would be invited to return, and so when Ronnie Hawkins dropped out of *Rock'n'Roll Festival '78* the organisers looked to the burly Smith as a worthy replacement.

The festival was somewhat disorganised, but after a chaotic start gradually gathered momentum during the afternoon as Flying Saucers, the Riot Rockers, Wee Willie Harris, Gina & The Rockin' Rebels, and Freddie 'Fingers' Lee performed to a rowdy audience of mainly Teddy boys. Freddie was especially outrageous, setting his hat

Photo by Paul Harris

Ubangi Stomp!

alight at the climax of his set. He was followed on stage by the popular Welsh band, Crazy Cavan & The Rhythm Rockers, who further raised the temperature and richly deserved their three encores.

The Dave Travis Band opened Warren's show with an instrumental, before Smith himself came on stage and burst into an energetic 'Ubangi Stomp', followed by 'Rock'n'Roll Ruby'. The act was unfolding according to plan, when suddenly fellow headliner Ray Smith made an unscheduled and unannounced appearance. Clearly the worse for wear, he strolled up to centre stage and planted a big kiss on the lips of a startled Warren Smith, much to his apparent embarrassment. The audience looked almost as bewildered as Warren, who struggled to regain his composure and continue through 'That's All Right' and a terrific version of 'Folsom Prison Blues'. Aside from this extraordinary interruption, his performance was entertaining, even though he had been complaining about a sore throat all day. The act was also rather short and Warren still did not seem to have prepared enough material.

Tragically his second trip to England proved to be his last. On 30 January 1980 he passed away in Longview, Texas following a massive heart attack.

RAY SMITH

November 1978		
11	Harlesden	New Roxy
13	Camden Town	Dingwalls
Tour organiser — GMC Promotions		

Ray Smith was one of rock'n'roll's crazy men. A Jerry Lee Lewis-styled piano-pounder and singer, he first recorded for Sun in 1958, but only made the US charts after Jud Phillips took him to Nashville to cut 'Rockin' Little Angel' for his Judd label the following year. Ray was never able to sustain his brief period of stardom and in later times had based himself in Burlington, Ontario, from where he played the clubs and bars and continued recording for a succession of small record companies.

This was Smith's first visit to Europe and he got off to a poor start, turning up for rehearsals on 10 November in a semi-inebriated state, which did not aid his concentration. Instead of spotting the danger signs, the organisers made the fundamental mistake of leaving him alone from 10.00 am on the day of the Harlesden festival, with nothing to occupy his time and a generous quantity of alcoholic beverage close at hand. It was a long show, and by the time the compere, Paul Barrett, announced him to the audience, Ray was seriously drunk.

He started strongly enough, belting out his rock'n'roll version of Mickey Gilley's country hit, 'Room Full Of Roses', but was in no state to follow the set list, nor even to perform the songs which had been prepared, leaving the Dave Travis Band with the impossible task of second-guessing his intentions. He pounded away at a rather inadequate piano and sounded fine on his own songs such as 'Right Behind You Baby', 'Rockin' Bandit' and 'Rockin' Little Angel', but was swaying about so alarmingly that

Photo by Paul Harris

Ray in high spirits at the New Roxy.

there seemed a real possibility that he would fall backwards off his piano stool and collapse in a drunken heap on the ground at any moment.

Between numbers, Ray rambled drunkenly at the audience, who seemed transfixed by this extraordinary display, and for reasons best known

to himself seemed anxious to perform some Dean Martin numbers to the assembled throng of rock'n'roll fans. He had a strong enough voice, as he ably demonstrated with an emotional 'It's Now Or Never' and snatches of several Dean Martin favourites, but overall the performance was a real embarrassment for all concerned. As the act eventually lurched to a close, the musicians fled the stage and the audience shuffled out into the cold night collectively scratching their heads in disbelief. There was no demand for an encore, but Ray was not to be put off so easily and he returned to his piano – minus his band and most of his audience – and hammered out a drink-sozzled 'Whole Lotta Shakin' Goin' On' to a near-empty auditorium.

Dave Travis made it clear that, unless the organisers could guarantee a sober Ray Smith, the show at Dingwalls two days later (on which he was again a late replacement for Ronnie Hawkins), would not go ahead. In fact, it could not have been a greater contrast. Ray was in fine fettle and delivered outstanding versions of 'Break Up', 'Why, Why, Why', 'So Young' and 'Red Hot', plus a belting 'Right Behind You Baby'. He joked with the audience, sang requests and went a long way towards salvaging his reputation.

CHAPTER SEVEN

1979

The Crazy Beat Just Stopped Me Dead

The success of Freddie Laker and his cut-price air fares was making travel between the USA and Britain much more affordable, and the dynamics of rock'n'roll tours to the UK were changing for ever. Back in 1957, Bill Haley and his Comets had sailed across the Atlantic on the *Queen Elizabeth*, a long, slow and expensive process. Now that the journey time and the costs were dramatically reduced, short tours or even single shows made economic sense. This state of affairs ensured that increasing numbers of American rock'n'rollers would continue to entertain British audiences for many years to come.

In September 1956, the first US act to perform live rock'n'roll in Britain, R.B. Shaw & His Melody Mountaineers, appeared at Butlin's Holiday Village in Clacton. More than twenty years later, the focus of live rock'n'roll returned to the holiday camps when the *1st International Rock'n'Roll Weekend Hop*, starring Ray Campi, was held at Ladbroke's Holiday Centre, Caister in March 1979. Enthusiasts would henceforth travel long distances – many from mainland Europe – so the self-contained, low-cost style of the British holiday camp, with its tacky, slightly seedy 1950s image made it the perfect venue. The Teds and rockabillies could dance, drink, fight and generally raise hell with only a minimum of interference. Rock'n'roll and holiday camps were perfect bedfellows and would remain inextricably entwined for evermore.

1979 saw the first British stage appearances by Billy Lee Riley, Hank Mizell, Tony Conn, Danny & The Juniors and Sleepy LaBeef, and from now on we would welcome more new and exciting names every year, many of whom would prove so popular that, despite an absence of hit records, nor any record company hype, they would return time and time again to Europe, enjoying a measure of adulation and respect that was totally lacking back home in the US. British popular music was currently in the midst of the heavy metal boom, but there was so much going on in the insular world of rock'n'roll that enthusiasts could close their ears to the discordant noise that was blasting out of Radio One and enjoy a veritable glut of rock'n'roll – had it ever been as good as this?

The *Oh Boy!* stage show opened at London's Astoria Theatre on

28 January with a cast that included Shakin' Stevens, Joe Brown, Alvin Stardust, Shades and Freddie 'Fingers' Lee, while many of the other British veterans were out gigging again. Even Tony Crombie was back, at least on the fringes of rock'n'roll, playing drums for Georgie Fame. Shakin' Stevens was clearly the man most likely to succeed and his name was in the frame at the end of July when some mysterious German investors were reportedly casting for a film of Eddie Cochran's life to be shot in Hollywood. We are all still waiting.

A fascinating show, *The Roots of Rock'n'Roll* took place at the Drury Lane Theatre, London on 24 April and featured Mickey Baker, Hal Singer, boogie pianist Sammy Price and Memphis Slim. Fats Domino's sax player, Herb Hardesty, on tour with Tom Waits, was in the audience but declined to get up on stage and play.

As always, live country music in Britain was centred around the massive Easter festival at Wembley, but interesting club and concert tours took place during the year featuring Bobby Bare, Red Sovine, Jimmy Driftwood, Gene Watson and Hank Williams' Original Drifting Cowboys.

Blues legend Charles Brown made his British debut at the 100 Club in April and other appearances of note included Albert Collins, J.B. Hutto, Rockin' Dopsie & The Cajun Twisters, Ry Cooder and Nina Simone.

DANNY & THE JUNIORS

January 1979		
11 Southgate	Royalty	
Tour organiser — Showstopper Promotions		

'At The Hop' by Danny & The Juniors, a doo-wop quartet from Philadelphia, was a smash hit in the UK during the early months of 1958 and remains a classic of the rock'n'roll era. The original line-up consisted of Danny Rapp, Joe Terry, Dave White and Frank Maffei. By the time of this, their first British stage appearance, however, they had shrunk to a trio. Rapp and White had left and the 1979 line-up comprised Terry, Maffei and Bill Carlucci.

It was originally intended that there would be a series of one-nighters around the country, but interest was only lukewarm and so they had to make do with a single performance at the Royalty Ballroom in Southgate, North London, which was now very much the UK's top rock'n'roll venue. The audience was a mixture of rockers, Teds and rockabilly rebels and they were noticeably unimpressed when the British backing group, Zigger Zagger, appeared on stage, neither looking nor sounding like a rock'n'roll band.

The situation never really improved. The Juniors appeared to have been beamed in direct from Vegas, complete with music stands and sheet music. They were slick and well rehearsed, but unhip, and as they honeycrooned and glee-clubbed their way through a lost era of doo-wop, schmaltz and high school weepies, the audience shuffled uncomfortably. They were more used to Crazy Cavan & The Rhythm Rockers at the Royalty, and neither the medley of Four Seasons songs, nor the twist numbers, were enough to get them moving. Just when it seemed that things could not get any worse, they threw in an attempt at comedy, stuffing cushions down the front of their frilly saffron shirts and donning Mothercare smocks for their rendition of Paul Anka's '(You're) Having My Baby'. It was rather pitiful, but the audience were pretty good-natured and even applauded when they finally dished up mild versions of 'At the Hop' and 'Rock And Roll is Here to Stay'.

RICK NELSON

It was announced in the music press early in January 1979 that a concert had been scheduled for London's Sadlers Wells Theatre on 28 January featuring Rick Nelson, Roy Clark and Buck Trent. This seemed an unlikely venue, as Sadlers Wells is the home of ballet and not generally available for rock'n'roll or country acts. Perhaps it was just as well that the project fizzled out, as the sight of hordes of drape-jacketed Teddy boys converging on their beloved theatre may have proved too much.

JOHNNY & THE HURRICANES

February 1979		
15	Southgate	Royalty
25	Ashton-under-Lyne	Tameside
	Tour organiser — Showstopper Promotions	

THE **Royalty** NITESPOT

Winchmore Hill Road, Southgate, N.14   01-886 4112
Opposite Southgate Underground Station
THE UK's LEADING
ROCK'N'ROLL VENUE
EVERY THURSDAY THE COUNTRYS LEADING BANDS
THURSDAY FEBRUARY 15th
FROM THE USA
JOHNNY & THE HURRICANS
Tickets on sale now £2.50   Doors open 8.00 till 12.00
4 Licenced Bars

The dear old *New Musical Express* reported that Johnny Paris and three other original members of the Hurricanes would be undertaking a series of one-nighters in Britain during February 1979. This was, of course, a complete fabrication as the original line up had long gone by the time of the first Johnny & The Hurricanes tour in 1963, and there was no prospect of them re-forming sixteen years later.

In reality, Johnny Paris had moved to live in Hamburg following a messy divorce, and was now working with a group of English musicians based in Germany. Screaming Lord Sutch provided the support for the gig at Ashton-under-Lyne.

THE RONETTES

February 1979		
17	Manchester	Pembroke
22	Colchester	Essex University
27	London	The Venue
	Tour organiser unknown	

Ronnie Spector made another short visit to the UK accompanied by two other anonymous Ronettes. The music press promised an exclusive one-off gig at the Venue in London's Victoria, but at least two other shows took place as well.

When the Ronettes first toured Britain in 1964, successive audiences were entranced by their sexy stage movements and provocative act. It was very much part of the attraction. However, fifteen years had taken their toll, and at the Venue the sight of Ronnie and her two stooges clad in tight black satin spray-on trousers and silver lurex boob tubes gave an almost seedy feel to the proceedings.

Ronnie burst straight into an unconvincing 'Be My Baby', which was sung in flat, nasal tones and despite twisting, squalking and begging the audience for kisses, the girls found great difficulty in inspiring the necessary level of nostalgia. The mainly male crowd were not really concentrating on the music, so much as their lewdly suggestive behaviour, although 'It's A Heartache', 'Walking In The Rain' and '(The Best Part Of) Breaking Up', containing high-pitched vocal harmonies, did hark back to better days.

Eventually, one drooling male admirer managed to climb on the stage and attempted to unzip Ronnie's trousers, much to her apparent delight, before being ushered away for a cold shower by the security team. The short set ended as it had begun with a reprise of 'Be My Baby', followed by flowers, curtseys and smiles all round.

RAY CAMPI

March 1979			14	Southall	White Hart
3	Caister	Ladbroke's Holiday Centre	15	Sheffield	Polytechnic
5	Sunderland	Boilermakers	16	Leicester	TUL
9	Swindon	Brunel Rooms	19	Rayleigh	Croc's
10	Leicester	University	22	Southgate	Royalty
11	London	Lyceum	23	Manchester	New Osborne
12	Camden Town	Dingwalls	24	Carshalton	Chick-a-Boom
13	Brighton	Top Rank Suite			
Tour organiser — David Harris (Rollin' Rock UK)					

The second Ray Campi tour was a resounding success. He flew into the UK with his Rockabilly Rebels, Jerry Sikorski and Kevin Fennell (lead guitars), Colin Winski (rhythm guitar) and Steve Clark (drums), and opened at the *1st International Rock'n'Roll Weekend Hop* at Caister in front of a capacity crowd, on a bill that included

Photo by Paul Harris

Ray tears it up at the Top Rank, Brighton.

the Jets, Crazy Cavan & The Rhythm Rockers, Flying Saucers, Matchbox and Freddie 'Fingers' Lee – the cream of the contemporary British scene.

This was the first rock'n'roll weekender, and it was captured on film in the documentary, *Blue Suede Shoes*, in which Ray can be seen smartly attired in a black-and-white Western shirt, belting out 'Rockabilly Rebel' in front of a seething mass of Teds, rockabillies and assorted lunatics. Periodically, he dabs at his face with a pair of black frilly knickers, kindly donated by one of the ladies at the front, and alternately climbs on top of his double bass or wheels it around his head like an axe. The atmosphere was electric and the excitement of the

occasion has been preserved on film for posterity. Jerry Sikorski can be seen sweating profusely as he delivers 'Jump, Jive And Wail', while Colin Winski, his long greasy hair hanging down over his face, teases the girls close to the stage as he performs an over-the-top version of 'Rock Therapy'.

Campi and his Rockabilly Rebels went down a storm and contributed enormously to the success of this first weekender. After Caister, they travelled around the UK on a series of one-nighters, at Leicester, Brighton and Sheffield co-starring with George Thorogood & The Destroyers, and at London's Lyceum with Bo Diddley.

The evening at Sunderland's Boilermakers Club was typical. An ecstatic crowd cheered widely as

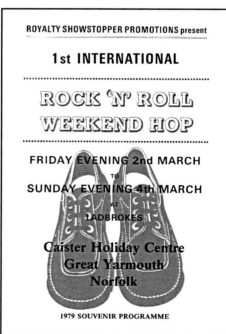

ROYALTY SHOWSTOPPER PROMOTIONS present

1st INTERNATIONAL

ROCK 'N' ROLL WEEKEND HOP

FRIDAY EVENING 2nd MARCH
TO
SUNDAY EVENING 4th MARCH
AT
LADBROKES

**Caister Holiday Centre
Great Yarmouth
Norfolk**

1979 SOUVENIR PROGRAMME

Campi reeled off 'It Ain't Me', 'Caterpillar' and his Rollin' Rock favourites, 'Rattlin' Daddy', 'How Low Do You Feel' and 'Rockin' At The Ritz', interspersed with vocals from his younger colleagues. Winski's Presleyesque gyrations had the girls squealing during 'Gone, Gone, Gone' and Sikorski ran him close with 'Alligator Come Across'. Ray even varied the pace and played some fine slide guitar on Bob Wills's 'Steel Guitar Rag'.

Radar Records released a new album by Campi & His Rockabilly Rebels, *Wildcat Shakeout*, to coincide with the tour.

FREDDY CANNON

It was announced in the music press that Freddy Cannon would appear at the Royalty, Southgate on 8 March along with Flying Saucers as the support for Bill Haley & His Comets, with the gig being shot by Kendon Films for a rock'n'roll documentary called *Blue Suede Shoes*. Plans were afoot for him to participate on the whole tour until a dispute over billing scuppered the entire scheme. It seems that Cannon wanted equal billing to Haley, and that this was not acceptable. So, he stayed at home and was replaced by the Wild Angels.

THE DRIFTERS

March 1979			May 1979		
7	Porthcawl	Stoneleigh	1	Jersey, CI	Behan's (West
9-10	Cardiff	Troubadour			Park Pavilion)
12-24	London	Talk of the Town	2-5	Usk	Stardust
26-31	Wythenshawe	Golden Garter	10-11	Farnworth	Blighty's
April 1979					
1	Wythenshawe	Golden Garter			
2-10	Purfleet	Circus Tavern			
11-14	Westcliff	Queen's Cabaret			
16	Sheffield	Fiesta			
18-19	Farnworth	Blighty's			
19-20	Windsor	Blazers			
21	Eastbourne	King's			
23-28	Birmingham	Night Out			
30	Jersey, CI	Behan's (West Park Pavilion)			
Tour organiser — Henry Sellers					

A reissued 45 of 'Save The Last Dance For Me' briefly returned the Drifters to the British charts during April, as the 1979 line-up comprising Ray Lewis, Clyde Brown, Joe Blunt and Billy Lewis were engaged in their umpteenth cabaret tour. It was built up around a fortnight at London's prestigious Talk of the Town, and even without their erstwhile leader, Johnny Moore, the sheer professionalism of the four men ensured customer satisfaction wherever they went.

BILL HALEY & HIS COMETS

March 1979					
8	Southgate	Royalty	17	Finsbury Park	Rainbow
10	Bournemouth	Winter Gardens	18	Preston	Guildhall
11	Bristol	Colston Hall	19	Glasgow	Apollo
12	Paignton	Festival	20	Sheffield	Fiesta
14	Harrogate	Royal Hall	21	Corby	Festival Hall
15	Birmingham	Odeon	22	Slough	Fulcrum Centre
Tour organiser — Patrick Malynn					

Over two years had elapsed since Bill Haley had last performed for British audiences. Nothing much had been heard of him during that period and he remained at home in Texas far away from the limelight, enjoying a well-earned rest after years on the road. It was the perseverance of promoter Paddy Malynn that finally got him back into the saddle, and it was announced early in 1979 that Bill and the Comets would play a series of concerts in the UK during March.

The Comets had, of course, long since ceased to exist as a working unit and Malynn's plan was for the first time to utilise local musicians, as this would result in considerable savings on air tickets and other expenses. In the end, Haley compromised by sending two of his American Comets, Ray Parsons (rhythm guitar) and Jim Lebak (bass) as an advance party. They linked up with Mal Gray, former vocalist with the Wild Angels, who had recruited four British Comets: Gerry Tilley (lead guitar), Steve Murray (drums), Geoff Driscoll (tenor sax) and Pete Spencer (rhythm guitar). Gray himself would share some of the vocal duties with Haley. After a week of rehearsals, Bill and his wife, Martha, flew into Heathrow on 6 March and the tour was soon underway with a press conference at a Knightsbridge hotel the following morning. Support acts were the Wild Angels and Flying Saucers.

The first night at the Royalty was filmed for the *Blue Suede Shoes* TV documentary and a capacity crowd enjoyed a typical Haley performance. Parsons vocalised on 'Rockin' Robin' and 'Memphis, Tennessee', while Gray chipped in with 'Promised Land', but Bill himself sang ten numbers – far more than in recent years. The show opened with 'Shake, Rattle And

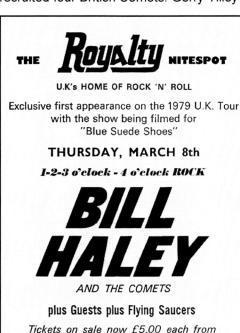

Photo by Paul Harris

Opening night at the Royalty.

Roll' and 'Razzle Dazzle', and included such long-time favourites as 'Burn That Candle', 'Rock-A-Beatin' Boogie' and 'Rip It Up'. He even harmonised with Ray Parsons on 'Me And Bobby McGee'. The instrumental antics of the Comets were replicated through 'Rudy's Rock' and 'Caravan', and a very lively evening concluded with Bill rocking his way through 'See You Later, Alligator', 'Rock Around The Clock' and 'Rock The Joint'.

This opening night was typical of the whole tour. Most shows were sold out or near capacity – Mal Gray had done a fine job in selecting the British Comets, who rose admirably to their task. The set list stayed fairly constant, although Jim Lebak sang 'Slippin' And Slidin' ' on several occasions and they sometimes included another instrumental, 'Guitar Boogie Shuffle'.

At the Rainbow Theatre in London, a mini-riot broke out, resulting in several seats being damaged, but there were more serious problems at Preston. Inadequate security arrangements meant that they were unable to prevent a mass invasion of the stage area and Bill fled the theatre during the instrumental, 'Caravan'. With the show cut short, the situation got out of hand and there were several arrests and substantial damage in the nearby shopping centre, with a number of people requiring hospital treatment. At the conclusion of the tour, Bill and the Comets recorded some original songs including 'Hail, Hail Rock And Roll', 'God Bless Rock And Roll' and 'I Need The Music' for Sonet Records before he finally departed on 28 March.

TV Appearances
Format V (ATV)   15 March 1979

BO DIDDLEY

March 1979		
11	London	Lyceum
15	Camden Town	Dingwalls
Tour organiser unknown		

Bo made a short visit to London as part of a month-long European tour which included shows in Norway, Sweden, France and Germany. He was accompanied by his own trio, Michael Flemming (drums), Gordon Vessell (guitar) and Richard E. Moore Jr. (bass).

He co-starred with Ray Campi and Whirlwind before a sizeable crowd at the Lyceum in London's Strand and performed a tight set which included a memorable 'Mona', a lengthy version of 'I'm A Man', plus 'Diddley Daddy', 'Road Runner' and 'Bo Diddley's A Gunslinger'.

The second show four days later was arranged at short notice and received only limited publicity, but again found Mr. Diddley in fine spirits and on top of his game.

JOHNNY CASH

March 1979			18	Manchester	Apollo
11	Brighton	Centre	20	Glasgow	Apollo
12-16	Wembley	Conference Centre	21	Belfast	Church
17	Birmingham	NEC			
Tour organiser unknown					

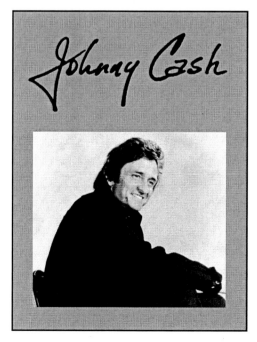

Johnny Cash returned to the UK after an absence of almost four years and proved as popular as ever. He was scheduled to play four nights at Wembley Conference Centre, but the demand for tickets was such that an extra night was added on 12 March.

Cash's mother-in-law, Maybelle Carter, had passed away in October 1978, so there was a different feel to the early part of the proceedings at Wembley, when long-time family friend Jan Howard opened with a couple of country songs. The Tennessee Three were augmented by guitarist Jerry Hensley and pianist Earl Poole Ball. Hensley was featured on 'Tulsa Time', after which eight-year-old John Carter

Cash was brought on stage and the audience squirmed in their seats and tried hard to cover their ears as the precocious little boy squealed his way through a couple of cringe-inducing ditties. It was a blessed relief when June Carter replaced him and served up a selection of Carter Family classics, including a fine rendering of 'Wildwood Flower'.

Photo by Paul Harris

Cash at Brighton.

Finally, it was the turn of the big man himself. Johnny Cash's appearance and remarkable charisma seemed to fill the whole stage, and for well over an hour he held the audience in the palm of his hand with a seemingly endless procession of great songs. A magnificent rendition of 'Ballad Of Ira Hayes' and lovingly re-created versions of 'Big River' and 'Get Rhythm' were among the high points. He closed with a slick and polished 'Will The Circle Be Unbroken'.

On 21 March Cash travelled to Northern Ireland and appeared at a church in Belfast. Despite all the tensions and religious differences within that troubled city, the audience comprised both Catholics and Protestants, who divided up and sat on opposite sides of the aisle – a quite extraordinary sight at that time. Johnny Cash and his music seemed capable of succeeding where successive generations of politicians and religious leaders had failed.

FREDDY FENDER

April 1979		
15 Wembley	Arena	
Tour organiser — Mervyn Conn		

More than 40 acts appeared at the *11th International Festival of Country Music*, held over three days during the Easter weekend, and inevitably some of them seemed to get lost as the audience struggled to soak up the sheer quantity of music being pitched at them. Freddy was halfway down the bill on the Sunday evening and had to compete for attention alongside Tammy Wynette, Ronnie Milsap, Moe Bandy, Barbara Fairchild,

Vernon Oxford, Floyd Cramer, Don Gibson, Jana Jae, Jeannie Denver, Frank Yonko, Ken & Billie Ford and Ray Lynam.

Reports of the show highlighted the successes and the failures, but made little mention of Fender. It was not that he had performed poorly, rather that his modest set had been eminently forgettable. It really only took off in the final stages when he moved away from contemporary country and closed his act with his old rock'n'roll ballads 'Wasted Days And Wasted Nights' and 'Mathilda'.

TV Appearances
Sing Country (BBC2)   15 April 1979 (screened 12 September 1979)

CONWAY TWITTY

April 1979		
16	Wembley	Arena
	Tour organiser — Mervyn Conn	

This was Conway's first appearance in the UK for seven years, during which he had enjoyed a continuous run of country hits and was now unquestionably one of the music's big hitters. Gone was his greasy rocker appearance and slightly gauche and nervous stage manner. He now sported a nattily permed coiffure and exuded confidence throughout his 35-minute set.

Working with his own six-piece band, he looked and sounded great, so it was all the more surprising that three numbers into his show the audience seemed unmoved by the whole experience. Conway then went for the safety of a Hank Williams medley and the whole atmosphere changed. From then on, he could not go wrong, and by the end of his act the crowd were on their feet and pandemonium reigned as stressed-out stewards battled to keep the excited fans in their seats. Highlights of the act were 'Linda On My Mind', 'You've Never Been This Far Before' and, despite the absence of his other rock'n'roll hits, the ever-popular 'It's Only Make Believe'.

TV Appearances
Sing Country (BBC2)   16 April 1979 (screened 28 May 1979)

SLEEPY LaBEEF

April 1979		
16	Wembley	Arena
26	Southgate	Royalty
27	Guildford	Star Hotel
28	Carshalton	Chick-a-Boom
Tour organisers — Mervyn Conn and Showstopper Promotions		

Sleepy at Southgate.

This was the British debut for the genial giant of rockabilly, Sleepy LaBeef. Born in Arkansas, he had recorded since the Fifties for a wide range of labels including Starday, Columbia, Wayside and, most recently, Sun International. With no hit records to his name, it was the reports of his high-energy stage act that led to interest by European promoters and Sleepy made his first trip across the Atlantic in March 1979 to co-star with Ray Smith at the *12th Rockhouse International Rock'n'Roll Meeting* at Eindhoven.

Three weeks later, he arrived in England along with his wife Linda and his American drummer, Clete Berg, to appear at the *11th International Festival of Country Music* along with Conway Twitty, Crystal Gayle, Jim & Jesse, Bobby Bare, Joe Stampley and Lonnie Donegan.

Advance reports had claimed that Sleepy was a human jukebox with a repertoire in excess of 4,000 songs and he seemed eager to sing them all during his Wembley spot, eventually squeezing fourteen numbers into his fifteen-minute allowance. Driven along by his own sledgehammer lead guitar, he moved effortlessly between 'Hello Josephine', 'Party Doll', 'Honey Hush', 'Blue Eyes Crying In The Rain', 'Wabash Cannonball' and a tremendous version of 'Tore Up'. He made a very strong impression on the Wembley audience and along with Crystal Gayle was one of the hits of the night.

With ten days between Wembley and his next UK date, Sleepy played shows in Sweden, the Netherlands and Spain, before returning to London to record an album, *Rockabilly Heavyweight*, with Dave Travis for Charly Records. He also revealed himself to be an interviewer's dream, having almost instant recall of every detail from his much-travelled life in rock'n'roll and country music, as well as providing a never-ending supply of stories about his contemporaries and life on the road.

Favourable reports of the Wembley show ensured a good turnout at London's Royalty Ballroom, and with Matchbox supplying the backing Sleepy had every opportunity to shine. An enormous man, smartly dressed in a dark suit topped off with an equally enormous stetson hat, he literally bludgeoned his audience into submission with a succession of rocking songs that came flying from the stage like bullets from a machine gun. Early in the act, he broke a guitar string during a pulsating 'Polk Salad Annie', but coolly extracted a new one from his breast pocket and proceeded to fit it while the song continued without even momentary hesitation.

His repertoire covered the full range of blues, country, gospel and rock'n'roll. A furious 'Boogie Woogie Country Girl' and a primitive-sounding 'Shotgun Boogie' contrasted with Duane Eddy's 'Detour' and the Sun sound of 'Rock'n'Roll Ruby'. With LaBeef no show is long enough for everything he wants to play and every performance is refreshingly different from the last. Here was a highly talented and vastly underrated performer who was virtually unknown to UK rock'n'roll fans. How many more such virtual stars were still hidden away out there just waiting to be discovered?

TONY CONN

April 1979		
16	Southgate	Royalty
19	Southgate	Royalty
23	Rayleigh	Croc's
24	Camden Town	Dingwalls
Tour organiser — David Harris (Rollin' Rock UK)		

After the successful tours by Ray Campi and Mac Curtis, Tony Conn became the third Rollin' Rock act to visit Britain. His stay lasted little more than a week and he only made limited impact, despite a highly animated stage act.

Conn originally came from Boston, Massachusetts and had been spotted on an amateur night at New York's Apollo Theater in 1958. This led to photo coverage in *Life* magazine in a feature about this up-and-coming rock'n'roll singer, and ultimately a record release, 'Like Wow', on Decca. In the Sixties, he moved out to California and dabbled in the movies for a while. However, after meeting Ronny Weiser of Rollin' Rock in 1974, he eagerly resurrected his career as a rock'n'roll singer.

> **Bank Holiday Monday**
> **APRIL 16th**
>
> # ALL DAYER
> 12 NOON — 12 MIDNIGHT
> Featuring
> **From The U.S.A.**
> **WILD MAN**
> ## TONY CONN
> ROLLIN ROCK RECORDING ARTISTE
>
> +
>
> **ALL THE TOP BRITISH GROUPS.**
>
> Winchmore Hill Road, Southgate, London N.14
> Opp Southgate Underground Station. 01-886 4112

Unfortunately, Conn proved to be a very limited stage performer, although nobody could fault his effort. At Dingwalls he wore a leopardskin jacket which he maintained had been given to him by the Big Bopper, and he literally threw himself around the stage utilising a great deal of sheer physical energy and enthusiasm on numbers such as 'Great Balls Of Fire', 'Dangerous Doll' and 'Like Wow'. He even included a tribute to Campi, titled 'Ramblin' Ray', but although the small crowd applauded politely in all the right places, it was clear that his earlier claim to be the 'white Little Richard' fell a long way short of reality. Backing was provided by Dynamite.

NEIL SEDAKA

April 1979			May 1979		
20	Poole	Arts Centre	3	Oxford	New
21	Brighton	Centre	4	Blackpool	Opera House
22-28	London	Palladium	5	Manchester	Apollo
			6	Glasgow	Apollo
			7	Birmingham	Odeon
			8	Liverpool	Empire
			9	Bridlington	Royal Hall
Tour organiser — Henry Sellers					

Neil returned to the UK after an absence of two years and once again did excellent business on the theatre circuit. His arrival created no interest at all amongst hard-core rock'n'roll fans, as his act was aimed squarely at middle-of-the-road audiences, although in fairness he never made any attempt to hide from his rock'n'roll roots.

His week at the London Palladium was slick, professional and unthreatening. 'Breaking Up Is Hard To Do' was performed at ballad tempo and he delivered 'Solitaire' solo at the piano with great impact, all the while enchanting his audience with the likes of 'Laughter In The Rain', 'You've Never Done It Like That' and 'The Other Side Of Me'. He kept thanking the 'wonderful London audience', which became somewhat irritating, but his talent and boyish personality shone through and eventually won over even the biggest cynic in the auditorium

As always, Sedaka found room in his show for the hits of his rock'n'roll youth and happily belted out 'Oh! Carol', 'I Go Ape' and the rest with a silly grin on his face and genuine enthusiasm.

An extra midnight performance was added at the Palladium on 27 April, with the proceeds going to the charity Help A London Child.

DEL SHANNON

May 1979		
17-19	Cardiff	Troubadour
20	Gainsborough	Chestnuts
23	Doncaster	Side Saddle
24	Chesterfield	Aquarius
25	Bristol	Pathway
26	Colchester	Copford Windmill
28	Derby	Talk of the Midlands
Tour organiser — Henry Sellers		

A year on from his last set of UK dates, things were looking up again for Del Shannon. He had weaned himself off both booze and dope, and was making an effort to exercise on a daily basis. His audiences still wanted to hear the old hits every night, but he seemed more accepting of the situation and less frustrated by the limitations placed on him by the cabaret circuit.

LINK WRAY

May 1979			June 1979		
24	Nottingham	Sandpiper	2	London	The Venue
25	Manchester	Factory			
26	Birmingham	Barbarella's			
28	Edinburgh	Tiffany's			
Tour organiser unknown					

Since splitting from Robert Gordon, Link had signed a new record deal with Charisma and was blasting his way across Europe on an extensive tour to promote his new album, *Bullshot*.

Much of his stage act comprised rock'n'roll standards and, in all honesty, his vocal delivery was only adequate at best as he worked his way through the likes of 'Johnny B. Goode', 'Roll Over Beethoven' and 'Peggy Sue' at Birmingham's Barbarella's. He really struggled when the pace dropped for a creaking version of 'Can't Help Falling In Love', but did better with a subdued 'Learning The Game'.

Wray looked his usual menacing self, wearing tight jeans, a studded belt, a silver cross and a vest containing a picture of the young Elvis.

Inevitably, it was the instrumental numbers like 'Rawhide' and 'Rumble', punched out on his well-worn Gibson, that earned him the most response from an unexpectedly youthful audience. His appeal seemed to extend across the generations to incorporate rock fans who would not otherwise attend a rock'n'roll concert.

JOHNNY & THE HURRICANES
DEL SHANNON

June 1979			18	Halifax	Civic Hall
1	Manchester	Valentines	19	Rochdale	Champness Hall
2	Gloucester	Bowden Hall Hotel	20	Lowestoft	Sparrow's Nest
11	Falkirk	Town Hall	21	Corby	Festival Hall
12	Kilmarnock	Grand Hall	22	Birmingham	Digbeth Civic Hall
13	Hamilton	Town Hall	23	Bexhill	De La Warr Pavilion
14	Musselborough	Broughton Hall	24	Ramsgate	Granville
15	Carlisle	Assembly Hall	**July 1979**		
16	Burslem	Queen's hall	4	Carshalton	Chick-a-Boom
Tour organiser unknown					

Del Shannon's May dates had now expanded into an old-style package tour via the inclusion of both British piano-pounder Freddie 'Fingers' Lee and sax man Johnny Paris, complete with a newly acquired set of UK Hurricanes – Steve Whalley (guitar), John Ashe (organ), John Levenson (bass) and Mike Small (drums).

The tour was unremarkable and did no more than average business, at least partly due to very scant publicity. The traditional music press such as *Record Mirror* and *Melody Maker* had long since ceased to be of interest to rock'n'roll fans, while magazines like *New Kommotion* or *Not Fade Away* which were aimed at the specialist market tended to appear infrequently and gave only limited column space to live rock'n'roll.

After the package tour concluded at Ramsgate, Johnny & The Hurricanes played a final gig at the Chick-a-Boom in Carshalton with support from Dynamite. Interestingly, a significant portion of the audience appeared to be around sixteen years of age and, despite the fact that Billy Lee Riley had appeared at the same venue only a week previously, the hall was near to capacity.

Johnny Paris arrived on stage at 10.50 pm and opened with a belting version of 'Crossfire'. The UK Hurricanes did a competent job, performing 'Down Yonder' and a bluesy 'Lazy' with gusto. 'Reveille Rock' really had the audience bopping around, but then Paris abandoned his saxophone and vocalised on a mediocre 'Johnny B. Goode', which was made worse by guitarist Whalley trying to imitate a Led Zeppelin solo. Johnny's vocals were pretty uninspiring, as he again demonstrated when he slaughtered 'Memphis, Tennessee', but happily he concentrated most of his energy on his instrumentals and 'Old Smokie', 'Buckeye'. 'Beatnik Fly' and 'Rocking Goose' all went over well. Their fairly short set closed with 'Ja-Da' and, as an encore, 'Red River Rock'.

ROCKY BURNETTE

June 1979	
26 London	Marquee
Tour organiser unknown	

Rocky Burnette, 'the son of rock'n'roll', was virtually unknown in the UK when he made his first, albeit brief cameo appearance on the stage of London's Marquee Club. Rocky is the son of Johnny and nephew of Dorsey Burnette. His father had died in a freak boating accident back in 1964, and after his death Rocky grew up in a tough ghetto area of the San Fernando Valley. He had dropped out of bible college and by 1979 was looking to make it in rock'n'roll.

After running into music publisher Bert Berman in Los Angeles, Rocky was advised to look him up if he ever came to England. Consequently, when he arrived on Berman's doorstep a few months later, Bert introduced him to the Pirates who were long-time fans of his father's music.

The Pirates had started out as Johnny Kidd's backing group, and the 1962 line-up of Frank Farley, Mick Green and Johnny Spence retained legal ownership of the group name after Kidd's death. They had built up a new audience during the Seventies with a more contemporary rock sound, but included several Johnny Burnette Rock'n'Roll Trio numbers in their show.

On the night of the Marquee gig, Johnny Spence was suffering with a sore throat and Rocky did not take much persuasion to sit in with them. He sang both 'Tear It Up' and 'Lonesome Train (On A Lonesome Track)' with the Pirates and remarked afterwards that 'it came off perfect, like we'd worked together for years.'

BILLY LEE RILEY

June 1979			July 1979		
27	Carshalton	Chick-a-Boom	1	Bristol	Trinity Centre
28	Southgate	Royalty	2	Broadstairs	Grand
29	Leicester	TUL	3	Leysdown	Island Hotel
30	Swindon	Town Hall	4	Southall	White Hart
			5	Camden Town	Dingwalls
			6	Plymouth	Circus Tavern
Tour organiser — Paul Barrett					

Billy Lee Riley from Pocahontas, Arkansas made some of the greatest recordings for Sun Records and gems like 'Red Hot' and 'Flyin' Saucers Rock & Roll' sit comfortably alongside the very best work by Elvis, Carl and Jerry Lee. It still seems desperately unfortunate that Riley did not enjoy the same degree of success as his illustrious contemporaries. He and his band, the Little Green Men, played on many of the classic Sun recordings and were an outstanding live act. In the early Sixties, Billy moved to the West Coast for a time and became a top sessionman. He carried on recording in a host of different styles, but lasting success always eluded him.

Riley's first British tour went well, though attendances were excellent

Billy Lee lays it down at the Southgate Royalty.

at some venues and less so at others. He gave an outstanding performance at Leysdown on the Isle of Sheppey. Smartly dressed in a dark-red jacket, black shirt and trousers and white shoes, he alternated between rhythm guitar and harmonica while excellent backing was provided (as it was throughout the tour) by Johnny & The Roccos, whose Bob Fish faithfully recreated the guitar licks from Billy's Sun recordings. There was only a small crowd, but they congregated in front of the stage and helped to create an atmosphere. The set list comprised the very cream of Riley's Sun material and he worked through 'Trouble Bound', 'Pearly Lee', 'Baby Please Don't Go' and 'Rock With Me Baby' to the delight of everyone present, even including the two harmonica instrumentals 'Itchy' and 'Thunderbird', which he recorded with Sonny Burgess in 1958. Inevitably though, it was the classic 'Flyin' Saucers Rock & Roll' and 'Red Hot' which closed a highly entertaining show.

At the conclusion of his British tour Billy travelled to Europe for further gigs in the Netherlands and Belgium.

ROBERT GORDON

There were two attempts to bring Robert Gordon back to Britain during the first half of 1979, but sadly they both failed. After his split with Link Wray, he had paired up with British guitarist Chris Spedding and recorded a new album, *Rock Billy Boogie*, for RCA. Vague plans were formulated for a UK tour during February, but this did not materialise.

Gordon and Spedding did make it over to Europe during June however, and assisted by Tony Garnier (slap bass) and Robby Shouinard (drums) played a highly successful gig at the Palais des Sports in Paris on the same bill as Ian Dury & The Blockheads. He was scheduled to play the Venue at London's Victoria on 30 June, but pulled out of this and other European dates claiming both exhaustion and family reasons. He was replaced at the Venue by British rockabilly band Whirlwind.

BOBBY LEWIS

Indianapolis-born Bobby Lewis had enjoyed a US No.1 hit in 1961 with 'Tossin' And Turnin' ', but strangely neither this nor its follow up, 'One Track Mind', made any impact with British record buyers at the time.

Lewis was booked by Jeff Davey of IPA Agency for a short tour of US military bases at the end of June and there was speculation in *Melody Maker* that he would also play a public show at the Venue in London's Victoria. Nothing materialised, and he slipped quietly in and out of the UK, restricting his appearances to the US bases at Alconbury, Lakenheath and Chicksands.

FATS DOMINO

Fats was in Europe during July for a string of personal appearances including the prestigious *North Sea Jazz Festival* in the Netherlands. He was also scheduled to play for two nights at the *Capital Radio Jazz Festival* at London's Alexandra Palace on 21 and 22 July, and was heavily advertised as one of the headliners.

By the time Norman St. John-Stevas, the Minister for Arts, hosted a reception at the Cabinet Office on 18 July, Fats had dropped out through ill health. B.B. King, Woody Herman, Lionel Hampton and Muddy Waters each enjoyed a glass of sherry with music-loving members of Margaret Thatcher's new government, but his replacement, that old rogue Chuck Berry, was noticeably absent as well.

MACK ALLEN SMITH

July 1979		
?	West Malling	Greenways
?	Chatham	Old Ash Tree
?	Detling	Kent County Showground
?	Brixton	Brockwell Park
?	Margate	*unknown venue*
25	Swansea	British Rail
Tour organiser — Martin Hawkins		

Mack Allen Smith from Carroll County, Mississippi was an unlikely candidate for a UK tour. A country and rockabilly singer who worked almost entirely in the clubs and honky tonks within the Mississippi Delta, he had run into British writer Martin Hawkins at a recording studio in Jackson during the spring of 1975. Hawkins was able to find British outlets for his recordings and albums were soon available for the European market on Checkmate, Redneck and later on Charly Records, although sales were generally unremarkable.

Smith was keen to visit Britain, however, so Hawkins contacted Lee Williams of Allen Promotions and attempts were made to set up a tour on the country circuit during April 1979. When nothing happened, he tried to make his own arrangements, but was very aware that he had neither the inclination nor the contacts to be a promoter.

A fellow *Country Music People* writer, Alan Cackett, helped set up the opening date at Greenways, near Maidstone. Mack was backed by the Roger Humphries Band and his own pianist, Jessie Yates, who accompanied him on the trip and provided vocal harmonies. The material ranged from rock'n'roll standards like 'Don't Be Cruel', 'Blue Suede Shoes' and 'It's Only Make Believe', to country ballads like 'If I Said You Had A Beautiful Body (Would You Hold It Against Me)' and a solid version of 'She Thinks I Still Care', all performed in a strong Presleyesque voice.

In the end, Smith spent a fortnight in England and made at least three radio broadcasts in the Kent and London area. Six gigs went ahead, each set up at short notice and with little advance publicity, but he returned home optimistically dreaming of a return visit the following spring.

CHUCK BERRY

July 1979		
21-22	Wood Green	Alexandra Palace
Tour organiser — George Wein		

When ill health prevented Fats Domino from performing at the ambitious *Capital Radio Jazz Festival* at Alexandra Palace, the organisers turned to Chuck Berry as his replacement. This seemed a sound decision, but unfortunately Chuck had his own problems which were a good deal more serious and which almost caused him to miss the festival as well.

On 10 July, a Los Angeles court sentenced Berry to four months in

prison after he pleaded guilty to income tax evasion. He had failed to declare nearly half of his income for 1973, thereby depriving the US Government of some $100,000 of tax. Fortunately, Supreme Court Judge Harry Pregerson allowed a stay of the sentence until 10 August, so that Chuck could conclude his European commitments (and, presumably, pay off some of his unpaid taxes).

The festival was a six-day open-air extravaganza and the brainchild of veteran US promoter George Wein. He had pioneered the famous *Newport Jazz Festival* in the USA in the Fifties, and had recently organised the *Nice Jazz Festival*, held in the ruins of a French castle. In Nice, the local authority made a £120,000 grant towards the event, while in London the GLC merely sent him a bill for hiring the Ally Pally. Wein needed 45,000 paying customers to break even.

Chuck appeared on the main stage on each of the final two nights. The Saturday line-up also included B.B. King, Dave Brubeck, Georgie Fame and the Willie Bobo Latin Band, while on the Sunday he shared billing with Muddy Waters, Dizzy Gillespie, Lionel Hampton's All Star Orchestra, Stephane Grappelli, Stan Tracey, Terry Callier and the Mike Carr Trio. Chuck was backed by his US bass player, Jim Marsala, and two British musicians, drummer Rod de'Ath and pianist Lou Martin.

Soberly attired in a suit and tie, Chuck's Saturday performance kept the audience on their feet for 50 minutes as he worked through his usual show, which included standout versions of 'School Day' and 'Sweet Little Sixteen'. He made several attempts, but never quite managed to get his guitar completely in tune, and lost his way with a rather shaky version of 'Baby What You Want Me To Do', though he recovered with 'Wee Wee Hours' and an unexpected and rockin' version of 'Bio'.

His performance on the Sunday was more subdued, but did include some different material. 'Around And Around' and 'Let It Rock' went over well, and he even threw in a snippet from 'You Can't Catch Me', but only seemed able to remember the lyrics to the first couple of verses. Considering the fate awaiting him upon his return to the States, Berry gave two solid performances and was very well received on both nights.

Sadly, it must be assumed that the numbers did not add up at the box office, because the dream of an annual jazz festival in London still had a long way to go before it could compete with similar, but already established events in Europe.

HANK MIZELL

August 1979			September 1979		
27	Southgate	Royalty	1	Burgess Hill	Martlets Hall
29	Carshalton	Chick-a-Boom	3	Rayleigh	Croc's
31	Mansfield	Swan	6	Derby	Talk of the Midlands
Tour organiser — Showstopper Promotions					

Three years after the farcical cancellation of the first Hank Mizell tour, British audiences finally got the chance to see him on stage, although inevitably the hysteria which had surrounded the chart success of 'Jungle Rock' had long since subsided. Backing was supplied by the short-lived British group, Mystery Train, featuring saxophone player Tommy Husky and guitarist Terry Clemson, both of whom had backed Chuck Berry and Bo Diddley with the Houseshakers at the *London Rock'n'Roll Show* in Wembley in 1972.

The first three dates on the tour were recorded and the German record label Razzle Dazzle issued an album, *Hank Mizell and Mystery Train... Live!* which suitably captured the occasion for posterity. Hank did not have a particularly strong voice, nor any noticeable charisma, but he fired out adequate versions of 'Ubangi Stomp', 'Folsom Prison Blues' and 'Ain't Got A Thing', plus a selection of Hank Williams songs – among which a speeded-up version of 'You Win Again' was a definite mistake. His 1976 single, 'Kangaroo

Rock' and the bouncy 'Singing In The Jungle' reminded the audience why they were there. Finally, on cue, he ripped his way through 'Jungle Rock' to bring the proceedings to a close.

Mizell never returned to Britain. His brief moment of glory was never likely to be repeated. He passed away in December 1992, two years after being severely disabled by a stroke from which he never fully recovered.

CHARLIE GRACIE

September 1979					
12	Carshalton	Chick-a-Boom	18	Camden Town	Dingwalls
13	Southgate	Royalty	19	Rhondda	Hibernian
14	Colchester	Embassy Suite	20	Wellingborough	British Rail
15	Leicester	De Montfort Hall	22	Manchester	Midland Hotel
16	St. Neots	WMC	23	Leeds	Fforde Green Hotel
17	Rayleigh	Croc's	24	Sunderland	Boilermakers
Tour organiser — Paul Barrett					

Charlie at the Chick-a-Boom.

A sure indicator that rock'n'roll was bubbling away healthily just below the surface of popular music was the steady increase in American visitors to the UK during 1979. None were more welcome than Charlie Gracie, returning for the first time since May 1958. He had toured Britain twice in the Fifties as a young man at the peak of his popularity as a chart act. Now, he was older and wiser. His talent and engaging personality had enabled him to keep working through the many lean years, but it is fair to say that, during the Sixties and much of the Seventies, his name had rarely been mentioned in the UK, nor his records played with any great regularity. To those who may have discounted him as being too lightweight, there was a sharp lesson to be learned.

The show at the Hibernian Club in South Wales was typical of the whole tour. A small venue, it had sold out and very quickly came alive as sweating, heaving, jiving bodies responded to the opening set by Dynamite. They backed the American throughout the tour and performed their task admirably.

Charlie himself just seemed pleased to be back in the UK after so long and made a tremendous start with a stomping 'Rockin' Is Our Bizness'. A small man, smartly dressed in black slacks and shirt, plus an off-white jacket and shoes, he clutched a huge Guild guitar and very quickly demonstrated that it was more than a stage prop. His guitar playing was quite magnificent as he worked his way through his old material, 'Ninety-Nine Ways', 'Tootsie', 'Fabulous' and a brilliant '(You Got) A Heart Like A Rock'. He interspersed other rock'n'roll favourites, of which 'You Mostest Girl', 'I'm Ready', 'Stagger Lee' and 'I'm Moving On' were among the highlights. Ironically though, as if time had stood still and just as on his first two UK tours all those years ago, it was the instrumental, 'Guitar Boogie Shuffle' which earned the biggest response and really won over the audience. He was not allowed to leave without three encores: 'Great Balls Of Fire', 'Whole Lotta Shakin' Goin' On' and 'Kansas City'. After twenty-one years, Charlie Gracie was back in style.

The gig at Leicester's De Montfort Hall was an all-dayer which also featured Crazy Cavan & The Rhythm Rockers, Shades, Freddie 'Fingers' Lee and the Riot Rockers. This was a return visit for Gracie, as he'd played the same venue on his first British tour in September 1957.

He then travelled to Belgium to cut an album, *The Fabulous Charlie Gracie*, which was released in 1981 by Black Jack Records, and also found time to co-star with Buddy Knox at the *13th Rockhouse International Rock'n'Roll Meeting* in Eindhoven, Holland.

British audiences were destined to see a whole lot more of the talented Mr. Gracie in the future.

THE CRICKETS
DON EVERLY

September 1979	
14 Hammersmith Odeon	
Tour organiser — Harvey Goldsmith	

The 1979 celebrations for *Buddy Holly Week* commenced with an exhibition at the Clarendon Hotel, Hammersmith on 13 September as a prelude to the concert the following night. As well as newspaper cuttings, photos, magazines and all things Holly-related, there were appearances by various guests, notably Buddy's widow, Maria Elena Holly Diaz, his one-time singing partner, Bob Montgomery, and Crickets Jerry Allison, Sonny Curtis, Joe B. Mauldin and Albert Lee, along with former Cricket Rick Grech. Maria Elena, in particular, sat and signed autographs for over an hour and demonstrated limitless patience despite some undignified scrambling by impatient fans eager for both photos and kisses.

The free concert at Hammersmith attracted plenty of media attention. Alan Freeman and Jimmy Savile compered, and the capacity audience were entertained during the first half by both Fumble and Mike Berry & The

Vol. 1 No. 4 — September 7th-14th 1979

Buddy Holly Week Raves On!

Outlaws. After an intermission, Maria Elena made a short speech and was presented with a bouquet of flowers. Then Sonny, Jerry and Joe B. got the second half properly underway with a jumping version of 'Oh Boy!'. This was followed by 'Maybe Baby', 'Rock Around With Ollie Vee', 'Everyday' and an excellent 'Think It Over'.

At this point Sonny introduced a new song, 'The Real Buddy Holly Story', which he had written the previous year, after which Albert Lee joined them and took lead vocal on 'Fool's Paradise'. The hits followed one by one as they moved through 'I Fought The Law', 'Well... All Right', 'Peggy Sue' and 'Keep A-Knockin' '. After 'That'll Be The Day', Bob Montgomery made his British stage debut, performing two songs that he co-wrote with Holly — 'Heartbeat' and 'Love's Made A Fool Of You'.

Montgomery gave way to Don Everly for Sonny's 'Walk Right Back', and with Albert substituting for Phil, they dueted on a bunch of Everly Brothers favourites including '('Til) I Kissed You', 'Cathy's Clown', 'All I Have To Do Is Dream' and a rollicking 'Bye Bye Love', with backing provided by the Crickets, just as it had been on the Everlys' UK tour of April 1960.

With the proceedings drawing to a close, Denny Laine, in a Teddy boy suit, joined in with an unusual interpretation of 'Raining In My Heart', before Paul and Linda McCartney harmonised on 'It's So Easy'. Finally, the whole cast returned to the stage for a prolonged jam session with 'Bo Diddley', Joe B. slapping his bass and sharing his microphone with McCartney, and looking just as impassive as ever while the audience went crazy. Albert Lee and the Crickets encored with 'Rave On'. This was a vintage night for live rock'n'roll in Britain and an abiding memory for everyone present.

BUDDY HOLLY WEEK

SEPTEMBER 7th — 14th, 1979.

THE CRICKETS

+ Mike Berry and Guests

at
HAMMERSMITH ODEON
LONDON W6
on
FRIDAY, SEPTEMBER 14th at 8.00pm.

THE DRIFTERS

September 1979			14-20	Luton	Caesar's Palace
22	Birmingham	Night Out	21	London	Grosvenor House Hotel
23-29	Wakefield	Theatre Club	November 1979		
October 1979			29-30	Watford	Bailey's
1-2	Stockport	Quaffers	December 1979		
3-6	Farnworth	Blighty's	1	Watford	Bailey's
10-13	Usk	Stardust	3-8	Wythenshawe	Golden Garter
Tour organiser — Henry Sellers					

The Drifters, in the shape of Clyde Brown, Ray Lewis, Joe Blunt and Billy Lewis returned for a further batch of cabaret dates. They had recently signed to Epic Records and had a new single, 'Pour Your Little Heart Out', to place in front of British audiences. It became a club favourite and was even featured in a Joan Collins sexploitation movie, but never threatened to dent the sales charts. The cabaret audiences wanted the old songs, and as always the Drifters were happy to oblige.

BUDDY KNOX

Buddy and his wife, Mitzi, arrived in the UK on 2 October and spent several days in the studio with Dave Travis, re-recording his old hits. No UK shows were arranged, but he did appear live in Eindhoven on 6 October and in Liege the following day. The latter was a great success and was described by Knox as one of his best concerts ever.

EDDY CLEARWATER

Big Bear Records organised a blues package to undertake a lengthy UK tour during October 1979 under the banner of *American Blues Legends '79*. The participants were originally listed as Lefty Dizz, Good Rockin' Charles, Little Smokey Smothers, Chico Chism, Lester Davenport and Eddy Clearwater. Whether Clearwater dropped out or was listed in error is open to conjecture, but by the time the package got underway he had been replaced by Eddie C. Campbell and Dizz by former Sun Records bluesman, Billy 'The Kid' Emerson.

RAY SMITH

October 1979		
10	Carshalton	Chick-a-Boom
11	Southgate	Royalty
Tour organiser — Showstopper Promotions		

Ray played two shows in the South of England as part of a three-week European tour. He still had something of a credibility problem after his drink-affected disaster at Harlesden the previous November, and this may be partly the reason why only a small crowd turned up at the Royalty, but those that stayed away missed a fine performance by the enigmatic Mr. Smith.

Backed by Johnny & The Roccos, he whipped up a rockin' storm, pounding away at the piano and intermingling his own material like 'Rockin' Bandit', 'Right Behind You Baby' and 'You Made A Hit' with standards such as 'Mystery Train' and 'Whole Lotta Shakin' Goin' On'. The tempo never flagged and he gave the piano some real punishment, even playing it with his feet at one point. He fully earned the sustained applause and his two encores at the end of the evening.

The impression given was that Ray Smith was enjoying himself and that his professional life was in good shape. Unfortunately, there were problems in his personal life which culminated in his death on 29 November 1979 from a self-inflicted gunshot wound at his home in Burlington, Ontario. This wild man of rock'n'roll was buried five days later in Woodlawn Cemetery, Paducah, Kentucky.

DEL SHANNON

October 1979			November 1979		
12-13	Manchester	Valentines	1	Cleethorpes	Bunny's Place
14	Whitehaven	Civic Hall	2	Derby	Talk of the Midlands
15	Borrowstounness	McTavishes	3	Norwich	Talk of the East
16-17	Dundee	Town Hall	4	Lowestoft	Sparrow's Nest
18	Edinburgh	Kirkliston			
19	Bellshill	Stuart & Lloyd's			
20	Dunfermline	Marconi's			
21	Galashiels	Waverley Castle Hotel			
24	Walsall	Bloxwich Memorial Hall			
	Oakengates	Town Hall			
25	Coventry	*unknown venue*			
	Stoke	Trentham Gardens			
26	Melton Mowbray	Painted Lady			
	Burton	Allied			
27	Carshalton	Chick-a-Boom			
28	Liverpool	Wooky Hollow			
Tour organiser unknown					

Immediately before flying to the UK, Del cut four new tracks at Leon Russell's studio in Los Angeles, produced by Tom Petty and with backing by the Heartbreakers, so he was in good spirits when he embarked on yet another round of the UK cabaret circuit, which on this occasion included a clutch of dates in Scotland.

At the conclusion of the British tour, Del and his wife, Shirley Westover, took off for Germany. As they drove between Hanover and Berlin, they were amazed at how similar the countryside was to that of their native Michigan. However, a long and intimidating delay at the border with East Berlin probably highlighted the differences.

MARVIN RAINWATER

October 1979			17	Doncaster	Moorend Hotel
20-28	Hemsby	Pontin's Holiday Centre	18	Bury St. Edmunds	Theatre Royal
			19	Langley	Hen & Chickens
November 1979			20	Bridgwater	Arts Centre
1	Great Torrington	Plough	21	Carshalton	Chick-a-Boom
2	Presteigne	Memorial Hall	22	Brighton	Stanford Arms
3	Keynsham	Fry's	24	Spalding	British Legion
5	Southsea	Rock Gardens	25	Cambridge	*unknown venue*
6	Basildon	Racquel's	27-29	Shetland Isles	*unknown venue*
7	Dagenham	Kimberley C&W	30	Invergordon	Royal British Legion
9	Great Yarmouth	New Beach Hotel	**December 1979**		
10	Basingstoke	Oak Ridge CMC	1	Diss	*unknown venue*
11	Hull	New	2	Southend	Minerva
12	Bishop Thornton	Chequers Inn	6	Southgate	Royalty
13	Spennymoor	Cornforth USC	7	Coventry	Red House Inn
14	Wakefield	Newton House WMC	8	Hemsby	Florida Cabaret
16	Coventry	*unknown venue*			

Tour organiser — Mike Storey

Marvin Rainwater had been a regular visitor to the UK throughout the Seventies, playing small clubs, pubs and country music venues. No booking was too small, no journey too long. Marvin and his guitar would show up and entertain the folks with his own distinctive brand of country music.

This, however, was the tour when things started to change for him. It commenced normally enough, with a booking alongside Jim Glaser on an eight-day country music festival at Pontin's Holiday Centre in Hemsby (Marvin would return to this venue years later as a fully born-again rockabilly singer). His itinerary continued along the same lines as his recent tours, taking in such unlikely venues as the Hen & Chickens at Langley and even three nights on the Shetland Isles – probably something of an ordeal during a cold and wet November. But it was the visit to Carshalton in Surrey on the evening of 21 November that really caught Marvin's attention.

The Chick-a-Boom was not a country music venue at all, but a rock'n'roll club which met regularly at the St. Helier Arms pub, near Croydon. It was a rough, tough place inhabited by Teddy boys and bikers. Fights were not uncommon and the requirements of the clientele were very specific: they wanted to hear Marvin's rock'n'roll songs, and not a bunch of country tunes. He was only too happy to oblige, or at least as far as was practically possible. Backing on the tour was provided by Jon Derek & Country Fever, who neither looked nor sounded like a rockabilly band. They were, however, competent musicians and made a decent stab at propelling Marvin through the likes of 'I Dig You Baby', 'Dance Me Daddy', 'Baby Don't Go' and 'Mr. Blues'. Throughout the show, Rainwater wore a puzzled expression on his face. He just could not comprehend that this audience, many of whom were teenagers, not only knew all his old songs, but were shouting requests for things that he had half-forgotten. This was not a polite country audience clapping to the latest Waylon Jennings or George Jones hit. It was him they were cheering for and his material that they wanted to hear.

The same thing occurred a couple of weeks later when the tour stopped at the Royalty in Southgate. Marvin later recalled, 'I finally found out what I was doing. The people started yelling for me to sing 'Mr. Blues', which was a rockabilly tune I cut 25 years ago. They banned it in the US and said it was rubbish. All of a sudden, it's in the bootleg charts in England. The kids were identifying with what I thought was great 25 years ago, so I thought, *Well I'm 25 years ahead of my time. Let me back my own mind up and go out and do what these people want me to do.* There was another song called 'Hot And Cold', which was the same type of thing. At first I used to refuse to do these songs, but then I realised that I was wrong and started to do them. There was a warp in time and suddenly a whole new world opened up to me. It's weird isn't it?'

MAC CURTIS

Early reports listed Mac as one of the headliners for the *2nd International Rock'n'Roll Weekend Hop* at Caister in November and the success of his two previous tours made him an attractive candidate. However, he dropped out at a fairly early stage and it was Sleepy LaBeef and Billy Lee Riley who eventually took the honours when the usually quiet Norfolk coast braced itself for another invasion of Teds, rockabillies and sundry rock'n'roll nuts over the weekend of 16-18 November.

SLEEPY LaBEEF

November 1979			12	Wimbledon	Nelson's
8	Southgate	Royalty	14	Carshalton	Chick-a-Boom
9	Leicester	TUL	15	Camden Town	Dingwalls
10	Rotherham	Clifton Hotel	16	Plymouth	Top Rank
11	Guildford	Star Hotel	17	Caister	Ladbroke's Holiday Centre
Tour organiser — Showstopper Promotions					

Sleepy returned for his second tour of 1979 to headline the *2nd International Rock'n'Roll Weekend Hop* at Caister along with Billy Lee Riley. Both Americans performed on the Saturday, along with Johnny & The

Roccos, Dynamite (who backed Sleepy throughout the tour), Matchbox and Freddie 'Fingers' Lee. The latter was in one of his more eccentric moods and climaxed his show while wearing a miner's helmet, which he set on fire as he was pounding away at the piano. Health & Safety was a good deal more relaxed in 1979.

Prior to the Caister show, Sleepy tore his way through a series of rock'n'roll club dates and enhanced his growing reputation as a powerhouse performer.

BILLY LEE RILEY

November 1979		
16	Wigan	Casino
17	Caister	Ladbroke's Holiday Centre
19	Carshalton	Chick-a-Boom
22	Southgate	Royalty
23	Leicester	TUL
24	Bristol	Trinity Centre
	Tour organiser — Showstopper Promotions	

Billy Lee was back in the UK only four months after his first visit and starred, along with Sleepy LaBeef, at the *2nd International Rock'n'Roll Weekend Hop* at Caister. Backed again by Johnny & The Roccos, his act was unchanged except that, on this occasion, he demonstrated his versatility by playing some lead guitar, as well as rhythm guitar and harmonica, on each show. This was particularly memorable, as Riley rarely played lead guitar in Europe again.

Prior to his first tour, Billy had recorded a new album, *Vintage*, on his own Mojo label, featuring rockabilly singer Larry Donn on piano, and copies were sold at each gig. More and

Billy Lee at Carshalton.

more people were turning out to hear those Sun classics, 'Red Hot', 'Flyin' Saucers Rock & Roll' and 'Pearly Lee', and the name of Billy Lee Riley was finally becoming known to a wider rock'n'roll audience.

BILL HALEY & HIS COMETS

November 1979		
16	Woolwich	Odeon
17-20	London	The Venue
23	Crawley	Leisure Centre
24	Cambridge	Kelsey Kerridge Sports Hall
26	London	Royal, Drury Lane
Tour organiser — Patrick Malynn		

Bill Haley's final UK tour proved to be a mixture of highs and lows. His four nights at the Venue in London's Victoria were very poorly attended, many of the potential audience having departed from London to attend the *2nd International Rock'n'Roll Weekend Hop* at Caister. In contrast, what proved to be his swansong before the British public was his appearance at the *Royal Variety Show*, one of the proudest moments of his long career.

The tour began in Amsterdam on 24 October and included live appearances in the Netherlands, Norway, Sweden, Denmark and Germany, Bill and his wife, Martha, finally arriving at London Heathrow on a flight from Berlin during the morning of 16 November.

Mal Gray had brought together and rehearsed a new set of Comets. Gerry Tilley (lead guitar) and Steve Murray (drums) were retained from the shows in March and joined by Pete Thomas (tenor sax) and John Gordon (bass). The only American was ex-Sha Na Na member Chico Ryan (rhythm guitar). Gordon was taken ill during the tour and replaced by Pete Spencer, who had also enjoyed an earlier spell as a Comet during March.

Surprisingly, Bill's act, which rarely exceeded 45 minutes in length, was expanded to around an hour, his own contribution being ten songs – a much better return than in earlier days. The show had not changed, of course. Bill was hardly likely to have made radical changes at this point in his life. All the old favourites were present when the UK segment of the tour got underway at Woolwich. 'Rip It Up', 'Shake, Rattle And Roll', 'Razzle Dazzle' and 'Burn That Candle' were each received with wild enthusiasm from the audience. He even sang one of his recent Sonet recordings, 'Hail, Hail Rock And Roll', while Mal Gray chipped in with 'Johnny B. Goode' and 'Promised Land'. The Comets were competent musically, both Tilley and Thomas solidly contributing the instrumental highlights on 'Guitar Boogie Shuffle' and 'Rudy's Rock' respectively, although the vocal expertise of Ryan on 'Rockin' Robin' and Gordon with 'Kansas City' left a little to be desired. Steve Murray was exemplary on the drums throughout.

The biggest criticism of these latter-day Comets was their appearance and general demeanour. Mal Gray was dressed in a yellow anorak, while Chico Ryan appeared on stage wearing ill-matching clothes, a cigarette dangling from his mouth and clutching a bottle of beer. Traditionally, the Comets had always appeared so smart and so professional that long-time Haley fans could only wince at the drop in standards which was only too noticeable. The highlight of the show at Woolwich, as every night, came at the end of the evening when Bill fired his way through 'The Saints Rock'n' Roll', 'See You Later, Alligator' and his own personal anthem, 'Rock Around

The Clock'. Yet another audience was sent home happy.

On 17 November, Haley did a two-hour interview for *The Sun* that appeared as a full-page article under the banner 'Rock Of Ages', in which they claimed that Bill had 'invented teenagers'! Two days later, he recorded four songs for BBC radio, while on 22 November he and Martha, along with UK fan club president Hugh McCallum, and his wife, Ruth, attended the London production of *Hello Dolly!*, starring Carol Channing, at the Theatre Royal, Drury Lane. Part of the attraction was that this would be the venue for the Royal Command Performance four days later. Haley was able to watch the musical from the Royal Box, thereby simulating the conditions under which the Queen would be watching him – no doubt a sobering thought for the quiet American.

The *Royal Variety Show* was a very big occasion indeed, and no other Fifties' rock'n'roller had been invited to participate since Pat Boone back in 1958. The star-studded line-up included Marti Caine, Millicent Martin, Hinge & Bracket, Boney M, Amii Stewart, Elaine Stritch, James Galway, James Mason, Gemma Craven and Jim Davidson. The Comets followed Boney M on stage and were introduced by Noel Edmonds who looked straight up at the Royal Box and announced that he wanted 'no dancing in the boxes or ripping up of seats, 'cos we are now gonna turn back the clock and we are gonna rock with the one and only Bill Haley & His Comets.'

There was a roar of welcome as the theatre curtains parted and they went straight into an abridged version of 'See You Later, Alligator'. The Queen was clearly visible clapping along to the beat as Bill performed, yet again in his own unique style, an extended version of 'Rock Around The Clock'. When the song finished, he stepped forward, bowed to the Royal Box and was gone. The whole cast congregated onstage one by one at the end of the evening and nobody got a bigger cheer than Bill and his Comets, before everybody sang 'God Save The Queen' to complete the proceedings.

Backstage, the cast lined up to be introduced to the Queen. When she drew level with Haley, she remarked, 'It was wonderful to hear that music again. I grew up on it and it reminds me of when I was young. It takes me back a bit and I enjoyed it.' Bill responded, 'It reminds me of when I was young too, ma'am.' If only someone had explained to Her Majesty that she could pop across to the Royalty Ballroom at Southgate and hear live rock'n'roll anytime she wanted!

Bill had been scheduled to appear for three nights in Paris to round off his tour, but an air traffic controllers' strike in France put paid to that plan. The tour came to an abrupt end and Bill flew out of the UK for the final time on 27 November.

TV Appearances
The Royal Variety Performance (ATV)   26 November 1979 (screened 2 December 1979)

BEN E. KING

November 1979			December 1979		
16	Norwich	Cromwell's	1	Melton Mowbray	Painted Lady
17	Colchester	Copford Windmill	17	Camden Town	Dingwalls
19	London	Aphrodite's			
26	London	The Venue			
30	Croydon	Fairfield Halls			
Tour organiser unknown					

Ben E. King had been absent from Britain's clubland since July 1977, an unusually long period for one of our most regular visitors. His return in November 1979 was considerably more low-key than many of his earlier tours and the datebook was far from full.

Only a small crowd turned up at the Venue at London Victoria, where Mirage opened the show. King was impressively backed by an anonymous British five-piece, his affable personality and easy-going style adding to the charm of numbers like 'Sing A Happy Song', 'This Magic Moment' and 'Spanish Harlem'. He did struggle a bit with 'Good Times', but recovered via an intense 'I (Who Have Nothing)' and 'Stand By Me', which he performed twice. An enjoyable set closed with 'Don't Stop Till You Get Enough'.

At Croydon Ben shared billing with Jimmy James & The Vagabonds.

JOHNNY & THE HURRICANES

December 1979		
29	Carshalton	Chick-a-Boom
Tour organiser unknown		

Johnny Paris had proved a big draw at Carshalton's Chick-a-Boom club in July, and so he was re-booked from his German base for a repeat performance only six months later. The act was largely unchanged, with his instrumental hits, 'Red River Rock', 'Beatnik Fly' and 'Reveille Rock' gaining the lion's share of the audience response. Support was provided by Bop Street.

CHAPTER EIGHT

1980

Move Around

For several years there had been speculation about the commercial future of rock'n'roll. With the popularity of rockabilly in Britain and the renewed interest in recordings from the Fifties, there was an obvious need for a figurehead to drive the music forward. Hank Mizell had carried rockabilly into the charts during 1976 with 'Jungle Rock', but had been no more than a novelty act, lacking any potential for sustained success. His more talented contemporaries like Billy Lee Riley, Sleepy LaBeef, or even Ray Campi, might have made more use of a hit record, but clearly if the interest of this new, young audience was to be sustained, a fresh personality would have to emerge who would capture and hold their imagination.

Everyone was in agreement that this was the way forward, but few anticipated the arrival of the Stray Cats, nor the level of impact that their music would exert. Love them or loath them, they would gradually transform live rock'n'roll in Britain and their influence is still clear to see at every rock'n'roll club or ballroom more than three decades later.

Chuck Berry had been released from Lompoc Prison in November 1979, and was therefore free to continue his non-stop touring schedule, which included a short tour of the UK in June. Carl Perkins, Jerry Lee Lewis and Charlie Gracie made welcome return visits, while Texas rockabilly threatened to dominate the club scene in the shape of debut tours by Gene Summers, Johnny Carroll, Sonny Fisher and Groovey Joe Poovey. Ronnie Hawkins finally made his European stage debut in the spring with appearances in Belgium and the Netherlands, and a contingent of his British fans crossed the channel for a riotous weekend of boozing and partying.

More and more venues in Britain were booking rock'n'roll acts and Matchbox were now at the forefront of the UK scene, scoring four hits during the year including 'When You Ask About Love', which reached the Top 10 in October, while both Shakin' Stevens and Darts were not far behind, each charting twice in 1980.

The expanding live circuit now regularly featured such names as Johnny & The Jailbirds, Bop Street, Johnny Storm & Memphis and Rockin' Louie, while rockabilly from the Rockats, the Polecats and Levi Dexter was visible, especially around the London clubs. An all-British rock'n'roll festival in September on the Isle of Man included Joe Brown, Shakin' Stevens, Flying Saucers, Crazy Cavan & The Rhythm Rockers, Screaming Lord Sutch, Heinz and Tommy Bruce. There seemed plenty of work for everybody and audiences craving for more.

Live country music in Britain was also expanding, but ultimately overextended itself. Interesting visitors during the year included Jean Shepard, Charlie Daniels, Skeeter Davis and Dave Dudley, while Joe Ely tried his hand at punk-country, touring with the Clash and Butch Hancock. and on one memorable occasion closing with a stormy duet on a rockin' 'Lipstick, Powder And Paint', accompanied by a very sexy Carlene Carter, provocatively dressed in a tiny miniskirt.

The country scene came close to imploding in August, however, when too many overambitious festivals were placed before the public. Those held in Peterborough and in Scotland did well, but Aberystwyth was abandoned midway through, a similar event scheduled for Chelmsford was cancelled at the last minute, and the Portsmouth extravaganza, which starred Johnny Cash, proved a major financial disaster.

Other notable visitors in 1980 included the Fabulous Thunderbirds, Billy Eckstine, Otis Rush and Queen Ida's Bon Ton Zydeco Band. There was now more good live music in the UK than could ever have been dreamed about in the past, and so much great rock'n'roll still to come.

JOHNNY CASH

Johnny, his wife, June Carter and son, John Carter Cash, spent the early part of January 1980 vacationing in England and Scotland before travelling on to Rome and Egypt. The media knew nothing of this visit, but some fans must have recognised them and were probably shocked to find 'The Man in Black' at their local bar, restaurant or supermarket.

FREDDY CANNON

The new era of affordable air travel meant that unlikely people could suddenly turn up in unexpected places. Visitors to the National Exhibition Centre in Birmingham in the middle of January 1980 would not have anticipated seeing Freddy Cannon as they strolled through the *Custom Car Show*, but he was in Britain for a promotional visit and talks with Hot Rock Records of Newport, who had already issued a new EP by Mac Curtis and were scheduling Freddy for a future release.

JERRY LEE LEWIS

February 1980			14	Slough	Fulcrum Centre
9	Sheffield	Fiesta	16	Chester	Deeside Leisure Centre
10	Manchester	Apollo	17	Finsbury Park	Rainbow
13	Newcastle	Mayfair			

Tour organiser — Jeffrey Kruger

Souvenir Programme 1980

Jerry Lee returned to Britain in fine spirits and good physical shape. Accompanying him were the Memphis Beats – Kenny Lovelace (guitar/fiddle), Joel Shumaker (guitar), Duke Faglier (bass) and Ron Norwood (drums). The supporting act was J.D. Sumner & The Stamps.

The opening night at Sheffield was a sell-out and Jerry confirmed the impression that he was in the mood to rock, opening with a steamy 'Mean Woman Blues' and blasting through 'Rockin' My Life Away', 'What'd I Say' and a torrid 'Tutti Frutti'. The set lasted for almost 70 minutes and also featured standout versions of 'Who Will The Next Fool Be' and 'There Stands The Glass', but probably the pick of the whole evening was an excellent 'Sweet Georgia Brown', not least because of some superb fiddle playing by Kenny. Jerry stayed the night in Manchester and went out to the Playboy Club after the show.

The following evening, much to everyone's surprise, he turned up at the venue at 6.00 pm to rehearse with the band and spent almost an hour putting everyone through their paces. As Jerry Lee's performances are so unpredictable and unplanned, it is rare for him to rehearse in this way, so perhaps it was almost inevitable that when the show commenced, he arrived stylishly attired in a silver and black jacket and jeans, then proceeded to perform an almost entirely different selection of songs.

RAINBOW THEATRE
FINSBURY PARK   **392**

JEFFREY S. KRUGER presents
ONLY 1980 LONDON APPEARANCE OF
JERRY LEE LEWIS
at 7.30 p.m.
Sun FEBRUARY 17
STALLS

Incl. VAT   **£7.50**

F 51

TO BE RETAINED   For conditions of sale see over

Highlights included 'Flip, Flop And Fly', 'Waiting For A Train' and a great version of 'Old Black Joe'.

Over the next two days, Jerry made a couple of television appearances, first performing 'Great Balls Of Fire' and 'Whole Lotta Shakin' Goin' On' on *Blue Peter*, then on 12 February flew up to Glasgow to record the same two songs for *The Old Grey Whistle Test*. On both spots he merely had his own piano accompaniment, as the rest of the band remained in Manchester.

There had been a gig scheduled for Derby on 15 February, but sadly the club went bankrupt and it had to be cancelled. A good many people who had purchased tickets lost money, as well as missing out on their evening's entertainment.

Jerry Lee stops by Manchester's Playboy Club.

Slough was probably the least successful night of the tour. The early house went well enough and included a nice version of 'Country Memories', but when the late performance got underway, Jerry became upset by the stage spotlights, which were disturbing his concentration. After complaining on several occasions, he stormed off in the middle of 'There Must Be More To Love Than This', only to return five minutes later and beat out 'Great Balls Of Fire' and 'Whole Lotta Shakin' Goin' On', thereby bringing the evening to a somewhat abrupt close.

After further shows at Chester, during which he responded to a request and sang 'I'll Sail My Ship Alone', and the Rainbow Theatre in London, where he closed with 'Good Golly Miss Molly' while lying stretched out on the keyboard, Jerry and his entourage moved on to Germany for an appearance at the legendary Star-Club in Hamburg, and later to the Netherlands, Belgium and France.

TV appearances

Blue Peter (BBC1)	11 February 1980
The Old Grey Whistle Test (BBC2)	12 February 1980

GENE SUMMERS

February 1980		
21	Southgate	Royalty
23	Carshalton	Chick-a-Boom
Tour organiser — Dick Grant		

Gene rockin' at Carshalton.

Few people in Britain had even heard the name of Gene Summers prior to the Seventies, when bootleg copies of his Jan record, 'School Of Rock'n'Roll' started to circulate. A tremendous pounding piano rocker, it became a fixture on the playlists at the pubs and record hops wherever rock'n'roll was heard, eventually creating a demand for a personal appearance by the man himself. This was now the formula. UK releases, legal or otherwise, would make available hitherto unknown and often totally obscure recordings, and if they became sufficiently popular a tour would very likely follow

Summers had been active around Dallas, Texas since the mid-Fifties, but although he had recorded for several local labels, he had never been able to break out to a national – let alone international – audience. This short trip finally gave him that opportunity.

He played a show at Lille in France on 16 February backed by Dynamite, then arrived in the UK for rehearsals at the St. Helier Arms in Carshalton, home of the infamous Chick-a-Boom Club. Backing for the two shows was to be provided by the exciting young rockabilly band, the Blue Cat Trio.

Problems arose almost from the start when Gene's wife, Dea, became ill and had to fly home to Texas, and then to make matters worse drummer Stef Edwards broke his arm. A replacement was found in time for a recording session at Frog Studio in Stanmore, but the decision had to be taken to bring in Dynamite to provide the backing for the Royalty show. Happily, Summers went down well on his British debut despite talking rather too much between songs. Then he was off to Sweden for a gig with the Teddy Hill Band in Gothenburg on 22 February before jetting straight back to play the Chick-a-Boom.

By now, the Blue Cat Trio had a replacement drummer, Dave Joice, and were augmented for the night by saxophone player Clive Osborne and pianist Geraint Watkins. Summers was smartly attired in a white suit and shoes and an open-necked black shirt. His energetic act commenced with 'Alabama Shake' and an exciting version of fellow Texan Sonny Fisher's 'Rockin' Daddy'. The irritating chat between numbers had been eradicated, and with the band performing admirably he stormed through 'Blue Suede Shoes', 'Back In The USA', and 'So Glad You're Mine', removing his jacket for 'School Of Rock'n'Roll', which was greeted with a roar of approval from the audience.

Sweat was pouring off Gene as he utilised the whole of the stage area for 'Dance, Dance, Dance' and he went down on his knees during 'High School Confidential'. The excitement continued through 'Wine, Wine, Wine' and, as encores, 'Straight Skirts', a second treatment of 'Alabama Shake' and finally, 'Twixteen'.

Gene Summers had proved himself a highly visual and hard-working entertainer. He had achieved a great deal in just a few days and his head must have been spinning as he flew home to Texas, a whole new career in Europe having opened up for him.

THE DRIFTERS

March 1980			17	Slough	Fulcrum Centre
1	West Malling	Greenways	18	Weston-super-Mare	Webbington
3-8	Wythenshawe	Golden Garter	19	Eastbourne	King's
13-15	Caerphilly	Double Diamond	20	Lewisham	Concert Hall
17-22	Birmingham	Night Out	23	Tottenham	Mayfair
24-25	Stockton	Fiesta	24-26	Southend	Queen's Hotel
26-29	Edinburgh	McTavish	30	Manchester	Fagin's
31	Stoke	Jollee's	**May 1980**		
April 1980			1-3	Manchester	Fagin's
2-3	Charnock Richard	Park Hall Hotel	5	Nottingham	Heart of the
5	Nottingham	Commodore			Midlands
6-12	Purfleet	Circus Tavern	10	Crawley	Leisure Centre
13	Wimbledon	Theatre	11	Reading	Hexagon
16	Stevenage	Leisure Centre			
Tour organiser — Henry Sellers					

Another year and another Drifters' tour, but one to put a smile back on the faces of their many fans: Johnny Moore had returned from his sabbatical and his distinctive tenor voice was again at the forefront of the Drifters' act. Controversy regularly rages over the relative authenticity of the many so-called Drifters performing around the world, but no group led by Johnny Moore could ever fail to be accepted. He, more than any other single man, was the voice of the Drifters.

There were, in fact, two changes for the spring 1980 tour, both Billy Lewis and Joe Blunt having departed and the second newcomer was Louis Price, a baritone who had previously worked with the Temptations. The new line-up therefore comprised Johnny Moore, Clyde Brown, Ray Lewis and Louis Price.

CHARLIE FEATHERS

March 1980		
6	Southgate	Royalty
7-8	Caister	Ladbroke's Holiday Centre
Tour organiser — Showstopper Promotions		

Photo by Paul Harris

Charlie at the Royalty.

Nearly three years on from the *Sun Sound Show*, the enigmatic Charlie Feathers returned to the UK for the *3rd International Rock'n'Roll Weekend Hop* at Caister, where he co-starred with Charlie Gracie before a highly charged audience reportedly numbering around 3,000.

Accompanied by his son, Bubba Feathers, on guitar and sessionmen Pete Miles (drums) and Bob Brunning (bass), he achieved a tight and authentic rockabilly sound which went down a storm, the crowd bopping along to the likes of 'Tongue-Tied Jill' and 'Bottle To The Baby'. He played twice over the weekend and was well received, despite his irritating habit of talking too much between numbers.

In contrast, Charlie's pre-Caister club date at the Royalty was an unmitigated disaster. Backed by the Rhythm Hawks, augmented by Bubba Feathers, he never seemed comfortable at all, merely performing segments from songs and continually wandering away from the set list, leaving the musicians with an impossible task trying to follow him. Eventually, he stopped playing altogether and told a long, rambling story, which had no apparent ending. The audience, who had greeted him with warm applause, had lapsed into disappointed silence by the time he shuffled off stage, his act having lasted a shade under 20 minutes.

After 25 years of comparative failure, Charlie Feathers seemed to be struggling to come to terms with his new-found fame in Europe.

CHARLIE GRACIE

March 1980		
8-9	Caister	Ladbroke's Holiday Centre
12	Carshalton	Chick-a-Boom
13	Southsea	Rock Gardens
14	Bristol	Turntable
15	Barkingside	Old Maypole
Tour organiser — Showstopper Promotions		

The *3rd International Rock'n'Roll Weekend Hop* at Caister was every bit as successful as its predecessors. Charlie Gracie and Charlie Feathers headlined and each performed twice, while the pick of the British contingent were the Cruisers, Flying Saucers, Johnny Storm & Memphis, Crazy Cavan & The Rhythm Rockers, the Blue Cat Trio and a particularly strong set from Shades on the Sunday evening.

Gracie was again paired with Dynamite, who worked well behind him. His guitar playing was excellent and his act a well-crafted mixture of his own hits like 'Fabulous', 'Wanderin' Eyes' and 'Butterfly', plus the instrumental 'Guitar Boogie Shuffle' and rock'n'roll standards 'Great Balls Of Fire' and 'You Mostest Girl'. He was likeable, highly professional and seemed to have assessed precisely what the audience required from him. The Caister weekenders may have been creating a time warp of Fifties music, fashions and lifestyle, but Charlie Gracie had effortlessly entered the time bubble and seemed to be thriving on the experience.

ROY ORBISON

March 1980					
			6	Bridlington	Royal Hall
21	Nottingham	Commodore	7	Blackpool	ABC
22	Manchester	Apollo	8	Nottingham	Commodore
23	Southport	New	9-10	Windsor	Blazers
26-29	Stoke	Jollee's	11	Ipswich	Gaumont
	Stockton	Fiesta	12	Chatham	Central Hall
30	Peterborough	ABC	13	Windsor	Blazers
31	Luton	Caesar's Palace	18	Brighton	Dome
April 1980			19	London	Dominion
1-3	Birmingham	Night Out	20	Portsmouth	Guildhall
4	Bournemouth	Winter Gardens	21	Croydon	Fairfield Halls
5	Birmingham	Night Out			
Tour organiser — Arthur Howes					

Roy was back in the US charts, thanks to his duet with Emmylou Harris, 'That Lovin' You Feelin' Again', and although it did not gain similar success in the UK market, he seemed as popular as ever, with the datebook for his latest tour full to the brim.

Two years earlier, one of Roy's fans, Michelle Booth, had fallen from a train and sustained life-threatening injuries. In a coma for several months at a hospital in Isleworth, she had responded to Roy's songs and he had sent a personal tape to her, as a result of which she recovered. Now back in Britian, Roy took the opportunity to visit her, and they both appeared on BBC TV's

Nationwide on 20 March.

Backed throughout the tour by the Price Brothers, Roy delivered his usual act and his unique voice was as magnificent as ever. They travelled to Germany and the Netherlands for further shows in mid-April, only to find that a confirmed booking in 's-Hertogenbosch turned out to be in a sex club! Orbison was furious but had to play the show, as he could not pull out of his contract. Newspaper headlines reported 'Orbison Among The Hookers'.

TV Appearances
Nationwide (BBC1)   20 March 1980

MAC CURTIS

Rollin' Rock UK organised a return visit for Mac and he was billed to appear at Wembley on the *12th International Festival of Country Music* on 7 April, with Matchbox providing the backing. This was to be only one leg of an ambitious programme scheduled to take both acts into Belgium, the Netherlands and France under the tour banner *Rockabilly '80*. Unfortunately, Mac's commitments as a radio presenter back home in Dallas, Texas made the timing impossible and the whole project had to be cancelled.

JOHNNY CARROLL
JUDY LINDSEY

March 1980			April 1980		
27	Southgate	Royalty	2	Southall	White Hart
28	West Runton	Pavilion	3	Bournemouth	Tiffany's
29	Carshalton	Chick-a-Boom	5	Salford	Willows
			7	Bristol	Locarno
Tour organiser — David Harris (Rollin' Rock UK)					

Johnny Carroll and his musical partner, Judy Lindsey, would become regular fixtures on the UK rock'n'roll scene over the next decade, but this short and highly embarrassing debut tour was a classic example of what can go wrong without adequate preparation.

A lifelong resident of Godley, a small township just south of Fort Worth, Texas, Johnny had recorded some classic rockabilly for Decca in 1956 and later had releases on Phillips International and Warner Brothers before moving into club management. In 1977, he met Judy Lindsey, a successful model with ambitions to become a singer, and together they formed the Johnny & Judy Band. By the time of their first UK visit, they were highly visible on the Dallas-Fort Worth music scene and in the midst of a long-term residency at the Fort Worth Hilton.

When Mac Curtis pulled out of his UK tour, Carroll, who had cut an album for Rollin' Rock in 1978, was an obvious replacement. Unfortunately, nobody explained to him that the requirements of a UK rockabilly audience were very different from those of the Fort Worth cabaret circuit and, to make matters worse, he and Judy were paired with a desperately inadequate backing band, Dixie Phoenix.

Not surprisingly, their opening night at Southgate's Royalty was a big disappointment. Johnny's songs like 'Crazy, Crazy Lovin'' and 'Wild Wild Women' were performed without any cutting edge and Judy, who had no background in rock'n'roll, seemed an irrelevance. It was not a good night and the ultra-critical Royalty audience were decidedly unimpressed.

By the time they played the White Hart in Southall, the situation had improved. Johnny seemed more at ease and 'Hot Rock', 'Crazy, Crazy Lovin'' and 'Blue Moon Of Kentucky' all went over well, as did their latest single, a duet of 'Honey Don't'. However, this whole painful experience was a sharp learning curve for Johnny Carroll. British audiences had yet to see the best of him.

CARL PERKINS

Carl was scheduled to appear on Mervyn Conn's *12th International Festival of Country Music* at Wembley on Easter Monday, 7 April, and for a club date at Dingwalls, Camden Town in North London three days earlier. He cancelled his trip quite late on owing to sinus problems.

BRENDA LEE
CHARLIE RICH

April 1980		
6	Wembley	Arena
	Tour organiser — Mervyn Conn	

Photo by Paul Harris

The Sunday line-up for the *12th International Festival of Country Music* included Bobby Bare, Jeanne Pruett, Stonewall Jackson, Barbara Fairchild, Tompall & The Glaser Brothers, Ronnie Prophet, Ray Lynam and Little Ginny, as well as two acts of special interest to rock'n'roll followers, Brenda Lee and Charlie Rich.

This was Brenda's first appearance in Britain since 1973 and she worked with her own band – Tom Wild (lead guitar), Chuck Spence (bass guitar), David Youen (keyboards), Bob Ballard (rhythm guitar) and Tommy Wells (drums). Her 30-minute spot mainly comprised her own hits, including

'As Usual', 'All Alone Am I', 'I'm Sorry' and an unexpectedly raunchy 'Sweet Nothin's'. She also threw in a medley of country standards and was generally well received, closing with her new single, 'The Cowgirl And The Dandy'.

Charlie Rich did not fare nearly so well. He had the disadvantage of following the newly reformed Tompall & The Glaser Brothers, always a popular act with the Wembley audience. They had created such a high level of excitement that Rich's quiet, bluesy style and awkward stage persona gave him little chance. His set never got going and sadly many of the audience walked out, further disrupting the enjoyment for those who remained. It was a shame, because he performed stunning versions of 'Sittin' And Thinkin' ' and 'Behind Closed Doors', but this was not his night.

TV appearances (Brenda Lee)
Sing Country (BBC2)   6 April 1980 (screened 30 May 1980)

TV appearances (Charlie Rich)
Sing Country (BBC2)   6 April 1980 (screened 13 June 1980)

DON EVERLY

April 1980		
7 Wembley	Arena	
Tour organiser — Mervyn Conn		

Easter Monday was designated 'Contemporary Country Night' at the *12th International Festival of Country Music*, although quite how Don Everly fitted that description was open to question. He appeared on the usual extensive bill along with the Bellamy Brothers, Commander Cody & His Lost Planet Airmen, Emmylou Harris, Kenny Serratt, Matchbox, Sonny Wright, Peggy Sue, Raymond Froggatt, Norway's Bjøro Håland, Colleen Peterson, Frank Ifield and Pete Sayers. His backing was provided by the Dead Cowboys – Phil Donnelly (guitar), Rachel Peer (bass), Tony Newman (drums) and Lamar Hill (piano) – plus the significant addition of Albert Lee, who contributed both guitar and harmony vocals.

To be frank, there was really nothing new or contemporary about Don's act. Increasingly chubby in appearance and his dark hair curlier than in the past, he stuck to the old favourites 'Walk Right Back', 'Bye Bye Love' and 'All I Have To Do Is Dream' as the cornerstone of his act, and did not seem to have made much real headway with his solo career since the split with his brother in 1973. He reminisced about the first Everly Brothers tour of Britain, paid homage to Lefty Frizzell and closed his uninspired spot with 'T For Texas'.

Probably the most rocking moment of the evening came during the set by Commander Cody & His Lost Planet Airmen, when guitarist Bill Kirchen let rip with some red-hot picking during Warren Smith's 'Ubangi Stomp'. The 'Keep It Country' contingent in the audience were apoplectic.

TV Appearances
Sing Country (BBC2)   7 April 1980 (screened 23 May 1980)

JOHNNY & THE HURRICANES

April 1980			May 1980		
9	Basildon	Locarno	31	Carshalton	Chick-a-Boom
10	Harlow	Tiffany's	**June 1980**		
12	Melton Mowbray	Painted Lady	6	Brighton	Lewes Road Inn
15	Leighton Buzzard	Unicorn	8	Slough	Alexander's
16	Carshalton	Chick-a-Boom			
17	Stoke	Tiffany's			
19	Colchester	Copford Windmill			
21	Middlesbrough	Priory			
22	Stockton	Fiesta			
23	Hartlepool	Corporation Welfare			
Tour organiser unknown					

Johnny Paris hauled his saxophone out on the road for another lengthy tour fronting a revamped Hurricanes comprising Ricky Gee (guitar), plus probably Mick Brady (drums) and Tony Raw (bass). After a clutch of one-nighters they spent most of May touring Germany, before returning to finish with three more UK gigs.

By the end of May, when the show reached the Chick-a-Boom in Carshalton, they had the act pretty much nailed-down. There was a sizeable crowd including a high proportion of Teddy boys, as the set opened to the strains of 'Crossfire'. The saxophone did develop a nasty buzz during the early stages of the proceedings, which affected 'Down Yonder', 'Reveille Rock' and 'Farewell Twist', but it miraculously disappeared as Johnny varied the pace with 'Old Smokie', 'Beatnik Fly' and a masterful 'Harlem Nocturne'. He vocalised on 'Maybe Baby', 'Johnny B. Goode' and 'You're Sixteen', but it was the instrumentals which scored best with an audience, who were initially slow to respond. By the climax of the set, however, the dancers were out on the floor and the Hurricanes received appropriate applause for a raunchy 'Red River Rock'.

Johnny found time for some recording while in England and cut two tracks, 'Don't Push' and 'Get It On', with the Jets.

ROCKY BURNETTE

April 1980			May 1980		
24-25	Glasgow	Apollo	1	Hammersmith	Odeon
26	Manchester	Apollo	2	Brighton	Centre
27	Liverpool	Empire	3	Finsbury Park	Rainbow
28	Birmingham	Odeon			
30	Hammersmith	Odeon			
Tour organiser — Danny Betesh					

Not many rock'n'roll fans were present when, six months after scoring a minor hit with 'Tired Of Toein' The Line', Rocky Burnette undertook his first lengthy UK tour – the reason being that he was support act for Dr. Hook, and it was mainly country fans that made up the bulk of the audience. *Sounds* were clearly confused as to Rocky's parentage and suggested erroneously that he was the son of Swedish piano player Hank C. Burnette!

Rocky knew who he was however. Every night he opened his short set with 'Rock Billy Boogie' and closed with a riotous 'Tear It Up' – classic songs from his father, Johnny Burnette's days with the Rock'n'Roll Trio. The whole tour had been sold out weeks in advance, although naturally it was Dr. Hook who were the principal draw. Rocky's contribution was criticised in the country press, where reference was made to the ear-shattering volume and vocals screamed out way beyond distortion level. Rocky had yet to find his audience in Britain, but his day would come.

SONNY FISHER

May 1980		
5	Southgate	Royalty
7	Carshalton	Chick-a-Boom
8	Catford	Squire
Tour organiser — Showstopper Promotions		

Sonny Fisher was a Texan rockabilly singer who recorded eight highly impressive songs for Starday Records during 1955. He was popular for a time in the nightclubs around Houston, but by 1961 had retired from music and for nearly 25 years had been earning his living as a self-employed flooring contractor. Ace Records had introduced British fans to Sonny's music through an album, *Texas Rockabilly*, issued in 1979, but when he flew into London for this short UK tour he was very much an unknown quantity.

Sonny thrills the Chick-a-Boom crowd with authentic '50s rockabilly.

He made his debut at the Royalty on an all-dayer, appearing with Flying Saucers, Freddie 'Fingers' Lee, Gina & The Rockin' Rebels, plus Johnny & The Roccos, who also provided backing throughout the tour. Fisher, perhaps more than any other rock'n'roller before or since, seemed totally stunned by the sudden and unexpected resurrection of his musical career and his head was clearly in a spin when he came out to meet his audience.

A craggy, gaunt figure, he certainly looked the part. His thick black hair was combed back with an impressive quiff; he sported a pair of thick, bushy sideburns and was dressed in a yellow jacket and black shirt. Not only did he look good, but he sounded superb. The set was built around his Starday recordings and the crowd were delighted to sing along with 'Pink And Black', 'Sneaky Pete', 'Little Red Wagon' and a sizzling 'Rockin' Daddy'. Sonny Fisher had been away from music a long time and had acquired no modern influences to taint his sound. As soon as he picked up his guitar, it was 1955 again. Credit must also be given to the Roccos, especially guitarist Bob Fish, for the restrained and authentic sound that they created for him.

During his short stay in the UK, Sonny found time to cut four tracks for Ace Records before departing to France for a show in Lille on 10 May.

CHUCK BERRY

May 1980			June 1980		
25	Middlesbrough	Town Hall	1	Poole	Arts Centre
27	Glasgow	Tiffany's	2	St. Austell	New Cornish Riviera
28	Blackburn	King George's Hall			
29	Finsbury Park	Rainbow			
31	West Runton	Pavilion			
Tour organiser unknown					

Strike action prevented publication of both *Melody Maker* and *New Musical Express* for a six-week period that stretched through May and the early part of June 1980. During the news blackout, and with no discernable publicity anywhere else, Chuck Berry entered the country and completed his umpteenth British tour, including an appearance at the Rainbow Theatre, scene of earlier triumphs, where on this occasion the Cruisers were his opening act. His daughter, Ingrid, and his trusty bass player, Jim Marsala, travelled with him. This was very much Chuck's 'lost tour' and has since been overlooked or forgotten by music historians and Berryphiles alike.

At the conclusion of the dates he flew to Scandinavia for further shows in Sweden and Norway.

FATS DOMINO

The second *Capital Radio Jazz Festival* was due to be held at Alexandra Palace in North London on the weekend of 12 July, and when the details were announced in March, Fats was one of the headline acts scheduled to appear. Sadly, for the second year running he dropped out and was replaced by Ray Charles, leaving only saxophone maestro Sam 'The Man' Taylor of interest to rock'n'roll enthusiasts.

On 10 July, a major fire broke out at Alexandra Palace destroying more than half of the building and the ill-fated festival had to be aborted.

THE STRAY CATS

Brian Setzer (guitar and vocals), Slim Jim Phantom (drums) and Lee Rocker (upright bass) were three teenagers from New York who arrived in London at the beginning of July with vague expectations of both gigs and accommodation, neither of which materialised. They ended up sleeping in Old Compton Street, on the office floor of music publicist Keith Altham, while he used his contacts to find work for them.

By the end of July, they were gigging around London and made an immediate impact with a wild and uncompromising, yet modern rockabilly act that drew heavily on the spirit of Gene Vincent and Eddie Cochran, but which was very much a product of 1980. Setzer played a semi-acoustic 1956 Gretsch, but it was the slapping bass and the minimalist drum kit – just snare, cymbal and bass drum – that gave the Stray Cats their distinctive sound. The rock'n'roll of the Fifties was in there, but it was only a part of the overall package. 'Punk rockabilly' was probably the best description of this new phenomenon.

Through August and September they worked constantly around London, appearing at Dingwalls, the Marquee, the Half Moon in Putney and the Hope & Anchor in Islington. They opened for US punk band the Mechanics at the Venue, tore up the Thomas à Becket at Camberwell and the Bridge House at Canning Town, and shared billing with the Fabulous Poodles at the Greyhound in Fulham. They also made an appearance at Bogart's in Birmingham, but otherwise rarely ventured far from London.

The music press were convinced they were on to something and shadowed their every move. Mick Jagger, Keith Richards, Ronnie Lane and members of the Clash, Siouxie & The Banshees and the Pretenders were among the faces spotted at their early gigs. The shows themselves became increasingly riotous, the music comprising rock'n'roll standards like 'Ubangi Stomp', 'Somethin' Else', 'Be-Bop-A-Lula' and 'Jeannie, Jeannie, Jeannie', plus original material such as 'Fishnet Stockings', 'Crawl Up And Die' and 'Rock This Town'.

By the end of September, they were already in the studios preparing to record their first album, although no deal had yet been finalised. An incredible two months were rounded off with an appearance at the Rainbow Theatre, Finsbury Park on 29 September as support for Elvis Costello & The Attractions.

DON EVERLY

July 1980			August 1980		
31	Southgate	Royalty	1	London	The Venue
Tour organiser unknown					

Don spent much of the summer in Europe working with the Dead Cowboys. The two London gigs came at the end of a month-long French tour, and his appearance at the Venue in London's Victoria was later described by him as 'one of my most successful evenings in show business'.

Later, he was billed to appear for two nights at the *Essex Country Music Festival* in Chelmsford on 16 and 17 August, along with Webb Pierce and the Wilburn Brothers. Only about 300 advance tickets had been sold when the decision was taken to pull the plug on the whole event, no doubt at considerable expense for the organisers.

JOHNNY CASH

August 1980		
10	Portsmouth	Airport
Tour organisers — Susan Fuller and Mike Moore (Fullmoore Festivals)		

An overambitious promotion, a three-day *Country Music Festival* at the 120-acre airport site was jointly organised by Portsmouth Council and Radio Victory, and was run on their behalf by Fullmoore Festivals. The outdoor stage was the centre point of a Wild West town, complete with a Hollywood movie-style saloon and store fascias erected in front of various Western clothing, merchandising and record stalls. The only thing missing was the public. Camping facilities were available for up to 150,000 visitors, but the actual crowd was less than 15,000 for the whole weekend, and inevitably this led to a massive financial disaster.

Cash appeared on the final night along with Hoyt Axton, Billie Jo Spears and Johnny Tillotson. His fee had been settled in full by the organisers, but when he learnt that the money had run out and that some of the other acts were not being paid, he generously agreed to return half of his entitlement, so that the other artists could be accommodated. He was accompanied by June Carter, John Carter Cash and the Great Eighties Eight – Bob Wootton (guitar), Marty Stuart (guitar), Joe Allen (bass), W.S. Holland (drums), Earl Poole Ball (piano), Jerry Hensley (guitar), and Jack Hale and Bob Lewin (horns). A noticeable absentee was his long-time bass player, Marshall Grant, a member of the original Tennessee Two, who had recently retired after a quarter of a century of service.

Johnny Cash proved to be the high point of a pretty dire weekend. He drew by far the biggest crowd and enchanted everyone with his usual act, stalwarts like 'Folsom Prison Blues', 'I Walk The Line' and 'Ring Of Fire' gathering the greatest applause, while 'A Boy Named Sue' still had the audience in fits of laughter as if they had never heard the song before.

Between 11 and 13 August, Cash remained in the UK and recorded a guest appearance on *The Muppet Show*, in which he sang 'Ghost Riders In The Sky' and a medley of railroad songs.

BUZZ & THE FLYERS

The Stray Cats were not the only young American rockabilly band to visit the UK during the summer of 1980. Dig 'Buzz' Wayne (vocals and guitar), Michael Gene Antle (lead guitar), Pete Morgan (upright bass) and Rocco DeRubeis (drums) were based in New York and, like the Stray Cats, heavily influenced by the music of Gene Vincent.

They shared billing with Ray Campi on a one-off gig at the Royalty Ballroom, Southgate on 25 August and let rip with frantic versions of 'Double Talkin' Baby', 'One Hand Loose' and 'Tore Up' in front of a young and highly enthusiastic audience.

RAY CAMPI

August 1980		
25 Southgate	Royalty	
Tour organiser — Showstopper Promotions		

Ray was considered enough of a box-office draw to be flown in specially to headline an all-dayer at the Royalty on Bank Holiday Monday, where he appeared along with the young New York band, Buzz & The Flyers, the Polecats, the Rhythm Hawks and Remember This. High ticket prices probably accounted for the less-than-capacity crowd, but Ray was on good form, his act as animated as ever.

Backed by the Rhythm Hawks, he included most of the Rollin' Rock favourites like 'Rockin' At The Ritz', 'Eager Boy' and 'Caterpillar', and was enthusiastically received by the surprisingly youthful audience.

BEN E. KING

A lengthy tour for Ben E. King was arranged, commencing at the Island Hotel in Leysdown on the Isle of Sheppey on 12 September, and including appearances in Manchester, Chester, Colchester and London Victoria. Unfortunately, he pulled out because of family illness and the whole project had to be scrapped.

WANDA JACKSON

September 1980			27	Ipswich	Gaumont
17	Southport	New	29	Bournemouth	Winter Gardens
18	Edinburgh	Playhouse	30	Eastbourne	Congress
19	Glasgow	Kelvin Hall	**October 1980**		
20	Aberdeen	Capitol	1	St. Austell	New Cornish Riviera
21	Inverness	Eden Court	2	Chatham	Central Hall
23	Wembley	Conference Centre	3	Gloucester	Leisure Centre
24	Reading	Hexagon	4	Chelmsford	Odeon
26	Peterborough	ABC	5	Norwich	Theatre Royal
Tour organiser — Mervyn Conn					

This was a welcome return for Wanda Jackson, headlining a lengthy tour that was aimed squarely at country music audiences. Billed as *Nashville Cavalcade*, the package also featured Tompall & The Glaser Brothers, Lloyd Green and Jimmy C. Newman. By and large the rock'n'roll enthusiasts had given up on Wanda at this stage, as it was accepted that her performance would contain only a countrified 'Let's Have A Party' and nothing else from her back catalogue of rockabilly recordings.

Wanda on stage at Eastbourne.

Photo by Paul Harris

Her performance at Edinburgh confirmed this fact. The highlights of her spot were an emotional 'Before The Next Teardrop Falls' and a gospel-flavoured 'One Day At A Time', but it was still 'Let's Have A Party' which earned the greatest applause.

One brief glimmer of hope arose when she guested on BBC Radio London's *Echoes* programme and was interviewed by Stuart Colman. He concentrated heavily on her rocking past and Wanda spoke enthusiastically about her rockabilly roots. Little did she realise that those days were far from over.

THE STRAY CATS

It was announced that the Stray Cats would spend the first half of October touring as support for the Specials, opening at Manchester's Apollo Theatre on 1 October. Although verbal agreement was allegedly reached, a spokesman for the band later claimed this to have been a 'premature assumption' and the dates were never taken up. The first priority seemed to be recording them and getting some product in the shops before media interest in the Stray Cats cooled down.

THE DRIFTERS

October 1980		
1-4	Watford	Bailey's
16-18	Frimley Green	Lakeside
20-25	Birmingham	Night Out
Tour organiser — Henry Sellers		

Johnny Moore, Clyde Brown, Ray Lewis and Louis Price undertook their second UK tour of 1980 with a small batch of cabaret engagements. Nothing remarkable to report – just the usual highly professional and cleverly choreographed stage act featuring an hour of great songs each night.

EDDY CLEARWATER

October 1980		
8	Camden Town	Dingwalls
10	Putney	Half Moon
Tour organiser unknown		

Eddy Clearwater had appeared briefly in the UK during July 1978 as a participant on the *Blues Festival '78* package and had shown enough of himself to warrant further attention from the rocking crowd.

Since the Fifties, he had been a stalwart in the blues clubs on Chicago's West Side with his slashing left-handed guitar playing, soulful vocals and a style that encompassed a mix of blues, rock'n'roll, country, gospel and rockabilly. He appeared at Putney along with his cousin, blues harmonica player Carey Bell, and backed by the Sunflower Blues Band. His act proved to be dynamic and action-packed, and contained more than a sprinkling of Chuck Berry. Indeed, several people in the audience were heard to compare his live show favourably with Chuck's sometimes lacklustre performances of late.

Clearwater performed songs from his latest album release – *The Chief*, on Rooster Records – including a fine rocker, 'I Wouldn't Lay My Guitar Down', the Berry-influenced 'Two Times Nine' and several of Chuck's classics including a sizzling 'Johnny B. Goode'. He seemed to have unlimited energy and enthusiasm, which resulted in a truly dynamic act.

Carl receives a warm welcome from the Royalty crowd.

CARL PERKINS

October 1980		
9	Southgate	Royalty
10-12	Caister	Ladbroke's Holiday Centre
16	London	The Venue
17-18	Caister	Ladbroke's Holiday Centre
19	Cambridge	Midsummer Common
Tour organisers — Showstopper Promotions		

Carl and his band, again including his sons, Greg and Stan Perkins, appeared at two weekenders during this short tour. Both were held at Caister, though the audiences were very different. After a storming rock'n'roll night at the Royalty, he was headliner at the *3rd International Country Music Weekend* at Caister along with Don Gibson, Carroll Baker and Linda Cassidy.

Then a week later, Carl was back at the same venue for the *4th International Rock'n'Roll Weekend Hop* along with Jack Scott, Matchbox, Shades, the Blue Cat Trio and all the usual suspects. However, not many people were aware that also travelling with Perkins, although not performing, was Marshall Grant, until recently bass player for Johnny Cash's Tennessee Three.

The final night of the tour was held in a big-top-styled circus tent, where Carl appeared with both the Cruisers and Matchbox. The latter joined him on stage for an enthusiastic workout on the song from which they had taken their name. The audience loved it.

Jack delivers a quality show at Southgate Royalty.

JACK SCOTT

October 1980			November 1980	
15	Carshalton	Chick-a-Boom	1 Stevenage	Bowes Lyon House
16	Southgate	Royalty		
17-18	Caister	Ladbroke's Holiday Centre		
26	Croydon	Greyhound		
Tour organisers — Showstopper Promotions and Paul Barrett				

Jack Scott had made his British debut at the *Sun Sound Show* in 1977, and was so good on that occasion that he stole the show on both nights. It was surprising, therefore, that nearly three years had elapsed before his return to the UK for a handful of club dates and joint top billing with Carl Perkins on the *4th International Rock'n'Roll Weekend Hop*. He was backed throughout by the Cruisers, who coped admirably, even making a decent stab at the vocal harmonies – so much a part of Scott's unique sound.

It has always been a mystery how a man with Scott's talent, his impressive tally of hit records and his charismatic stage act failed to sustain the success that came to him in the early years of his career. He should have been a major star in 1980, but at least the rock'n'roll audiences knew the truth even if the wider world were unaware of what they were missing.

THE STRAY CATS

The Stray Cats were back gigging in London during the second half of October, including appearances at Camden's Music Machine, the Tramshed in Woolwich and as support for the Pretenders at Hammersmith Palais on 20 October. They finished the month on the college circuit, playing university gigs at Uxbridge, Coventry and Birmingham.

Their first record, 'Runaway Boys', produced by Dave Edmunds, was released by Arista early in November, following which they expanded their activities nationwide with club and college dates as far afield as Newcastle, Edinburgh, Exeter, Cardiff and Norwich. They continued gigging right up to 13 December, when the tour terminated after an appearance at Blackpool's Norbreck Castle.

'Runaway Boys' entered the UK charts on 29 November and during a ten-week run peaked at an impressive No.9 over the Christmas period. The Stray Cats were enormously popular at this time, but more importantly were highly influential to a new generation of teenagers, for many of whom rockabilly music would become a lifetime obsession.

JOHNNY & THE HURRICANES

October 1980		
22 Harrow Weald Jules		
Tour organiser unknown		

German resident Johnny Paris and his Hurricanes were ideally located to undertake live shows within Europe and consequently there was no element of surprise when he turned up on a bill with fellow American Gary 'US' Bonds.

This must have been an emotional reunion for the two men who had been intense rivals on the British charts almost twenty years earlier.

GARY 'US' BONDS

October 1980	November 1980	
22 Harrow Weald Jules	1 Carshalton Chick-a-Boom	
Tour organiser unknown		

Bonds was an unlikely figure to appear in England during the autumn of 1980. He had not played live here since touring with Duane Eddy, Gene Vincent and the Shirelles back in 1963, and in truth his records were rarely played on the rock'n'roll club circuit.

On the show at Harrow Weald, he shared billing with Johnny & The Hurricanes, but performed a considerably more contemporary act than his old fans expected. His repertoire still included his early hits like 'Quarter To Three' and 'New Orleans', but his overall sound was now closer to Bruce Springsteen than Chubby Checker. It was the eternal problem: Bonds had moved on, but his audience had not.

CHUBBY CHECKER

It was announced that Chubby Checker would be making a one-off UK appearance at the Venue in London's Victoria on 29 October. The show must have been more than just an idle rumour, as it was advertised briefly in the music press, but without any explanation the adverts disappeared. His place at the Venue was taken by Tom Paxton, hardly a worthy replacement for twist enthusiasts.

MICKEY GILLEY

Mickey Gilley flew into London during the last week in October to promote his new country album, *That's All That Matters To Me*, and the hit movie, *Urban Cowboy*. A sizeable feature was printed in *Melody Maker*, while listeners to BBC Radio London heard him interviewed by Stuart Colman on his *Echoes* programme.

Gilley was well-known to rock'n'roll enthusiasts both as a cousin of Jerry Lee Lewis, and for a series of recordings made in similar style. Like Charlie Rich, however, his rock'n'roll days seemed to be over and his current popularity as a country artist did not inspire much confidence that his old rockers like 'Drive-In Movie' would be on the set list, were he to appear live in the UK. Nevertheless, he seemed keen to set up some concerts, even offering to waive his usual $15,000 a night fee and play for expenses. His British fans are still waiting for him to return, however.

BUZZ & THE FLYERS

After the success of their UK stage debut at the Royalty in August, Buzz & The Flyers returned for further gigs in the autumn, including an appearance at Dingwalls on 2 November. They again went over well and included 'Little Pig', 'You Crazy Gal You', Sonny Fisher's 'Pink And Black' and a country-flavoured 'Scars Of Love' in a varied and enthusiastic act.

GROOVEY JOE POOVEY

November 1980		
13	Southgate	Royalty
14	Coventry	*unknown venue*
15	Carshalton	Chick-a-Boom
Tour organiser — Dick Grant		

The arrival of the magnificently named Groovey Joe Poovey for a short UK tour followed the now-familiar pattern. A native of Dallas, Texas, Joe had been a regular performer on the *Big D Jamboree* radio show in the Fifties, and had cut both rockabilly and country for a string of small labels, as well as pursuing a parallel career as a disc jockey. His 1958 Dixie recording, 'Ten Long Fingers', had become available to British collectors through a 45 released on the tiny Injun label in 1972, and was now a firm favourite with the rockin' crowd.

Joe arranged a seven-day absence from his duties with Radio KJIM in Fort Worth and made his European stage debut in Belgium. He was overwhelmed by the interest in his otherwise dormant career as a rock'n'roller but initially performed mainly standards, fearing that his own material would not be recognised so far from home.

By the time Joe had spent a couple of days recording in London with the Dave Travis Band, he seemed more relaxed and his three UK dates all went well. Backing on the live shows was provided by the Blue Cat Trio and by the time they reached Carshalton's Chick-a-Boom Club, Poovey was right in the groove. As well as 'Good Rockin' Tonight' and 'Great Balls Of Fire', he now included his own songs like 'Move Around' and 'Sweet Louella', before climaxing with a powerful 'Ten Long Fingers' and a prolonged version of the gospel classic, 'Will The Circle Be Unbroken'.

BILL HALEY & HIS COMETS

A lengthy European tour had been arranged for Bill Haley, commencing at the beginning of November in Germany and including two English dates at the Hammersmith Odeon on 20 November and then three days later at Carshalton's Chick-a-Boom Club, but sadly time had run out for the father of rock'n'roll.

The bombshell news of Haley's failing health was contained in the *News of the World* of 26 October. In a front-page story, they claimed that he was seriously ill in hospital with a suspected brain tumour, and although his UK manager, Paddy Malynn, was guarded in his comments, the German promoter, Wolfgang Rocksch was considerably more outspoken, claiming, 'Bill will never perform again.' Tragically, his prediction proved to be correct.

On 9 February 1981, Bill Haley died in his sleep of an apparent heart attack at his home in Harlingen, Texas. Six typed chapters of his unfinished life story were found beside him. The man who brought rock'n'roll to the world was gone for ever, but his music and the memories of his fabulous live shows will live on far into the future.

ERNIE MARESCA

Now, this is an interesting one! Maresca was primarily a songwriter and responsible for rock'n'roll classics like Dion's 'Runaround Sue' and 'The Wanderer'. Like Dion, he was brought up in the Bronx district of New York and in 1962 released his own single, 'Shout! Shout! (Knock Yourself Out)', which became a smash hit in the States. It fared less well in the UK, but did receive a good deal of radio play at the time.

In 2004 *Now Dig This* printed an interview with Maresca by writer/broadcaster Spencer Leigh, in which Ernie talked about his brief career as a recording artist. He concluded by mentioning that he did a show in England during 1979 or 1980, which remains a complete mystery and of which no corroborative evidence has so far been found...

CHAPTER NINE

1981

Nothin' Shakin'
But The Leaves On The Tree

Rock'n'roll had acquired a new problem. There had been a substantial increase in attendances at rock'n'roll events since the rise of rockabilly, as a result of which fashion-conscious teenagers wearing 'cat clothes' in the style of Fifties' America were now mixing uneasily with the traditional rock'n'roll audiences.

Ironically, it had been the generation gap which had helped create rock'n'roll in the first place, but the teenagers of the Fifties and Sixties had grown up and were now aged in their thirties or even forties. They had beaten off the mods and the hippies and studiously ignored the disco dancers. A completely self-contained rock'n'roll circuit had been created with venues, bands, magazines and specialist record companies catering for every rocking need.

Not surprisingly therefore, the Teddy boys objected to the influx of young cats who had been brought to the music by the sounds of Ray Campi, Mac Curtis or the Stray Cats, and who were changing the format within the club scene by introducing more and more obscure rockabilly music. Fights were not uncommon. Resentment and prejudice were building, and over the next few years the live rock'n'roll scene would split in two as parallel weekenders catered for the two factions.

The well-established Caister festivals were at the heart of the problem. As time went on, more and more rockabilly cats had attended and the older rock'n'roll fans eventually felt sufficiently excluded that the Bristol Rock'n'Roll Society launched a rival weekender at Brean Sands in April 1981, capturing a good slice of the Teddy boy audience with a line-up which starred Charlie Gracie, Sonny Fisher and Eddie Fontaine.

This was Fontaine's first trip to the UK, and 1981 also saw British stage debuts by Frankie Ford, Jimmy McCracklin and the highly popular Johnny Burnette Rock'n'Roll Trio, featuring original guitarist, Paul Burlison.

Within the club scene there was now an extraordinary range of choices. Venues were everywhere and established acts like Flying Saucers, Johnny & The Roccos and Matchbox had all the work they could handle. Shakin' Stevens finally cracked the big time with 'This Ole House' in February and took his own brand of rock'n'roll into the pop music mainstream, where he would enjoy an incredible ten years of hits, but sadly he found it necessary to turn his back on the rock'n'roll circuit, never to return. A young group, the Jets, charted during the year, first with 'Sugar Doll' and then in October took 'Yes, Tonight Josephine' into the Top 30. New bands were springing up all around the country.

Rockabilly and neo-rockabilly groups continued to prosper in the wake of the Stray Cats, with the Rockats, Blue Cats, Polecats and Flash Cats all active in the UK during 1981. The Shakin' Pyramids toured with Shaky, as well as recording an album with Lonnie Donegan.

In addition, the London pub circuit featured a number of fine bands which were not strictly rock'n'roll acts: Diz & The Doormen, Juice On The Loose, the Electric Bluebirds and Red Beans & Rice all contained plenty of rock'n'roll within their shows, and each commanded an enthusiastic following.

There was so much rock'n'roll to find during 1981 that there was no need to look elsewhere for live music. Nevertheless, US visitors as diverse as Ella Fitzgerald, Buddy Rich, John Sebastian and the Sir Douglas Quintet performed here, as did Ray Charles, Louisiana Red, the Staple Singers, Muddy Waters and James Brown. For country fans there were visits by Emmylou Harris, Bobby Bare, Tammy Wynette, Boxcar Willie and Skeeter Davis. Without doubt, 1981 had something for everyone.

BOBBY HELMS

Indiana-born Bobby Helms enjoyed a long career in country music, where he is remembered for hit records such as 'Fraulein' and 'My Special Angel'. He recorded rockabilly during the Fifties, including 'Long Gone Daddy' and 'Tennessee Rock'n'Roll', and eccentric small-time promoter Dick Grant had him lined up for a British tour in January 1981.

Helms was scheduled to arrive on 27 January and the Dave Travis Band cancelled other work so as to be available to tour with him up to 15 February. Nothing materialised, however, and Grant claimed that lack of bookings caused the late cancellation.

Bobby did finally make it to Britain in 1993 for a country festival in Yorkshire, but never performed his rockabilly act in the UK. He died on 19 June 1997 in Bloomington, Indiana.

MARVIN RAINWATER

February 1981			March 1981		
19	Southgate	Royalty	7	Carshalton	Chick-a-Boom
Tour organiser — Showstopper Promotions					

Marvin was back in Europe again and played two rockabilly shows for his British fans backed by the Blue Cats. His last appearances at the Chick-a-Boom had been something of a watershed, in that he had finally realised that there was an audience for his old-style rocking material and now he had the advantage of a young, energetic and highly competent group behind him.

The Blue Cats really drove him on through an act containing the very best of his rocking repertoire including 'Baby Don't Go', 'I Dig You Baby', 'Roving Gambler', the hypnotic 'Mr. Blues' and even obscurities like 'Hot And Cold' and 'Boo Hoo', which he would never have included a few years earlier. The boisterous reaction of the audience indicated that they knew all the songs extremely well and from the look on Marvin's face he was enjoying the experience as much as they were.

Whole lotta Marvin at the Southgate Royalty.

THE STRAY CATS

Brian Setzer, Lee Rocker and Slim Jim Phantom were back for a lengthy tour of colleges and ballrooms, which commenced at Southampton University on 27 February. They headlined wherever they played and were supported throughout by the Barracudas. Four nights at the Lyceum in London at the end of March, which also featured the Pirates, were completely sold out and the Stray Cats were now unquestionably the hottest ticket in town. The tour ended in Jersey on 28 March.

Their second single, 'Rock This Town', followed 'Runaway Boys' into the UK Top 10 and their Dave Edmunds-produced debut album, *Stray Cats*, was released by Arista on 20 February. This also proved a massive seller and spent five months in the British charts.

ROY ORBISON

It was reported that some dates were being set up for Roy in March 1981 and that he would fly into the UK after taping an episode of *Dukes Of Hazzard* in Los Angeles. The itinerary would include appearances in Birmingham, at the Circus Tavern in Purfleet, and a week at Blazers in Windsor from 15 to 21 March. The project did not come to fruition and Orbison fans in the Windsor area had to make do with the Stylistics instead.

JERRY LEE LEWIS

Jerry Lee Lewis has never appeared at a rock'n'roll weekender in the UK and it is increasingly unlikely that he ever will. The sheer cost of transport and accommodation for his sizeable entourage, plus his not-inconsiderable fee, make it a financial non-starter. Back in March 1981, however, a very real attempt was made for Lewis to headline the *5th International Rock'n'Roll Weekend Hop* at Caister and for a short period it seemed that the promoters had got their man.

Showstopper Promotions announced that Lewis would appear over the weekend of 20-22 March along with Mac Curtis and the young rockabilly band, Buzz & The Flyers. Interestingly, below Jerry Lee's name, it was stated: *'The living legend playing a wild 100% rock'n'roll show'*.

Before long, an announcement was made that Lewis had withdrawn following a contractual problem concerning the guarantee of a purely rock'n'roll performance. Apparently, he now intended to pursue a country music career and had no plans to undertake a rock'n'roll tour at this time. This was an interesting contrast to the country music venues, where he was regularly criticised for playing too much rock'n'roll. There are some talents which are just too large to be boxed-in and pigeonholed in this way. Jerry Lee will not be told.

MAC CURTIS

March 1981		
19	Southgate	Royalty
21	Caister	Ladbroke's Holiday Centre
24	Carshalton	Chick-a-Boom
Tour organiser — Showstopper Promotions		

Mac rocks! Carshalton, 24 March.

When Jerry Lee Lewis withdrew from the *5th International Rock'n'Roll Weekend Hop* at Caister, it was first rumoured that Carl Mann would replace him as headliner. This did not work out either, so eventually Mac Curtis and New York rockabilly band Buzz & The Flyers headed up the weekender along with Crazy Cavan & The Rhythm Rockers, the Polecats, Flying Saucers, the Jets, Shades, CSA and the Stargazers.

Mac was backed by the Rhythm Hawks and gave

a classy performance including 'Granddaddy's Rockin' ', 'You Ain't Treatin' Me Right' and 'If I Had Me A Woman', interspersed with his more recent recordings such as 'Hot Rock Boogie' and 'The Hucklebuck'.

His stay in the UK was brief, but Curtis found time to squeeze in a recording session for Hot Rock Records before travelling to Caister.

BUZZ & THE FLYERS

Unlike their contemporaries, the Stray Cats, there were no hit records to generate media interest when Buzz & The Flyers made their third UK visit within a year.

They played the Royalty, Southgate on 12 March and subsequently clocked up London appearances at Camden, Fulham, Victoria and Canning Town, while at Carshalton's Chick-a-Boom they opened for Mac Curtis. The only time that they ventured far from the capital was for the *5th International Rock'n'Roll Weekend Hop* at Caister, and here again they were billed alongside Mac Curtis. The Caister audience loved them and they provoked the greatest frenzy of the weekend, with at one point seemingly more people on stage than off.

THE DRIFTERS

March 1981			May 1981		
27	Enfield	Starlight	1	Cleethorpes	Pepper's
29	Poole	Arts Centre	6-8	Caerphilly	Diamond
30	London	Talk of the Town	13-16	Luton	Caesar's Palace
April 1981			21	Inverness	Eden Court
1-25	London	Talk of the Town	22	Aberdeen	Capitol
			23	Edinburgh	Playhouse
			26-30	Frimley Green	Lakeside
			June 1981		
			1-6	Birmingham	Night Out
Tour organiser — Henry Sellers					

All seemed quiet within the ranks of the Drifters. The line-up of Johnny Moore, Clyde Brown, Ray Lewis and Louis Price had now remained constant for more than a year, while the efforts of promoter Henry Sellers ensured a full datebook of cabaret bookings, so, on the face of it, everything was fine and dandy. However, problems were bubbling away below the surface. The Drifters were no longer the Number One draw on the circuit, and before long there would be major changes for this most enduring group whose roots stretched back to the great Clyde McPhatter in 1953.

TV appearances
Unknown (ITV)   7 May 1981

JIMMY McCRACKLIN

March 1981		
29 London	100 Club	
	Tour organiser unknown	

Photo by Paul Harris

Pianist, blues shouter and rock'n'roller Jimmy McCracklin preceded four dates in Scandinavia with a short visit to London and an entertaining gig at the 100 Club, along with lanky tenor saxophonist Wild Willie Moore.

McCracklin proved to be a fine pianist and, although much of his act was 12-bar blues, he varied the mood, threw in some vibrant instrumentals, had the audience clapping and yelling, and sent the rock'n'roll fans home happy thanks to some superb piano pounding on 'Georgia Slop' and a fine rendition of his 1958 hit, 'The Walk'.

SONNY FISHER

April 1981		
4-5	Brean Sands	Pontin's Holiday Village
9	Southgate	Royalty
10	Catford	Squire
	Tour organiser — Bristol Rock'n'Roll Society	

Sonny's second UK visit was almost a mirror image of his first. The only significant difference was that this time he jointly headlined the *International Rock'n'Roll Festival* at Brean Sands along with Charlie Gracie and Eddie Fontaine, in addition to his club dates in the London area. The Brean Festival was a rival event to the now well-established Caister weekender and followed the same holiday camp format.

He was again paired with Johnny & The Roccos and powered his way through his Starday recordings including 'Sneaky Pete', 'Pink And Black', 'Hold Me' and 'Little Red Wagon'. Also included in his act were the songs that he had cut in London on his first visit, and 'Mathilda', 'If You Leave Me Tonight I'll Cry' and 'Shake That Thing' blended well with the older material. Sonny had grown a nifty moustache and, allied with his habit offstage of smoking through a long cigarette holder, now appeared suspiciously like a rocking

Terry Thomas.

Fisher never returned to Britain, which is extraordinary given the quality shown on his two short tours. He did, however, enjoy some measure of success in France and even visited Spain as late as 1993. Long periods of ill health and a habit of disappearing completely from time to time did not help his cause, but it is probably fair to say that even the adulation heaped upon him by European audiences did not fully compensate for the disillusionment he felt towards the music business in general. He passed away in Texas on 8 October 2005.

CHARLIE GRACIE

April 1981		
4-5	Brean Sands	Pontin's Holiday Village
11	Carshalton	Chick-a-Boom
	Tour organiser — Bristol Rock'n'Roll Society	

Charlie Gracie worked with Johnny & The Roccos on this short tour, appearing as joint headliner with Eddie Fontaine and Sonny Fisher at the *International Rock'n'Roll Festival* at Brean Sands. Others on the bill included Gina & The Rockin' Rebels, Flying Saucers, Crazy Cavan & The Rhythm Rockers, Johnny Storm & Memphis, Freddie 'Fingers' Lee, the Blue Cats, the Jets and Blackcat.

All three Americans performed on the Saturday, and Gracie, smartly attired in a white jacket and black slacks, managed to generate the same level of excitement as at the Caister weekender the previous year. As well as his usual act, he included superb versions of 'Bo Diddley' and 'Get A Job', further enhancing his reputation with an exhilarating performance.

Each of the Americans proved so popular at Brean that they were brought back at 4.00 pm on the Sunday for an extra couple of numbers each. After Eddie Fontaine's slot, Gracie led the three on stage together for a knockabout version of 'Shake, Rattle And Roll', which was fully appreciated by the enthusiastic audience.

EDDIE FONTAINE

April 1981		
4-5	Brean Sands	Pontin's Holiday Village
15	Carshalton	Chick-a-Boom
	Tour organiser — Bristol Rock'n'Roll Society	

Eddie Fontaine was best known to British audiences as a result of his brief appearance in the classic rock'n'roll movie, *The Girl Can't Help It*. In addition to a singing career which extended into sophisticated nightclubs, he was also a well-respected character actor who regularly made guest appearances in the top television dramas of the day.

His British debut was at the *International Rock'n'Roll Festival* at Brean

Sands, where he appeared alongside Sonny Fisher and Charlie Gracie, all three Americans performing their main shows on the Saturday night.

Fontaine had movie-star looks and an assured, confident manner about him, although he admitted to being inwardly nervous as to the likely response to his appearance. He opened with 'Cool It Baby', and gave a highly polished performance, working through 'Rock Love', 'Honky Tonk Man', a rocking 'Goodness, It's Gladys' and the slower 'On Bended Knee'. His voice was magnificent, and other highlights of his fine act were 'One And Only', 'It Ain't Gonna Happen No More' and to close, his 1958 US hit, 'Nothin' Shakin' '. He was backed by Johnny & The Roccos.

As he prepared to leave the stage, a stunned Fontaine looked out into the audience and told them, 'I haven't experienced anything like this in 25 years.' He was overwhelmed by the reception.

NEIL SEDAKA

April 1981					
5	Bristol	Colston Hall	18	Aberdeen	Capitol
7	Bournemouth	Winter Gardens	20	Glasgow	Apollo
9-12	Hammersmith	Odeon	22	Manchester	Apollo
14	Liverpool	Empire	23	Birmingham	Odeon
15	Newcastle	City Hall	24	Brighton	Centre
17	Edinburgh	Playhouse	25	Wembley	Conference Centre
Tour organiser — Derek Block					

Neil Sedaka was no longer a chart act but still had a significant following within the UK. He had retained many of his original audience from the Fifties, who had grown up with 'Oh! Carol', 'Breaking Up Is Hard To Do' and 'Happy Birthday, Sweet Sixteen'. His later batch of hit records such as 'Laughter In The Rain' and his 1975 US No.1, 'Bad Blood', had added to his fan base and enabled him to not only perform in theatre venues, but to fill some of the most prestigious concert halls in the land.

If you wanted to hear some commercial rock'n'roll mixed in amongst more contemporary soft rock music, Neil was your man. Not directly relevant to the live club scene as such, he nevertheless remained a positive force, always appearing proud of his rock'n'roll youth and never failing to include at least some of his early hits on each night of the tour.

RICK NELSON

Early in March, adverts appeared in the music press promising three nights at the Venue in London Victoria on 10-12 April, featuring Rick Nelson & The Stone Canyon Band. Tickets went on sale at £4 each and were scheduled as the only UK dates on a lengthy European tour.

By the beginning of April the whole project appeared to have been shelved and he was replaced at the Venue by the Members.

MARVIN RAINWATER

April 1981		
11-17	Prestatyn	Pontin's Tower Beach
18	Wembley	Arena
	Tour organiser — Mervyn Conn	

Marvin was a very late addition to the Saturday bill for the newly sponsored *Silk Cut International Festival of Country Music*. He had started to perform rockabilly again, but this short tour was strictly for the country crowd. He was already working a week-long engagement at Pontin's in Prestatyn when he was pulled into the Wembley line-up along with Bobby Bare, Marty Robbins, Don Gibson, Tom Gribbin, Doc Watson and Melba Montgomery.

Rainwater had the difficult task of following that great showman Marty Robbins, but handled his task admirably, including fiery versions of both 'I Dig You Baby' and 'Whole Lotta Woman'. His moving interpretation of Red Sovine's 'Teddy Bear' was especially well received.

WANDA JACKSON
JERRY LEE LEWIS
CARL PERKINS

April 1981		
17	Wembley	Arena
	Tour organiser — Mervyn Conn	

SOUVENIR BROCHURE
1981

There was a large contingent of rock'n'rollers mingling uncomfortably with the hard-core country fans at Wembley Arena on Good Friday for the *Silk Cut International Festival of Country Music*. The reason was the inclusion of Jerry Lee Lewis, Carl Perkins, Wanda Jackson and Matchbox on a bill that already promised George Jones, Gene Watson, Hank Thompson, Skeeter Davis, Vern Gosdin, Razzy Bailey, Carey Duncan and compere Frank Ifield. From time to time over the years promoter Mervyn Conn had been criticised for the sometimes uneven content of his festivals, but bringing together this formidable array of talent, all on one day, must surely have been his finest hour.

Carl and Jerry Lee share the stage at Wembley.

The running order was segregated, with the rock'n'roll acts closing the show, therefore many of the rockers remained in the bar during the first half, for once allowing the country contingent to enjoy their favourites without the usual interruptions.

Wanda was still a few years shy of reinventing herself and acknowledging her place as perhaps the greatest female rock'n'roller of them all. She stuck with her routine Wembley act, only letting rip on 'Let's Have A Party' – a raunchier version than usual – which was met by tumultuous applause.

After a solid and rocking set from the group Matchbox, Carl Perkins opened with 'Matchbox', and with his four-piece band including sons Greg and Stan, proceeded to enchant the Wembley audience, dropping the pace for 'Turn Around' and belting through 'Boppin' The Blues', 'Rockabilly Fever', 'Honey Don't ' and, inevitably, 'Blue Suede Shoes'.

Kenny Lovelace (guitar and fiddle), Joel Shumaker (guitar), Randy Wilkes (bass) and Ron Norwood (drums) were already in place at 10.00 pm when Jerry Lee strolled on stage unannounced and sat down at the piano. 'I'm Jerry Lee Lewis. Glad to be back in London, England,' he drawled and then raced into a new rocker, 'Keep My Motor Running'. Dressed in a black sweater, blue jeans and cowboy boots, he varied the tempo of the act, moving from a gentle 'Middle-Aged Crazy', into a storming version of 'What'd I Say', including two lengthy piano solos. Then it was back down for 'Over The

Rainbow' and straight into a rhythmic 'Folsom Prison Blues'. Many of the audience were on their feet dancing, while several of the country fans were heading for the exits. There was some friction between the two factions at this point, but when had rock'n'roll, and Jerry Lee in particular, not provoked strong reactions of this type?

He roared through 'High School Confidential', then frustrated the masses by slowing again into 'Thirty-Nine And Holding', before closing out with 'Great Balls Of Fire' and 'Whole Lotta Shakin' Goin' On'. The piano stool was dispatched across the stage and Jerry, with microphone in hand, clambered on top of the piano for the final verses.

With the crowd at fever pitch, Carl returned and Jerry delighted everyone present with the words, 'We'd like to do a couple of Carl's tunes,' and then launched into a prolonged medley of 'Matchbox' and 'Blue Suede Shoes', Perkins adding his distinctive vocals and guitar to the proceedings. This was a highly enjoyable night, only marred by some sound problems from time to time.

TV appearances (Jerry Lee Lewis)
Sing Country (BBC2)   17 April 1981 (screened 13 July 1981)

TV appearances (Carl Perkins)
Sing Country (BBC2)   17 April 1981 (screened 13 July 1981)

JOHNNY CASH

April 1981		
20 Wembley	Arena	
Tour organiser — Mervyn Conn		

Easter Monday's line-up for the *Silk Cut International Festival of Country Music* was headlined by the Johnny Cash Show. The remainder of the acts included Joe Sun, Jimmy C. Newman, Diane Pfeifer, Jim & Jesse, Paul Kennerley, Frank Ifield and Raymond Froggatt. Clearly, this was not one of Mervyn Conn's strongest line-ups, but presumably the box office strength of Cash meant that there was no requirement for expensive support.

Dressed in black and backed by the Great Eighties Eight, Johnny opened with 'Ring Of Fire' and 'Sunday Morning Coming Down'. He included a new song, 'Without Love', written by his son-in-law, Nick Lowe, and in a lengthy set also performed memorable versions of 'Forty Shades Of Green', 'Folsom Prison Blues', 'Ghost Riders In The Sky' and 'Orange Blossom Special', the latter a duet with June Carter. It was truly a family occasion, with daughter Cindy Cash performing 'City Of New Orleans', eleven-year-old John Carter Cash butchering 'Battle Of New Orleans', and the whole family including Carlene Carter singing 'Will The Circle Be Unbroken' as the grand finale.

TV appearances
Sing Country (BBC2)   20 April 1981 (screened 27 July 1981)

FATS DOMINO

| **April 1981** |
| 19-20   Hammersmith   Odeon |
| Tour organiser — Patrick Malynn |

Photo by Paul Harris

More than three years had slipped away since Fats Domino last played for British audiences and he returned to Hammersmith with a nine-piece band which comprised Lee Allen (sax), Walter Kimble (sax), Herb Hardesty (sax), Roger Lewis (sax), Mac Davies (trumpet), Jimmy Moliere (guitar), Carlton 'Frog' McWilliams (bass), David Douglas (guitar) and Mike Brown (drums). The supporting act was Shades.

Domino's stay in London was brief, as his two dates at Hammersmith were part of a wider European tour. The second show fell on Easter Monday and drew a sizeable, if not quite capacity, crowd. The band opened with a jazzy instrumental before Fats joined them on stage, smartly attired in a three- piece white suit and brown tie. All of his fingers were adorned with a selection of chunky diamond rings.

The show opened with 'I'm Walkin'' and moved effortlessly through the many hit records, including fine interpretations of 'Walking To New Orleans', 'Blue Monday' and 'Blueberry Hill'. At one point, Gerry Tilley, guitarist for Bill Haley's Comets on the 1979 tours, joined the proceedings while Domino briefly left the stage for refreshment.

The act climaxed with a New Orleans-style 'When The Saints Go Marching In', during which the brass section paraded through the theatre while Fats hammered away at the piano. This led into a more restrained 'Sentimental Journey', in which Domino bounced the grand piano across the stage and walked off to thunderous applause.

Two standard-length encores were succeeded by a further 30 minutes of unscheduled rock'n'roll as Fats and his band responded to the wishes of the audience. By the time he finally departed, he had performed 23 songs in a set that lasted only a little short of two hours. This was one of Fats Domino's finest performances in the UK.

DON EVERLY

May 1981		
10-16 Caerphilly	Diamond	
Tour organiser unknown		

This was another of rock'n'roll's forgotten moments. Don flew into the UK for a week of cabaret in Caerphilly, backed by the Dead Cowboys, yet received no publicity whatsoever. The management of the Diamond club were flexing their muscles and booking a string of international stars, much as the Batley Variety Club had done just a few years earlier.

However, the elder Everly Brother was still making little headway with his solo career, and the audience craved the old hits and not an evening of contemporary material. This was a conundrum for which he would never find a satisfactory solution.

At the conclusion of the final performance of the week, the Welsh audience rose to its feet and serenaded Don with a burst of 'We'll Keep A Welcome In The Hillsides'.

LINK WRAY

May 1981		
26 Wembley	Arena	
Tour organiser — Harvey Goldsmith		

This was just a cameo appearance, but a pretty high-profile one nevertheless. Bruce Springsteen & The E Street Band were bludgeoning their way through a marathon concert at Wembley, when, to the surprise of everybody in the auditorium, the menacing figure of Link Wray joined them onstage for a prolonged version of Sonny Curtis's 'I Fought The Law'.

JOHNNIE ALLAN

Swamp pop rocker Johnnie Allan had spent a week in the UK in March 1978 when his recording of 'Promised Land' was bubbling under the British charts. He returned for a few days in mid-June 1981 as part of a European holiday and took the opportunity to engage in some promotional work, which included a radio appearance in the London area on Stuart Colman's *Echoes* show.

CHUCK BERRY

July 1981		
26	Knebworth	Festival Site
Tour organisers — George Wein and Capital Radio		

The ill-fated second *Capital Radio Jazz Festival,* having been wiped out in 1980 following the serious fire at Alexandra Palace, reinvented itself twelve months later under the banner, *Capital Jazz on Clapham Common.* This year they were going for broke with over 100 names allegedly confirmed, including Chuck, Muddy Waters, Herbie Hancock, Lightnin' Hopkins, Jimmy Witherspoon, Mel Torme, Nellie Lutcher and Lionel Hampton. The event was to take place over a nine-day period, with Berry performing on the opening and closing nights, 18 and 26 July.

Disaster struck again when Scotland Yard received information that serious disturbances were being organised and that persons unknown were planning to disrupt the concerts. The promoters were forced to cancel the first weekend altogether, and after much soul-searching shrank the event down to just the final two days and relocated to Knebworth Park in Hertfordshire. Chuck headlined on the final night as scheduled, on a bill which also contained Muddy Waters, George Melly, Zoot Money and Sarah Vaughan.

Berry made little concession to the jazz flavour of the occasion, performing his usual act, but did throw in a reflective 'Everyday I Have The Blues'. He did not seem to be concentrating very much and performed 'Let It Rock' twice, the second version coming only five songs after he had already sung it! Ingrid Berry did her usual 'Tina Turner' spot and the backing musicians included Jim Marsala (bass) and Lou Martin (piano).

JOHNNY LEGEND

The highly eccentric figure of Johnny Legend turned up in London during mid-August looking for gigs. He was well-known in the seedier parts of Los Angeles as a broadcaster, pornographer, wrestling promoter, movie historian and Rollin' Rock recording artist.

His UK debut took place at Dingwalls in Camden Town on 18 August backed by Shotgun (masquerading as the Skull Caps). Legend himself had a long, straggly beard and was dressed in the full uniform of a Confederate army officer, while his act was very much on the theatrical side of rock'n'roll, mainly featuring songs that were decidedly unsuitable for a family audience. He was joined onstage by members of the Polecats and the Blue Cats, and perhaps inevitably by rock'n'roll's other great eccentric, Screaming Lord Sutch. There was also a scantily clad young lady who draped herself in turn around the various band members, microphone stands and indeed anything vertical that she could find. The whole chaotic proceedings concluded with everyone up on stage for a truly original rendition of 'Tear It Up'.

Legend hung out in Europe until early November, making a few other appearances in the UK, including gigs at Southend, Carshalton and Fulham.

GARY 'US' BONDS

August 1981	
14-15 London	The Venue
Tour organiser unknown	

Suddenly Gary 'US' Bonds was back in fashion, entirely as a result of his association with Bruce Springsteen, a long-time fan who had produced and played on his comeback album, *Dedication*, and had appeared with him on stage as recently as 11 July at Big Man's West, a nightclub in New Jersey. Any connection with Springsteen, a genuine rock music superstar, could only help to drag Bonds back into the spotlight, and the capacity audiences who turned out for his two nights at the Venue were mainly Springsteen followers curious to see what all the fuss was about, rather than the rock'n'roll contingent, who in the main showed little interest in his re-emergence.

Backed by his own six-piece band, perhaps unsurprisingly the set list included contemporary rock material like Bob Dylan's 'From A Buick 6', Jackson Browne's 'The Pretender' and a R&B workout on 'Just Like A Child', a song written by his daughter. Despite the modern slant to his act, Bonds still closed the proceedings with a rip-roaring 'Quarter To Three'.

RAY CAMPI

August 1981			September 1981		
26	Carshalton	Chick-a-Boom	3	Wellingborough	British Rail
27	Camden Town	Dingwalls	4	Chelmsford	Odeon
29	Yate	Stars and Stripes	5	Stevenage	Bowes Lyon House
31	Southgate	Royalty	**October 1981**		
			31	Fulham	Greyhound
Tour organiser — David Harris (Rollin' Rock UK)					

Since his first trip to the UK in 1977, Ray Campi had managed to successfully pursue his revitalised career as a rockabilly performer and recording artist while at the same time maintaining the security of his full-time job as an English teacher in Los Angeles. Overseas tours had been scheduled during school vacations and until now Ray had enjoyed very much the best of both worlds. Decision time came in Spring 1981, when he received a substantial offer from a booker in Finland for a massive tour of that country linked in with additional shows in Sweden, the Netherlands and England that would prove financially very lucrative and would keep him working in Europe from July through to the end of 1981.

After much soul-searching, he negotiated an unpaid leave of absence for the fall semester, thereby forfeiting his position of seniority within the school system and took off along with fellow Rollin' Rock artist Jimmie Lee Maslon for what turned into something of a nightmare. The arrangements were chaotic. Both men slept on a floor for several nights, while there were continual squabbles over money and, perhaps worst of all, they were landed with musicians who seemed more interested in heavy metal than rockabilly, and more interested in furthering their own careers than providing backing for the two Americans. Maslon was fired by the Finnish promoter and departed to try and find some gigs in France, leaving Ray to battle on with little cooperation and often open hostility from two members of the band. Finally, they arrived by boat at Harwich for the English leg of the tour, only to find that the organisation was just as chaotic and that the Finnish booker, who was supposed to be taking care of the arrangements, had elected to stay at home, leaving them to fend for themselves.

In addition to Ray and the now-reinstated Jimmie Lee Maslon, another Rollin' Rock act, Ravenna & The Magnetics, were in London. They too were struggling to find enough gigs to keep themselves afloat, and for all concerned this was a highly difficult and often embarrassing time trying to find work, accommodation and some semblance of order while a long way from home. It did, at least, successfully come together at the Greyhound in Fulham for Campi's final performance of this highly forgettable tour. Yet another Rollin' Rock act, Johnny Legend, joined Campi, Ravenna & The Magnetics and Jimmie Lee Maslon for a wild, rockin' evening which did at least ensure that they departed back to Finland in high spirits, if considerably poorer than they had anticipated.

JIMMIE LEE MASLON

Minnesota-born Maslon moved with his family to California in 1972 and at the age of fourteen became the first artist to record for Ronny Weiser's Rollin' Rock label. Later, he participated on several of Ray Campi's sessions, also for Rollin' Rock.

Jimmie Lee accompanied Campi on his chaotic tour of Finland in the summer of 1981, eventually being fired by the promoter in some desperate cost-cutting measure. He linked up with Campi again for his British dates, performing his own set, as well as accompanying Ray on guitar. The fragmented nature of the tour gave British fans very little opportunity to assess the ability of Jimmie Lee Maslon, a lost opportunity for all concerned.

BUDDY KNOX

Buddy had planned to visit the UK during August to further an album project with the Dave Travis Band. Willie Jeffery set up a few live dates for him to cover the expenses for his visit, including an appearance at Dingwalls in Camden Town which was scheduled for 28 August. Late on, he withdrew and the recording session had to be shelved until a future date.

JERRY LEE LEWIS

Shortly after Jerry Lee's Wembley appearance at Easter, it was announced that he would return to the UK for a six-night engagement at the Diamond club in Caerphilly, South Wales from 6 to 12 September 1981.

Sadly, this booking was never fulfilled, because on 30 June, he was rushed to hospital in Memphis with a two-inch tear to his stomach which required immediate surgery. Despite predictions that he had a less than 50/50 chance of survival, he came through two major operations, eventually leaving hospital on 29 August.

Lewis explained: 'God is with me in many strange ways. He's taken two of my kids and my mama and daddy, but he ain't never whipped me like this.' He celebrated by instructing his road manager, J.W. Whitten to purchase two new cars, a Corvette and a customised Cadillac. The computerised hospital bill for his 61-day stay was eight foot long and totalled $69,000. Jerry signed it without more than a cursory glance at the details. The man has always had style.

RAVENNA & THE MAGNETICS

The Magnetics were based around Seattle, Washington and performed for several years with a constantly changing line-up, which at one time briefly included bluesman Sunnyland Slim on piano. Gradually, they evolved into a rockabilly outfit fronted by the exotically named Ravenna du Mane (alias Freda Johnson), and in 1981, when their second Rollin' Rock album was released, travelled to Europe for a promotional tour.

The line-up which arrived in Britain during early September was Ravenna (vocals), Al Kaatz (guitar), Darnell Kellman (saxes), Bob Connole (drums) and Steve Flynn (piano), along with British bass player, Paul Diffin. They opened their tour at the Greyhound, Fulham in support for the Roy Sundholm Band. The problem was that they were just not well enough known, even amongst the rockabilly crowd, and, unlike the Stray Cats a year earlier, were unable to generate sufficient publicity to kick-start their careers in Britain.

They played several poorly publicised and often chaotic gigs around the London area, and also found work in Germany, but it was always a struggle to even cover their food and accommodation. They finally departed mid-November shortly after a gig at Dingwalls, Camden Town where they supported the new British rockabilly band, Restless. On 31 October, they shared billing with fellow Rollin' Rock artists Ray Campi, Jimmie Lee Maslon and Johnny Legend at the Greyhound, Fulham.

Charlie whips up the crowd at the Southgate Royalty.

CHARLIE GRACIE

September 1981		
17	Camden Town	Dingwalls
18	Leeds	*unknown venue*
19	Leicester	De Montfort Hall
24	Southgate	Royalty
Tour organiser — Paul Barrett		

Charlie's second UK visit of 1981 was primarily for the purpose of recording a new album with Dave Travis, and between 21 and 25 September, they were hard at work at Southern Music in London on the *Amazing Gracie* project.

A short tour was set up to offset Charlie's travel and living expenses, with backing supplied by Johnny & The Roccos. The most notable gig took place at Leicester, where he headlined on a sizeable package along with Freddie 'Fingers' Lee, Shades, the Strollers and the Dragons.

THE CHIFFONS

September 1981		October 1981	
27-30 Caerphilly	Diamond	1-5 Caerphilly	Diamond
Tour organiser unknown			

It was announced during August that New York girl group, the Chiffons would be visiting the UK and that RCA planned to reissue their 1963 hit, 'One Fine Day', to tie in with the tour. Sometimes in such circumstances sufficient interest can be generated to revive otherwise dormant careers, but there was no such luck for the Chiffons. This was only their second time in Britain, their first tour having taken place in 1967, and the group had since shrunk to a trio. Judy Mann had departed, leaving Barbara Lee, Sylvia Peterson and Pat Shelley to perform in cabaret, and the wider public remained blissfully unaware of their presence.

THE DRIFTERS

September 1981		November 1981	
28-30 Wythenshawe	Golden Garter	19-21 Farnworth	Blighty's
October 1981		22 Southport	New
1-3 Wythenshawe	Golden Garter	25 Chippenham	Golddiggers
5-10 Birmingham	Night Out	27 Cleethorpes	Pepper's
12-17 Watford	Bailey's	28 West Malling	Greenways
21-22 Charnock Richard	Park Hall Hotel	30 Purfleet	Circus Tavern
23-24 Enfield	Starlight	**December 1981**	
25-31 Windsor	Blazers	1-5 Purfleet	Circus Tavern
		9-12 Caerphilly	Diamond
Tour organiser — Henry Sellers			

This long tour of all the top cabaret venues in the UK brought down the curtain on the Drifters line-up of Johnny Moore, Clyde Brown, Ray Lewis and Louis Price. Confusion reigned as manager Faye Treadwell ended the eleven-year agreement with promoter Henry Sellers, who had worked tirelessly for so long to keep the ever-changing group among the top earners on the cabaret circuit.

Johnny Moore, who was plainly exhausted, initially headed home to New York, but by 1982 was back in the UK, where, along with Clyde Brown and another ex-Drifter, Joe Blunt, he formed a new group, Johnny Moore & Slightly Adrift.

Meanwhile, the future of the Drifters was now uncertain.

JON & THE NIGHTRIDERS

Surf guitarist Jon Blair had created California's second wave of guitar instrumental rock'n'roll in 1979, when their recording 'Rumble At Waikiki' exploded onto the club scene in Hollywood, giving them a regional hit and, for a while, something of a cult following.

The Dutch Rockhouse label issued an album by the band, and they made a brief promotional visit to the UK, as well as playing one live show at Dingwalls in Camden Town on 15 October. Then as now, surfing proved to be a more popular pastime in California than in Camden.

JOHNNY CASH

October 1981					
			20	London	Royal Albert Hall
17	Edinburgh	Playhouse	21	St. Austell	Cornwall Coliseum
18	Manchester	Apollo	22	Poole	Arts Centre
19	Sheffield	City Hall	23-24	Caerphilly	Diamond
Tour organiser unknown					

Johnny Cash spent six days in Scotland between 12 and 17 October recording material for a 1981 Christmas TV Special. Despite biting winds, filming took place at Falkland Palace in Fife, during which he sang 'Footprints In The Snow' and performed a duet with Andy Williams on 'Greensleeves'. Filming was also held in Kinghorn, Elie and St. Monans, while the Edinburgh concert was recorded as part of the same project. US television broadcast *Christmas In Scotland* on CBS on 9 and 10 December, with Cash also performing 'Ring Of Fire', 'Keep On The Sunny Side' and 'Reverend Mr Black'. June Carter, John Carter Cash and Carlene Carter also appeared.

Backing on the live shows was provided by the Great Eighties Eight, featuring Bob Wootton and W.S. Holland.

FATS DOMINO

October 1981	
31	Hammersmith Odeon
Tour organisers — Patrick Malynn and Straight Music	

New Musical Express, with their usual eye for detail, announced this one-off London date as Domino's first appearance in the UK for a year, seemingly unaware that he had appeared at the same venue as recently as Easter Monday. This was just the sort of misinformation that rock'n'roll fans had to contend with on a regular basis and was extremely frustrating.

Fats delivered his usual show with no surprises. His ten-piece band were as tight as ever and the audience were served up a quality act climaxing with a superb 'Ain't That A Shame'. There was a danger that Domino was being taken for granted, such was the overall quality of his live work.

RONNIE HAWKINS
LONNIE MACK

Several abortive attempts had been made over the years to bring Rompin' Ronnie to Britain, but he had yet to appear live on a British stage. This state of affairs seemed to have finally been resolved when it was announced in June that Hawkins would jointly headline with Frankie Ford at the *6th International Rock'n'Roll Weekend Hop* at Caister over the weekend of 6-8 November.   He would be accompanied by his band, the Hawks, comprising John Lewis (guitar), Stan Szelest (piano), Dave Lewis (drums), Ken King (bass) and, as an unexpected bonus, Lonnie Mack, architect of guitar instrumental hits 'Memphis' and 'Wham!', who was taking a sabbatical from his own career and temporarily working as a sideman for Ronnie.

The initial negotiations with the Caister organisers, Showstopper Promotions, were conducted by Willie Jeffery, a long-time Hawkins fan, one-time president of his UK fan club, and himself a future rock'n'roll promoter. When it became clear that a firm deal was in the offing, Steve Thomson, Hawkins's Canadian manager, flew into the UK to iron out the details.   To book Ronnie and his entourage involved considerable financial outlay and, although initially everyone seemed satisfied, the project gradually unravelled as the full impact of the financial cost hit home.

Ronnie Hawkins & The Hawks were replaced at Caister by Rocky Burnette, Paul Burlison and a reconstituted line-up of Johnny Burnette's Rock'n'Roll Trio, while the long-suffering fans of the Hawk were left to lick their wounds and wait still longer to see the big man perform.

FRANKIE FORD

November 1981		
5	Southgate	Royalty
6-7	Caister	Ladbroke's Holiday Centre
Tour organiser — Showstopper Promotions		

New Orleans piano rocker Frankie Ford was far from just another in the ever-lengthening parade of 'great unknowns' being placed before British rock'n'roll audiences.   There were hit records, even million sellers, on his CV and he was a confident and experienced entertainer.   However, he had never enjoyed the luxury of a British chart hit and therefore had still to build his reputation as a live performer on this side of the Atlantic.

His UK stage debut took place at the Royalty, Southgate on the eve of the Caister weekender.   The piano was covered in flowers as a welcoming gesture and Frankie, contrasting an orange scarf with his otherwise all-black stage clothes, created an immediate impression with a piano style reminiscent of Fats Domino and a strong vocal delivery.   His act included several of Domino's hits but it was Ford's own material like 'You Talk Too Much', 'Roberta' and 'Alimony' which went over best.   His closing number was 'Sea Cruise', his signature tune and a fitting climax to an outstanding performance.

Backing was provided by Johnny & The Roccos both at Southgate

Frankie at Caister.

and at Caister, where Frankie co-starred with Johnny Burnette's Rock'n'Roll Trio on a bill which also included, Blackcat, the Deltas, Shades, Flying Saucers and Crazy Cavan & The Rhythm Rockers.

JOHNNY BURNETTE'S ROCK'N'ROLL TRIO

November 1981	
7 Caister	Ladbroke's Holiday Centre
Tour organiser — Showstopper Promotions	

The Rock'n'Roll Trio originally comprised brothers Johnny and Dorsey Burnette and guitarist Paul Burlison. Based in Memphis, Tennessee they were early exponents of the rockabilly sound and in April 1956 travelled to New York to seek their fortune, landing a spot on the national TV show, *Ted Mack's Amateur Hour*. This break led them to a recording contract with Coral and a series of superb recordings which are now regarded as some of the finest rockabilly ever committed to wax. Sadly, they were not commercially successful at the time and the Rock'n'Roll Trio disintegrated all too soon. However, both of the Burnette brothers went on to enjoy solo success, Johnny even touring the UK in 1962 and 1963, before his death in a tragic

Johnny Burnette's Rock'n'Roll Trio at Caister.
Left to right: Johnny Foster, Tony Austin and Rocky Burnette wearing his dad's jacket!

boating accident the following year. Dorsey passed away in 1979. Paul Burlison had been largely inactive as a performer prior to the relaunch of the Trio for the *6th International Rock'n'Roll Weekend Hop* at Caister some twenty-five years after their original shot for fame.

It was an inspired decision to re-form the Rock'n'Roll Trio. Their classic recordings were now universally acclaimed throughout the rock'n'roll world, and in addition to Burlison, Johnny's son, Rocky Burnette, was brought in as vocalist, along with drummer Tony Austin, bass player Johnny Black and guitarist Johnny Foster. British guitarist Bob Fish was also added to the line-up, making it a six-man trio, but nobody was about to query such mathematical inaccuracies.

It was about as authentic as was possible: Johnny Black, the younger brother of Bill Black, had replaced Dorsey in the later days of the Trio and even appeared with them in the movie, *Rock, Rock, Rock*. Tony Austin, a cousin of Carl Perkins, had played drums for the Trio many times on the road, while for Rocky Burnette this was the opportunity for him to claim his birthright.

Their show was a great success. Johnnny and Dorsey had not lived long enough for British audiences to enjoy the privilege of hearing the likes of 'The Train Kept A-Rollin' ', 'Rock Billy Boogie' and 'Tear It Up'. Rocky made up for this by including all the Rock'n'Roll Trio classics in the act and, with three guitars whipping up a storm, the sizeable crowd were swept away as 'Lonesome Train (On A Lonesome Track)', 'Honey Hush', 'Please Don't Leave

Me' and 'You're Undecided' washed over them. This was like a rebirth for Rocky Burnette, who is enormously proud of his family heritage and, although he and Paul would return many times to play for European audiences, this was unquestionably the most authentic line-up of the Rock'n'Roll Trio ever to appear in Europe.

For one man however, the weekend was destined to finish on a sour note. Johnny Foster, a friend of Burlison, enjoyed his trip to Europe a little too much, getting very drunk after the show and being mugged for all his money. Perhaps not surprisingly, he got hell from his wife when he arrived home and never returned to Europe again.

JOHNNY & THE HURRICANES

November 1981		
12	Carshalton	Chick-a-Boom
13	London	Rock Garden
19	Stroud	Marshall Rooms
20	Brighton	Lewes Road Inn
22	Melton Mowbray	Painted Lady
Tour organiser unknown		

Decca had recently issued a *Best of Johnny & The Hurricanes* album and this was therefore an ideal opportunity for a few UK dates to be included as part of a wider European tour.

The latest line-up of Hurricanes comprised Johnny Paris (saxophone and vocals), Terry Clemson (guitar), Keith Evans (bass), Rod de'Ath (drums) and Lou Martin (keyboards) and at Carshalton's Chick-a-Boom, it was the volume of their playing that made the greatest impression. As the band commenced the opening number, a tsunami

Johnny & The Hurricanes blast Carshalton.

of sound enveloped the audience, forcing them to collectively step backwards as if in response to a physical attack. Paris worked through his usual repertoire, but the oppressive volume was never addressed and by the end of the evening the dazed crowd staggered into the street, each checking that their ears were not bleeding from the onslaught.

For the performance at London's Rock Garden, Johnny & The Hurricanes were supported by the rockabilly band, Restless.

THE BMT's

Another young New York rockabilly band, the BMT's (short for Brooklyn-Manhattan Transfer) played some club dates including London venues at the Rock Garden and Dingwalls during November. Described as 'a punked-up rockabilly band', they were a vehicle for vocalist Freddy Frogs, who had developed a stunning version of 'Crazy Little Mama', which was generally the high point of their act, alongside a more restrained interpretation of Johnny Ace's 'Pledging My Love'.

GARY 'US' BONDS

November 1981		
24	Hammersmith	Odeon
25	Manchester	Free Trade Hall
27	Edinburgh	Odeon
28	Newcastle	City Hall
Tour organiser — Harvey Goldsmith		

As part of a European tour, Bonds returned to Britain with the same six-piece band who had backed him on his two sell-out London gigs in August. Ensign Records released a *Greatest Hits* album, and once again his Bruce Springsteen connection ensured both publicity in the music press and healthy ticket sales, the Hammersmith concert selling out several days in advance.

It was the newer songs that Bonds was anxious to perform, and at Hammersmith 'Jole Blon', 'From A Buick 6', his latest single 'It's Only Love', and a saxophone-inspired 'This Little Girl' were highlights, along with his early hits 'New Orleans', 'Quarter To Three' and 'School Is Out'. He had taken several steps to update both his music and his image, but he still rocked like crazy.

TV Appearances
The Old Grey Whistle Test (BBC2)   3 December 1981

THE STRAY CATS

Now firmly positioned in the big league, the Stray Cats had recently completed a world tour and a series of gigs in the US with the Rolling Stones, before arriving in December for their first British shows since March. 'Stray Cat Strut' had given them a third major hit in the UK, and although record sales were now levelling off on this side of the Atlantic, they were still highly popular in France and Japan.

Eight gigs were played between 13 and 22 December, commencing at Bristol Locarno and concluding at Rock City in Nottingham, where Screaming Lord Sutch supplied the support. Their second album, *Gonna Ball*, was released by Arista to tie in with the tour.

CHAPTER TEN

1982

Crackerjack

By 1982, the craze for rockabilly music had largely subsided and even the Stray Cats were moving towards more of an R&B sound. Popular music never settles long in one place and rockabilly was no longer the coolest trip for the teenage trendies. This situation was inevitable, but even though the main spotlight had moved elsewhere, what remained was a significantly larger audience for all forms of authentic rock'n'roll music than had existed a few years earlier.

The Caister weekender was now into its fourth year of operations but seemed to be slowly losing momentum. The organisers, Showstopper Promotions, were pulling in much larger crowds for soul weekenders and were not perhaps as committed long-term to the cause of rock'n'roll as the Teddy boy promoters John Hale and Ken Hersey who fronted the Bristol Rock'n'Roll Society and their rival weekender, which in 1982 moved down to Cornwall. Hale publicly queried the need for 'businessmen' to be running rock'n'roll at all, but sadly there were to be several examples in the years to come of fans-turned-promoters who demonstrated no business skills at all. What was really wanted, of course, was a combination of both fan and businessman.

Another example of the changing times was the rebranding of the Royalty Ballroom in Southgate, which for several years had been London's premier rock'n'roll venue. By the end of 1982, it had been completely refurbished and was now boasting nightly cabaret in the main auditorium, a disco and cocktail lounge, its name changed to the Elephant Fun House (later the Pink Elephant). Rock'n'roll fans could see that the writing was on the wall and the great days at the Royalty were over.

The competing weekenders inadvertently brought about a ludicrous clash of dates when, on the second weekend of October, fans had to choose between a massive line-up of more than twenty acts at Perranporth in Cornwall, headed by Buddy Knox, Janis Martin and Ronnie Hawkins, or the chance to witness the newly re-formed Blue Caps at the Caister weekender, which had relocated a few miles along the coast at Great Yarmouth. Then, to make matters worse, Hawkins and the Blue Caps went head-to-head on club dates in London four days later. Intense and not always friendly rivalry between rock'n'roll weekenders would become a feature of the rocking world for many years to come.

The Jets enjoyed further chart success in 1982 and their album, *100% Cotton* reached the Top 30. They embarked on a nationwide tour in May with support from Coast To Coast. Shakin' Stevens was churning out hit singles with unfailing regularity and took 'Oh Julie' to the very top of the British charts, while Darts starred in a musical, *Yakety Yak*, which opened in November. It was based on the lives of record producers Jerry Leiber and Mike Stoller, and both men put in an appearance on opening night.

A fascinating array of talent was to be seen in Britain from outside the rock'n'roll world. Acts as diverse as Barry Manilow, Frankie Laine, Doug Sahm, Gene Pitney and Stevie Ray Vaughan rubbed shoulders on the concert trail, while the choice for country music lovers included the likes of Porter Wagoner, Willie Nelson, Ferlin Husky and Stonewall Jackson.

There was an even more interesting choice for lovers of black music. As well as club dates by Etta James, Louisiana Red, Fontella Bass and Esther Phillips, a *San Francisco Blues Festival* at Dingwalls in June included Troyce Key, Little Frankie Lee and J.J. Malone. Saxophonist Hal Singer serenaded the diners at Pizza Express in London's Soho, while on a memorable evening at the 100 Club in May, B.B. King came out of the audience to jam with former Sun bluesman, Rosco Gordon. Once again, live music enthusiasts could enjoy an abundance of good music and plenty of rock'n'roll.

THE BMT's

The BMT's were holed up in London for the first three months of 1982. Eddie Von Bach (lead guitar), Tommy Byrnes (rhythm guitar), Luigi Scorcia (bass) and Vinni Matland (drums) spent four weeks out on the road backing Bo Diddley, as well as playing several gigs on their own at Victoria, Camden Town, Islington and Fulham. It is probable that vocalist Freddy Frogs joined them for their own shows.

THE COASTERS

January 1982		February 1982	
22 Caerphilly	Diamond	4 Camden Town	Dingwalls
24-30 Frimley Green	Lakeside		
31 Harrow Weald	Middlesex & Herts		
Tour organiser — Henry Sellers			

Carl Gardner, Earl Carroll and Ronnie Bright returned to the UK as a trio, Jimmy Norman having left the group since their last visit in December 1974. They were scheduled to open with two nights at Caerphilly, but persistent rain resulted in severe flooding and the cancellation of the second show. At Lakeside Country Club their efforts were hampered by an inadequate backing group, but for the performance at Dingwalls everything finally came together, so the audience were treated to the full Coasters experience and the humour contained in such classic songs as 'Charlie Brown', 'Yakety Yak' and 'Poison Ivy'.

It remains a mystery why the Coasters, with the depth of material available to them and the theatrical nature of their act, were never able to get closer to the level of popularity attained by the Drifters, who at their peak were by far the most popular club act in the UK.

BO DIDDLEY

February 1982						
11	Camden Town	Dingwalls		24	Brentwood	*unknown venue*
	London	100 Club		25	Aberdeen	*unknown venue*
12	London	School of African &		26	Dundee	*unknown venue*
		Oriental Studies		27	Liverpool	Adam's
	Brixton	Fair Deal		28	Redcar	Coatham Bowl
13	Norwich	Univ. of East Anglia		**March 1982**		
14	Harrow Weald	Middlesex & Herts		2	Brentford	Red Lion
15	Putney	Half Moon		3	Manchester	University
17	Derby	Blue Note		4	London	100 Club
18	Sunderland	Close Encounters		5	Reading	Hexagon
19	Birmingham	Carlton		6	Greenham	
20	Coventry	General Wolfe			Common	USAF
22	Deptford	Albany Empire		7	London	Lyceum
23	Croydon	Sinatra's			Camden Town	Dingwalls
				8	Putney	Half Moon

Tour organiser — Stallion Artists

Bo's many British fans had seen little of their man over the past decade. Two club dates in London during March 1979 and a short spot on the Carl Perkins package a year earlier were inadequate exposure for one of rock'n'roll's true originators. This lengthy tour did much to redress such a sorry state of affairs and was generally successful. Backing was provided by the BMT's from New York.

The quality of the shows was somewhat uneven. At his best, Diddley was unstoppable and at the exotically named London School of African and Oriental Studies, he won over the audience with a masterful display of hypnotic guitar work and dramatic vocals. At East Anglia University, he attracted a sizeable and varied crowd who seemed intrigued by this large man wearing an equally large, wide-brimmed hat and carrying a strange oblong guitar. He alternately played up to the audience, meandering into guitar histronics and feeding them scraps of brilliance from 'Road Runner' and 'I'm A Man', before concentrating fully for a superb 'Mona'.

The show at Brixton was somewhat spoiled owing to lengthy problems with the amps, but included a steamy 'I'm A Man', a long, rambling 'Just Like Bo Diddley Do' and an exciting 'Hey Bo Diddley' as an encore. This was the pre-opening night at the Fair Deal, which was being touted as London's newest and most ambitious music venue.

Bo was appealing not just to the rock'n'roll faithful, but also to the sizeable punk movement, and the climax of the tour found him at London's Lyceum Ballroom headlining over the Meteors and Roddy Radiation & The Tearjerkers. At Dingwalls, the support was provided by the Cannibals.

TV Appearances
Unforgettable (Channel 4)   23 February 1982 (screened 8 July 1983)

JOHNNY & THE HURRICANES

February 1982			27	Carshalton	Chick-a-Boom
17	Harrow Weald	Middlesex & Herts	28	Putney	Half Moon
18	Brighton	Lewes Road Inn	**March 1982**		
19	Camden Town	Dingwalls	3	Blackpool	Norbreck Castle
20	Twickenham	Black Dog	4	Swindon	Brunel Rooms
23	Leeds	Fforde Green Hotel	5	Tolworth	Recreation Centre
24	Coventry	General Wolfe	17	Brixton	Fair Deal
Tour organiser unknown					

Johnny Paris and his UK Hurricanes, Terry Clemson (guitar), Keith Evans (bass), Rod de'Ath (drums) and Lou Martin (keyboards), returned for further dates commencing in Harrow on 17 February.

Paris had also been scheduled to perform at London's newest music venue, the Fair Deal in Brixton, on 22 February, but that gig had to be cancelled as the decorators were still painting the building. The show at Dingwalls also featured Johnny Storm.

He did finally make it to the Fair Deal on 17 March on a bill with Sixties' beat groups the Tremeloes, the Troggs and the Merseybeats, immediately following dates in the Netherlands, Belgium and Germany. It seems likely that, on a few of the British shows, Paris worked with local pick-up bands if the budget would not stretch to include the UK Hurricanes.

ROY ORBISON

March 1982			April 1982		
26	Crawley	Leisure Centre	1	Middlesbrough	Town Hall
27	Caerphilly	Diamond	2	Bridlington	Royal Hall
28	Poole	Arts Centre	4	Southport	New
29	St. Austell	Cornwall Coliseum	5-8	Windsor	Blazers
30	Southend	Cliffs Pavilion	9	Frimley Green	Lakeside
31	Jersey, CI	Behan's (West Park Pavilion)	12	Wembley	Arena
Tour organiser — Mervyn Conn					

Roy arrived back in the UK on 24 March for a series of one-nighters. His band comprised Bucky Barrett (lead guitar), Jackie Cook (rhythm guitar), Jim Johnson (bass), Marshall Pierson (drums), Jim Kirby (keyboards) and backing vocalists Kim Cole, Barbara South and Richard Law. His personal

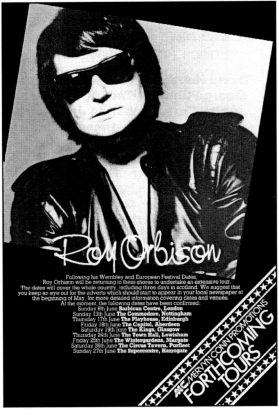

Following his Wembley and European Festival Dates,
Roy Orbison will be returning to these shores to undertake an extensive tour.
The dates will cover the whole country, including three days in scotland. We suggest that
you keep an eye out for the adverts which should start to appear in your local newspaper at
the beginning of May, for more detailed information covering dates and venues.
At the moment, the following dates have been confirmed:
Sunday 6th June **Barbican Centre, London**
Sunday 13th June **The Commodore, Nottingham**
Thursday 17th June **The Playhouse, Edinburgh**
Friday 18th June **The Capitol, Aberdeen**
Saturday 19th June **The Kings, Glasgow**
Thursday 24th June **The Town Hall, Lewisham**
Friday 25th June **The Wintergardens, Margate**
Saturday 26th June **The Circus Tavern, Purfleet**
Sunday 27th June **The Supercentre, Harrogate**

manager Terry Elam (percussion) completed the line-up, while support for much of the tour was provided by Carey Duncan.

His act rarely changed and audiences knew precisely what to expect. At Caerphilly he looked fit and slim. Dressed completely in black from head to toe and playing a black guitar, Roy opened with 'Only The Lonely'. The capacity crowd went wild and he seemed taken aback by the reception. One by one he worked through the familiar hits of the Sixties: a superb 'In Dreams' led into a surprisingly raunchy 'Mean Woman Blues', then on through 'Blue Angel', 'Lana' and 'Candy Man'. The end of 'Crying' created such a roar of approval from the audience that he sang it again.

Except for a few mumbled words of thanks, Orbison did not speak, letting his songs communicate for him. His Elvis tribute, 'Hound Dog Man', a rocking 'Ooby Dooby' and a brilliant 'Working For The Man' kept up the momentum. Then it was on to 'That Lovin' You Feelin' Again', 'Down The Line', 'It's Over' and two renditions of his show-stopper, 'Oh, Pretty Woman'. The crowd, which included many young people, enjoyed a memorable evening in the presence of a consummate performer.

Following his appearance at Camberley, Roy was whisked over to Europe for shows in Sweden and the Netherlands before returning to appear at Wembley on the *Silk Cut International Festival of Country Music* on Easter Monday. He co-starred with Don Williams, Jeannie C. Riley, the Nashville Superpickers and Lonnie Donegan, and proved enormously popular, earning no fewer than six standing ovations from the notoriously difficult Wembley audience.

The following day he flew to Germany and then Switzerland, returning to his home in Hendersonville, Tennessee in time to celebrate his 46th birthday with his family on 23 April.

TV Appearances
Sing Country (BBC2)   12 April 1982 (screened 26 July 1982)

JOHNNY MOORE & SLIGHTLY ADRIFT

March 1982			May 1982		
27	Burton	Allied	1	Batley	Frontier
28	Harrow Weald	Middlesex & Herts	3	Birmingham	Millionaires
30-31	Batley	Frontier	5-6	Chesterfield	Aquarius
April 1982			9	Harrow Weald	Middlesex & Herts
1-3	Batley	Frontier	12	Camden Town	Dingwalls
7	Chippenham	Golddiggers	13	Rhyl	CJ's
25	Nottingham	Commodore	14-15	Farnworth	Blighty's
27	Cleethorpes	Pepper's	27	Norwich	Talk of the East
28-31	Batley	Frontier	30	Frimley Green	Lakeside
			June 1982		
			1-5	Frimley Green	Lakeside
Tour organiser — Henry Sellers					

The UK's most consistently popular touring group, the Drifters, had imploded at the end of 1981. Presumably, the unbearable pressures of the road had finally taken their toll because their mentor, Faye Treadwell, widow of long-term manager George Treadwell, returned to the States with no apparent plans for the group to continue.

Back home, she found that the position was even more complex. If the UK Drifters, fronted by Johnny Moore, were the direct descendants of the group which recorded for Atlantic Records, then there were still plenty of rival 'Drifters' who were eager to exploit the situation for their own gain. Benny Anderson, Albert Fortson and Wallace Ezzard had toured the UK in 1967 as members of Bill Pinkney's 'Original Drifters'. Fifteen years later, they were in Charleston US District Court trying in vain to convince a jury that they were not in breach of patent by using that name. Other groups of 'Drifters' still performed openly throughout North America with varying degrees of authenticity.

Meanwhile Johnny Moore, Clyde Brown and Joe Blunt now rebranded as Johnny Moore & Slightly Adrift were soon back out on Henry Sellers' cabaret circuit. For Moore, it was always a constant struggle to project himself as a separate entity from the Drifters, with whom his whole career was entwined. 1982 would be his last real attempt to succeed as a solo performer.

EDDIE BOND

April 1982		
2-3	Caister	Ladbroke's Holiday Centre
10	Tadcaster	Forge Inn
Tour organisers — Showstopper Promotions and Dick Grant		

Eddie Bond was a well-respected figure in the Memphis area, having enjoyed a long career working as both a radio deejay and a country music artist. Back in the mid-Fifties, he had toured with Elvis, Carl Perkins and Johnny Cash, and during 1956 recorded rockabilly for Mercury Records. He made his British stage debut at the *7th International Rock'n'Roll Weekend*

Hop at Caister, backed by the Dave Travis Band.

He arrived in the UK on 29 March, which allowed valuable rehearsal time and the first show at Caister went over well.

Bond was an undemonstrative performer, but a fine country singer and the quality of his Mercury material carried him home, as the audience loved 'Flip, Flop Mama', 'Boppin' Bonnie', 'Slip, Slip, Slippin'-In' and his version of Sonny Fisher's 'Rockin' Daddy'.

The following night was less successful. A large section of the audience were psychobillies impatiently waiting to see the Polecats, and they succeeded in disrupting Eddie's portion of the show.

After Caister, Bond stayed in London and commenced work with Dave Travis on an album project for Rockhouse Records, before travelling up to Yorkshire for a gig at the Forge Inn at Tadcaster – a most unlikely venue for authentic Memphis rockabilly. That evil ole rock'n'roll music they said would never last was still spreading out across the globe and turning up in the most unlikely places.

RAVENNA & THE MAGNETICS

The Magnetics had only just about survived their highly chaotic debut tour of the UK in September and October 1981. Even though they had struggled to make any real impact with British audiences, they did at least alert Showstopper Promotions, organisers of the Caister weekenders, as to their potential and earned themselves a spot on the *7th International Rock'n'Roll Weekend Hop* in April 1982.

They appeared on a varied bill which was headlined by Eddie Bond, and which also included Crazy Cavan & The Rhythm Rockers, Dynamite, the Polecats, the Cruisers, the Strollers, Rebel Rouser and the Fantoms. The split within the rock'n'roll world was exacerbated by further friction between the Teddy boy followers of Cavan and the rockabilly supporters of the Polecats, making for a highly charged and at times edgy weekend.

BILLY SWAN

Four years on from Billy's last appearance in the UK, he was still a part of the Kris Kristofferson show, contributing rhythm guitar as well as performing an opening set before Kris came on stage.

When Kristofferson headlined the *Silk Cut International Festival of Country Music* on Good Friday, 9 April on a bill which also included Guy Clark, Jerry Foster, the Dillards, Carey Duncan and Cynthia Clawson, Swan was allocated only enough time for three songs, but included a lovely ballad, 'Lay Down And Love Me', and a raunchy 'I Can Help' before his boss took over the proceedings.

TV appearances
Sing Country (BBC2)   9 April 1982 (screened 26 July 1982)

JERRY LEE LEWIS

April 1982		
11 Wembley	Arena	
Tour organiser — Mervyn Conn		

After Jerry Lee's tremendous success in 1981 on the *Silk Cut International Festival of Country Music*, he was rebooked for Easter Sunday and flew into Gatwick Airport on 8 April with an entourage which included his eighteen-year-old daughter, Phoebe, and musicians Ken Lovelace (guitar and fiddle), Joel Shumaker (guitar), Randy Wilkes (bass) and Ron Norwood (drums).

The Wembley festival had now been a regular fixture in the calendar for fourteen years and was probably at its peak in the early Eighties. The event had expanded across Europe, and Jerry Lee played in Rotterdam, Frankfurt, Berlin, Gothenburg and Zurich as well as Wembley, and was in good form throughout.

An amusing example of Lewis's unpredictable behaviour was demonstrated at the pre-festival banquet in London. Photographer Graham Barker leaned across the table to engage him in conversation and made reference to his 1981 duet with Carl Perkins. Jerry took exception to his comments, grabbed his tie and pulled him down onto the table while pointedly explaining that he

The Killer raises hell at Wermbley.

did not want to hear talk of other singers in his presence.

At Wembley, Lewis closed the show on a bill which included Marty Robbins, Lloyd Green, Terri Gibbs, Razzy Bailey and Ronnie Prophet. He wore a black velvet jacket, white shirt, tie and jeans and opened with a longer-than-usual version of 'Rockin' My Life Away'. A beautiful rendition of 'You're The One Rose' had been requested by Chas Hodges and was followed by another ballad, 'Thirty-Nine And Holding', before the tempo increased for 'Me And Bobby McGee' and – unexpectedly – 'Good News Travels Fast', a song that he had never performed in the UK before.

A bluesy treatment of 'Georgia On My Mind' was followed by some great piano-work on 'What'd I Say' and a punchy 'C.C. Rider'. The pace dropped for three more country songs before 'Drinking Wine Spo-Dee-O-Dee' got the full rocking treatment and led into a superb 'Old Black Joe'. Just as the audience were starting to get out of control, he cut back on the throttle for 'Over The Rainbow' and then roared into 'Great Balls Of Fire'.

Jerry seemed in no hurry to finish and moved into a surprisingly tight version of 'Chantilly Lace' with some tasty piano solos and then the pick of the whole night, a haunting 'I'm So Lonesome I Could Cry'. At that point, promoter Mervyn Conn walked on stage and explained that the show was running well over schedule. Lewis gave him a withering look before hammering out an abbreviated 'Whole Lotta Shakin' Goin' On' and a tempting snippet of 'You Can Have Her' to close off another excellent appearance.

Shortly after this European tour, further tragedy struck Jerry Lee Lewis. His estranged fourth wife, Jaren, drowned in a friend's swimming pool in Collierville, Tennessee on 10 June 1982.

TV Appearances
Sing Country (BBC2)   11 April 1982 (screened 19 July 1982)

THE BLASTERS

A Californian rockabilly band with strong blues, R&B and country influences, the Blasters were the support act for Nick Lowe on a lengthy tour of colleges and ballrooms commencing at Leeds Polytechnic on 29 April. The group comprised Dave Alvin (vocals and guitar), his brother Phil Alvin (vocals and guitar), John Bazz (bass), Gene Taylor (piano) and Bill Bateman (drums).

F-Beat Records released their 1981 album, *The Blasters*, and a single, 'I'm Shakin' ', to coincide with the tour. They gave a good account of themselves with a high-energy act that included 'American Music', 'So Long Baby, Goodbye' and Dave Alvin's own composition, 'Marie Marie', which had given Shakin' Stevens his first UK Top 20 hit in 1980.

The Nick Lowe package wound up on 17 May at Hammersmith Palais, but the Blasters remained in London and played two further dates at Dingwalls and at the Venue.

THE DRIFTERS

May 1982			June 1982		
7-8	Enfield	Starlight	1-5	Watford	Bailey's
9	Lewisham	Concert Hall	6	Newmarket	Cabaret
11	Stockton	Fiesta	7-12	Wythenshawe	Golden Garter
12-15	Batley	Frontier	13	Ashington	Leisure Centre
16	Warrington	Parr Hall	14	Derby	Assembly Rooms
17-18	Glasgow	Morley's	15	Chippenham	Golddiggers
19	Lochgelly	Centre	16	Worthing	Pavilion
20	Preston	Guildhall	17-19	Purfleet	Circus Tavern
24-29	Birmingham	Night Out			
30	Southend	Cliffs Pavilion			
31	Watford	Bailey's			
Tour organiser — Derek Block					

With long-time Drifters manager Faye Treadwell back in the States and Johnny Moore, Clyde Brown and Joe Blunt working the live music circuit for promoter Henry Sellers under the name Johnny Moore & Slightly Adrift, the two other current members of the long-running group were understandably feeling similar sentiments themselves. Ray Lewis and Louis Price were left without management, bookings or any worthwhile prospects. However, not for the first time, the strong brand name of the Drifters ensured that the group would rise from the ashes and eventually carry on as if nothing had happened.

Two high-profile ex-Drifters, Ben E. King and Bill Fredericks, returned

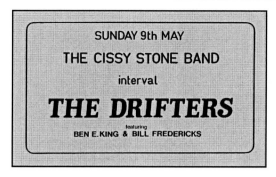

SUNDAY 9th MAY

THE CISSY STONE BAND

interval

THE DRIFTERS

featuring
BEN E.KING & BILL FREDERICKS

to the fold and promoter Derek Block had little difficulty in setting up a sizeable tour of concert and cabaret venues with the new line-up of King, Fredericks, Lewis and Price. At Lewisham Concert Hall they delivered an entertaining and highly energetic act, containing the pick of the Drifters' favourites. King's rich tenor voice and Fredericks' warm and pleasing personality ensured a successful evening, and the sheer professionalism of the four men overcame the internal conflicts which had so nearly brought about the end of the legendary group.

TV Appearances
The Big Top Variety Show (Thames)   21 July 1982
The Video Entertainers (Granada)   3 August 1982

LEE ALLEN

May 1982		
20 Camden Town	Dingwalls	
21 London	The Venue	
Tour organiser unknown		

Saxophonist Lee Allen was a giant of New Orleans rock'n'roll who had played on classic hits by the likes of Fats Domino, Lloyd Price and Little Richard. More recently, he had featured on the Blasters' album and now flew into London to appear with them on their two club dates. He was, of course, employed as a sideman, but on each show took centre stage to perform his 1958 US hit, 'Walkin' With Mr. Lee', hence his inclusion within these pages.

Allen also undertook some promotional work on his own account during his short stay in the UK, taping an interview with Stuart Colman for his *Echoes* show, which was aired on BBC Radio London on 27 July.

THE STRAY CATS

The wheels on the Stray Cats bandwagon may not have quite fallen off, but were clearly loosening when Brian Setzer, Slim Jim Phantom and Lee Rocker flew into London for two gigs at the Marquee Club on 24 and 25 May. The second album, *Gonna Ball*, had not been the massive seller that had been predicted and Setzer was not slow to make his views known.

He openly admitted to personality clashes within the group and revealed that he did not talk to the other two very often. Legal problems had arisen with their former management, so Lee was handling their bookings until everything was resolved. The Marquee Club was a small venue for an act of their stature and the discord within the ranks was plain for all to see.

They sounded tired, disillusioned and empty, even though the more partisan sections of the audience conspired to believe otherwise. The recent move from rockabilly towards R&B was clearly a mistake and their version of Jimmy Reed's 'Baby What You Want Me To Do' was lamentable. Familiar material like 'Rumble In Brighton', 'Stray Cat Strut' and 'Rock This Town' went down well enough, even though Setzer's guitar seemed uncharacteristically glum but they did at least close strongly with a steamy version of Eddie Cochran's 'Somethin' Else'.

ROY ORBISON

June 1982					
6	London	Barbican	20	Glasgow	King's
10	Scarborough	Futurist	24	Lewisham	Concert Hall
11	Ipswich	Gaumont	25	Margate	Winter Gardens
12	Chatham	Central Hall	26	Purfleet	Circus Tavern
13	Nottingham	Commodore	27	Harrogate	Conference Centre
14	Batley	Frontier	29	Bristol	Colston Hall
17	Edinburgh	Playhouse	30	Birmingham	Odeon
18	Aberdeen	Capitol	**July 1982**		
			3	Brighton	Dome

Tour organiser — Mervyn Conn

While Roy was in Britain back in March/April, promoter Mervyn Conn was already planning a more extensive tour for June 1982. He rightly assessed Orbison as a consummate professional who always delivered a quality performance, as well as being an artist with enduring popularity at the box office.

His band was unchanged from his earlier visit, namely Bucky Barrett (lead guitar), Jackie Cook (rhythm guitar), Jim Johnson (bass), Terry Elam (percussion), Marshall Pierson (drums), Jim Kirby (keyboards), plus Kim Cole, Barbara South and Richard Law on background vocals.

The tour was enjoyable if unremarkable. Orbison did not deal in surprises, but sent each successive audience home happily humming along to his hit records. It was an exercise in nostalgic entertainment of the highest order.

BO DIDDLEY

June 1982		
9	Camden Town	Dingwalls
10	Nottingham	Rock City
11	Edinburgh	Playhouse
12	Leeds	Fforde Green Hotel
13	Gillingham	Coach House

Tour organiser — Stallion Artists

Like London buses which seem always to arrive in pairs, so too, the charismatic Mr. Diddley. Only three months after concluding a gruelling month of one-nighters, he was back in the UK for a further five nights which

Bo at Nottingham's Rock City, with daughter Tammi on drums.

took him from London to Edinburgh and then back down to Kent – a very tiring experience, but nothing out of the ordinary for a man who had lived on the road for more than a quarter of a century.

Bo's act had not, of course, changed since March but his backing group on this occasion were Offspring, comprising Scott Smith (guitar), Ron Haughbrook (bass) and his daughters Tammi McDaniel (drums) and Terri McDaniel (keyboards), who gave his music a funkier edge.

DON EVERLY

June 1982		
19 Lincoln	Sincil Bank	
Tour organiser — Lincoln City FC		

David Mitchell, commercial manager of Lincoln City, was the driving force behind an ill-fated two-day 'Country & Western' festival held at the football club's Sincil Bank Stadium. Billie Jo Spears and Skeeter Davis headlined the opening night, Friday, 18 June, while Spears and Don Everly topped the bill on the Saturday, appearing with an array of British country acts like Poacher and the Frank Jennings Syndicate.

The weather was appalling. There were two days of torrential rain and, with the Friday a normal working day, the attendances were way below the projected numbers. Don Everly performed a pleasing set and was reported to be underrated as a solo act, but all the newspaper coverage of the

BILLIE JO SPEARS
DON EVERLY
Plus top British Country and Western acts

LIVE ON STAGE
at

LINCOLN CITY FOOTBALL CLUB
Saturday, 19th June, 1982
Commencing 12 noon to 10.30 p.m.

Tickets in advance from only £4.
Lincoln City FC Commercial Department, Sincil Bank, Lincoln.
Tel. 42333 or at the door.

event concentrated on the heavy losses incurred by the already cash-strapped football club. Mitchell was suspended by the club amidst claims of bouncing cheques and one emotive headline read 'Billie Jo gets the bad cheque blues'. The total loss was reported to have been £40,000.

CLARENCE 'FROGMAN' HENRY

The Frogman's visits to the UK had been few and far between, and at one point he had vowed never to return, so upset was he about bogus acts impersonating him in the Northern clubs. This all changed however, following a chance meeting with record producer Geoffrey Gill in New Orleans.

Clarence flew into the UK during September and spent a week recording a new album for Stuge Music, a company directed by Gill and Stuart Littlewood, the Manchester-based manager of Max Boyce and Cannon & Ball.

TV Appearances
Unforgettable (Channel 4)   ? September 1982 (screened 6 January 1983)

LINK WRAY

September 1982		
17 London	The Venue	
Tour organiser unknown		

Link Wray was always something of a mysterious figure and, despite his connections with the rock'n'roll of the 50's, his appeal extended to a much wider audience, which included contemporary rock music fans and even some brain-damaged lovers of heavy metal.

This one-off gig at London Victoria's Venue created little interest amongst rock'n'roll enthusiasts and even less coverage by the music press, who conspired to ignore it completely.

NEIL SEDAKA

September 1982			14	Edinburgh	Playhouse
30	Bristol	Colston Hall	15	Sunderland	Empire
October 1982			16	Wembley	Conference Centre
1	St. Austell	Cornwall Coliseum	18	Reading	Hexagon
4	Manchester	Apollo	19	Brighton	Dome
6-7	London	Dominion	20	Cardiff	St. David's Hall
9	Birmingham	Odeon	22	Scarborough	Futurist
11	Glasgow	Apollo	23	Harrogate	Conference Centre
12-13	Aberdeen	His Majesty's	24	Liverpool	Empire
Tour organiser — Derek Block					

The activities of Neil Sedaka were of little interest within the increasingly insular world of rock'n'roll. Much of his act contained the contemporary pop music which had restored his name to the charts during the Seventies, but his obvious affection for the early material ensured that on every live show he would find space to include at least some of his original rock'n'roll hits. For this reason, he continues to warrant our attention.

This was another quality tour playing sizeable venues. Every night, Sedaka's audiences would file out of the theatre having been fully entertained by a master showman and with the sounds of 'Oh! Carol', 'Breaking Up Is Hard To Do' or even 'I Go Ape' ringing in their ears.

BUDDY KNOX
JANIS MARTIN

October 1982		
9-10	Perranporth	Perran Sands Holiday Village
Tour organisers — Bristol Rock'n'Roll Society and Willie Jeffery		

This very ambitious project titled *The Great International Rock & Roll Festival* was the brainchild of John Hale and Ken Hersey, Teddy boy promoters who had previously organised the Brean Sands weekender in April 1981. This time they had put together a formidable line-up. There were three American headliners – Buddy Knox, Janis Martin and Ronnie Hawkins – plus an extensive support including Crazy Cavan & The Rhythm Rockers, Screaming Lord Sutch, Freddie 'Fingers' Lee, the Dave Travis Band, Shades, Blackcat, Dynamite, the Bel Airs and Hot Rod Gang. Also billed to appear was Peter Singh, an Indian Elvis impersonator from Wales, but he withdrew after a series of threats and the realisation that his act would be disrupted. An Indian Elvis in a white Las Vegas jumpsuit was never going to have an easy ride at a rock'n'roll weekender.

Buddy and Janis were to be backed by the Dave Travis Band, and they both rehearsed at his Barnet home on 6 October before travelling down to Cornwall by train the following day. The show followed the holiday camp format so successfully pioneered at Caister and drew a sizeable crowd, despite the geographical limitations which made travel from mainland Europe something of a nightmare.

This was Buddy Knox's third visit to the UK and his first since the *Sun Sound Show* in 1977. His main spot was on Saturday, 9 October and it turned out to be the best show he ever gave in the UK. Conservatively dressed in a grey suit, white shirt and black tie, he performed all of his most popular songs, including 'Hula Love', 'Rock Your Little Baby To Sleep', 'Lovey Dovey', 'Ling Ting Tong' and, of course, 'Party Doll'. The

Dave Travis Band did a fine job with the backing and it was one of those occasions when everything came together for the amiable Texan who had not always been fully appreciated on his previous UK dates.

Until recently, Janis Martin had been something of an unknown quantity to British rock'n'roll fans. Born in Sutherlin, Virginia, she recorded for RCA Victor in 1956 at the tender age of sixteen and was groomed to become 'the female Elvis'. Unfortunately, marriage distractions and the public's reluctance at that time to accept a raunchy female rock'n'roller brought an early close to what should have been a glittering career for Janis. Sadly, not one of her RCA recordings was even released in the UK until decades later. After many years of retirement she had made her European stage debut at Eindhoven, The Netherlands in March 1982 and was now on British soil in the company of her husband, Wayne Whitt and about to show an unsuspecting audience that, as a live performer, she was the greatest female rock'n'roller of them all.

She could not have made a better impression. This

lady could rock in a way that surpassed every other female artist who had appeared in Britain. The act was based around her RCA Victor recordings, and as she tore through 'Let's Elope Baby', 'Drugstore Rock And Roll' and 'Crackerjack' the audience were mesmerised by her rasping vocals and raunchy, confident stage manner. Still aged only 42, Janis was tall, slim and attractive. Dressed in a white jacket and dark slacks, she was in complete control, and even a stage invasion by a member of the Bum Biters' motorcycle gang did not faze her. High points of a fabulous act were a rocking take on Roy Orbison's 'Ooby Dooby', a song which Janis had herself recorded in 1956, 'Barefoot Baby' and her best known number, 'My Boy Elvis'. At the end of her show, she borrowed a guitar and led the band through a riotous 'Johnny B. Goode'.

On the Sunday, each of the Americans performed again, climaxing with an informal jam session which included Buddy, Janis, Ronnie Hawkins, Dave Travis and guitarist Bob Fish on a rousing 'Whole Lotta Shakin' Goin' On'.

Janis and her husband returned home to Virginia straight after the weekend, while Buddy Knox stayed in London and spent five days in the studio working on a new album with Dave Travis.

RONNIE HAWKINS

October 1982		
9-10	Perranporth	Perran Sands Holiday Village
14	Camden Town	Dingwalls
Tour organisers — Bristol Rock'n'Roll Society and Willie Jeffery		

Ronnie Hawkins had visited the UK on a few occasions, most notably in January 1960 when he appeared on British TV in *Boy Meets Girls*, but only now, nearly 23 years later, did he finally get to play live for a British audience. For a brief period, work permit problems threatened to sabotage the tour, but happily these were resolved and Ronnie flew into London along with his band, the Hawks, comprising Stan Szelest (piano), Dave Lewis (drums), Steve Hogg (bass), Rheal Lanthier (guitar) and John Gibbard (guitar), plus his Canadian manager, Steve Thomson.

Thomson had been unwilling to forego a well-paid gig in Canada, which left the travelling schedule to Cornwall extremely tight. The inevitable happened and they were delayed by Customs at Heathrow, thereby missing the train connection and were left stranded at Reading railway station to await a later train.

When Hawkins and his entourage finally arrived at Perran Sands, they were greeted by John Hale of the Bristol Rock'n'Roll Society who was understandably angry at the disruption to his schedule. Irrationally, he insisted that they perform immediately, despite the fact they hadn't slept for the past 24 hours, so not surprisingly Ronnie's UK stage debut was extremely lacklustre. Even the audience could see that he was exhausted and simply going through the motions.

On Sunday, 10 October and after a good night's sleep, Ronnie took Janis Martin, Buddy Knox, and a party of his closest friends and fans totalling 39 people to a local restaurant for a long and enjoyable lunch at his expense. Then, fully refreshed and in a better frame of mind, he played his second set which was altogether a much better experience for all concerned.

Pianist Szelest was one of the last of the many great musicians to play in the Hawks, and with a few days free before the Dingwalls gig, he was hastily drafted in to play on Buddy Knox's new album which was being recorded in London by Dave Travis.

Steve Thomson had decided to record the Dingwalls show for a live album, which added greatly to the tension of the occasion, especially when Ronnie went walkabout for a few hours on the day of the gig, leaving his manager in a state of increasing panic.

The imposing figure of Rockin' Ronnie at Perranporth.

However, all turned out well with Ronnie and the Hawks in fine form and the audience responding well to a show which included 'Dizzy Miss Lizzy', 'Ruby Baby' and 'Down The Line'. Ronnie's giant personality and sharp wit were in evidence throughout, as when he introduced his 1959 US hit, 'Forty Days': 'This is the one that took us from the hills and the stills and put us on the pills!' Other highlights of a memorable evening were 'Odessa', 'Wild Little Willie' and 'Mary Lou'.

The live album was issued first in Canada as *The Hawk and Rock* on Trilogy, and later in the UK as *The Hawk* on Magnum Force.

THE BLUE CAPS

October 1982		
9-10	Great Yarmouth	Seashore Holiday Village
14	Tottenham	Mayfair
15	Birmingham	Golden Eagle
16	Langford	Yew Tree
17	Newcastle	Bierkeller
Tour organisers — Showstopper Promotions and Paul Barrett		

It was now eleven years since the tragic death of Gene Vincent, yet his dark shadow still loomed large within the world of rock'n'roll. Idolised not only by the legions of his old fans, but also by the younger Teddy boys who were drawn in by his rebel image and captivated by the amazing quality of the records that he left behind. Gene was gone, but the musicians who had toured and recorded with him were still out there living normal lives, with only memories remaining of their misspent youth. It was time for the Blue Caps to re-form.

On 8 October Johnny Meeks, Dickie Harrell, Bobby Jones, Paul Peek and Tommy 'Bubba' Facenda arrived at Gatwick Airport for their first British tour. In 1957, these same five men had worked alongside Vincent at the peak of his popularity and had been part of one of rock'n'roll's wildest stage acts. Other than one brief rehearsal this was the first time they had been together for twenty-five years.

They travelled first to a reception held at the Royalty – newly renamed the Pink Elephant – in Southgate, and then on to Great Yarmouth where they were to headline the *8th International Rock'n'Roll Weekend Hop* the following evening on a bill which also included Flying Saucers, the Stargazers, Johnny & The Roccos, Crazy Cavan & The Rhythm Rockers, a French band called the Alligators, and the Wild Ones from Belgium.

Rock'n'roll agent Paul Barrett introduced the Blue Caps to an already overexcited audience and they burst straight into 'Lotta Lovin' ' with Paul Peek on both lead vocals and rhythm guitar. Johnny Meeks, resplendent in a magnificent leopardskin jacket which had once belonged to Gene, tore straight into the first guitar solo, while Tommy Facenda whirled around the stage acting as both 'clapper boy' and background vocalist. Bobby Jones was a study in concentration as he picked out the familiar bass notes over on the far right of the stage, while behind them all the massive frame of Dickie Harrell was clearly visible hammering out a solid beat on the drums. Peek and Facenda were dressed in the same turquoise shirts they had worn in the Fifties' movie, *Hot Rod Gang*.

Each song was greeted with near-hysteria and wild applause as they thrashed through 'Dance To The Bop', 'I Got It', 'Yes I Love You Baby' and a feverish 'Rollin' Danny' with Bobby Jones on vocals. Harrell periodically left his drums and wandered around the stage throwing water over Paul Peek or punching the air. Meeks ripped through a tremendous 'I Got A Baby' taken at breakneck speed, while on 'Baby Blue', Facenda demonstrated the freeze, his crazy-shaking dance, before rolling around on the floor of the stage egged on by an equally frantic Paul Peek.

Blue Cap Johnny Meeks snapped at Langford.

After 16 numbers, and with each man close to exhaustion, Peek and Facenda led the audience through 'Be-Bop-A-Lula', but they were still not finished. Three encores were demanded and the Blue Caps eventually wrapped up their set with a great version of 'Rocky Road Blues'.

Following the two shows at Great Yarmouth, the boys spent a couple of days recording an album at Horseshoe Studios in Gwent, South Wales, which was later released by Magnum Force with the title *Unleashed*.

At the Mayfair, Tottenham, Flying Saucers were the support act and their vocalist, Sandy Ford, joined the Blue Caps onstage to sing 'Baby Blue', while Vincent stylist Dave Phillips also made a brief appearance. Meeks provided the vocals on a stunning 'Who's Pushing Your Swing'.

The Birmingham show had been poorly publicised and was relatively unmemorable, but at Langford, near Bristol, there was a stage invasion during 'Be-Bop-A-Lula'. Dave Phillips again guested and sang 'Teenage Partner', while Facenda provided one of the high spots with a terrific 'Dance In The Street'.

Travelling to the final show at Newcastle, the Blue Caps were stranded just north of Leeds when their van broke down, but they arrived in time to deliver another storming session which included standout versions of 'Blue Jean Bop' and 'Lovely Loretta' from Paul, and 'Say Mama' with Johnny on vocals. Even fan club secretary Steve Aynsley guested on three numbers. The Bel Airs were the support act at Newcastle.

JOHNNY MOORE & SLIGHTLY ADRIFT

October 1982			18	Norwich	Talk of the East
31	Nottingham	Commodore	20	Warrington	Owl
November 1982			24-27	Caerphilly	Diamond
2	Liverpool	Adam's	**December 1982**		
3-6	Batley	Frontier	5-11	Frimley Green	Lakeside
12-13	Farnworth	Blighty's			
Tour organiser — Henry Sellers					

Towerbell Records released a solo recording by Johnny Moore, 'Your Broken Heart', in October, but the song lacked any realistic chance of becoming a hit because the material was just not strong enough. What the public wanted to hear was the sound of the Drifters, but (presumably for legal reasons) Moore, Clyde Brown and Joe Blunt would not allow Towerbell to use the Drifters' name and they soldiered on as Johnny Moore & Slightly Adrift.

It was as if Moore were trying to push a boulder up a hill. There was a lot of hard work and perspiration, but everyone else could see that it would soon come rolling back to the bottom.

THE DRIFTERS

November 1982			December 1982		
15-20	Watford	Bailey's	5	Llandudno	Astra
22-27	Wythenshawe	Golden Garter	7	Norwich	Norwood Rooms
			13-18	Birmingham	Night Out
Tour organiser — Derek Block					

A further batch of cabaret dates for Ben E. King, Bill Fredericks, Louis Price and Ray Lewis kept the Drifters busy as 1982 drew to a close. They had recorded a session for UK Atlantic and a 45, pairing 'You Better Move On' and 'Save The Last Dance For Me', had been issued, with the promise of an album to follow. Naturally, both songs were prominently featured in the stage act.

TV Appearances
Rod and Emu's Saturday Special (BBC1)   Nov or Dec 1983 (screened 1 January 1983)

LINK WRAY

December 1982		
14	Camden Town	Dingwalls
Tour organiser — Harvey Goldsmith		

Top concert promoter Harvey Goldsmith had recently taken over Dingwalls, one of London's most popular music venues, and had plans to open similar clubs in Bristol, Liverpool, Sheffield and Newcastle. This would give each act their own mini-tour playing around the Dingwalls outlets and, as rock'n'roll had often been featured in the past, this seemed like very good news indeed.

Meanwhile, guitarist Link Wray played a one-off UK gig in Camden Town, supported by the Poor Boys.

CHAPTER ELEVEN

1983

Gonna Shake This Shack Tonight

With live rock'n'roll increasingly centred around the holiday camp weekenders, 1983 must be viewed as a year of transition. Caister celebrated its tenth anniversary with the British stage debut of Texan rockabillies Sid & Billy King, but was no longer attracting the same numbers as in the early years. The Bristol Rock'n'Roll Society were still licking their wounds after heavy losses incurred at their Perran Sands weekender in October 1982. They had promoted a magnificent event, but had not drawn enough people. Perranporth, in Cornwall, is a beautiful location but geographically unsuitable if you want to attract your audience from all parts of the UK and the mainland of Europe.

For one glorious summer's night in August, a small corner of North London was transformed into 1950s Los Angeles, as in turn Willie Egan, Chuck Higgins, Big Jay McNeely and Young Jessie brought their own unique brand of rock'n'roll to Britain. Honking saxes dominated an enterprising and highly enjoyable show titled *1950's R&B Jamboree*.

With hindsight, one of the most significant happenings of 1983 occurred in April with the publication of a new monthly rock'n'roll magazine, *Now Dig This*. It was the brainchild of two youngsters from the North-East, Trevor Cajiao and Mickie Downey, and when the first issue went on sale at the Caister weekender there was no hint that *NDT* would quickly grow into an indispensable read for anyone wishing to keep abreast with the increasingly insular world of rock'n'roll.

Billy Fury, perhaps Britain's greatest rock'n'roller, passed away in January. His health had been a concern for many years. but he had recently come out of temporary retirement and had featured in the UK charts with 'Devil Or Angel' in November. His final album, *The One And Only Billy Fury*, became a posthumous hit shortly after his death. A tribute concert starring Mike Berry, Danny Rivers, Marty Wilde, Joe Brown and Alvin Stardust was held at the Beck Theatre in Hayes, with the proceeds donated to research into heart disease.

Outside of rock'n'roll, live music followers had plenty to choose from. Country music veterans Hank Snow, Roy Acuff and Bill Monroe were included on the Wembley bill at Easter, while bad boy David Allan Coe and the delectable Dolly Parton both hit the concert trail during the year.

Blues fans could overdose on Albert King, John Lee Hooker, Buddy Guy and Junior Wells at the *London Blues Festival* in May, or seek out appearances by Johnny Copeland with his five-piece band at Dingwalls or James Cotton at Crystal Palace Park.

Other American visitors included Gene Chandler, Johnny Mathis, Dean Martin and Dionne Warwick. There was an appearance in London by the Mighty Clouds of Joy gospel group, while Dr. John flew in from New Orleans to join in the 25-year celebrations of the Marquee Club. He played several gigs, including some with the Chris Barber Band, and at the 100 Club closed his show with rocking versions of 'Lights Out' and 'Stagger Lee'.

TONY ORLANDO

Since his hit period with Dawn in the early Seventies, one-time rock'n'roller Tony Orlando had rarely been heard of in Britain, so he seemed a strange choice as a guest on ITV's weekly variety show, *Live From Her Majesty's*. Nevertheless, he appeared alongside Joe Longthorne and Jimmy Tarbuck on 13 February, though few rock'n'roll fans bothered to tune in.

TV appearances
Live From Her Majesty's (LWT)   13 February 1983

CLARENCE 'FROGMAN' HENRY

March 1983			11-13	Inverness	Eden Court
4-16	Bristol	Hippodrome	15	Kendal	Leisure Centre
17	Oxford	Apollo	16	Middlesbrough	Town Hall
19	Coventry	Apollo	18-19	Cardiff	New
20	Ipswich	Gaumont	20	Leicester	De Montfort Hall
21-22	Norwich	Theatre Royal	21	Wolverhampton	Civic Hall
25-26	Norwich	Theatre Royal	22	Gloucester	Leisure Centre
27-28	Croydon	Fairfield Halls	23-24	Birmingham	Odeon
29-31	Frimley Green	Lakeside	26-27	St. Austell	Cornwall Coliseum
April 1983			28-29	Torquay	Princess
2	Blackpool	Opera House	30	Portsmouth	Guildhall
3	Nottingham	Royal Concert Hall	**May 1983**		
4	Skegness	Embassy Centre	1	Worthing	Pavilion
5-6	Sunderland	Empire	6-7	Frimley Green	Lakeside
8-10	Aberdeen	Capitol	14	Putney	Half Moon
Tour organiser — Stuart Littlewood					

Throughout his long career, Clarence Henry has rarely strayed far from his home in New Orleans, preferring to work the local clubs rather than endure a life on the road. In 1983, with an exciting new album awaiting release, he temporarily changed the habits of a lifetime and spent much of the year in the UK, having hitched his wagon to the comic duo Cannon & Ball, who were probably at the peak of their popularity at this time.

The duo were embarking on a lengthy theatre tour commencing in Bristol on 14 March and the Frogman was signed up as the main support act. The connection which brought about this unlikely pairing was Cannon & Ball's manager, Stuart Littlewood, a director of Stuge Music, who had set up the recording of the *Legendary Clarence 'Frogman' Henry* album released by

Silvertown Records in early April.

Clarence stayed on in the UK after the final night with Cannon & Ball in Worthing and made further appearances at the fashionable Lakeside cabaret venue, plus a highly enjoyable and rocking show at Putney's Half Moon along with Diz & The Doormen.

TV appearances
Chas & Dave's Knees-Up (LWT)   25 June 1983

BO DIDDLEY

March 1983			April 1983		
23	Camden Town	Dingwalls	26	Brixton	Ace
24	Bristol	Dingwalls	27	Camden Town	Dingwalls
25	Liverpool	Dingwalls	28	Newcastle	Dingwalls
26	Sheffield	Dingwalls	29	Birmingham	Carlton
27	Leeds	Fforde Green Hotel	30	Hull	Dingwalls
29	Manchester	Gallery	**May 1983**		
30	London	The Venue	1	London	Lyceum
			2	Derby	Blue Note
			3	London	100 Club
Tour organiser — Stallion Artists					

Bo looks like he means business! – Hull Dingwalls.

Bo returned for a ballroom tour which was centred around Harvey Goldsmith's recently expanded Dingwalls chain, and for which backing was provided by the excellent Welsh band, the Red Hot Pokers. After a week of one-nighters at the end of March, he played gigs around Europe for more than three weeks before completing a further set of dates in the UK.

At Newcastle Dingwalls, which until recently had been the Bierkeller, there were continual problems with the sound system which effectively wiped out the efforts of the support band, the Ray Stubbs R&B All Stars, and caused Bo to stop playing completely during the early part of his act. He seemed about to walk off the stage but happily the problem was finally resolved, after which the night was sheer magic. Bo was on fine form, opening with 'Bo Diddley' and including memorable versions of 'Road Runner', 'I'm A Man', 'You Can't Judge A Book By The Cover' and 'Hey Bo Diddley'. At times he extended the songs beyond tolerance level but the audience seemed enchanted by the hypnotic jungle rhythm. The act ran for more than 90 minutes and finished with Mr. Diddley playing drums, to the delight of the crowd.

The support act at the first Camden gig were the Cobras. Dutch bluesman Hans Theesink opened at Bristol, Liverpool and Sheffield, and the Pirates at the Lyceum.

JOHNNY CARROLL
JUDY LINDSEY

April 1983		
2	Brighton	Centre
8	Caister	Ladbroke's Holiday Centre
10	Caister	Ladbroke's Holiday Centre
Tour organisers — Showstopper Promotions and Willie Jeffery		

Johnny Carroll had not fared well on his debut tour of the UK in 1980, so this second visit was an important opportunity to repair his reputation as a live performer and show British audiences that he was among the best of the Texan rockabillies. His singing partner, Judy Lindsey, was also anxious to contribute more to the act and had worked up some Brenda Lee and Wanda Jackson numbers for her spot.

They flew into London ahead of the Caister weekender and worked on an album project with Dave Travis for Seville Records which was later released under the title *Screamin' Demon Heatwave*.

The gig at Brighton produced a much more rocking performance and less of a cabaret act, with Carroll belting out fine versions of 'Rock'n'Roll Ruby', 'Crazy, Crazy Lovin'' and 'Hot Rock' and benefiting from some inspired backing by the Dave Travis Band. Judy chipped in with 'Let's Have A Party' and 'Let's Jump The Broomstick' and added a touch of glamour to the otherwise all-male proceedings. Support was provided by Blackcat.

For the Caister weekender, Johnny and Judy's main set was scheduled for the Friday evening and Carroll was very concerned

Johnny at Caister.

that the band selected to back them may not be up to the task. Fearing a repetition of 1980, he ruffled a few feathers and stubbornly insisted that they work with Johnny & The Roccos, who were already backing Billy Lee Riley. The outcome was a very successful performance and undoubtedly Carroll's best UK showing up to that point. He finished an exhilarating set bathed in perspiration and minus his shirt.

NARVEL FELTS

April 1983		
3	Wembley	Arena
Tour organiser — Mervyn Conn		

The Sunday evening bill for the *Silk Cut International Festival of Country Music* had been built around George Jones and Tammy Wynette until George became ill and had to be replaced by Jimmy C. Newman. The other acts included Tompall & The Glaser Brothers, Barbara Fairchild, John D. Loudermilk, Matchbox, Tom Gribbin, Linda Cassidy, Terry McMillan and Narvel Felts.

Narvel performed early in the proceedings and was backed by his son, Albert 'Bub' Felts, on drums, along with the Raymond Froggatt Band. Stylishly attired in a pink shirt and black jacket, he opened with 'Drift Away' and delivered emotional versions of both 'Reconsider Me' and 'Lonely Teardrops' in his short but effective spot.

TV appearances
Sing Country (BBC2)   3 April 1983 (screened 8 September 1983)

JERRY LEE LEWIS

April 1983				17	Cardiff	St. David's Hall
5	Belfast	King's Hall		18	Nottingham	Royal Concert Hall
15	Plymouth	Theatre Royal		19	Bristol	Colston Hall
16	Hammersmith	Odeon		21	Farnworth	Blighty's
Tour organiser — Mervyn Conn						

Jerry Lee Lewis flew into Brighton at the beginning of April along with Ken Lovelace (guitar and fiddle), Ron Norwood (drums), Joel Schumaker (guitar), Bill Strom (organ) and Randy Wilkes (bass).

The tour kicked off with a country gig in Belfast on a bill which also featured Bobby Bare, Billie Jo Spears, Rattlesnake Annie and Boxcar Willie. They then flew out for concerts in Germany, with the main UK tour commencing ten days later in Plymouth. Support on most of the shows was provided by young British rockabilly band the Polecats, although black American doo-woppers Fourteen Karat Soul did the honours at Nottingham. The efforts of the Polecats were not always appreciated by the rock'n'roll purists and at Hammersmith there appeared to be more people in the bar than in the stalls during their set.

At Plymouth, Jerry was in an expansive mood and included both 'Money' and 'Lewis Boogie' in a varied and highly enjoyable show. Bill Strom's organ was mixed too loud and drowned out the piano on 'Would You Take Another Chance On Me', but this problem was soon rectified and the act also included a masterful interpretation of Ernest Tubb's 'Let's Say Goodbye Like We Said Hello', a rocking 'Ubangi Stomp' and a top version of 'Old Black Joe'.

The Hammersmith show was sold out and again Jerry mixed country and rock'n'roll, highlights being a storming version of 'Sweet Georgia Brown', Carl Mann's 'Mona Lisa' and an energetic 'High School Confidential'. He even joked with the audience, 'I've got a list of songs here to do. I ain't done one of them!'

At Nottingham, he wore a black cowboy shirt and dark glasses and opened with 'Drinking Wine Spo-Dee-O-Dee'. There were two excellent gospel numbers, 'Life's Railway To Heaven' and 'A Picture From Life's Other Side', as well as 'I'll Sail My Ship Alone', a beautiful 'You Belong To Me', 'Working Man Blues' and flat-out takes of 'Blue Suede Shoes' and 'Mean Woman Blues'. A portion of the Bristol show was incorporated in the BBC's *Arena* special.

Every performance was refreshingly different and the master showman seemed to have enormous reserves of energy. The final night at Farnworth, near Bolton, was another sell-out and another great performance. Long-time fans proclaimed his rendition of 'What'd I Say' as the best they had ever heard, while other memorable moments included 'Brown Eyed Handsome Man', 'Why Don't You Love Me Like You Used To Do' and an uptempo 'Mexicali Rose'.

There had been concerns about Jerry's health, but, although somewhat frail, he appeared to be generally in good spirits. His latest girlfriend, 25-year-old Sharon Stevens, flew into London in time for the

Another piano stool goes south – JLL in action at Blighty's.

Hammersmith show. She and Jerry wed on 7 June at his home in Nesbit, Mississippi, but tragically the marriage was to be brief, because on 24 August the fifth Mrs. Lewis was found dead in bed after a methadone overdose.

TV appearances

Wogan (BBC1)	1 April 1983 (screened 2 April 1983)
Arena (BBC2)	19 April 1983 (screened 27 March 1984)

BILLY LEE RILEY

April 1983		
9-10	Caister	Ladbroke's Holiday Centre
Tour organisers — Showstopper Promotions and Paul Barrett		

Showstopper Promotions had hoped to secure another Sun rockabilly artist, Sonny Burgess, to headline the *9th International Rock'n'Roll Weekend Hop*, but he was reluctant to leave his day job as a lace salesman in Arkansas, and his former stablemate at Sun, Billy Lee Riley, was brought in for his second Caister, this time alongside Texan rocker Johnny Carroll.

Riley flew into the UK on Thursday, 7 April and stayed that night in Orpington, Kent before completing his journey to Caister by road the following day. His main spot was on the Saturday evening, backed by Johnny & The Roccos, and on a bill which also included Blackcat, Shades and the Flash Cats.

The end of a great weekend.

Conservatively dressed in a dark jacket and tie with white shirt and cream trousers, Riley was in good form vocally, scoring positively with 'Red Hot', 'Flyin' Saucers Rock & Roll' and 'Trouble Bound'. Disappointingly, he did not play guitar at all, restricting his instrumental activity to some bluesy harmonica on 'Itchy' and 'Thunderbird'. It was a competent performance, but perhaps a little less exciting than many of the shows on his 1979 tours.

On the Sunday afternoon, following a typically outrageous set by Screaming Lord Sutch, both Riley and Johnny Carroll took part in a jam session, belting out a prolonged version of 'What'd I Say?'.

THE DRIFTERS

April 1983			June 1983		
9-30	Enfield	Starlight	1	Swindon	Brunel Rooms
May 1983			2	Fareham	Collingwood
1	Lewisham	Concert Hall	3	St. Austell	Cornwall Coliseum
9-14	Watford	Bailey's	4	Eastbourne	King's
15	Stockport	Davenport	8	Hull	City Hall
17-21	Birmingham	Night Out	9	Oldham	Queen Elizabeth Hall
22	Kendal	Leisure Centre	10-11	Enfield	Starlight
25	Cardiff	St. David's Hall			
26-28	Purfleet	Circus Tavern			
31	Nottingham	Royal Concert Hall			
Tour organiser — Arthur Howes					

The Drifters had another shake-up in 1983. Johnny Moore's attempt at a solo career had proved unsuccessful, so once again he returned to the safe haven of the group with whom his name was so closely identified, bringing with him his loyal cohorts, Clyde Brown and Joe Blunt. Faye Treadwell retained Ben E. King from the 1982 line-up and sent the newly restyled group out on a long spring tour. This next period in the Drifters' history would be the last occasion that two of their heavyweight names – King and Moore – performed together on a regular basis.

PHIL EVERLY

1983 had started well for Phil, his duet with Cliff Richard, 'She Means Nothing To Me', nudging into the UK Top 10 in February. He made a short visit in April to promote the follow-up, 'Sweet Pretender', which included an appearance on BBC-TV's popular magazine programme, *Nationwide*. In the course of an interview with Sue Lawley, he announced that both he and Don were looking forward to singing together again, which was welcome news to the many fans of the Everly Brothers, who had once feared that they would never again perform together. There had been rumours of a reconciliation for several months, but now it seemed that something would finally happen.

TV appearances
Nationwide (BBC1)   22 April 1983

DEL SHANNON

May 1983			June 1983		
20	Newmarket	Cabaret	2	Corby	Stardust Leisure
21	Burton-in-Kendal	Crowthorne Hall	3-4	Stanley	Castles
22	Frodsham	Mersey View	5	Birmingham	Wedley Castle
25	Minehead	Butlin's	6	Putney	Half Moon
26	London	Lyceum	7	Camden Town	Dingwalls
27	Portsmouth	Cowplain Social	8	Chesterfield	Aquarius
28	Yeovil	Gardens	9	Norwich	Tudor Hall
29	Deptford	Albany Empire	10	Mildenhall	USAF
30	Coventry	Walsgrove Hotel	11	Eastbourne	King's
Tour organiser unknown					

Del had been a regular and welcome visitor to the UK through much of the Seventies, but now had been absent from the cabaret circuit since 1979. His highly rated new album, *Drop Down And Get Me*, had finally secured a UK release on Demon Records and had been given an enthusiastic review in *New Musical Express*. This lengthy tour of clubs and ballrooms was a good opportunity to promote the album and Del was in fine form throughout.

At Putney, where backing was provided by the Bikinis from Leicester, he dressed in a pink shirt, black cord trousers and a stripped-down zip-up leather jacket. He opened with 'Hats Off To Larry' and 'Handy Man', and it was immediately apparent that his guitar playing was as good as ever. As well as his hits there were memorable versions of 'Crying', 'I Go To Pieces' and Hank Williams' 'Long Gone Lonesome Blues', and from the new album, 'Sea Of Love', 'Cheap Love' and 'Life Without You'. It was clear that his distinctive voice had never sounded better and he thoroughly deserved the enthusiastic audience response, encoring with 'Do You Wanna Dance' and 'Runaround Sue'.

Sonny King & The Sons of Swing were the support act at Deptford, and the Tremeloes at London's Lyceum Ballroom.

Screamin' Jay puts a spell on the crowd at Camden Town Dingwalls.

SCREAMIN' JAY HAWKINS

June 1983		
9	Camden Town	Dingwalls
10	Bristol	Dingwalls
11	Brixton	Ace
Tour organiser unknown		

Screamin' Jay Hawkins toured the UK twice in the Sixties and after a gap of seventeen years returned for three club gigs in June. For many people, this was a first opportunity to see the great eccentric in action, while long-time fans were anxious to establish whether he still displayed the same level of craziness.

On the opening night, he made an immediate impression. A tall, imposing figure with thick, wavy hair and a neatly trimmed beard, he emerged wearing an extraordinary African-style brown-patterned suit with an equally garish cloak, a necklace of animal teeth, and carrying a stick on top of which was perched his skull, 'Henry'.

His wonderful, deep voice was as strong and imposing as ever as he worked through a set containing his best-known songs, sometimes singing *bel canto* before lapsing into his own unique brand of vocal insanity. He prowled around the stage shaking maracas, pounding at the piano and eyeballing members of the audience in an extraordinary display of rock'n'roll circus. High points of a marvellous evening included 'Little Demon', 'Little Bitty Pretty One', 'Alligator Wine' and, inevitably, 'I Put A Spell On You'.

Support, at least on the two London dates, was provided by Gaz's Rebel Blues Rockers.

Photo by Paul Harris

Genial Frogman at the Half Moon, Putney.

CLARENCE 'FROGMAN' HENRY

July 1983			September 1983		
8-31	Scarborough	Futurist	1-10	Scarborough	Futurist
August 1983			**October 1983**		
1-31	Scarborough	Futurist	13	Camden Town	Dingwalls
			30	Putney	Half Moon
Tour organiser — Stuart Littlewood					

Summer seasons by the seaside are not really an appropriate setting for rock'n'roll, and rarely have American visitors been placed in that situation. Clarence Henry, having supported Cannon & Ball on a lengthy spring theatre tour, was retained as part of their package show when they settled down on the East Coast for a nine-week season at Scarborough's Futurist Theatre. It was an old-style variety show and Clarence closed the first half. There were two performances each day at 6.10 and 8.40, and the remainder of the bill comprised Peter Saint, the Alan Harding Dancers, Franklyn James and the Mike Ryal Orchestra.

Surprisingly, the Frogman did not stray far from his usual club act, mixing his own hits like 'But I Do' and 'You Always Hurt The One You Love' with a selection of New Orleans rock'n'roll. He had appeared on Chas &

Dave's *Knees-Up* TV show in June, and apparently hit it off with the duo, as he regularly included their 'Ain't No Pleasin' You' in his show.

He also recorded the Chas & Dave composition, 'That Old Piano', which was released as a 45 on their Rockney label at the end of July and generated quite a lot of radio interest, but did not make the charts. While in Scarborough, Clarence was a guest at the opening of what was claimed to be the world's 'first and only Rock'n'Roll Museum', the brainchild of writer and broadcaster Chas 'Dr. Rock' White.

When the summer season came to an end, he played a couple of club dates in the London area, including a highly successful night at Dingwalls backed by Juice On The Loose. The audience were looking for uptempo rock'n'roll and were rewarded with a thumping 'Got My Mojo Working' and exciting versions of 'Lucille' and 'Johnny B. Goode', but it was the song which gave Clarence his 'Frogman' tag, 'Ain't Got No Home', that earned him the most enthusiastic audience response.

TV appearances
Pebble Mill At One (BBC1)   28 September 1983

FATS DOMINO

July 1983		
18 London	Royal Festival Hall	
Tour organisers — Capital Radio and Patrick Malynn		

Capital Radio's *Great American Blues Party* was headlined by Fats and his band and also featured Jimmy Witherspoon along with Jay McShann and the Kansas City Quartet.

What promised to be an entertaining evening was very nearly a massive disaster owing to appalling sound problems that effectively killed off McShann's efforts completely. Some instruments were inaudible, while others could be heard, but only in conjunction with a continuous whine. For this to happen at a quality venue like the Royal Festival Hall was quite unacceptable. Jimmy Witherspoon did fare a little better, but by the time Domino's ten-piece band opened the second half, the audience's patience had worn thin and there were shouts of protest from the stalls.

Somehow or other Fats managed to overcome the inadequacies of the equipment and led the audience through his usual array of classic New Orleans rock'n'roll. The sound had not really improved to any significant degree, but it was as if the strength of his personality overcame the distractions and by the end of the evening he had the audience in the palm of his hand. 'Blueberry Hill', 'Ain't That A Shame', 'Jambalaya (On The Bayou)', 'My Girl Josephine' and 'I Want To Walk You Home' were among the best of a superb act which ended with a mass invasion of dancers, young and old, up on the stage.

BUDDY KNOX

July 1983			August 1983		
23	Shoreham	Community Centre	3	Lakenheath	USAF
25	Southgate	Pink Elephant	4	Bentwaters	USAF
30	Putney	Half Moon	5	Camden Town	Dingwalls
31	Harlesden	Mean Fiddler			

Tour organisers — Willie Jeffery and Paul Barrett

Photo by Paul Harris

Buddy at the Half Moon, Putney.

Buddy's visit was primarily to complete an album project which had commenced in October 1982 and which was being produced by Dave Travis. He flew into London on 18 July and went into the studio for five days, although time was found to celebrate his 50th birthday with a party at drummer Howard Tibble's home in Finchley on 20 July. The album, *Texas Rockabilly Man*, was eventually released by Rockstar Records in 1987.

The Sussex Rock'n'Roll Society have been promoting live music for around thirty years, which makes them one of the UK's longest-running rock'n'roll clubs. Although they mainly feature local acts, they made an exception on 23 July when they hosted the first of Knox's live dates. It was a gorgeous sunny day and Buddy's entourage stopped for a barbecue lunch at a Sussex pub, the Bolney Stage. By an extraordinary coincidence, the landlady was not only a long-time fan of Knox, but they both hailed from the same tiny area of West Texas, and she had even worked briefly in California for his erstwhile colleague, Jimmy Bowen! When lunch was over, the afternoon was spent visiting the Bluebell steam railway, and a memorable day concluded with a fine performance by both Buddy and the Dave Travis Band at Shoreham.

The only low point of the short tour was the visit to USAF Lakenheath, where Buddy played two sets, one for the troops and the second for the officers. The young servicemen were generally unresponsive and did not seem interested in rock'n'roll or country music. At Putney however, everything clicked and 'Hula Love', 'Rockhouse', 'Somebody Touched Me' and 'Party Doll' were the pick of an excellent set.

With a few free days, sightseeing trips were made to Windsor and London and, after a proposed gig in Bristol on 6 August was cancelled, Buddy spent the evening at the cinema watching *Return Of The Jedi* before flying home the following day.

WILLIE EGAN
CHUCK HIGGINS
YOUNG JESSIE
BIG JAY McNEELY

August 1983		
28	Camden Town	Electric Ballroom
Tour organiser — Rock On		

Rockabilly had been the focus of so much attention that black rock'n'roll had been largely overlooked in the scramble to unearth increasingly obscure rockabilly cats from the Fifties. This situation was at least partially remedied during one summer evening in North London, thanks to the efforts of Ted Carroll, proprietor of leading oldies record shop Rock On and a director of reissue label Ace Records. The four participants were flown into London from Los Angeles and, thanks to splendid backing from Juice On The Loose and Red Beans & Rice each gave an excellent account of themselves on a show titled *1950s R&B Jamboree*.

First on stage was Willie Egan, a native of Louisiana who had lived in Los Angeles since the age of nine. He had recorded for the Mambo and Vita labels in Pasadena during the mid-Fifties, his name variously credited as Egan, Egans or even Eggins. Later, he had worked with Marvin

Photos by Paul Harris

Willie Egan.   Chuck Higgins.

Phillips as one half of the Marvin & Johnny act, before leaving music to earn his living as a hospital porter. A tall man in a white jacket, he was not helped by the fact that the piano was situated in the far corner of the stage, but he opened brightly with his own 'Wow Wow', very much in the style of Fats Domino. He appeared somewhat bewildered by the whole experience, but rocked his way through 'Chicken Shack Boogie' and an explosive 'She's Gone Away', ably assisted by some fine backing from Juice On The Loose. He seemed more relaxed by the time he reached 'Rock And Roll Fever', and on 'Wear Your Black Dress' eagerly pounded out a memorable piano break. His portion of the show concluded with 'Linda Lu' and 'Lawdy Miss Clawdy'.

Next, it was the turn of Chuck Higgins, something of a veteran at the age of 59. Born in Gary, Indiana, he had been resident in Los Angeles since 1940 and had enjoyed a long and varied life as saxophonist and bandleader, his recording career dating right back to 'Pachuko Hop' in 1952. An extrovert character with a steady stream of slightly risqué jokes and comments, he wore a gaudy black-and-white check jacket and blew up a storm on his saxophone while Red Beans & Rice rocked away behind him. His opening number, 'Oh Yeah', set the scene for a lively act and he showed himself to be a competent vocalist with 'Blind Man' and 'Baby What You Want Me To Do', but it was the saxophone instrumentals that really got the audience excited. He closed with a long version of 'Aw Shucks'.

Obediah Jessie, known as Young Jessie, has an impeccable rock'n'roll pedigree. Born in Dallas, Texas, his family moved to California when he was an infant and he attended school in Los Angeles. His first group, which included Cornel Gunter and Richard Berry, became the Flairs and in 1955 he enjoyed solo success with 'Mary Lou'. Later, he was briefly a

Young Jessie.   Big Jay McNeely.

member of the Coasters as well as cutting several fine rock'n'roll and R&B records. He looked a very slick dude in a white suit and dark glasses. On 'Lonesome Desert' he played piano, but otherwise he prowled around the stage singing with a powerful and emotional voice. His set seemed short, but included 'Twenty-Four Hours Of The Day', 'Don't Happen No More' and a very rocking 'Mary Lou', which gained perhaps the best audience reaction of the night. He closed with 'Hit, Git And Split', the backing again provided by Red Beans & Rice.

The final act was the man they call 'King of the Honking Tenor Sax', Big Jay McNeely. Another veteran of the Los Angeles R&B scene, Jay was born in the LA suburb of Watts and was recording as early as 1949 with 'The Deacon's Hop'. Thanks to his flamboyant style, he remained popular throughout the Fifties, eventually scoring a national pop hit with 'There Is Something On Your Mind' in 1959. He drifted out of music during the Seventies and had been working as a postman, but had clearly lost none of his old style and panache. Backed by Juice On The Loose, he honked his way through 'Big Jay's Shuffle', 'Night Train' and a flat-out and exciting '3-D', sang his big hit 'There Is Something On Your Mind' and left the stage, which was darkened so that when he returned during 'Dixieland Funk', all that was visible to the audience was his luminous saxophone, and the gyrating, also luminous chest of a female dancer. Jay proved himself an old-style showman and no mean sax player.

The evening concluded with a chaotic and obviously unrehearsed finale during which Egan sat at the piano looking bemused while the other three jumped from song to song, honking and singing, commencing with 'Big Fat Mama' and ending up with 'Flip, Flop and Fly' and 'Kansas City'. All in all, it was a unique and highly entertaining evening for all concerned.

A live recording of the historic event was released by Ace Records as *1983 R&B Jamboree* later that year. McNeely and Egan also recorded studio albums, *From Harlem to Camden* and *Going Back To Louisiana*, which both appeared in 1984. Sadly, while McNeely's popularity grew, Egan's brief spell back in the limelight was not sustained, at least in part due to his liking for the taste of gin.

Although Big Jay and Young Jessie would both visit the UK again, neither Chuck Higgins nor Willie Egan managed a return trip. Higgins died of lung cancer in Los Angeles on 14 September 1999, and Egan followed on 5 August 2004

CHUCK BERRY

August 1983		
30	St. Ives	Penwith Festival Site
September 1983		
1	Irvine	Magnum Centre
3	Peterborough	Embankment
6	Portsmouth	Guildhall
7	Margate	Winter Gardens
Tour organiser — Derek Block		

HEREWARD RADIO PRESENTS

Chuck Berry Concert

SATURDAY, 3rd SEPTEMBER, 1983

PRICE £8.50   7.00 p.m.

Concert Organisers accept no responsibility for loss or damage to property or accident or injury to persons however caused.   N⁰   0268

Chuck's 1983 tour must have been a very tiring experience, and few would relish the amount of travelling involved. Flying into the UK from Switzerland, the first gig was in Cornwall as part of the *Penwith '83* festival, which also starred Meat Loaf, 10cc and Renaissance. Next came a single date in Scotland at the Magnum Centre in Irvine, before a flight to Belgium for a show on 2 September.

Back in England the following day, Chuck headlined a *Rock'n'Roll Spectacular* in Peterborough, which was held in a circus tent on the bank of the River Nene, on a bill which also included Billy J. Kramer, Screaming Lord Sutch, Billie Davis and Tommy Bruce. Then it was off to the Netherlands for a show on 4 September, followed by Italy the next night, and then two final appearances in Portsmouth and Margate. Ingrid Berry opened for her father and backing included Billy Peek (guitar) and Jim Marsala (bass).

CHUCK BERRY
FATS DOMINO
JERRY LEE LEWIS
LITTLE RICHARD (and others)

The April 1983 programme for the Caister weekender contained an extraordinary advert for a concert to be held at Wembley Arena on 17 and 18 September under the title *The Legends of Rock'n'Roll*. It promised a two-day festival of the world's greatest living legends. Negotiations were apparently underway for Chuck Berry, Fats Domino, Jerry Lee Lewis, Little Richard, Carl Perkins, Bo Diddley, Duane Eddy, Chubby Checker, Freddy Cannon, Danny & The Juniors, Johnny & The Hurricanes, and many more US and British support acts yet to be announced.

Such an ambitious project had to be speculative at best, and Showstopper Promotions, with their Caister weekenders slipping into decline, were perhaps gambling with one final throw of the rock'n'roll dice. Needless to say, the negotiations for so many big names could not have gone well, as the whole glorious enterprise soon sank like the *Titanic*, never to be mentioned again.

THE STRAY CATS

Brian Setzer, Lee Rocker and Slim Jim Phantom made a brief UK visit to promote their new Arista album, *Rant 'n' Rave with the Stray Cats*. They played one live gig on 18 September at London's Lyceum Ballroom, which was packed out and literally dripping in a temperature that was reported in excess of 100 degrees. Setzer's voice was shot and nearly failed completely towards the end, but not before the amiable but unruly crowd had caused a mini-riot during 'Sexy And 17'.

Other highlights included 'Your Baby Blue Eyes', 'Tear It Up' and Gene Vincent's 'Double Talkin' Baby'. They were called back for an impressive six encores, during which Dave Edmunds joined them onstage for 'The Race Is On'.

EVERLY BROTHERS

September 1983	
22-23 London	Royal Albert Hall
Tour organisers — Terry Slater and Mel Bush	

Since parting company in 1973, Don and Phil Everly had each pursued solo careers, but with only limited commercial success. It was an open secret that the two brothers had barely been on speaking terms, but suggestions of a reunion had started to gather momentum towards the end of 1982. An Everly Brothers concert was first rumoured for February, but as the project grew, so too did the complexities of the organisation. Eventually, the scene was set for a two-night engagement at the Royal Albert Hall, and with

Don and Phil at press reception in London, 19 September.

around 12,000 seats available, there were reported to be in excess of 60,000 ticket applications.

The brothers arrived in the UK early in September and undertook a series of media interviews. They were still considered of interest to the national press and the reunion received generous coverage. The backing band for the live shows comprised Albert Lee (guitar), Martin Jenner (guitar), Mark Griffiths (bass), Pete Wingfield (piano) and Graham Jarvis (drums), while support was provided by Paul Brady. The show on 23 September was recorded and an album, *Reunion Concert*, was issued by Impression Records in December.

The concerts themselves were inevitably highly emotional occasions and Don was reportedly so nervous the night before that, unable to sleep, he pounded the streets of Knightsbridge trying to mentally prepare himself for the experience. Once the nerves were overcome, however, the shows were

ROYAL ALBERT HALL
GENERAL MANAGER: D. CAMERON McNICOL

THE FACE OF THIS DOCUMENT HAS A COLOURED BACKGROUND

FRIDAY 23RD SEPTEMBER 1983
AT 7-30 P.M.DOORS OPEN AT 6-45

MEL BUSH
PRESENTS
THE EVERLY BROTHERS.
ADMIT TO:-

STALLS *M*

ENTER BY DOOR NO.9.
PRICE (INC. VAT) ROW SEAT

260 1242 L £15.00 10 1718

THE BACK OF THIS DOCUMENT CONTAINS AN ARTIFICIAL WATERMARK
TO BE RETAINED   See Reverse

extremely successful. After all, they were playing to loyal and committed audiences who were just delighted that the brothers were back together after so long.

They opened with 'The Price Of Love', and for well over an hour worked through 'Bye Bye Love', 'Walk Right Back', 'Claudette' and as many more of their classic recordings as could be fitted into the time available. Everyone was floating on air. The Everly Brothers were back together and it was 1960 again. 'Cathy's Clown', 'So Sad', 'All I Have To Do Is Dream', even a segment of 'Ebony Eyes' were included. Dressed in matching black tuxedos, white wing collar shirts and fancy bowties, admittedly the brothers had aged, but their voices, especially the harmonies, were as powerful and unique as ever.

They finished up with a solemn rendition of Sam Cooke's 'You Send Me', '('Til) I Kissed You' and a rocking 'Lucille'. For an encore, it was a note-perfect 'Let It Be Me' and then straight into 'Good Golly Miss Molly'. The audience would not let them go and they responded with Jimmy Reed's 'Baby What You Want Me To Do'. It was a magical experience for all concerned.

THE DRIFTERS

September 1983		
24 Stanley	Castles	
Tour organiser — Dexter Reed		

Not so many years ago, the Drifters had been the biggest draw on the UK club and ballroom circuit and with promoter Henry Sellers looking after their bookings and publicity, they had succeeded in maintaining a high profile with the public, even though the individual members of the group were regularly changing.

By September 1983, the Drifters had gone underground. Publicity was nil and it became increasingly difficult for long-time fans to track their movements. Johnny Moore was interviewed by *Now Dig This* magazine prior to this cabaret booking in the North-East. He appeared to be working as a trio along with Clyde Brown and Joe Blunt, but of one thing there was no doubt: the quality and high level of entertainment were undiminished. Any set of Drifters fronted by Johnny Moore always guaranteed a great evening of rock'n'roll.

WAYLON JENNINGS

October 1983		
18	Hammersmith	Odeon
20	Belfast	Grosvenor Hall
Tour organiser unknown		

Waylon's rock'n'roll days were behind him, but he still remained of more than passing interest to those who remembered his early connections to Buddy Holly.

Now a major country star and leader of the Outlaw movement, he headlined at the Hammersmith Odeon with support from his wife, Jessi Colter, and backing by the Waylors, comprising Gary Scruggs (guitar), Jerry Gropp (guitar), Jerry Bridges (bass), Ralph Mooney (steel), Floyd Domino (keyboards) and Dan Lusgow (drums). The band were outstanding as Waylon worked through his repertoire of hits including 'I've Always Been Crazy', 'Luckenbach, Texas' and 'Are You Sure Hank Done It This Way?'. His five encores closed with 'Mental Revenge' and 'Lonesome, On'ry And Mean'.

TV appearances
In Concert (Channel 4)   18 October 1983 (screened 1 July 1984)

BRENDA LEE

October 1983		
23	Lewisham	Concert Hall
24	Eastbourne	Congress
Tour organiser — Jeffrey Kruger		

Brenda Lee flew into London for a week-long promotional tour during which she played two live shows, made two television appearances and set up a full tour scheduled for March 1984. Jess Conrad and Les Howard were the support acts on the live shows.

TV appearances
Pebble Mill At One (BBC1)   19 October 1983
Des O'Connor Tonight (Thames)   ? October 1983 (screened 6 December 1983)

SID & BILLY KING

November 1983		
9	Harlesden	Mean Fiddler
10	Putney	Half Moon
12-13	Caister	Ladbroke's Holiday Centre
Tour organisers — Showstopper Promotions and Paul Barrett		

Sid King & The Five Strings were a popular live act in Texas during the mid-Fifties, performing both hillbilly and rockabilly and recording for Columbia Records. They never achieved more than regional success, but

Billy *(left)* and Sid King at the Mean Fiddler.

toured extensively and appeared regularly on big shows like the *Louisiana Hayride* and the *Big D Jamboree*. The group disbanded in 1958, following which Sid and his guitar-playing younger brother, Billy, gradually drifted out of show business. For nearly twenty years they ran a barber shop in Dallas, Texas, prior to dusting off their rock'n'roll shoes for a short UK tour on which they were backed by Red Beans & Rice.

The *10th Anniversary International Rock'n'Roll Weekend Hop* at Caister followed the usual tried and tested formula and also featured Crazy Cavan & The Rhythm Rockers, Flying Saucers, Rockin' Louie, the Bel Airs, the Blue Rhythm Boys, Red Beans & Rice and the Questionnaires.

Sid and Billy came on stage shortly after 11.00 pm on the Saturday evening and opened their set with 'Let 'Er Roll'. Both men are short in stature, and Sid was sporting a beard and moustache. He sang with a very pronounced Texan drawl, and in addition to their own Columbia recordings like 'Booger Red', 'When My Baby Left Me' and 'Gonna Shake This Shack Tonight', included 'Rave On' as a tribute to their fellow Texan, Buddy Holly. Red Beans & Rice did a fine job interpreting the Five Strings' sound, and an enjoyable set also included 'Drinkin' Wine Spo-Li-Oli', 'I Like It' and 'Sag, Drag And Fall'.

The split within the rock'n'roll ranks between the Teddy boys and the rockabilly cats was again apparent over the Caister weekend. Around 50 chalets were trashed and it was reported that there were 61 people arrested over the three days. Sid and Billy King performed for a second time at 3.00 pm on the Sunday, but on this occasion only a small crowd were in the ballroom. For some reason, Crazy Cavan joined them on stage for a couple of numbers, and with Cavan's somewhat vociferous followers calling the shots, it became somewhat embarrassing for the brothers.

Nevertheless, Sid and Billy King showed themselves to be fine exponents of authentic Texan rockabilly and worthy headliners for Caister. The problem of the escalating violence was becoming a concern, however.

JOHNNY CASH

November 1983		
10	Nottingham	Royal Concert Hall
11	Birmingham	Odeon
12	Hammersmith	Odeon
Tour organiser — Adrian Hopkins		

Johnny was at the end of a long and tiring European tour by the time he arrived in the UK from Belgium on 10 November accompanied by his wife, June Carter, daughter Tara Cash, plus Bob Wootton (guitar), W.S. Holland (drums), Jimmy Tiddle (bass), Earl Poole Ball (piano) and Marty Stuart (fiddle and guitar). All three concerts were sold out several days in advance.

At Nottingham, the great man was on superb form, the show lasting for well over two hours. In addition to his regular act, he included 'Any Old Wind That Blows', 'The Old Rugged Cross' and 'Johnny 99'. There was even an affectionate attempt at some rock'n'roll with 'Johnny B. Goode', during which he performed an impressive imitation of Chuck's duckwalk. A young fan called out for 'Rock'n'Roll Ruby', and he obliged with a fine version and then added a raunchy 'Blue Suede Shoes' as well. He sang 'Rock'n'Roll Ruby' again at Hammersmith two nights later.

Cash was at the height of his popularity and provided top-quality entertainment on every show. He stayed on for a short family holiday in Scotland before returning to Nashville in time for surgery for an ulcer, which was performed at the Baptist Hospital on 22 November.

CHAPTER TWELVE

1984

We Wanna Boogie

This was the year when Johnny Hale established Weymouth as the leading rock'n'roll weekender, supplanting Caister as the place to go for a hell-raising few days of non-stop partying and with live rock'n'roll from both the UK and USA. Initially, he succeeded by booking support acts that would only appeal to the Teddy boy crowd, thereby ensuring that the rockabilly cats would not attend and eliminating the friction between the two factions. Later on, he tried to cater for both sides of the rock'n'roll divide by promoting two events on consecutive weekends, which proved altogether more troublesome.

Sun Records legend Sonny Burgess made his UK stage debut at Weymouth in April, and another artist with Sun connections, Hayden Thompson, made his first European trip in October, jointly headlining with Carl Mann at the *23rd Rockhouse International Rock'n'Roll Meeting* in Eindhoven, as well as starring at an ill-fated weekender on the Isle of Wight.

Leading British acts on the pub-and-club circuit included established names like Crazy Cavan & The Rhythm Rockers, Flying Saucers, the Rapiers and Freddie 'Fingers' Lee, along with CSA, Johnny & The Roccos and Blackcat. There were also newer names jostling for attention such as the Firebirds, the Kingbeats, the Rimshots and Red Hot & Blue. Veteran British rocker Vince Eager toured Britain during the early part of the year in *Elvis – The Musical*.

Away from rock'n'roll there were country tours in 1984 by Emmylou Harris, Barbara Fairchild and Joe Sun. Los Lobos performed in a Tex-Mex style, while Jason & The Scorchers brought together country rock and punk under the dubious heading of 'cowpunk'.

Black music was represented by Roberta Flack, Al Green, Memphis Slim and Mary Wells, and the gospel sounds of the Edwin Hawkins Singers. Other notable performers who appeared in Britain were Paul Butterfield, Queen Ida's Bon Temps Zydeco Band and the Cramps, exponents of psychobilly and garage punk, who sold out an incredible four nights at the Hammersmith Palais. But perhaps most bizarre of all were Big Daddy, a Los Angeles-based pop group who claimed to have been kidnapped by Laotian guerrillas while entertaining US troops in Vietnam and not rescued until 1983! Their act comprised modern songs performed in a 1950s style, and for their UK tour they included British rock'n'roll pianist Dave Taylor in their line-up.

CLARENCE 'FROGMAN' HENRY

January 1984		
14	Putney	Half Moon
Tour organiser — Stuart Littlewood		

The Frogman returned to the UK during January for what was effectively a promotional visit, although one live gig did take place at the Half Moon in Putney, where he was backed by Juice On The Loose. This was his third appearance at this popular London venue within twelve months and he gave another excellent performance with a feast of New Orleans music and went over extremely well.

GROOVEY JOE POOVEY

February 1984					
4	Brighton	Lewes Road Inn	12	Haywards Heath	Clair Hall
5	Matlock	Pavilion	13	Godstone	Bell
10	Mildenhall	USAF	17	Crowborough	Cross Hotel
11	Westminster	Tower	18	Wormelow	Park Ballroom
			19	Harlesden	Mean Fiddler
Tour organisers — Willie Jeffery and Lee Williams					

Photo by Paul Harris

Groovin' with Joe at the Lewes Road Inn.

Joe returned for his second UK tour on 2 February and was again backed by the Dave Travis Band. After rehearsals at Dave's home in Barnet and interviews for both Radio London and Radio Sussex, the tour got underway at the less-than-glamorous Lewes Road Inn, a popular rocker venue on the outskirts of Brighton.

He looked somewhat smarter than his surroundings, in Western clothes, an exotic pair of cowboy boots and a pale-blue stetson hat, and included 'You Are My Sunshine', 'Lightning 'Cross The Sky' and 'Great Balls Of Fire' in a pleasing set. His warm personality and engaging sense of humour helped to win over the audience, and when he finaly closed the show with 'Ten Long Fingers' and 'That's All

Right', a good time had been had by all.

Country music promoter Lee Williams had obtained some bookings for Joe on the country circuit, while on 13 February he played an acoustic set at the Bell, a pub in Godstone, Surrey, accompanied only by his own guitar and bass player Terry Nicholson. Two nights earlier, he had visited writer Bill Millar in a London hospital, where he was recovering from a heart attack.

When the British dates were completed, Poovey travelled into Europe and played further shows in Belgium, the Netherlands and Sweden before flying home to Texas on 6 March.

BO DIDDLEY

February 1984			20	Aberdeen	Ritzy
14	Camden Town	Dingwalls	21	Dundee	Fat Sam's
March 1984			22	Newcastle	Mayfair
12	Rayleigh	Pink Toothbrush	23	Manchester	Carousel
13	Slough	Fulcrum Centre	24	Croydon	Cartoon
14	Bath	Chemies	25	Harrow Weald	Middlesex & Herts
15	St. Austell	Cornish Leisure	27	Brentford	Red Lion
		Centre		Harlesden	Mean Fiddler
16	Coventry	General Wolfe	28	London	The Venue
17	Carlisle	Creeps	29	Dartford	Orchard
18	Glasgow	Henry Afrika's	30	Leeds	Bierkeller
19	Edinburgh	Playhouse			
Tour organiser — Stallion Artists					

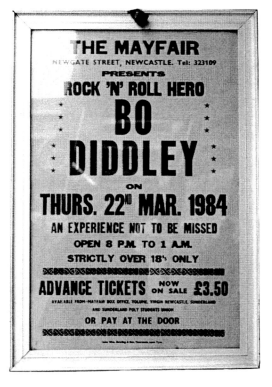

Another long tour by Bo Diddley opened at Dingwalls and drew a sizeable crowd. Backing was courtesy of Mainsqueeze, a blues rock band comprising Eric Bell, ex-Thin Lizzy (guitar), Dick Heckstall-Smith (saxophones), Dave Moore (keyboards), Keith Tillman (bass) and Leonard 'Stretch' Streching (drums). Not surprisingly, they provided a somewhat heavier sound than usual, but went over well enough because Bo was now appealing to a wider range of fans than just the rock'n'rollers. College types and rock music enthusiasts who would not have contemplated a weekend at Caister were turning out to see Diddley, and his move away from a strictly Fifties' sound reflected this development.

Even cynical old *New Musical Express* was practically swooning with excitement as their writer showed off his ability to string long words into sentences with such memorable phrases as *'paroxysms of delight'* and, as a description of Bo's guitar playing, *'rhythmic epilepsy wrestling with squelching solos'.* As for his vocals, he apparently *'turned somersaults of joyous affection'.* Long-time Diddley fans reading this review were left scratching their heads and wondering if they had been at the same concert.

There were not, of course, any significant changes to the act and old favourites like 'Road Runner', 'Diddley Daddy' and 'You Can't Judge A Book By The Cover' were belted out with the usual extended solos and increasingly irritating guitar gimmickry. A long 'Bo Diddley Put The Rock In Rock'n'Roll' tested the patience of the audience to the limit, but a superb 'Hey Bo Diddley' closed the proceedings strongly (or, as the *NME* preferred, *'its climax reached proportions of almost zen-like simplicity'*).

Diddley headed off to Europe for a month of one-nighters before returning on 12 March for the bulk of the UK dates. There was now plenty of work for one of rock'n'roll's greats, who for too long in the past had been undervalued in the UK.

TV Appearances
Good Morning Britain (TV-AM)	12 March 1984
The Tube (Channel 4)	23 March 1984

BRENDA LEE

March 1984		
12-17	Watford	Bailey's
20-22	Birmingham	Night Out
23	Frimley Green	Lakeside
24	Birmingham	Night Out
Tour organiser — Derek Block		

This tour was originally set up by promoter Jeffrey Kruger and, along with the expected cabaret venues, included a booking to headline the *3rd International 1950's Rock'n'Roll Weekend Festival* at Weymouth on 25 March along with Terry Dene. This would have been a most interesting experience for Brenda, and quite a contrast to her usual audiences. Unfortunately, a clash of dates between the competing Caister and Weymouth festivals resulted in Weymouth moving back to the end of April, when Brenda was no longer be available.

Kruger cancelled the tour completely, only for rival promoter Derek Block to take over the arrangements at short notice. Despite her having been rebranded as a modern country act, Brenda still included a surprising number of Chuck Berry and Ray Charles numbers in her repertoire, and it would have been fascinating to see how she would have gone over to a fanatical rock'n'roll audience at this point in her career. We will never know, and to date she has still never played a UK rock'n'roll weekender.

TV Appearances
Live From Her Majesty's (LWT)	18 March 1984

NEIL SEDAKA

Neil Sedaka had not appeared in the UK for more than a year when he joined Brenda Lee on ITV's top variety programme, *Live From Her Majesty's*, as part of a star-studded bill which also featured David Essex, Grace Kennedy, Danny La Rue, Jimmy Cricket and compere Jimmy Tarbuck.

TV Appearances
Live From Her Majesty's (LWT)   18 March 1984

FRANKIE FORD

March 1984			April 1984		
28	Camden Town	Dublin Castle	5	Cardiff	Earlswood
29	Putney	Half Moon	6	Ebbw Vale	Leisure Centre
30	Camden Town	Dingwalls	7	Bristol	Trinity Centre
31	Great Yarmouth	Seashore Holiday Village	8	Harlesden	Mean Fiddler
Tour organisers — Paul Barrett and Showstopper Promotions					

Frankie had made a big impression when he first appeared in Britain for the Caister weekender in November 1981, and it was therefore no surprise when he was rebooked for the same event, this time in Great Yarmouth, nearly 2½ years later. He again worked with Johnny & The Roccos, on a bill that also featured Big Jay McNeely, Hailey & The Hailstones and the Keytones.

His show had not fundamentally changed and contained several Fats Domino numbers. Perhaps a little more of his own material might have served him better, for 'Roberta', 'Alimony' and 'You Talk Too Much' were all well received. Inevitably, he closed with a rip-roaring 'Sea Cruise'.

There were club dates arranged around the weekender, and the Firebirds provided the support at Bristol and Sugar Ray Ford & The Hotshots at Harlesden.

A recording session took place at Livingston Studio in London on 2-4 April, which resulted in the album, *New Orleans Dynamo*, for Ace Records. Producer Mike Vernon did an excellent job and tracks like 'Whiskey Heaven', 'Don't Drop It' and 'Bony Moronie' are every bit as good as Ford's classic recordings from the Fifties.

Photo by Paul Harris

Fun at the Half Moon, Putney.

BIG JAY McNEELY

March 1984			April 1984		
29	Stoke Newington	Pegasus	3	Harlesden	Mean Fiddler
30	Putney	Half Moon			
31	Great Yarmouth	Seashore Holiday Village			
Tour organisers — Paul Barrett and Showstopper Promotions					

Big Jay McNeely and Frankie Ford were the joint headliners of what was exotically billed as the *11th International New Orleans Mardi Gras Rock'n'Roll Weekend Party*, but was in fact the final Caister weekender. Despite moving back to the Seashore Holiday Village at Great Yarmouth, there was a poor turnout, and from those who did attend, considerable criticism of the heavy-handed approach adopted by the security team.

Jay was scheduled to perform at 2.30 pm but arrived late, so his spot was moved back until 10.00 pm. Backed by Johnny & The Roccos, he worked extremely hard and gave a most energetic display, the highlights of which included 'Night Train', 'There Is Something On Your Mind' and 'Kansas City'. At one point, he jumped down off the stage and continued to play his saxophone whilst dancing around the hall, much to the delight of his audience, and the act climaxed with an extended version of 'All Night Long'.

YOUNG JESSIE

Plans were put in place for Young Jessie to record an album in London for Ace Records. He was advertised to play club dates in Stoke Newington, Putney, Kennington and Harlesden between 29 March and 3 April backed by Juice On The Loose, and on at least one occasion was to share billing with Big Jay McNeely. The whole project fell apart at the last minute and many years would elapse before Jessie returned to the UK.

THE DRIFTERS

April 1984			May 1984		
4	Liverpool	Rendezvous	21-26	Salford	Willows
6-7	Manchester	Fagin's	27-31	Watford	Bailey's
9-14	Watford	Bailey's	**June 1984**		
24-28	Birmingham	Night Out	1-2	Watford	Bailey's
			5-9	Birmingham	Night Out
Tour organiser — Derek Block?					

The Drifters were back out on the cabaret trail for much of the spring. It appears the line-up on this occasion was Johnny Moore, Ben E. King, Clyde Brown and Joe Blunt, although some show adverts mention Bill Fredericks. Either way, it was a quality set-up and audience reaction was as positive as ever, even though the music press ignored them completely.

For their TV appearance on 1 April, they shared billing with Shakin' Stevens, Charley Pride and Cannon & Ball.

TV Appearances
Live From Her Majesty's (LWT)   1 April 1984
The Rock Gospel Show (BBC1)   3 June 1984

FREDDY FENDER

April 1984		
21	Wembley	Arena
Tour organiser — Mervyn Conn		

The *Silk Cut International Festival of Country Music* featured Freddy Fender in the Saturday line-up, which also included Slim Whitman, Lynn Anderson, Ronnie Robbins, Jim Glaser and Ray Pillow. He was only allocated a short spot, but showed up well on 'You're To Blame' and 'Secret Love'. He closed strongly with a vigorous 'My Rancho Grande', on which the audience clapped along enthusiastically.

TV Appearances
Sing Country (BBC2)   21 March 1984 (screened 12 September 1984)

SONNY BURGESS

April 1984		
28-29	Weymouth	Ladbroke's Blue Waters
		Holiday Village
Tour organisers — Bristol Rock'n'Roll Society, Paul Barrett and Willie Jeffery		

The Bristol Rock'n'Roll Society, having survived heavy financial losses at their Perran Sands weekender in 1982, returned with the *3rd International 1950s Rock'n'Roll Weekend Festival*. This was direct competition for the ailing Caister weekender and was aimed squarely at the Teddy boy crowd. It was originally inked in for the weekend of 24-25 March with Brenda Lee headlining, but the Caister organisers had a time-barring agreement in place with Ladbroke's which forced Weymouth to be rescheduled 30 days or more from the Caister event. Brenda Lee would no longer be available, so a new headliner had to be found.

Sonny Burgess from Newport, Arkansas had been one of the stalwarts of Sun Records in the Fifties. His wild and primitive records like 'Red Headed Woman' and 'We Wanna Boogie' had not been hits, but, as with his Sun stablemates Billy Lee Riley and Warren Smith, Sonny's music had eventually found an enthusiastic audience in the UK and demand for a live appearance was considerable.

His group, the Pacers, had been one of the most visual acts in the South during the Fifties. Their original drummer, Russ Smith, had accompanied Jerry Lee Lewis on his first fateful tour of the UK, while Joe Lewis had played bass for Conway Twitty at Wembley in 1969. Sonny himself, however, had been working outside the music business for some time and had been singularly reluctant to put on his rock'n'roll shoes again. It took a phone call from Ronnie Hawkins made from the home of rock'n'roll agent Willie Jeffery to persuade him, and more than a year of negotiation before he finally boarded the flight to London, along with his bass player, Gary Grady.

Burgess was scheduled to play two sets, appearing on both the Saturday and Sunday at Weymouth along with support from Terry Dene, Crazy Cavan & The Rhythm Rockers, Flying Saucers, the Rapiers, Freddie 'Fingers' Lee, Rocky Trent, Bonneville and the ever-dependable Johnny & The Roccos who would also provide his backing. In the end, Terry Dene failed to show up, so Sonny covered his set as well.

As he opened with 'We Wanna Boogie', the crowd went crazy at the sound of Sonny's

unique, growling vocals. The Roccos had been augmented by a trumpet player to achieve the most authentic sound possible and the set list was a namecheck of all those classic Sun records – 'Going Home', 'My Bucket's Got A Hole In It', 'Sadie's Back In Town' – interspersed with rock'n'roll standards like 'Memphis, Tennessee', 'C.C. Rider' and 'That's All Right'. The audience enthusiastically joined in the call-and-response of 'Ain't Got A Thing', while Sonny underlined his inexperience of the UK rock'n'roll scene by thanking all the teddy bears, rather than Teddy boys, for their support. In truth, sound distortion and an excess of feedback from the stage did mar the enjoyment of the show, but by the time the act closed with a roistering 'Red Headed Woman', it was clear to everyone that another major rock'n'roll talent had emerged from the shadows.

EDDIE BOND

May 1984		
6	Harlesden	Mean Fiddler
Tour organiser — Willie Jeffery		

Eddie Bond was booked for a show in Belgium on 5 May, and with only seven days notice a one-off gig was set up in Harlesden for the following night. The Mean Fiddler was shaping up to be a worthy successor to the Royalty Ballroom for rock'n'roll gigs in London, although it would never attract quite the same numbers. There was a late-drinking licence, however, and this attraction, plus some local radio plugs, helped ensure a sizeable audience for Bond's show.

Dressed in a smart suit and a stetson hat, he looked more like a prosperous businessman than a rock'n'roll singer. He did not play an instrument and was a fairly static performer, relying solely on his strong voice and pleasing stage personality to see him through. Backed by the Dave Travis Band, the show opened with 'I Got A Woman' and continued with a mixture of country and rockabilly material. By the time the act climaxed with 'Rockin' Daddy' and 'Slip, Slip, Slippin'-In', he had the audience eating out of his hand.

CHUCK BERRY

May 1984		
7-8	London	The Venue
9	Swansea	Leisure Centre
10	Portsmouth	Guildhall
Tour organiser — Derek Block		

The irrepressible Mr. Berry flew into London on 7 May following a concert in Vienna, accompanied by his trusty bass player, Jim Marsala.

For his show at Swansea Leisure Centre he seemed in an exceptionally good mood and joked with the audience throughout the evening. Dressed in a green flowered jacket, beige trousers, white shirt and bootlace tie, unusually he opened with 'Havana Moon' and a subdued 'No Money Down', before belting through 'School Day' and a melodic 'Ramblin' Rose'. He then informed the audience that there would be no more slow numbers, only rock'n'roll and accelerated straight into 'Let It Rock'.

Much to everybody's surprise, he then called for requests and obliged with 'Memphis, Tennessee', 'Nadine' and 'Rock And Roll Music'. On 'Maybellene', he duckwalked across the stage before cutting back for 'Wee Wee Hours', complete with new risqué lyrics. 'Carol', 'Little Queenie' and 'Johnny B. Goode' were other highlights of the act, which closed on an extended 'Reelin' and Rockin' ' that left the crowd screaming for more. Chuck merely unplugged his guitar and was gone.

CLARENCE 'FROGMAN' HENRY

May 1984			June 1984		
26	Putney	Half Moon	3	Harlesden	Mean Fiddler
27	Westminster	Tower	4	London	100 Club
Tour organiser — Stuart Littlewood					

Clarence recorded a television appearance on *Hall Of Fame* at the Granada Theatre, Manchester and then hung around for a trio of club dates in London with Juice On The Loose.

At Putney, he opened with 'But I Do' and a medley of Fats Domino numbers, before responding to a request from the audience and delivering a powerful 'Lawdy Miss Clawdy', which went over extremely well. The set continued with 'Little Suzy', 'Basin Street', 'Troubles, Troubles' and a riotous 'Ain't Got No Home'. An overlong version of 'Whole Lotta Shakin' Goin' On' was augmented by some shapely dancers, but the high point of a mammoth set lasting some 90 minutes was a pair of Huey Smith numbers, 'Don't You Just Know It' and 'High Blood Pressure', which had the audience singing along with great enthusiasm. An excellent night of rock'n'roll was only slightly marred by some sound problems, an unusual occurrence at the Half Moon.

TV appearances
Hall of Fame (Granada)   ? May 1984
Chas & Dave's Knees-Up (LWT)   13 May 1984

BILLY RICHARD'S COASTERS

June 1984			July 1984		
?	Stratford	Granada Bingo	1	Yeovil	Westland Helicopter
?	Willesden	Granada Bingo			Social
30	Greenwich	Granada Bingo	3-4	Lakenheath	USAF
Tour organiser — Wayne Kennedy					

1984 BRITISH ROCK-N-ROLL FESTIVAL

ON SATURDAY JULY 14th
BLUE BOAR FESTIVAL SITE,
HUCKNALL, NOTTINGHAM.
GATES OPEN 12noon (FIRST BAND ON 1p.m.)
Featuring from Los Angeles U.S.A. the legendary

COASTERS
plus

THE RAPIERS   FREDDIE 'FINGERS' LEE
JOHNNY   CLIVE OSBOURNE
& THE ROCCOS   & THE CLEARNOTES
BLUE JEAN BOP

HOSTED BY BBC RADIO'S **BIG BOPPER** & GUEST D.J.'S
LICENSED BAR, FULL CATERING FACILITIES, HUGE AUXILIARY
MARQUEES
TICKETS ONLY £6.50 in advance £8 on the day
FREE ADMISSION TO ACCOMPANIED CHILDREN UNDER 10
FREE PARKING FOR COACHES AND CARS

Tickets and Enquiries SAE to Rock it. 107 Park Road, Ilkeston,
Derbyshire DE7 5DN. Tel: (0602) 305110.
CHEQUES/POSTAL ORDERS PAYABLE TO:- BRITISH ROCK-N-ROLL FESTIVAL

PLEASE SUPPLY .... TICKETS AT £6.50 EACH   NAME......................
TOTAL £ ....   ADDRESS.................
CHEQUE or P/O NUMBER ....
FOR THE 1984 BRITISH ROCK-N-ROLL FESTIVAL
on JULY 14th IN NOTTINGHAM

This was not the authentic Carl Gardner-led Coasters who had toured the UK as recently as 1982, but a group comprising Billy Richard Jr, Bobby Sheen, Randy Jones and Sherman James, who, if they were not exactly what it said on the tin, were nevertheless significant players within the tangled web of US vocal groups.

Richard Jr is nephew of Billy Richard, one of the original Robins, and he and Bobby Sheen joined that group in 1958. A few years later, both men were to be found in Bobby Nunn's Coasters. Nunn was himself a former Robin and an original member of the Coasters. In 1966, Randy Jones joined, with Richard Jr taking over leadership of the group when Nunn retired in 1970.

Bobby Sheen had also recorded for Phil Spector under the name of Bob B. Soxx and scored a Top 10 hit in 1963 with 'Zip-A-Dee-Doo-Dah', while Jones had been a founder member of the Meadowlarks, later bouncing around numerous LA vocal groups including the Penguins and the Flairs. Sherman James had no previous connection with the Coasters, but had toured the UK in 1972 as one of Buck Ram's Platters. Therefore, even if this version of the Coasters was not strictly the real deal, they were close enough for most people. As usual, of course, the general public had no idea as to the identity of the four men onstage and were only concerned about the quality of the show.

Backing was provided by Johnny & The Roccos, comprising Bob Fish (guitar), Ian Bell (double bass), Jim Fisher (drums) and Martin Winning (saxophone), and rehearsals took place at the Dublin Castle in North London. Straight off there was friction between the Roccos and Sherman James who favoured disco-style arrangements of the Coasters' hits and the inclusion of Lionel Richie numbers in the set. At one point, Bob Fish threatened to withdraw the Roccos from the tour altogether, but things settled down and they completed shows at such diverse locations as the Westland Helicopter Factory Social Club and a trio of London bingo clubs.

Tension had also built up between the Coasters and tour organiser Wayne Kennedy, who was also vocalist with the Flash Cats. Things came to a head after a booking at the US military base in Lakenheath. They played the officers' mess on the first night and then on 4 July took part in a massive show in front of some 20,000 troops at a baseball field as support for Grand Funk Railroad. By then they had received a letter inviting the group to appear on American television and so took the decision to split for home without completing the remaining UK dates, which included headlining the *1984 British Rock'n'Roll Festival* at Hucknall, near Nottingham on a bill which included Sleepy LaBeef.

SLEEPY LaBEEF

July 1984					
7	Salisbury	Grange Hotel	15	Streatham	Big Top Marquee
8	Aston	Holte Hotel		Oxford	Caribbean Hall
10	Harlesden	Mean Fiddler	17	Harlesden	Mean Fiddler
11	Brighton	Lewes Road Inn	18	Godstone	Bell
14	Hucknall	Blue Boar Festival Site	24	Rayleigh	Pink Toothbrush
	Leeds	Astoria			

Tour organisers — Willie Jeffery and Ian Wallis

Sleepy flew into London on 5 July for what proved to be an arduous three weeks of rock'n'roll. He travelled straight to Dublin for a gig the following night, then back to kick-start the UK dates at Salisbury on 7 July.

Salisbury proved a big disappointment. The enthusiastic but inexperienced tour organisers had relied on local advertising, which had been promised but never materialised, and only a handful of people turned out at showtime. Sleepy was not best pleased, but delivered an energetic and professional performance to a near-empty room. Happily, things improved considerably after that.

Backed throughout by Dave Taylor (piano), Alan Wilson (bass) and Rob Godwin (drums), Sleepy's boundless energy and marathon sets tested the endurance and ability of the musicians, and his steamroller approach invariably left the audience exhausted at the end of the night.

On one memorable weekend, he made an early evening appearance at Hucknall, near Nottingham on the *1984 British Rock'n'Roll Festival* along with the Rapiers, Freddie 'Fingers' Lee, Clive Osborne & The Clearnotes and Blue Jean Bop, before racing up the motorway for a club date in Leeds. After a few hours sleep, it was back to London for the *Rock'n'Roll Jubilee Party* being held in a giant marquee on Streatham

Photo by Paul Harris

Rockin' at the Lewes Road Inn.

Common and also featuring Marty Wilde, Terry Dene, Screaming Lord Sutch, Tommy Bruce, Heinz, the Jets, CSA, the Firebirds and a host of others. The weekend was rounded off with a fourth gig, a late-evening club appearance in Oxford. It was daylight when they finally got back for a couple of hours' sleep, following which the tour organisers had day jobs to attend. Rock'n'roll either kills you or keeps you young.

At the Bell in Godstone, Sleepy appeared with just bass player Terry Nicholson and performed an acoustic set. The following day he flew to Sweden where he headlined a rock'n'roll festival in Vargarda. This exhilarating and high-energy tour concluded with a final UK club date at Rayleigh after which Sleepy returned to the US on 25 July.

Rock 'n Roll   Rockabilly

SOUNDS OF THE 50'S

Rhythm & Blues   Jive

EVERY SUNDAY

Holte Hotel
Trinity Road
Aston Birmingham

plus live on stage:

Sun. July 8th.
from the U.S.A...
SLEEPY LA BEEF

JULY 22nd. ROCKETS
JULY 29th. RED HOT & BLUE
AUGUST 12th. CAT TALK

BO DIDDLEY

August 1984		
27	Cardiff	Butetown Bay Festival
28	Wimbledon	Theatre
29-30	Camden Town	Dingwalls
Tour organiser — Stallion Artists		

Peter Jacobs of Stallion Artists brought Bo back to the UK for four nights as part of another lengthy European tour and he was again backed by Mainsqueeze.

He was on excellent form throughout this period, headlining the open-air *Butetown Bay Festival* in Cardiff, and then going down extremely well the following night at Wimbledon. The acoustics at this fine, old South London theatre were superb and Bo was in a bluesy mood, treating a really responsive audience to a vintage performance.

His stay in Britain may have been brief, but there was plenty of demand for Mr. Diddley's services throughout Europe and this tour continued for much of September eventually winding to a close after a festival in Bochum, West Germany.

CARL MANN

September 1984		
23	Harlesden	Mean Fiddler
Tour organisers — Dave Travis and Willie Jeffery		

Photo by Paul Harris

More than six years after his British stage debut at Dingwalls, Carl returned to Europe for a short tour that was built around his appearance at the *23rd Rockhouse International Rock'n'Roll Meeting* in Eindhoven on 6 October.

He flew into London on 21 September along with his bass player, Rick Martin, and spent the day rehearsing in Barnet with the Dave Travis Band. The following evening, they played live in Dublin, before returning to London for his UK gig at Harlesden's Mean Fiddler. Hank Wangford was the opening act, while the sizeable crowd included Rory Gallagher and Van Morrison, plus a veritable who's who of faces from the rock'n'roll scene. A lot of people regretted missing Carl Mann's first show in London and made very sure not to miss out this time.

Smartly attired in a dark suit and bow tie, plus the addition of a bushy moustache, he did not look very rocking at all, but as soon as he hit the stage and burst into 'Ubangi Stomp', the audience were held spellbound by the energy and power of his performance. He stormed through 'Kansas City', 'Gonna Rock'n'Roll Tonight', 'Pretend', 'I'm Coming Home' and 'Baby I Don't Care'. Two Teddy Redell numbers, 'Judy' and 'Knockin' On The Backside', went over well, as did 'Ain't Got No Home' and 'Matchbox', but the greatest applause was saved for 'Mona Lisa' and, as a well-deserved encore, 'Look At That Moon'.

On 26 September, Carl flew to Finland for two shows, before returning briefly to the UK on 1 October, and then on to the Netherlands and Belgium to complete his tour.

HAYDEN THOMPSON

October 1984		
9	Rayleigh	Pink Toothbrush
19	Harlesden	Mean Fiddler
20-21	St. Helens, IoW	Nodes Point Holiday Village
Tour organisers — Sun Session, Paul Barrett and Willie Jeffery		

Hayden Thompson from Booneville, Mississippi was another of the young rock'n'rollers who built their reputation at Sun Records in the mid-Fifties. He recorded the magnificent 'Love My Baby' in 1956 and toured extensively with Billy Lee Riley and Sonny Burgess before relocating to Chicago in 1958, eventually moving into country music. Like so many of his contemporaries, he now found himself in demand as a rock'n'roll singer once again and travelled to Europe for the first time to jointly headline the *23rd Rockhouse International Rock'n'Roll Meeting* in Holland with Carl Mann on 6 October.

Dave Travis had set up a recording session at Southern Music and between 9 and 11 October they cut twelve sides

Whole lotta shakin' at the Mean Fiddler.

which were released by Charly Records the following year on an album titled *Booneville, Mississippi Flash*. He was then dispatched to Sweden on 12 October and played three shows before returning to complete the remaining studio work on 18 October. A proposed gig at the New Cross Palais that evening did not materialise.

At the Mean Fiddler, the Dave Travis Band, comprising Eddie Jones (guitar), Dave Taylor (piano), Terry Nicholson (bass), Rob Godwin (drums) and Travis (vocals and guitar) played their own set before Thompson opened with a blistering 'Fairlane Rock'. Few other rock'n'rollers could match the quality of his vocals, somewhat Presleyesque but still very much his own style, as he worked through 'My Baby Left Me', 'I'm So Lonesome I Could Cry' and 'My Babe', mixing country and rockabilly favourites with his own recordings, including 'One Broken Heart' and 'You Are My Sunshine'. An extremely friendly and genuine man, Hayden's personality came across to the audience, who let him know just how they felt, especially when he delivered his ace card, a blistering 'Love My Baby'. He then took over at the piano for 'Whole Lotta Shakin' Goin' On' and 'Mean Woman Blues', before encoring with 'Shake, Rattle And Roll'.

If the Mean Fiddler show was a great success, the attempt to establish a rockabilly weekender on the Isle of Wight was a good deal less so. At the *1st International Just A Rockin' Weekend Jamboree* Hayden headlined on a bill specifically slanted towards the rockabilly cats rather than the Teddy boys which included the Blue Rhythm Boys, the Keytones, Cat Talk, the Sureshots, Sugar Ray Ford & The Hotshots, the Crazy Quavers, the Rhythmaires and the highly eccentric Rochee & The Sarnos. He played two sets, appearing on both the Saturday and the Sunday, but unfortunately it was not the quality of acts that made the headlines, but the trail of devastation caused by a minority of the audience and which left the organisers with a bill in excess of £3,000 for damage to the holiday camp.

It seemed as if every crazy on the rock'n'roll scene had found their way to the Isle of Wight. The level of lunacy involved became clear to Hayden and his wife, Georgia, as they took a morning stroll and ran into two rockabillies, naked except for some strategically placed seaweed, which they had presumably found on the beach. The upshot of all this madness was that the second proposed weekender at Nodes Point, to star Sonny Burgess, was cancelled and the perceived divide between the cats and the Teds seemed wider than ever.

ROCKY BURNETTE

In November 1981, Rocky Burnette had fronted a newly reconstituted Rock'n'Roll Trio, along with the one surviving original member, Paul Burlison, plus Johnny Black, Johnny Foster and Tony Austin. They had been a smash hit at the Caister weekender and it seemed only a matter of time before they returned to play for UK audiences again.

It was announced that Rocky and the Rock'n'Roll Trio would headline at the Weymouth weekender along with Frankie Ford on 12-14 October, but negotiations stalled, probably because of the expense involved and eventually Terry Dene was brought in as their replacement.

FRANKIE FORD

October 1984		
13-14	Weymouth	Ladbroke's Blue Waters Holiday Village
Tour organisers — Bristol Rock'n'Roll Society and Paul Barrett		

Billed rather curiously as the *Weymouth '84 — No. 2 Rock'n'Roll Weekend Festival*, the Bristol Rock'n'roll Society celebrated the demise of the Caister weekender by expanding to run a second event in the space vacated by their erstwhile rival. Ironically, Frankie Ford, who had headlined at the final Caister, was booked to return at Weymouth on a bill that was aimed squarely at the traditional rock'n'roll crowd. Terry Dene & The Dene Aces were joint headliners along with the likes of Flying Saucers, the Rapiers, the Firebirds, Rock Therapy, Clive Osborne & The Clearnotes and Breathless. The problems between the Teddy boys and the rockabilly cats had led to a segregation policy and a brand new weekender would be floated on the Isle of Wight for the rockabilly crowd seven days later.

Backed once again by Johnny & The Roccos, now featuring no fewer than three saxophones, Frankie Ford commenced his main act at 8.20 pm on the Saturday evening, opening with 'Roberta'. Interspersed with his classic songs like 'You Talk Too Much' and 'Alimony' was material from his new album including 'Sick And Tired', 'Don't You Know Yockomo', 'Whiskey Heaven' and 'A Certain Girl', all of which were enthusiastically received. A very powerful set closed, as always, with the ever-popular 'Sea Cruise'.

EVERLY BROTHERS

October 1984			November 1984		
18	Belfast	New Victoria	1	Harrogate	Conference Centre
21-22	Wembley	Arena	2-3	Manchester	Apollo
24	Cardiff	St. David's Hall	4	Liverpool	Empire
26	Glasgow	Apollo	6	Birmingham	NEC
27	Aberdeen	Capitol	8	Birmingham	NEC
28-29	Edinburgh	Playhouse	9	St. Austell	Cornwall Coliseum
30	Newcastle	City Hall	10	Bournemouth	International Centre
			11	Brighton	Centre
			14	Hammersmith	Odeon

Tour organiser — Derek Block

THE BRIGHTON CENTRE

SUNDAY, 11th NOVEMBER, 1984
at 5.15 p.m.

DEREK BLOCK presents

THE EVERLY BROTHERS
PLUS SUPPORT

⌐⌐ 60   **RAISED CENTRE STALLS
£10.00**

(Magnificent Sea View)
Skyline RESTAURANT   Open two hours prior to most performances
Reservations: Telephone 203130

Neither the Council or their officers accept any responsibility for any loss or damage (howsoever caused or sustained) to any property whatsoever brought on to these premises. *tickets cannot be exchanged or refunded.*

The taking of unauthorised photographs during an artiste's live performance is a breach of the Copyright Act 1956. Cameras being used in defiance of this regulation will be removed to the cloakroom for the duration of the performance. The Management may also exercise the right to expose film if so requested by the artiste.

Inspired by the enormous interest in their *Reunion Concert* at the Royal Albert Hall, Don and Phil recommenced touring in July with a mammoth 48 shows across America and Canada. Billed as the *Everly Brothers World Tour '84*, they reached the UK three months later to find that most of the venues had sold out at the box office, further evidence of the goodwill and enthusiasm from their army of fans.

Backed by Albert Lee (guitar), Phil Donnelly (guitar), Philip Cranham (bass), Larry Londin (drums) and Pete Wingfield (keyboards), the whole tour was enormously successful on all levels. The brothers still seemed to be enjoying the experience of performing the old songs again and there was a freshness about the act which had been sadly lacking prior to the split in 1973.

At Newcastle, they opened with 'The Price Of Love', and then worked through the inevitable procession of hits, including 'Walk Right Back', 'Crying In The Rain', 'Love Is Strange' and 'Bye Bye Love'. They spoiled 'Bird Dog' by playing it a little too fast, and 'When Will I Be Loved' rocked rather more than on the record, but generally they kept to the original arrangements. The new single, 'Wings Of A Nightingale', was enthusiastically received and they closed strongly with 'Cathy's Clown', 'Lucille' and 'Let It Be Me'. An encore was demanded and fully justified so they belted out 'Temptation', following which Don announced, 'This one is for Gene Vincent,' and they roared into a frantic 'Be-Bop-A-Lula' which finally brought the evening to a very satisfactory conclusion.

CHUCK BERRY

October 1984		
25	Watford	Bailey's
26	Oxford	Polytechnic
	Watford	Bailey's
27	Watford	Bailey's
Tour organiser — Derek Block		

Chuck made a short trip to the UK for a three-night cabaret engagement at Watford. Accompanied by his bass player, Jim Marsala, this was strictly routine for the charismatic Mr. Berry, who could play this type of gig in his sleep and on a bad night could appear as if he were doing just that.

After his brief stay at Watford's finest nightspot, he was whisked off to Sweden for a show in Norrköping the following evening, where, interestingly, he was joined on stage by Johnnie Johnson, his original pianist. This was the very first time that Johnson had appeared with Chuck in Europe.

JOHNNY CASH

October 1984			6	Nottingham	Royal Concert Hall
31	Oxford	Apollo	7	Sheffield	City Hall
November 1984			8	Preston	Guildhall
1	Cardiff	St. David's Hall	9	Aberdeen	Capitol
5	Croydon	Fairfield Halls	11	Glasgow	Apollo
Tour organiser — Adrian Hopkins					

The extraordinary popularity of Johnny Cash had created an endless demand for his live show, and his touring schedule during the Eighties was positively breathtaking. This short tour was typical. Not only did it involve the usual round of one-nighters, but also, during the four-day break at the beginning of November, he flew out to Scandinavia for additional appearances in Finland and Sweden. Accompanied by June Carter, Anita Carter and his All Star Band, which included Bob Wootton (guitar), W.S. Holland (drums) and Earl Poole Ball (piano), Cash was on a seemingly endless treadmill of pressure.

In Croydon, his show lasted for two hours and included a cross-section of the many great songs from his near-thirty-year career. 'Ring Of Fire', 'Orange Blossom Special' and 'Forty Shades Of Green' were among the most popular with an audience who were already committed fans and sang along with every number. As an acknowledgement of the new video age, a large screen above the stage re-created a train wreck during 'Wreck Of The Old 97', a gambling scenario for 'The Baron' and a suitably humorous video for the latest single, 'Chicken in Black'. Interspersed with the new came old favourites like 'Folsom Prison Blues' and 'Big River'. An impassioned plea was made on behalf of the coal miners, which led into 'Dark As A Dungeon', and when the evening finally concluded with 'I Walk The Line' every person in the theatre had enjoyed a magnificent concert from a truly great entertainer.

Between 12 and 16 November, Cash was in Montreux, Switzerland taping a CBS Christmas special with guests that included Waylon Jennings, Willie Nelson and Kris Kristofferson, and it was during this period that the idea for their joint involvement as the Highwaymen was fashioned.

TV Appearances
Breakfast Time (BBC1)   31 October 1984

CHARLIE FEATHERS

November 1984		
10 Bristol	Trinity Centre	
Tour organisers — John Hale, Bob Brookes and Jan Blok		

This one-off UK show by the inimitable Charlie Feathers came at the commencement of a proposed European tour masterminded by eccentric Dutch promoter Jan Blok. Booked by his son, Bubba Feathers (guitar), Blok himself (harmonica) and two of the Firebirds, Tony Biggs (slap bass) and Steve Evans (drums), it proved to be one of Feathers' very best UK performances.

Smartly dressed in a pale blue suit, he opened with 'Stutterin' Cindy' and a very authentic-sounding 'Too Much Alike' on which Bubba and Jan provided the vocal harmonies. Authenticity was so important to Feathers, and the purist European fans loved him for it. He tried to re-create the sound of rockabilly exactly as it had been in mid-Fifties' Memphis and worked through 'Folsom Prison Blues', 'Tear It Up', 'When You Come Around' and even the folksy 'South Of Chicago', which was quite excellent.

His patter between numbers, which had been somewhat embarrassing on earlier shows, seemed less intrusive and Charlie himself seemed more relaxed and in control. His great songs are mainly unknown obscurities to the wider public, but shine like uncut jewels to the committed rockabilly fan. 'When You Decide', 'Peepin' Eyes' and 'One Hand Loose' all went over well, as did the early Presley numbers 'Good Rockin' Tonight' and the song which bears Charlie's name as co-writer, 'I Forgot To Remember To Forget', which he rather fancifully introduced as Elvis's biggest record. A very tidy and absorbing show closed with a raucous 'Tongue Tied Jill', but sustained applause from the sizeable crowd ensured that the evening was far from over.

He encored with 'Bottle To The Baby' and was brought back again for

'Everybody's Lovin' My Baby'. This was followed by perhaps the high point of the show. Steve Evans was ordered to the front of the stage, with brushes and a single drum, while the other musicians were repositioned in front of a lone microphone as Charlie demonstrated how rockabilly should really sound, with a superb rendition of 'Rain'. A third encore provided 'She Knows How To Rock Me', but even that was not the end. Compere Trevor Cajiao coaxed him back for a fourth and final time and a memorable evening concluded with 'Will The Circle Be Unbroken'.

Sadly, the rest of the tour did not proceed. Charlie had verbally agreed dates in France and the Netherlands, and several more in Germany, but had not signed any contracts. Before arriving in Bristol, he was already aware that the German shows had been cancelled and flew home the following day, leaving Jan Blok with heavy financial losses and no option but to cancel the other European dates.

BUDDY KNOX

Willie Jeffery had set up dates for Buddy Knox, including an appearance at the Mean Fiddler on 23 November, when, in a repeat of his aborted 1981 tour, he pulled out. This time it was because his wife, Mitzi, was having a baby and his presence was required at home in Canada.

THE DRIFTERS

December 1984		
5	Chippenham	Golddiggers
Tour organiser unknown		

By the end of 1984, the Drifters had disappeared completely off the rock'n'roll radar. Their dates were no longer listed in the music press, nor were they given any degree of coverage in the specialist blues or rock'n'roll magazines. They continued to find work on the cabaret circuit and, with a line-up of Johnny Moore, Ben E. King, Clyde Brown and Joe Blunt, audiences were rarely disappointed. The difficulty at this juncture was tracking them down at all. This performance at Chippenham is unlikely to have been their only one in the UK in December 1984.

LINK WRAY

December 1984		
27	Camden Town	Electric Ballroom
Tour organiser unknown		

What better way to conclude 1984 and the period covered by this book, than with a full-blooded assault on the senses by the Linkster himself?

An audience who had spent a couple of days eating and drinking to excess and watching reruns of *The Wizard of Oz* or *The Sound of Music*, would have been brought sharply back to reality with this one-off post-Christmas gig in North London at which Link Wray was supported by the Screaming Blue Messiahs, the Milkshakes and the Hatchetmen. Earlier that day, the venue had hosted a huge international record fair.

Postscript

By the end of 1984, live rock'n'roll had been performed in Britain for close to thirty years. True, those days when the music transformed society and changed the attitudes and values of a generation were now a distant memory, while the original fans were reaching middle age, as of course were the performers themselves. There did not seem to be any sign of the music dying though.

The rockabilly craze had introduced a significant number of young people to rock'n'roll during the late Seventies. They were born too late to have seen Buddy Holly, Eddie Cochran or even Gene Vincent on stage, but were no less committed to the music that they loved than their older counterparts. While the surviving stars of the Fifties like Fats Domino, Chuck Berry and Jerry Lee Lewis continued to fill theatre venues and play to audiences of all ages, the live scene in the UK was now fully established in the pubs, clubs and holiday camps. That is where the real action would now be found and where the new stars of live rock'n'roll like Janis Martin, Ray Campi and Sonny Burgess would ply their trade.

Our story is far from over. Names such as Ronnie Dawson, Johnny Powers, Ruth Brown, Dale Hawkins and the Collins Kids were known through their recordings but had yet to set foot on a British stage... and who exactly was Joe Clay? That mystery had yet to be solved. In addition, aside from the Drifters, Coasters and Platters the US vocal groups were almost an unknown quantity. Who in 1984 could have dreamed of seeing live performances by the Cadillacs, the Five Keys, the Del Vikings and the Olympics?

I am already conducting the necessary research to carry *American Rock'n'Roll – The UK Tours* on through the Nineties and into the new millennium. I hope that you will make that journey with me.

Any feedback, corrections, additions or comments about the period 1973-84 would be welcomed. I can be reached through Dixie Fried Music, 111 Worlds End Lane, Orpington, Kent BR6 6AW.

And finally... the answer to my challenge set in the *Introduction* was 'God Save The Queen', sung by Bill Haley and the rest of the cast of the 1979 *Royal Variety Show*!

BIBLIOGRAPHY

In addition to all the magazines and newspapers mentioned in the Acknowledgments, the following books were consulted and proved helpful:

Tony Allan, *Save The Last Dance For Me* (J.A. Allan, Glasgow) 2005

Johnnie Allan, *A Souvenir Book* (Jadfel Publishing, Lafayette, Louisiana) 2003

Howard & Dennis De Witt, *Stranger In Town*
                    (Kendall Hunt, Dubuque, Iowa) 2001

Chris Groom, *Rockin' Croydon* (Wombat Publishing, Croydon) 1998

John W. Haley with John Von Hoelle, *Sound And Glory*
                    (Dyne American, Wilmington, Delaware) 1990

Diane Ilka, *The Cal Album* (Book Castle, Dunstable) 2005

John Ingman, *Crickets Fact File* (Ingman Music Research, Brimington) 1998

Myra Lewis with Murray Silver, *Great Balls Of Fire*
                    (Virgin Books, London) 1982

Peter Lewry, *I've Been Everywhere* (Helter Skelter, London) 2001

Bill Millar, *The Coasters* (W.H. Allen & Co, London) 1975

Morten Reff, *The Chuck Berry International Directory (Volume 2)*
                    (Music Mentor Books, York) 2008

Fred Rothwell, *Long Distance Information* (Music Mentor Books, York) 2001

Ian Wallis, *American Rock'n'Roll: The UK Tours 1956-72*
                    (Music Mentor Books, York) 2003

Ian Wallis, *The Hawk* (Quarry Books, Kingston, Ontario) 1996

George R. White, *Bo Diddley – Living Legend*
                    (Castle Communications, Chessington) 1995

ADDITIONS & AMENDMENTS TO 'AMERICAN ROCK'N'ROLL'

I invited readers of *American Rock'n'Roll – The UK Tours 1956-72* to provide me with feedback, additions and corrections and would like to thank those who took the trouble to contact me, especially Derek Henderson, Barry Holley, John Hollyman, Geoff Kember, Peter Kent, Bill Millar and Eddie Muir. Below are listed additions and amendments to the first volume:

JOHNNY BURNETTE

Page 147	Delete:	12 November 1963	Cardiff	*unknown venue*
	Add:	19 November 1963	Cardiff	Discs A-Go-Go

DON & DEWEY
See LITTLE RICHARD

DUANE EDDY

Page 252	Add:	1 June 1968 *(with Marmalade)*	Dunstable	California

THE G-CLEFS

Page 250	Add:	6 April 1968 *(with the Fifth Dynasty)*	Dunstable	California
Page 275	Add:	8 March 1969	Dunstable	California

BILL HALEY & HIS COMETS

Page 172	Add:	23 September 1964	Glasgow	Barrowlands
	Delete:	11 October 1964	London	New Victoria
	Add:	11 October 1964	Kings Heath Handsworth	Ritz Plaza
		(a double gig, replacing London New Victoria)		
	Add:	12 October 1964	Windsor	Ricky Tick

JERRY LEE LEWIS

Page 159   Add: 31 March 1964   Bristol   Colston Hall

Page 221   Add: 9 November 1966   Stevenage   Locarno.
(Early evening show)

LITTLE EVA

Page 174   Add: 1 October 1964   Liverpool   Cavern

LITTLE RICHARD
DON & DEWEY

Page 162   Add: 14 May 1964   Bridlington   Spa
(doubling with Scarborough)

BUCK RAM'S PLATTERS

Page 356   Add: 30 January 1973   Stoke   Tiffany's

   Add: 1 February 1973   Stafford   Top of the World
(doubling with Birmingham Barbarella's)

   Add: 3 February 1973   Whitworth   Civic Centre
(doubling with Birmingham Barbarella's)

GENE VINCENT

Page 79   Add: 3 May 1960   Liverpool   Stadium

Page 91   Add: 4 June 1961   Bristol   Colston Hall
(with the Brook Brothers, Sylvia Sands, the Red Peppers and the Semi-Tones. Gene was backed by Sounds Incorporated.)

Page 102   Add: 7 May 1962   Brighton   Essoldo
(This was a Jerry Lee Lewis gig. Gene was a late addition to the bill and was backed by the Echoes.)

Page 109   The 6 July 1962 show at Gravesend was at the Co-op Hall.

Page 124   Add: 11 March 1963   Darwen   Baths Assembly Hall
(with Ricky Day and the Mustangs)

   Add: 8 April 1963   Bath   Pavilion
(backed by the English Blue Caps)

   Add: 11 April 1963   Bristol   Hippodrome
(with Michael Holliday)

   Add: 5 May 1963   Letchworth   Broadway
(with Sounds Incorporated, Suzy Cope and Johnny Temple)

Page 129	Add:	19 May 1963	Liverpool	Cavern
	Add:	26 May 1963 *(with Peter Jay & The Jaywalkers)*	Handsworth	Plaza
Page 134	Add:	13 July 1963 *(with Danny Havoc & The Ventures and the Denver Six)*	Northwich	Memorial Hall
	Add:	10 August 1963 *(with Eddie Martin & the Champions)*	Dunstable	California
	Add:	27 August 1963	Southport	Marine
Page 150	Add:	28 December 1963 *(with Ray Pilgrim & The Minute Men. Gene was backed by the Outlaws.)*	Dunstable	California
Page 154	Add:	5 February 1964 *(Gene was backed by the Shouts.)*	Newcastle	Top Rank
	Add:	8 February 1964 *(with the Apollos. Gene was backed by the Shouts.)*	Aylesbury	Assembly Hall
Page 162	Add:	9 May 1964	Bishops Stortford	Rhodes Centre
Page 171	Add:	10 October 1964	Bishops Stortford	Rhodes Centre

In addition to these missing gigs, one mystery has been solved and a new one posed to take its place:

THE ORIGINAL DRIFTERS

The identity of the fourth, previously anonymous Drifter, who accompanied Bill Pinkney, Gerhart Thrasher and Bobby Hendricks on a short club tour in December 1966 was none other than David Baughn. This makes them the most authentic line-up of Drifters ever to appear together in the UK, as all four men had been members of the group during the 1950s and Baughn was lead singer for a short period in 1955. The source of this information was Bobby Hendricks, who visited England to appear as a solo singer at the Hemsby weekender in October 2004.

THE BOBBETTES

This New York girl vocal group comprised sisters Emma and Jannie Pought, Helen Gathers, Laura Webb and Reather Dixon, and in 1957 they had a US Top 10 hit with 'Mr. Lee'. Four more chart records followed but they made no impact whatsoever in the UK market, where they remained virtually unknown.

In May 2004, Reather and Emma visited the UK with a new line-up of Bobbettes to appear at Hemsby and revealed that they had been here before, playing a series of club dates for promoter Roy Tempest in either 1968 or 1969. Both ladies had clear memories of performing in the UK as a trio with

Laura Webb and appearing in Manchester, Norwich, Liverpool, Scotland and specifically at the Bag O' Nails club in London. They even recalled hanging out with Clyde McPhatter whilst they were in Manchester, but despite extensive research, no evidence of this visit has materialised. Tempest was infamous for his 'bogus tours', but both Emma and Reather were adamant that they were billed at all times as the Bobbettes and were not masquerading as Shirelles, Crystals or the like.

This is therefore one mystery that remains unresolved... unless of course you know better.

SUMMARY OF VISITS BY ARTIST

☐ = TV appearance, recording session or promotional visit only.

Ford, Frankie
November 1981 237
March-April 1984 293
October 1984 305

Gilley, Mickey
☐ October 1980 215

Gordon, Robert
January-February 1978 *(with Link Wray)* 138
June 1978 *(with Link Wray)* 147

Gracie, Charlie
September 1979 181
March 1980 200
April 1981 223
September 1981 234

Haley, Bill, & His Comets
February-May 1974 36
December 1976 104
March 1979 165
November 1979 189

Hawkins, Ronnie
October 1982 259

Hawkins, Screamin' Jay
June 1983 274

Henry, Clarence 'Frogman'
☐ September 1982 256
March-May 1983 266
July-October 1983 275
January 1984 290
May-June 1984 298

Higgins, Chuck
August 1983 *(with Willie Egan, Young Jessie and Big Jay McNeely)* 278

Hyland, Brian
☐ July 1975 73
September 1975 75

Jackson, Wanda
April 1974 41
March 1975 66
September 1975 76
April 1976 90
October 1976 103
September-October 1980 210
April 1981 *(with Jerry Lee Lewis and Carl Perkins)* 225

Jennings, Waylon
October 1983 285

INDEX OF VENUES

Page numbers of venues listed in tour itineraries are shown in normal type.
Page numbers of show reports are shown in **boldface**.

INDEX OF PEOPLE'S NAMES

INDEX OF SONGS & ALBUM TITLES

■ = LP Title

INDEX OF FILM & SHOW TITLES

ILLUSTRATIONS & PHOTO CREDITS

Ads on pages 65, 156, 172, 183, 247, 253 and 296 from Author's collection; ads on pages 161, 162, 171, 245, 278 and 310 courtesy Music Mentor Archives; ad on page 256 courtesy Lincoln City Library.

Back cover photos all by Paul Harris, except Chuck Berry by Jean-Pierre Ravelli.

Flyer on page 20 courtesy Bill Greensmith; flyers on pages 89, 125, 127, 165, 186, 249, 258, 268, 293, 299, 300, 301, 303 and 309 from Author's collection.

Front over photo by Graham Barker.

Magazine cover on page 131 courtesy of John Beecher/Rollercoaster Records; magazine cover on page 183 courtesy Music Mentor Archives.

Photo on page 15 courtesy Mercury Records/Bill Millar; photos on pages 23, 35 and 142 from Author's collection; photos on pages 26 and 88 courtesy Bill Millar; photos on pages 29 and 62 by Jean-Pierre Ravelli; photos on pages 40 and 53 courtesy of Brian Young/delshannon.com; photos on pages 75 and 149 by Bill Greensmith; photo on page 101 courtesy Batley Variety Club/Music Mentor Archives; photos on pages 113, 117, 121, 123, 124, 126, 134, 135, 140, 141, 145, 146, 153, 154, 155, 157, 163, 166, 168, 179, 199, 202, 210, 222, 228, 234, 238, 275, 277, 283, 290, 294, 301, 302 and 304 by Paul Harris; photo on page 138 by Arjan Deelen/courtesy Trevor Cajiao/*Now Dig This*; photos on pages 169, 170, 176, 188, 208, 212, 213, 226, 239, 251, 260, 271, 272, 279, 280 and 286 by Graham Barker; photos on pages 181, 197, 205, 220, 240, 262 and 274 by Ian Wallis; photo on page 196 by Colin Phillips; photo on page 219 by Ian Tilbury; photo on page 230 by Martin Davis; photos on pages 255, 267 and 291 by George R. White/courtesy Music Mentor Archives; photos on pages 258 and 269 by Jackie Wallis; photo on page 297 by Trevor Cajiao/courtesy *Now Dig This*.

Programmes on pages 16, 41, 63, 77, 78, 94, 104, 111, 115, 117, 119, 120, 133, 157, 163, 167, 180, 195, 225, 250 and 284 from Author's collection.

Tickets on pages 17, 22, 38, 46, 51, 77, 105, 110, 176, 195, 281, 283, 306 and 307 from Author's collection.

OTHER TITLES FROM MUSIC MENTOR BOOKS

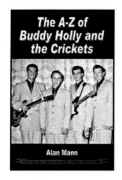

The A-Z of Buddy Holly and the Crickets
Alan Mann
ISBN-13: 978-0-9547068-0-7 *(pbk, 320 pages)* £19.99

The A-Z of Buddy Holly and the Crickets draws together a mass of Holly facts and info from a variety of published sources, as well as the author's own original research, and presents them in an easy-to-use encyclopaedic format. Now in its third edition, it has proved to be a popular and valuable reference work on this seminal rock'n'roller. It is a book that every Holly fan will want to keep at their fingertips. It is a book about a musical genius who will never be forgotten.

American Rock'n'Roll: The UK Tours 1956-72
Ian Wallis
ISBN-13: 978-0-9519888-6-2 *(pbk, 424 pages)* £19.99

The first-ever detailed overview of every visit to these shores by American (and Canadian!) rock'n'rollers. It's all here: over 400 pages of tour itineraries, support acts, show reports, TV appearances and other items of interest. Illustrated with dozens of original tour programmes, ads, ticket stubs and great live shots, many rare or previously unpublished.

Back On The Road Again
Dave Nicolson
ISBN-13: 978-0-9547068-2-1 *(pbk, 216 pages)* £12.99

A third book of interviews by Dave Nicolson in the popular *On The Road* series, this time with more of a Sixties flavour: Solomon Burke, Gene Chandler, Bruce Channel, Lowell Fulson, Jet Harris, Gene McDaniels, Scott McKenzie, Gary S. Paxton, Bobby 'Boris' Pickett, Martha Reeves & The Vandellas, Jimmie Rodgers, Gary Troxel (Fleetwoods), Leroy Van Dyke and Junior Walker.

The Big Beat Scene
Royston Ellis
ISBN-13: 978-0-9562679-1-7 *(pbk, 184 pages)* £11.99

Originally published in 1961, *The Big Beat Scene* was the first contemporary account of the teenage music scene in Britain. Written before the emergence of the Beatles, and without the benefit of hindsight, this fascinating document provides a unique, first-hand insight into the popularity and relevance of jazz, skiffle and rock'n'roll at a time when Cliff Richard & The Shadows were at the cutting edge of pop, and the social attitudes prevailing at the time.

The Chuck Berry International Directory (Volume 1)
Morten Reff
ISBN-13: 978-0-9547068-6-9 *(pbk, 486 pages)* **£24.99**

For the heavyweight Berry fan. Everything you ever wanted to know about Chuck Berry, in four enormous volumes compiled by the world-renowned Norwegian Berry collector and authority, Morten Reff. This volume contains discographies for over 40 countries, plus over 700 rare label and sleeve illustrations.

The Chuck Berry International Directory (Volume 2)
Morten Reff
ISBN-13: 978-0-9547068-7-6 *(pbk, 532 pages)* **£24.99**

The second of four volumes in this extensive reference work dedicated to rock'n'roll's most influential guitarist and composer. Contains details of bootlegs; radio albums; movies; TV shows; video and DVD releases; international tour itineraries; hits, achievements and awards; Berry's songs, roots, and influence on other artists; tributes; Chuck Berry in print; fan clubs and websites; plus annotated discographies of pianist Johnnie Johnson (post-Berry) and the ultimate Berry copyist, Eddy Clearwater.

Cook's Tours: Tales of a Tour Manager
Malcolm Cook
ISBN-13: 978-0-9562679-4-8 *(pbk, 324 pages)* **£18.99**

Throughout his 44 years in the entertainment industry, Malcolm Cook met and worked with some of the biggest names in show business. In this humorous, fast-paced biographical account, Cook lifts the lid on what it takes to keep a show on the road and artists and audiences happy. It's all here: transport problems, unscrupulous promoters, run-ins with East German police, hassles with the Mafia, tea with the Duke of Norfolk, the wind-ups, the laughter, the heartbreak and the tears. A unique insight into what really goes on behind the scenes.

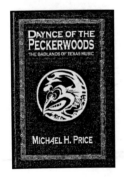

Daynce of the Peckerwoods: The Badlands of Texas Music
Michael H. Price
ISBN-13: 978-0-9547068-5-2 *(pbk, 350 pages)* **£18.99**

From a childhood spent among such key roots-music figures as Bob Wills and Big Joe Turner, and an extended dual career as a musician and journalist, Michael H. Price has forged this frenzied chronicle of life among the denizens of the vanishing borderlands of Texas' indigenous music scene over the past half-century. Contains essays on Billy Briggs, Ornette Coleman, the Light Crust Doughboys, Big Bill Lister, Rudy Ray Moore, Eck Robertson, Ray Sharpe, Robert Shaw, Major Bill Smith, Stevie Ray Vaughan and many more.

Elvis & Buddy – Linked Lives
Alan Mann
ISBN-13: 978-0-9519888-5-5 *(pbk, 160 pages)* **£9.99**

The achievements of Elvis Presley and Buddy Holly have been extensively documented, but until now little if anything has been known about the many ways in which their lives were interconnected. The author examines each artist's early years, comparing their backgrounds and influences, chronicling all their meetings and examining the many amazing parallels in their lives, careers and tragic deaths. Over 50 photos, including many rare/previously unpublished.

The First Time We Met The Blues – A journey of discovery with Jimmy Page, Brian Jones, Mick Jagger and Keith Richards
David Williams
ISBN-13: 978-0-9547068-1-4 *(pbk, 130 pages)* **£8.99**

David Williams was a childhood friend of Led Zeppelin guitar legend, Jimmy Page. The author describes how they discovered the blues together, along with future members of the Rolling Stones. The climax of the book is a detailed account of a momentous journey by van from London to Manchester to see the 1962 *American Folk-Blues Festival*, where they got their first chance to see their heroes in action.

Jet Harris – In Spite of Everything
Dave Nicolson
ISBN-13: 978-0-9562679-2-4 *(pbk, 208 pages)* **£12.99**

As a founder member of the Shadows, and a chart-topper in his own right, bassist Jet Harris scaled the heights of superstardom in the 1960s. A helpless alcoholic for most of his adult life, he also sank to unimaginable depths of despair, leaving a string of broken hearts and shattered lives in his wake. In this unauthorised biography author Dave Nicolson examines his eventful life and career, and how he eventually overcame his addiction to the bottle.

Last Swill and Testament
– The hilarious, unexpurgated memoirs of
Paul 'Sailor' Vernon
ISBN-13: 978-0-9547068-4-5 *(pbk, 228 pages)* **£12.99**

Born in London shortly after the end of World War II, Paul 'Sailor' Vernon came into his own during the 1960s when spotty teenage herberts with bad haircuts began discovering The Blues. For the Sailor it became a lifelong obsession that led him into a whirlwind of activity as a rare record dealer, magazine proprietor/editor, video bootlegger and record company director. It's all here in this one-of-a-kind life history that will leave you reaching for an enamel bucket and a fresh bottle of disinfectant!

Let The Good Times Rock!
– A Fan's Notes On Post-War American Roots Music
Bill Millar
ISBN-13: 978-0-9519888-8-6 *(pbk, 362 pages)* **£18.99**

For almost four decades, the name 'Bill Millar' has been synonymous with the very best in British music writing. This fabulous new book collects together 49 of his best pieces — some previously unpublished — in a thematic compilation covering hillbilly, rockabilly, R&B, rock'n'roll, doo-wop, swamp pop and soul. Includes essays on acappella, doo-wop and blue-eyed soul, as well as detailed profiles of some of the most fascinating and influential personalities of each era.

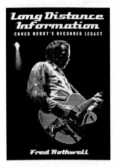

Long Distance Information: Chuck Berry's Recorded Legacy
Fred Rothwell
ISBN-13: 978-0-9519888-2-4 *(pbk, 352 pages)* **£18.99**

The lowdown on every recording Chuck Berry has ever made. Includes an overview of his life and career, his influences, the stories behind his most famous compositions, full session details, listings of all his key US/UK vinyl and CD releases (including track details), TV and film appearances, and much, much more. Over 100 illustrations including label shots, vintage ads and previously unpublished photos.

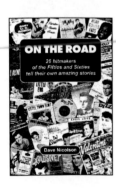

On The Road
Dave Nicolson
ISBN-13: 978-0-9519888-4-8 *(pbk, 256 pages)* **£14.99**

Gary 'US' Bonds, Pat Boone, Freddy Cannon, Crickets Jerry Allison, Sonny Curtis and Joe B. Mauldin, Bo Diddley, Dion, Fats Domino, Duane Eddy, Frankie Ford, Charlie Gracie, Brian Hyland, Marv Johnson, Ben E. King, Brenda Lee, Little Eva, Chris Montez, Johnny Moore (Drifters), Gene Pitney, Johnny Preston, Tommy Roe, Del Shannon, Edwin Starr, Johnny Tillotson and Bobby Vee tell their own fascinating stories. Over 150 illustrations including vintage ads, record sleeves, label shots, sheet music covers, etc.

On The Road Again
Dave Nicolson
ISBN-13: 978-0-9519888-9-3 *(pbk, 206 pages)* **£12.99**

Second volume of interviews with the stars of pop and rock'n'roll including Freddie Bell, Martin Denny, Johnny Farina (Santo & Johnny), the Kalin Twins, Robin Luke, Chas McDevitt, Phil Phillips, Marvin Rainwater, Herb Reed (Platters), Tommy Sands, Joe Terranova (Danny & The Juniors), Mitchell Torok, Marty Wilde and the 'Cool Ghoul' himself, John Zacherle.

Railroadin' Some: Railroads In The Early Blues
Max Haymes
ISBN-13: 978-0-9547068-3-8 *(pbk, 390 pages)* £18.99

This groundbreaking book, written by one of the foremost blues historians in the UK, is based on over 30 years research, exploration and absolute passion for early blues music. It is the first ever comprehensive study of the enormous impact of the railroads on 19th and early 20th Century African American society and the many and varied references to this new phenomenon in early blues lyrics. Includes ballin' the jack, smokestack lightning, hot shots, the bottoms, chain gangs, barrelhouses, hobo jungles and more.

Music Mentor books are available from all good bookshops or by mail order from:

Music Mentor Books
69 Station Road
Upper Poppleton
YORK YO26 6PZ
England

Telephone/Fax: **+44 (0)1904 330308**
Email: **music.mentor@lineone.net**
Website: **http://musicmentor0.tripod.com**